The Unholy Grail

A Social Reading of Chrétien de Troyes's
Conte du Graal

Figurae:

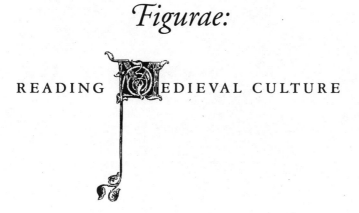

READING MEDIEVAL CULTURE

The Unholy Grail

A Social Reading of
Chrétien de Troyes's
Conte du Graal

Brigitte Cazelles

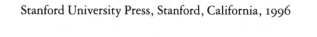

Stanford University Press, Stanford, California, 1996

Stanford University Press
Stanford, California
© 1996 by the Board of Trustees of the
Leland Stanford Junior University
Printed in the United States of America

CIP data are at the end of the book

Stanford University Press publications are
distributed exclusively by Stanford University Press
within the United States, Canada, Mexico, and
Central America; they are distributed exclusively
by Cambridge University Press throughout
the rest of the world.

Original printing 1996
Last figure below indicates year of this printing:
05   04   03   02   02   01   00   99   98   97   96

This book is dedicated to my uncles

Jean Cazelles (1908–1992)
Henri Cazelles (1912–)
Michel Cazelles (1916–1945)
Raymond Cazelles (1917–1985)

and, especially, to my father

Général Bernard Cazelles (1910–1991)

Contents

The Unholy Grail

A Social Reading of Chrétien de Troyes's

Conte du Graal

Introduction

In view of the extensive literature to which the Grail legend
has already given birth it may seem that the addition of another
volume to the already existing *corpus* calls for some words of
apology and explanation.
— Jessie L. Weston, *From Ritual to Romance*

Literary historians have long signaled the importance of Chrétien de
Troyes's final romance, *Perceval ou Le Conte du Graal*, as a turning point
in the development of medieval romance. Chrétien's earlier romances
explored the secular tensions generated by chivalric and courtly life in
the twelfth century.[1] The *Conte du Graal*, in contrast, has appeared to
most critics to seek to surmount such tensions by offering to its audience
a spiritualized ideal of a new kind of chivalry governed by a univer-
sal vision of chivalry's redemptive mission in the world. Whether seen
as a result of the "christianization" of chivalry's secular character or,
in Erich Köhler's analysis, as the paradoxical product of a profound
sense of alienation on the part of feudal society,[2] the *Conte du Graal* has
been almost unanimously interpreted as introducing a novel orientation
in chivalric romance. According to these interpretations, the *Conte du
Graal* is the first symptom of a long-term transformation in chivalric
ideology within vernacular romance, in which the codes and mores of
knightly society were progressively reinscribed in light of the values of a
pervasive Christian ethos. Seen in this perspective as a pivotal moment
in the history of imaginative writing, Chrétien's work anticipates the
development of a spiritual rather than secular assessment of chivalry's
mission in thirteenth-century romance.

At the core of this interpretation is the narration of Perceval's adven-
tures in what constitutes the first part of Chrétien's twofold romance,
the second of which focuses on the adventures of Gauvain. As the fol-

lowing outline indicates,[3] this first part of the *Conte* introduces the motif of the Grail, indicating that Perceval's story is, indeed, paramount for the significance of Chrétien's "Story of the Grail":

A young Welsh lad has been brought up by his mother in a house in a forest in total ignorance of chivalry and all social life because her two other sons have died in tournaments and her husband, himself wounded, has died of grief as a result. One day he meets five Arthurian knights riding in the forest and is so dazzled by their armor that he takes them for angels and asks their leader: "Are you God?" Returning home, he tells his mother of his intention to go to Arthur in order to become a knight. Reluctantly, she helps prepare for his departure and showers advice on him: he is to honor ladies and maidens and to pray to God in church. But this only provokes the question "Mother, what is a church?" As he rides off, he glances back and sees that his mother has fallen to the ground in a faint. He continues at a gallop without turning back. That night he sleeps in the forest. The next day he comes to a splendid tent, which he takes to be a church. He enters, intending to pray, but inside finds a girl in bed. Under the impression that his mother has told him to kiss girls, this he proceeds to do, against her will, and seizes the ring on her finger. He makes off after helping himself to food in the tent. The girl's lover (Orgueilleux de la Lande) returns from the woods, accuses her of infidelity, and they ride off, the knight swearing he will have the Welsh lad's head. The lad makes a clownish entry into Arthur's court, riding into the hall on his horse, but he soon distinguishes himself by killing the Red Knight, who has insulted Arthur and the queen. At the castle of Gornemant de Gohort, he learns much about weapons and chivalry and is told among many other things not to keep on saying "My mother told me . . . ." Remembering how he left his mother, he decides to return home. On the way he rescues a damsel, Blancheflor, from the clutches of a cruel knight (Clamadeu), and to her he owes his first experience of love. On leaving her he comes to a river; two men in a boat invite him to stay the night in the nearby castle. At table the young man sees a strange procession pass through the hall but, mindful of Gornemant's advice to restrain curiosity, asks no questions. First comes a young man carrying a lance, from the tip of which a drop of blood flows down to his hand (the Bleeding Lance); next come two young men holding candelabra of pure gold, each with at least ten candles; next is a damsel bearing a grail (*graal*), which gives off a light so bright that the candelabra are as stars to the sun; finally there is a damsel bearing a silver platter. The procession passes through the hall during each change of course, and each time the young man remains silent. Next morning the castle is empty, and the drawbridge is raised the moment he leaves. In the forest he meets a maiden (his cousin). When she asks him his name, he guesses that it is Perceval the Welsh and is right without knowing it. He learns from her that he has spent the night at the castle of the Fisher King, who, wounded between the thighs, is unable to ride a horse and fishes in a boat as a distraction. Had he asked questions about the Grail procession, the king would have been cured, but this could not happen because of his sin in abandoning his mother, who has died of grief in his absence. Perceval receives the news calmly and suggests that the damsel, whose knight has been killed, can follow him. She refuses, and he rides off. He meets the damsel whom he kissed in the tent and brings about a reconciliation between her and her lover. On his way again, he comes across three drops of blood in the snow where a falcon had caught a wild goose. The bright colors remind him of Blancheflor's complexion, and he becomes lost in contemplation as he stares at the drops. Arthur's court is nearby. Several of his knights (Keu, then Sagremor) make fun of Perceval, who easily unhorses them and returns to his contemplation. Only Gauvain is able to bring him to his senses, and he is well received by Arthur.

To the court comes an ugly damsel (the Hideous Damsel), who reproaches Perceval bitterly for his silence at the castle of the Fisher King, as a result of which the whole kingdom will suffer. Hearing from her that a maiden is in distress, Gauvain decides to help her, but Perceval leaves on a quest to find the Grail, despite the warning that the Fisher King will never hold his kingdom in peace now that the opportunity has been lost. The story then follows Gauvain's adventures for some time before returning to Perceval and his quest. For five years Perceval has not entered a church, but one Good Friday he meets a group of barefoot penitents who send him to a hermit in the woods to confess his sins. Once more he learns that his sin in not returning to his mother has caused him to remain silent in the castle of the Fisher King. He also learns that the *graal* served the Fisher King's father, the hermit's brother, and that the Fisher King was Perceval's cousin. The Host carried in the Grail had kept the Fisher King's father alive for many years, "such a holy object is the *graal*." Perceval remains for two days with the hermit and at last expresses true repentance. The story returns to the mundane adventures of Gauvain and, not completed by Chrétien, leaves Perceval's quest unfinished.

Intrinsic to the view of the *Conte du Graal* as introducing a novel orientation in chivalric romance is the hermit's interpretation of the Grail as a holy symbol, notably as containing the Host, itself the commemorative sign of Christ's redemptive role for humanity and thus, by analogy, a sign of the regenerated chivalry that Perceval, in the course of his maturation as a knight, will come to represent. Perceval's search for the Grail as emblem of redemption thus becomes, in turn, emblematic of a chivalric pilgrimage for spiritual maturity and salvation.

The question that has rarely been asked, however, is whether the hermit's revelation concerning the nature of the Grail is trustworthy and, if trustworthy, whether it represents Chrétien's views or merely those of a character in his romance. This book begins with such questions.[4] They were stimulated by a rereading of the *Conte du Graal* with a group of Stanford University undergraduates who so uncritically accepted the prevailing view that the hermit speaks for a religious understanding of medieval chivalry and its functions that they seemed to be effacing completely his role as a guide to and chronicler of the family ties that link him to Perceval's mother and to the holy recluse of the Grail castle. It is precisely this story of family ties that traditional interpretations of the *Conte du Graal* have tended to leave out in their focus on the spiritual significance of the Grail serving dish. Yet an awareness of the patterns of lineage the hermit articulates suggests that his discourse may function in the text as a strategic attempt to bind Perceval to the prosecution of the cause of his own lineage, rather than as a fully "true" and credible revelation either of the Grail's significance or of Chrétien's intended meaning for the *Conte* as a whole. If the hermit's discourse is not to be trusted, but represents only an ideological parti pris in support of a particular faction on whose behalf the hermit is seeking to enlist Perceval's aid, then the meaning of the Grail remains enigmatic, for there is no clearly authorized interpretation of it within the *Conte*, one untainted by the imperatives of lineage.

The lineal histories and conflicts that the hermit's discourse discloses also suggest that the *Conte du Graal* might usefully be approached with one eye on contemporary aristocratic society, for whom questions of lineage, affiliation, and allegiance were paramount. Written between 1181 and 1190 for Philippe of Alsace, count of Flanders,[5] the *Conte du Graal* appeared at a moment of particular crisis for the Flemish aristocracy. Philippe of Alsace's reign (1157/67–91)[6] marks the beginning of the decline of the Flemish nobility and an important turning point in the history of the county. Initially, however, Philippe's administrative acumen, together with the economic prosperity of his land, appeared to augur well for his emergence as one of the most powerful feudal princes of northern Europe in the last part of the twelfth century. Recognition of the brilliance of his rule, which, Gabrielle Spiegel notes,[7] brought medieval Flanders to the apogee of its power, inspired not only contemporary chroniclers[8] but also Chrétien himself to salute in Philippe the epitome of chivalric values, thus affirming in the dedication to the *Conte du Graal*

Qu'il le fait por le plus preudome
Qui soit en l'empire de Rome.
C'est li quens Phelipes de Flandres,
Qui valt mix ne fist Alixandres.[9]

that he composes [his *Conte*] for the most noble man to be found in the empire of Rome, namely, the count Philippe of Flanders, who is even more worthy than Alexander.

Philippe's action in support of the economic development of Flanders, his creation of a system of governmental agents (the *baillis*) to ensure the maintenance of his rule throughout the land, and the territorial advantages that were potentially his when he married Elizabeth of Vermandois all placed him in a position to attain political preeminence.

Yet Philippe's unstable relations with his neighbors, the kings of England and France, contributed to the erosion of his power and the eventual failure of his reign, while the power of the French kings steadily increased, enabling Philip Augustus (1179–1223) finally to reduce Flanders to a fief of the crown.[10] The death of Philippe of Alsace in 1191 while accompanying Philip Augustus on the Third Crusade marks that moment when the balance of power between monarchy and aristocracy tipped decisively, and irreversibly, in favor of the king.

Confronted, like Philippe of Alsace, by Philip Augustus's political ambitions, other territorial princes attempted to affirm and protect their autonomy. Resistance to the French king was at first facilitated by the fact that his rivals had much greater wealth and territory. During the opening years of his reign, the Capetian monarch thus had to contend with powerful enemies, all the more threatening when their lands ringed the comparatively small royal domain of Ile-de-France (as was the case, to the west, of the duchy of Normandy, ruled by the Plantagenets;[11] of the county of Blois-Champagne, to the south and east; and of the county of Flanders, to the north) and all the more dangerous when these princes joined forces against Philip Augustus, as they did, for example, in 1181.

It is not coincidental that Chrétien's literary career is rooted in those sites of resistance to the French monarchy. We know from Chrétien's own prologues that he composed at least two of his five extant romances, *Yvain* and *Lancelot*, while at the court of Marie of Champagne (whose spouse, Count Henry I, ruled over Champagne from 1164 to 1181) and that he eventually served Philippe of Alsace, to whom he dedicated his last extant romance.[12] Some scholars[13] have also suggested that before entering the service of the countess of Champagne, Chrétien was at the court of the Plantagenets and wrote *Erec et Enide*, and perhaps *Cligés*, for Henry II, king of England from 1154 to 1189. Thus, two if not three of Chrétien's noble patrons were linked to, or actively involved in, the movement of resistance to the Capetians. These courts also entertained close relationships with one another, thereby placing Chrétien within a network of political opposition to the French monarchy. Lineal ties, for example, connected the house of Champagne and the Plantagenets because Marie of Champagne was the daughter of Eleanor of Aquitaine.[14] Strong relations also existed between the houses of Flanders and Champagne: Philippe of Alsace, Chrétien's last known noble patron, was a frequent visitor at Marie's court and even proposed marriage to her after the death of Count Henry in 1181. It appears, therefore, that Chrétien's career evolved at the courts of some of the most powerful and virulent of Philip Augustus's opponents.

The movement of resistance to the French monarchy, however, was far from ensuring stable and harmonious interaction among its main actors. Although the troubled history of the last decades of the twelfth century deserves more attention than it can be given here, it is important to stress that alliances such as those linking the Plantagenets to the house of Champagne and the latter to the house of Flanders were in constant flux. Strategic marriage settlements, dynastic uncertainties, and the fortunes of warfare created a constantly changing social world, attesting to the complex world in and for which Chrétien composed his romances. It is thus difficult to determine the significance of King Arthur (who is only one among many royal characters introduced in Chrétien's *Conte du Graal*) in the context of the struggle between aristocracy and monarchy. Should we recognize in Arthur the figure of Philip Augustus,[15] of Philippe of Alsace,[16] or even of Henry II?[17] Was Chrétien indirectly siding with Philip Augustus or with Philippe of Alsace, his current benefactor? Although no definitive response to these issues exists, they indicate the profoundly unstable and fractured character of feudal society in the last decades of the twelfth century. In that connection, dating Chrétien's *Conte du Graal* between 1181 and 1190 is of crucial importance. Consciously or not, Chrétien's text records a critical moment in the history of Franco-Flemish society in particular and, in a broader sense, of the nobility of northern Europe, as aristocratic ambitions clashed with, and were finally overwhelmed by, Philip Augustus's ambitions.

The failure of the chivalric world, so evident in the *Conte du Graal*, therefore appears to have its analogue in the social world for which it was intended and in the histories of the patron for whom it was composed. Thus, although most scholars have argued that Chrétien's text points to a future redemption of chivalry through the elaboration of a new code of chivalric conduct and endeavor, it is also possible to see in it a displacement to the past of a contemporary context of rivalry. It is present in the work both in its form (most especially in its bipartite structure) and in its content, in terms of an inferred prediegetic past (*prediegetic* referring to events that occurred prior to the temporal setting of the *Conte*) that is constantly, if somewhat ambiguously, invoked in the course of the narration. Although a long tradition, beginning with medieval readers of Chrétien's tale, calls for an allegorical reading of literary works such as the *Conte du Graal*, this tradition should not preclude an attempt to situate the text in its sociocultural context. Chrétien's criticism of traditional chivalry resonated powerfully in the context of contemporary medieval society. The meaning of the Grail may be rooted in part in the predicaments of nobles who, like Philippe of Alsace, patronized vernacular romances.

This book attempts such a social reading of the *Conte du Graal*. It views Grail society not as the embodiment of a regenerated chivalry, but rather as an illustration of Chrétien's awareness of the failure of traditional chivalry. The bipartite structure of the *Conte du Graal*, the division of its *matière* between Perceval, representing, we learn ultimately, the Grail lineage, and Gauvain, champion of the Arthurian realm, suggests that if the *Conte* achieves any degree of coherence, it lies in factionalism, the setting at odds of two principal political forces, figured in the main protagonists. A "social" reading of the *Conte du Graal* suggests that, far from articulating a transcendent, unified, and spiritual ideal of chivalry, this last of Chrétien's romances instead acknowledges the failure of traditional chivalric values to inhibit factionalism and the violence that is its ever-present companion. In the absence of a resolution to the *Conte* that would shed light on a possible connection between Perceval's story and Gauvain's story, hence on any possible unifying function of the Grail motif, the bipartite structure of the text reinforces the view that this is a world fractured by factions in constant, unresolved strife with one another. Whereas traditional interpretations of the *Conte* see in Gauvain the image of a deeply flawed Arthurian society, rectified by Perceval as the embodiment of a regenerated chivalry, I suggest that both Arthurian chivalry and Grail chivalry in the *Conte du Graal* are to be understood as promoting violence and aggression, and that the effort to construe their relationship in terms of a narrative of lineal progress, whereby the defects of Arthurian chivalry are emended and transcended by Perceval, ultimately fails.

Three earlier interpretations of the *Conte du Graal* deserve special mention in the context of my approach because they also call attention to the centrality of factionalism in Chrétien's work. The first is "Perceval et les 'Illes de Mer,'" by Madeleine Blaess. According to Blaess, the enigma of Chrétien's romance revolves around Perceval's family, which demands that the reader pay close attention to its members. From the family chronicle that Perceval's mother relates to her son, we learn that she and her husband are from "the Isles of the Sea." Along with many other nobles of the Isles, they fell into great poverty when Utherpendragon died. The fact that they took refuge in the Welsh "forest gaste," where Perceval's father had a manor, suggests that the latter was originally from Wales, hence Chrétien's occasional identification of the son as "Perchevax li Galois." Perceval's family includes two elder brothers, the older of whom went to reside with the king of Escavalon. There he was trained as a knight and dubbed, but he died on his return to the Welsh forest. The younger went to King Ban de Gomorret, and he too was killed soon after being knighted. Noting that Gauvain is accused of having murdered the king of Escavalon and that Ban is identified in Grail literature after Chrétien as Lancelot's father, Blaess posits that both courts are hostile to Arthur. And so, it appears, is the clan of the Isles, which includes not only Perceval's maternal lineage, but also King Rion,[18] whom Arthur defeats shortly before the time in which the opening of the *Conte du Graal* is set.

While on his way to Arthur's court, Perceval learns that the king and his companions have just killed Rion, king of the Isles, and that Arthur's men have henceforth returned to their respective domains. In Blaess's view, this information presents the young protagonist with a unique opportunity to avenge the defeat of his clan. However, Perceval not only fails to seize this opportunity, but—worse still—offers his service to Arthur. The "pechiez" invoked by the hermit, his uncle, thus refers to Perceval's decision to align himself with Arthur, neglecting to avenge his lineage, a failure repeated and confirmed later in his indifference to the plight of another uncle, the wounded king of the Grail castle. According to Blaess, the ambiguous character of the *Conte du*

Graal lies in Chrétien's attempt to "Arthurize" what is fundamentally anti-Arthurian material.

My reading of the *Conte* concurs at many points with Blaess's, but I take issue with her conclusion that Chrétien intended to "Arthurize" the Grail material. Rather, I show that interactions between Arthurian society and the Grail lineage remain hostile throughout the *Conte du Graal*. Second, I believe the ambiguity of Chrétien's tale lies in the ambiguous nature of Perceval's situation as his service is simultaneously solicited by two antagonistic systems of authority. Third, I believe Chrétien was fully aware of the profoundly factional nature of contemporary aristocratic life and used ambiguity to suggest the contending forces that weighed upon contemporary knights and vied for their allegiance. From this perspective, the enigma of the *Conte du Graal* lies not in a problematic mingling of two vastly different literary traditions—the Arthurian legend and the Grail motif—but in a predicament that, for Perceval, as for similarly impoverished young nobles throughout Europe in the late twelfth century, consisted of having to choose between service and loyalty to aristocratic and royal rulers.

The second interpretation of Chrétien's *Conte du Graal* to which I am indebted is that of Philippe Ménard, proposed in his article "Problèmes et mystères du *Conte du Graal*." Underscoring the dynastic component of Perceval's story, Ménard asserts that the protagonist's mission is to restore Grail kingship to its previous strength and prosperity. For Ménard, it is not the Grail dish with its implied religious value that functions as the central and unifying motif of Chrétien's tale, but rather the lame king of the Grail castle. The king's wound bespeaks a history of violence, calling for the identification of the enemies of the Grail lineage. For various reasons too detailed to rehearse here, Ménard identifies the realm of Escavalon as the principal threat to Grail society, responsible both for the wounding of the king of the Grail and for the death of Perceval's elder brother. It is to prevent further aggression against his lineage that Perceval must become the new king of Grail society. In this context Gauvain's role is to help Perceval first to identify and then to overpower his family's foes. Ménard's interpretation of the dynastic history subtending the *Conte du Graal* thus posits a prediegetic narrative of aggression pitting the Escavalon faction against the Grail lineage.

Although I share Ménard's view concerning the central importance of the wounded king of the Grail, I read the events that take place at Escavalon as indices of a dispute not between the Escavalon faction and the Grail lineage, but between Grail kingship and Arthurian kingship. The fact that Perceval's father entrusted his eldest son to the king of Escavalon rather than to Arthur, as is usual in the context of Arthurian literature, suggests that both the Welsh nobleman and the king of Escavalon are hostile to Arthur. Indeed, a tension between Arthur and all rival sources of authority, whose alliance with one another is based on their unanimous desire to oppose the king's drive for dominance, is at the core of the *Conte du Graal*.

A final interpretation I have found particularly useful in understanding the role of revenge in Chrétien's romance is an article published in 1987 by Jean-Claude Lozachmeur. Adopting Roger S. Loomis's thesis on the legendary Celtic origins of the Grail story in *Arthurian Tradition and Chrétien de Troyes*, Lozachmeur distinguishes between two principal archetypes of the Grail legend. Archetype A, which designates the primitive stage of the legend, has as its central theme the vengeance that Perceval is expected to take against those who harmed the wounded king of the Grail castle. Archetype B represents a later stage in the development of the legend, in which the theme of vengeance has disappeared and been replaced by the quest motif. In Chrétien's romance— inspired by or itself the origin of Archetype B, according to Lozachmeur—Perceval's quest is essentially a quest for knowledge. As in the case of many texts produced on the model of Archetype B, Chrétien eliminates episodes that, in the plot following an A model, deal with the hero's combat against the enemies of Grail kingship. Some of the original elements of A, however, *are* preserved, notably Gauvain's adventures in Galvoie, which lead him to fight against the enemies of the Grail king. Lozachmeur's interpretation of the *Conte du Graal* thus identifies the "Pays de Galvoie" as a site of forces hostile to Perceval's lineage, suggesting that Gauvain, hence Arthur, aligns with Perceval against the enemies of Grail kingship.

My reading of Chrétien's romance entertains a completely different interpretation of the relationship between Arthur and the Grail lineage. In terms of Lozachmeur's categories, it views the *Conte du Graal* as closer to Archetype A than B, at least insofar as the revenge motif appears to me to stand at the forefront of both Perceval's and Gauvain's stories. In my opinion, the motif of the quest does not replace the theme of vengeance but is integral to Perceval's mission as avenger of the Grail lineage. Gauvain's story, in contrast, begins and ends with an accusation, thus focusing on his role as Arthur's champion and articulating the point of view of forces hostile to Arthur and determined to challenge his authority.

As in the case of the three interpretations I have summarized, at the core of my reading lies an analysis of Chrétien's hero, Perceval, whose main characteristic is his ignorance of chivalric society. That Chrétien chose to tell his story through the eyes of an ignorant protagonist, who has misperceptions and misapprehensions concerning the chivalric world he devoutly wishes to enter, implies something of the blindness and unawareness that, Chrétien seems to suggest, determine the deeply flawed character of traditional chivalry. At the same time, the fragmentary nature of the information provided to Perceval and, through him, to Chrétien's public is in large part the reason for the multiplicity of interpretations that his romance has inspired and continues to inspire.

The challenge posed by Chrétien's romance is therefore not that it lacks intrinsic meaning—and the multiplicity of readings to which it is subject testifies to its complex character—but that it hides that meaning deliberately. What confronts Perceval, Chrétien's ignorant protagonist, is a plethora of intratextual interpretations regarding his chivalric mission. Particularly confusing in that respect is the multifold significance of the Grail, at once a spectacular work of art, a serving dish, a symbol of the wounded king and his domain, a reference to Perceval's lineage, and the sacred holder of the Host. The variety of intratextual viewpoints concerning the value of the Grail points to its function as an ideological discourse sustaining specific lineal ambitions, rather than a mere object of impartial splendor, although the spectacular artistry of the serving dish is not in question. Given this, I attempt to decipher its meaning for its intratextual interpreters rather than to establish a transcendent significance that would somehow represent the sum of Chrétien's intentions. Because Chrétien narrates his tale through the eyes of Perceval, and because Perceval is ignorant, the reader of the romance must pursue clues whose full meanings are not entirely clear to the protagonist himself. In this sense, the *Conte du Graal* often functions rather like a detective story, compelling its readers to construe the language of Perceval's interlocutors in order to uncover their respective motives and aims. Perhaps the most striking "mystery" in the *Conte du Graal* is why the representatives of Arthurian society never mention the Grail, whereas spokesmen of the Grail lineage insist on its fundamental value. Part of the enigma of the Grail derives from the exegetical language— exegetical in the sense that it ascribes sacred meaning to Perceval's quest for the Grail—that these spokesmen employ to persuade Perceval to enlist in the defense of the Grail lineage. And of no one is this as true as of his uncle, the hermit. Those representing the Arthurian realm are singularly silent concerning the Grail, so this imbalance in the distribution of discourse relating to the putatively holy dish suggests that the Grail is first and foremost *their* Grail, that is, less an object or symbol of an overarching Christian eschatology than a strategic argument articulated to advance a partisan conception of chivalry.

Some comments need to be made about my choice of version for this study. The manuscript tradition mediates the text of Chrétien's *Conte du Graal* and thus poses a challenge for the recovery of its original meaning. One difficulty it presents is the existence not only of a relatively large number of manuscripts [19] for a text dating from the twelfth century, but also of a large number of variants from one manuscript to another. Because each codex represents a specific stage—hence form—of the text's transmission, each also constitutes, as Alexandre Micha observes,[20] the medieval equivalent of an "edition" of the *Conte*'s first version. Noting that the entire manuscript tradition of the *Conte* is characterized by continuous rewriting,[21] Micha questions the possibility of ever retrieving Chrétien's original romance. What further complicates the task of both editors and commentators of the *Conte* is the fact that, as Rupert Pickens remarks, "a high number of medieval copies existed that have not survived to modern times."[22] This loss renders virtually impossible the establishment of textual filiation. In his extensive comparative analysis of the *Conte*'s manuscript tradition, however, Micha succeeded in grouping the texts in clusters of affiliated versions, thus elaborating a complex relational scheme, on the basis of which Pickens identifies four major clusters.

It appears that the texts in each of these four clusters "all descend from a common exemplar and that the four exemplars descend from an original executed by Chrétien de Troyes."[23] The fourth of these clusters—cluster Delta in Pickens's designation[24]—owes its prestige to the fact that the northern dialect characterizing the texts links them to scriptoria in territories governed by Philippe of Alsace, for whom Chrétien wrote his last extant romance. But it is the primary model of cluster Alpha—Bibliothèque Nationale, fonds français 794[25]—that has attracted the attention of editors,[26] due to the relative antiquity of the codex (which dates from the second quarter of the thirteenth century), the renown of its scribe (Guiot, who lived in Paris but came from a region of Ile-de-France bordering Champagne),[27] and the Champenois cast of Guiot's text, resembling "what may have been Chrétien's own language."[28] That Guiot's copies of Chrétien's four other romances are universally praised for their reliability convinces Pickens that the scribe's version of the *Conte du Graal*, "as problematic as it is, deserves to be taken seriously."[29] This view corroborates both Micha's assessment of the relative merit of Ms. A and his emphasis on the necessity of controlling Guiot's text through examination of those manuscripts that share with Ms. A similar peculiarities in terms of variants, readings, and lacunae.[30]

Yet not all scholars share Micha's and Pickens's qualified preference for Ms. A. Tony Hunt, for example, believes that "the value of the Guiot texts has been overestimated or uncritically accepted."[31] A larger problem regarding the *Conte du Graal*, according to Hunt, is the lack of a reliable edition, despite the previously cited works of Baist, Hilka, and Lecoy, along with those of Potvin[32] and, more recently, William Roach,[33] none of which provides a complete version of its respective base texts. Until scholars collaborate to produce a new critical edition of Chrétien's romances, Hunt concludes, "studies will no doubt continue to ignore editorial problems, to proceed inconsistently, or to move from one edition to another."[34]

My study leaves itself open to Hunt's justified criticism. Acknowledging the distance that separates any modern or medieval "editions" of the *Conte du Graal* from Chrétien's original text, and recognizing the virtual impossibility of taking into account all the variations and alterations characterizing the process of textual transmission, I opted to ground my analysis on a specific form or stage of that transmission— William Roach's edition of Ms. T—primarily for three reasons: first, because of the generally acknowledged reliability of the codex;[35] second, because the dialect of Ms. T is Francien-Picard (a dialect close to the local language of Chrétien's patron, Philippe of Alsace), suggesting that this specific version of the *Conte du Graal* might have been produced in a location close to the territories in which the text originated and might thus represent a stage relatively close to what Chrétien composed;[36] third, because Roach's edition is prepared in such a way as to facilitate comparison of version T with that of Guiot as edited by Hilka.

The version of Ms. T is often at variance with those preserved in other manuscripts.[37] Among other examples[38] are the twenty lines (inserted between lines 3926 and 3927 of Roach's edition) that narrate how Perceval breaks the Grail sword when fighting against Orgueilleux de la Lande.[39] Two other manuscripts, Ms. H and Ms. P, amplify the incident of Perceval's breaking of the sword and link it to the lame king of the Grail, recounting how the king sends a *valet* to recover the pieces, which the latter carries back to the castle. In Ms. H, the lame king then announces to the members of his household that he will be cured of his wound on the day when "the best knight in the world" comes and asks about the lance and the *graal*, thus effecting the mending of the sword:

> S'en avera grand los e grand pris,
> Sur trestouz ceus de cest païs,
> Voir del realme le roi Arthurs.
> (Ed. Hilka, app. 2, ll. 375–77)

This will gain him great honor and value, over and beyond all the knights in this region, indeed, in Arthur's kingdom.

Yet the king sadly remarks, "The shores of the salted sea will come together" before such a knight can be found (ll. 322–23).

Two factors may account for the specificity of version T—as opposed to the *Conte*'s main manuscript tradition—in narrating the episode of Perceval's breaking of the Grail sword. At the intratextual level, first, this episode verifies the prediction, made to Perceval by his own cousin, that the sword he was given by his host at the Grail castle is bound to break in battle.[40] A second factor, at the extratextual level, is the reduction of Perceval's role in Grail literature after Chrétien.[41] Perceval's breaking of the Grail sword in version T anticipates, in that sense, the substitution of Galahad for Perceval as the ultimate hero of the quest. The influence of this later textual tradition is even more in evidence in version H, which implies that it is not Perceval, but a knight still to come, who will effect the restoration of both the king and the kingdom of the Grail. Yet the predicted resolution of the quest in the interpolation of Ms. H (the latest—mid fourteenth century—of the codices in which the *Conte* is preserved) shares none of the spiritual quality that distinguishes many of the Grail narratives after Chrétien.

That Chrétien's text is here last in a series of chronicles relative to the history of England (signaling that its producer sought to exalt King Arthur as a noteworthy figure of English history) puts forward a social rather than ethical interpretation of Perceval's story.[42] In this perspective, the interpolated passage articulates implicitly, and perhaps unintentionally, a tension between two distinct principles of sovereignty: Arthur's and the Grail.[43] Paradoxically, considering the pro-Arthurian tenor of this historiographical codex, the lame king of the Grail predicts the coming of a knight, better than any one of Arthur's knights, who will restore the power and status of both king and kingdom. Does this interpolation inadvertently reflect Chrétien's intentions in composing his final romance? Should we read Perceval's breaking of the Grail sword and the lame king's ensuing lament as indicating the existence of a strife between him and Arthur, which will end only with the appearance of a champion strong enough both to realize the Grail king's ambitions and inhibit Arthur's?

Too concise to provide a response to these questions, the interpolation of Ms. H, along with the shorter one present in both Mss. T and P, is nonetheless noteworthy for giving the character of the Grail king more narrative weight than he has in most other versions preserved in the manuscript tradition. Significantly, editors tend to view and treat these added lines as an unwarranted interpolation because the Grail king, particularly in the case of Mss. H and P, loses in the process some of his mysterious quality. Indeed, the primarily seigneurial tenor of the king's lament in the interpolation of Ms. H appears not to cohere with the sacred aura that the character possesses in the discourse of Perceval's eremitic uncle. Also noteworthy in that connection is the rather confused and confusing identity that the Grail king acquires in the course of Perceval's story. At issue here is how all the manuscript versions at times distinguish between father (the Maimed King of the Grail) and son (the Fisher King) while at other times identifying the Grail king as a single royal figure. This issue, which I further analyze in Chapter 3, emblematizes the kind of difficulties facing commentators of the *Conte du Graal*. To focus as I do on the text of Ms. T—in William Roach's edition—amounts to privileging one specific version in this complex manuscript tradition. Resorting to what Hunt considers an inadequate procedure, I occasionally move from one edition to another, consulting other versions of the romance when they contain passages germane to the perspective developed here.

Because this perspective addresses the social rather than transcendent significance of Chrétien's *Conte du Graal*, it is noteworthy that both the organization and iconographic program of Ms. T bear the marks of a religious interpretation of the Grail legend. Not only is the *Conte du*

Graal first in a series of texts that includes the *Continuations* of Gerbert de Montreuil and of Manessier, both of which imbue Chrétien's romance with spiritual significance, but the codex also ends with the Renclus de Moiliens's romances, *Miserere* and *Carité*, thus inspiring Micha to compare the Grail story (quest for the Grail) and the message of the Renclus (quest for charity).[44] Is Micha correct in taking the religious tenor of the codex as a sign that in Chrétien's version, too, the *graal* had a transcendent significance?

A preliminary answer to this question lies in the distance that separates the *Conte*'s date of composition from that of the manuscripts in which the text is preserved. Considering that no manuscripts survive from Chrétien's own time and that the earliest manuscript containing the *Conte* (Ms. B) probably dates from the second quarter of the thirteenth century, as Alison Stones observes, the manuscript tradition does not provide "aspects of Chrétien's own thinking as presented by the author himself."[45] Rather, this tradition provides information on the values and expectations of the specific public for which each codex was intended. In this connection, Ms. T constitutes a stage in the reception of Chrétien's works as it had evolved by about 1250 and reflects the intents and purposes of its producer.

Regarding the producer's textual selection, those intentions are not altogether clear. In inserting the two moralistic narratives by the Renclus de Moiliens, the planner of the codex, according to Lori Walters, "may well have wished to emphasize Perceval's ultimate choice of the spiritual over the worldly life."[46] Alison Stones disagrees with this view: because blank folios separate the Renclus's narratives from the rest of the codex and because the Renclus's texts begin a fresh quire, they "are unlikely to have been planned as a sequel to the *Continuations*."[47] Whether they were inserted by the producer of Ms. T or added later, the inclusion of the Renclus's texts articulates a Christian recasting of Perceval's story, stressing the value of repentance and charity in effecting the protagonist's spiritual transformation.

This recasting is amplified by the iconographic program of Ms. T, which begins its version of Chrétien's *Conte du Graal* with a multicompartment opening miniature that summarizes Perceval's story as it is interpreted by the texts contained in the codex. The upper register of the miniature shows Perceval's encounter with a group of knights; the lower register comprises a left-hand compartment, which depicts Perceval's arrival at Arthur's court, and a right-hand compartment, which illustrates Perceval's slaying of the Red Knight (the latter brandishes the gold cup he stole from Arthur).[48] In Lori Walters's view, the cup depicted in this last picture "foreshadows Perceval's role as seeker of the Grail."[49] That the producer of the codex intends to emphasize the episode in Chrétien's romance narrating Perceval's discovery of the serving dish at the Grail castle and to present it as a prologue to his quest for the Grail in the *Continuations* is confirmed by another illustration, located after the concluding line of the last of the Perceval *Continuations* (folio 261).[50] From right to left, it shows a figure holding a lance, a figure kneeling before the Grail, and a figure giving the Grail (here, a chalice) to an angel.[51] According to Emmanuèle Baumgartner, for whom the kneeling figure of the illustration represents Perceval, this final image of the Perceval Cycle in Ms. T both encapsulates and enlightens the message conveyed by the quadripartite miniature opening the text of Chrétien's *Conte du Graal*. Whereas the opening image calls attention to the lethal effect of Perceval's actions when he enters the realm of chivalry, the illustration concluding the Perceval Cycle depicts the protagonist's eventual transformation as it is narrated in some sequels of Chrétien's romance, thus showing him dressed in clerical garb and adoring the Grail as a holy relic.[52]

The text of Chrétien's romance contains only six illustrations, five of which relate to Perceval and emphasize the elements in his story that present him as both a warrior and a knight.[53] A remarkable aspect of this iconographic program is that Ms. T provides no depiction of Perceval's adventure at the Grail castle and thus deliberately ignores the part of Chrétien's romance that connects Perceval to the Grail.[54] In Baumgartner's view, the visual silence of the *Perceval* manuscripts with respect to the protagonist's Grail adventure in Chrétien's *Conte du Graal* reflects the illustrators' reticence in representing the *graal* as a serving dish and not as a holy relic.[55] Taken together, the illustrated manuscripts in which Chrétien's romance is preserved, including Ms. T,[56] articulate an interpretation of the Grail legend that recognizes the secular character of Chrétien's romance, in contradistinction to the spiritual recasting of its sequels.

The religious tenor of Ms. T therefore derives not from Chrétien's version of the Grail legend, but from the texts it inspired. Because this is potentially the case for all the codices in which Chrétien's romance is preserved,[57] any attempt to retrieve its meaning must take into account the retrospective character of each medieval "edition" of the *Conte du*

Graal. In this connection, the alternative reading that I propose here tries to recapture some possible intentions of Chrétien as the author of a text that Guiot, before proceeding with the transcription of the *First Continuation*, designates as "Percevax le viel."[58] It is Chrétien's "old," inaugural Grail story that I attempt to retrieve from the versions provided by Ms. T and by Roach's edition of the *Conte du Graal* contained in that codex.

As the massive body of Grail literature dating from the late twelfth century to the fifteenth century testifies, Chrétien's *Conte du Graal* clearly attracted the attention of both his contemporaries and successors. It continues to hold its fascination for us today, in part because its enigmatic character still excites our curiosity and commands our interest. This book represents a modest attempt to offer one possible reading of Chrétien's much read and much interpreted work. Although differing from existing interpretations in its focus on the "social" implications of Chrétien's narrative, it does not seek so much to replace those earlier views as to supplement them. Any text as rich as this opens itself for multiple kinds of readings, no one of which can possibly hope to account for the text in its entirety. I hope that this reading, in foregrounding some novel aspects of the work, will ultimately enrich our understanding of both the imaginative power and complex relations with the world in which it appears that constitute the enduring fascination of medieval literature in general and of the romances of Chrétien de Troyes in particular.

Chapter I

In Pursuit of Power

Prominent among the factors that have ensured the popularity of the Grail legend from the Middle Ages until today is the universal character of a quest whose destination bespeaks the attainment of excellence and perfection. The quest for the "Holy Grail" owes its enduring currency to its significance as the emblem of man's relentless attempt to rise above the human condition. Its reinscriptions in fiction and cinema are recent confirmations of the wide appeal and lasting fascination the legend exerts.

Returning to the moment, around the years 1180–91, at which the legendary quest appeared on the literary scene, I explore its genesis in the earliest extant Grail romance: Chrétien de Troyes's *Conte du Graal*. At issue is whether this inaugural text coheres with the tradition, developed by Chrétien's literary heirs, according to which the goal of the quest is a transcendent, "Holy" Grail. Although Grail literature after Chrétien sustains an interpretation of the *Conte du Graal* endowing both the Grail and its quest with ideal value, one cannot assume that these sequels represent a gloss of the text faithful to Chrétien's intentions. Nor can the Grail, even in the generally idealized perspective developed after Chrétien, be seen as a monolithic emblem. Taking into account the variable character of the Grail throughout the medieval tradition, this book, which in no way claims to represent the final word on the Grail according to Chrétien, assesses the *Conte du Graal* in the light of the specific sociocultural moment inscribed and internalized in this earliest extant Grail romance. My goal is to use a "social" reading of Chrétien's work to provide an alternative explanation for a romance whose hallmark is and will remain its highly complex and enigmatic character.

Part of the enigma posed by Chrétien's romance lies in the multiple meanings assigned to the "Grail" in the course of the narrative. With one exception ("Ce est li Contes del Graal," l. 66 of Roach's edition),[1] the 24 occurrences of the word *graal* in Chrétien's *Conte* refer to the serving dish that Perceval sees during his sojourn in the Grail castle. In the context of the romance, however, the word also takes on a metaphoric significance and designates, successively or simultaneously, a locus (the Grail castle itself), a kingdom (that of the royal recluse who lives at the castle), a sacred food (the Host served to the recluse), and a destination, in reference to Perceval's potential return to the Grail castle. The latter two meanings of Chrétien's *graal* were to have a lasting influence, for the sacred content of the dish stands at the origin of the traditional view of the Grail—henceforth capitalized[2]—as both an ideal quest and the quest for an ideal.

Another reason for the enigmatic character of Chrétien's *Conte du Graal* is its lack of narrative resolution. In the state of the text as preserved by the extant manuscript tradition,[3] the story of Perceval "ends" at the moment when the hermit's revelation of the eucharistic content of the *graal* prompts Perceval to repent and recognize Christ as the savior of mankind:

> Icele nuit a mengier ot
> Ice qu'al saint hermite plot;
> Mais il n'i ot se betes non,[4]
> Cerfueil, laitues et cresson
> Et mill, et pain d'orge et d'avaine,
> Et iaue de clere fontaine.
> Et ses chevax ot de l'estrain
> Et de l'orge un bachin tot plain.[5]   6506
> Issi Perchevax reconnut   6509
> Que Diex el vendredi rechut
> Mort et si fu crucefiiez.
> A le Pasque communiiez
> Fu Perchevax molt dignement.
> De Percheval plus longuement
> Ne parole li contes chi,
> Ainz avrez molt ançois oï
> De monseignor Gavain parler
> Que rien m'oiez de lui conter.
>   (Ed Roach, ll. 6499–518)

That night he ate that which pleased the holy hermit; but he was offered only beets, chervil, lettuce and watercress, and millet, and barley and oat bread, and clear spring water. And his horse had straw and a full bucket of barley. Here Perceval acknowledged that God was condemned to death on the Friday and was thus crucified. On Easter Sunday Perceval was given communion with due respect. The story here no longer talks about Perceval, and you will have heard a great deal about my lord Gauvain before I speak of Perceval again.

Considering that Chrétien here states his intention eventually to resume the recounting of Perceval's adventures, there is no question of narrative closure. Yet because the passage marks Perceval's last appearance in the romance, it has a terminal rather than transitional effect. At this point in his story, Perceval seems to have reached a level of maturity propitious to future success in his quest, but we do not know whether and, if so, how he will recover the Grail. Nor do we know the significance of Perceval's achievement in relation to Gauvain's story, which Chrétien proposes now to narrate in what constitutes the second part of his romance.

The inconclusiveness of Chrétien's *Conte du Graal* played a crucial part in the sustained fascination the legend exerted during the Middle Ages. Within a decade, several sequels were in circulation, followed by a vast corpus of Grail literature, ranging from Wolfram von Eschenbach's *Parzival*, through verse and prose renditions of the quest in various vernacular languages, and culminating with Malory's *Morte Darthur* in 1485. At the core of the rewriting and recycling of Chrétien's romance is a desire to elucidate the meaning of his *Conte du Graal* by providing a coherent narrative resolution. In the context of a story line inferring Perceval's eventual recovery of the Grail, a natural conclusion is the completion of the quest, which remains the ultimate achievement throughout the Grail medieval tradition. At the same time, however, Grail narratives after Chrétien, particularly the Vulgate Cycle,[6] tend to value not only the completion of the quest but also—if not primarily—the search itself, which they conceive of as a voyage conducive to self-improvement. An indication of the importance granted to the act of searching in the Vulgate Cycle is that, in contrast with the *Conte*, whose narration appears to assign to Perceval alone the mission of finding the Grail, it introduces a plethora of "questers." Galahad alone attains full knowledge of the Grail and thus emerges as the sole successful hero of the quest, so each of the other questers' achievements are, by comparison, imperfect or incomplete. What is meritorious, then, is not the questers' completion of the journey so much as each protagonist's attempt to draw nearer to an ideal image of himself. The result is an emphasis on the personal significance of the quest as a voyage toward maturity or as a pilgrimáge toward redemption, the final stage of which entails a kind of individual eschatology.

The amplification of the inner value of the act of questing in Grail literature after Chrétien is commensurate with the discovery, in John Benton's word, "rediscovery,"[7] of the individual in twelfth-century Europe, leading to a renewal of personal ethics. According to Colin Morris, a dominant interest in the private and personal, rather than the public and communal, aspects of the self emerged during the period. Provoked by the challenges posed by an increasingly complex society, which demanded a capacity for individual evaluation, criticism, and initiative, the rebirth of the individual in the twelfth century reflects an awareness of the existence of a range of options within which "there was no clear or simple ethic."[8] That the nature of true knighthood, for example, was an object of intense discussion testifies to the difficulty of determining one's place and function in a society whose values were increasingly experienced as varied and unstable. But these uncertainties also contributed to a resurgence of interest in inner growth and personal choice, leading to the development of a sense of identity that contemporary thought, according to Morris, understood in terms of dynamic self-realization.

The renewed focus on personal ethics in twelfth-century thought contributed to the reinscription of the later vernacular *roman* according to the values of a pervasive Christian ethos, as attested by the emphasis on the inner value of the act of questing in the Vulgate Cycle, but the question is whether this "rediscovery of the individual" exerted a comparable influence on the portrayal of the knightly protagonist in twelfth-century romance. Considering the authors' tendency to present the narration of their heroes' adventures from the latter's perspective, as is notably the case of Chrétien de Troyes, the representation of knightly society in twelfth-century imaginative literature seems to qualify as an individual-centered realm. In contrast to traditional epics such as the *Chanson de Roland*, whose focus is not the hero's inner motivation but his adherence to a pre-established code of conduct, the essential quality of the protagonist of chivalric romance appears to be his capacity to confront, understand, and control the world that surrounds him. What characterizes chivalric romance, in Robert Hanning's view, is thus a biographical, rather than familial, tribal, or national, narration that is constructed of linked critical moments punctuating the hero's progress as a self-determined individual.[9]

At the same time, this biographical narration takes its full significance only in the social context within which the protagonist achieves his heroic destiny. The hero's journey typically takes him away from the society of Arthur's court into the forest; there he will prove his worth through heroic exploits. The ultimate goal of these exploits is to earn him the reputation that will ensure his preeminent value at Arthur's court.[10] Also noteworthy is the role of amorous pursuits in relation to the protagonist's quest for honor and glory: although love and chivalry are frequently the two essential motifs of the story line developed in Chrétien's romances, the protagonist's amorous experience tends to remain subordinate to, and governed by, his determination to prove that he is the best of all knights.[11] Essentially, the primary force that induces the protagonist to undertake the series of exploits awaiting him in the forest is his desire to fashion for himself a public persona that will elicit the admiration—and envy—of his peers. In the masculine context of the chivalric society depicted in Chrétien's Arthurian romances, love is not an end in itself; instead, it is one of the means by which an impoverished knight, as is often the case of Chrétien's protagonists, can hope to realize his dream of social promotion. Feats of arms and amorous conquests are, in that sense, two similar manifestations of the self-advancing impulses that prompt the protagonist to demonstrate his knightly preeminence on the stage of ritualized masculinity.

The hero's prevailing concern for his public persona as knight puts forward a construal of the self that is intricately linked to one's status and renown within the chivalric community. The emphasis is not on an autonomous and unencumbered entity, what social psychology describes as "an independent self," but rather on "the interdependent self."[12] Indeed, the mark of the society depicted by traditional romance is a "fundamental connectedness of human beings to each other," indicating that the individual acts "primarily in accordance with the anticipated expectation of others and social norms rather than with internal wishes and personal attributes." From this perspective, the hero achieves his quest for prominence and visibility to the extent that he adheres to— and surpasses—the "normative imperatives" of what qualifies as a "collectivist culture."[13] Rather than entailing a conflict between his inner self (love) and his external self (chivalry), the hero's dilemma consists of a confrontation between love and chivalry as two contradictory, yet equally self-advancing, impulses, both of which are paramount for his successful transformation from an impoverished and peripheral knight at court into the champion of Arthur's companions. Erec, for example, must prove himself a superior lover by acquiring the most desirable lady, yet without losing in the process his knightly worth. Yvain must demonstrate that he is a superior knight through feats of arms, yet without losing in the process both his lady and her domain.

To be resolved, this dilemma calls upon the hero's capacity to control the outer and inner circumstances of his story in a manner ensuring that he will attain social preeminence. In a community whose members possess equal martial valor and are each eagerly in quest of the most desirable lady, cleverness (*engin*) thus emerges as one of the hero's primary assets. *Erec et Enide*, for example, is a typical illustration of the value of cleverness in enabling the protagonist to turn the contrary forces of love and prowess into a self-advantageous complementary alliance. This Erec achieves by removing Enide and himself from court to forest once he realizes that the adventure world is the only proper setting in which to prove his excellence as both knight and husband.[14] By enabling Erec to determine his own destiny, intelligence or even craftiness in manipulating the world that surrounds him also effects his transformation from an insignificant member of the Arthurian community into the most valorous knight at court.[15] At the biographical level, therefore, the happy ending of the narrative is evidence that Erec has realized his personal ambitions. Yet this ending also creates the inherent danger that Erec, as the best of all knights and the newly enthroned "king of Nantes," will rival Arthur's authority.[16] At the sociopolitical level, therefore, "happy endings" such as the ones elaborated in the concluding episodes of Chrétien's *Erec* and *Yvain* have a deproblematizing effect, indicating that it is not by solving but by circumventing the inherent predicament of Arthurian society that the hero liberates himself from the constraints of that society and contrives to satisfy his personal desires.

The self-centered character of the hero's quest in traditional chivalric romance is at the core of the reinscription of the genre in thirteenth-century narratives, particularly the five texts of the Vulgate Cycle. Although they, too, exploit the motif of the quest as a central narrative device, these Grail texts also ascribe to it a profoundly different meaning and orientation. Particularly noteworthy is how they articulate a radical condemnation of the social values extolled in traditional chivalric romance. Whereas the quest for excellence initiated by the hero of twelfth-century romance typically concludes with his success in reconciling his amorous impulses with his martial impulses, thus leading to his glorious reinsertion within Arthurian society in the final episode of his story, in the Vulgate Cycle, the search for the Grail presupposes that the quester distance himself from the sphere of chivalric society. Not only do these thirteenth-century narratives call into question the ideal and idealizing combination of love and chivalry that marks the ending of Chrétien's *Erec et Enide* and *Yvain*, they also present love and prowess as two contrary forces that coalesce in a way that fosters hostile and, in the end, lethal relationships among the members of the chivalric community. Thus, instead of projecting the vision of a society whose refinement renders possible the knight's domestication of his sexual and aggressive impulses, the Vulgate Cycle questions and even condemns that vision by bringing out the inherently disruptive instability of chivalric society.

Although one might assume that, taken together, the respective journeys of the questing protagonists, who share an affiliation with Arthur, will contribute to the progress of Arthurian society toward peace and harmony, narratives in the Vulgate Cycle, such as the *Mort le roi Artu*, describe instead the cataclysmic battle in which Arthur dies. This outcome indicates that the ultimate (if elusive) goal of the quest for the Grail is to effect the quester's internal betterment, rather than to further terrestrial chivalry. To the extent that "success" in searching for the Grail depends on the quester's willingness to relinquish such power and glory as knighthood confers on its adherents, the intended result of the quest is clearly a disempowerment of chivalric society. As the tragic conclusion of Arthur's history illustrates, the Grail material clashes with the Arthurian material in a manner that discloses the presence of an irreconcilable conflict between self and society. With the exception of Galahad, sole among the questers to complete the quest and receive full revelation of the mystery of the Grail, the protagonists of the Vulgate Cycle serve as exemplars of the fallibility of human nature. In contrast to the hero of traditional romance, whose success in chivalric society results from his capacity to manipulate and control the world that surrounds him, for most of the questers introduced in Grail literature after Chrétien, progress entails repudiating the realm of self-interested pursuits and recognizing one's imperfection as a human being.

What emerges from the openly anti-individualistic character of this literary production, in Robert Hanning's view, is the "fatalistic knowledge that history rules man, that time rules history, and that divine providence, by imposing a high duty on the Christian, makes the pursuit of pleasure or self-fulfillment on earth transitory and ultimately delusory."[17] That self-driven pursuits inexorably provoke both personal failure and universal collapse is confirmed by the effect of Lancelot's adulterous relationship with Guinevere in transforming Arthur's best knight into one of the least worthy questers of the Grail.[18] Once Lancelot's love for Guinevere becomes public knowledge, he and Arthur "fall out, the inhabitants of the Arthurian world divide into two warring camps, and the way is finally open for the kingdom to fall prey to Mordred's baser treachery."[19] Far from contributing to the regeneration or redemption of traditional Arthurian chivalry, the insertion of the Grail material in the Vulgate Cycle thus discloses its most problematic components. The lesson here is that terrestrial chivalry does not domesticate but on the contrary exacerbates the knight's sexual and aggressive impulses,[20] whence the introduction of a radically different notion of chivalry, one whose primary values include humility, abnegation, and service to others, requiring of the questing knights that they relinquish the tradition of violence and rivalry constitutive of chivalric society.

The condemnation of traditional chivalry in the hands of Chrétien's successors is a well-known aspect of the evolution of romance from the twelfth to the thirteenth century.[21] What is less clear are the reasons that prompted romance writers to abandon the optimistic assessment of selfhood in traditional chivalric narratives and to stress instead the faults and failure of Arthurian society. Although both the dating of the *Conte du Graal* and its role in inaugurating the Grail literary tradition situate Chrétien's romance at a turning point within that evolution, it still remains to determine whether the *Conte* influenced the pessimistic vision articulated by Chrétien's successors. Does Chrétien's romance, marking the beginning of a new era, articulate a concept of quest that anticipates the anti-Arthurian tenor of the thirteenth-century Vulgate Cycle? Contrarily, does Perceval's quest represent a promise that Arthurian chivalry can and will evolve toward a superior, regenerated form? Or is the quest for the Grail in Chrétien's *Conte* the very metaphor of the self-driven type of pursuits that govern traditional chivalry, thus encapsulating its fractious and ultimately destructive effects?

In the present state of the text, these are open issues, just as the issue of Perceval's quest for the Grail remains open, because indefinitely postponed. For Hanning, who admits to being puzzled by Chrétien's unfinished romance, the *Conte* "seems to be turning toward a new imaginative paradigm of the quest for individual fulfillment, involving service to a Christian social and personal ideal rather than the pursuit of a perfection best represented by the purely private experience of love." [22] A characteristic of Chrétien's last romance is that it appears to play down the value of love in contributing to the emergence of the hero as a fully realized individual. Whether the reduced importance of the motif in Perceval's story represents Chrétien's admission that love has no part in the making of a knight, except in the world of make-believe inferred from the "happy endings" of traditional romance, or whether it signals the substitution of divine love—*caritas*—for human love,[23] there is no question that the *Conte du Graal* constitutes an innovative use of romance at the level of writing techniques, plot, and characterization.

Testimony to Chrétien's capacity to reinvent the rules of the genre is, first, the determination he expresses in the prologue of the *Conte* to give a new impetus to what had by then become traditional material. Although Chrétien does allude to a "book" entrusted to him by Philippe of Alsace ("Ce est li Contes del Graal, / Dont li quens li bailla le livre"),[24] he also amplifies, as Michel Zink remarks, his own role as originator of the story: "Crestïens seme et fait semence / D'un romans que il encomence." [25] Even more openly than in the prologues of his previous romances, Chrétien here affirms his originality in creating, virtually ex nihilo, an artifact of unsurpassable quality. No longer dependent on an authoritative tradition, "truth" is now contained in the story itself, which seeks to provide its public with instruction valid in the present, rather than with information on a fictitious past. A second innovation is Chrétien's introduction of a novel protagonist, Perceval, whose main distinction is his ignorance of chivalry, an ignorance semantically underscored by the text's repeated qualification of Perceval as *niche* (from *nescius*, "one who does not know").[26] Also noteworthy is the manner in which love, as previously noted, appears to have much less of a role in Chrétien's last romance than in his four previous ones. In the *Conte du Graal*, prowess becomes the central topic of exploration. Instead of focusing on the dual demands made on Erec or Yvain as both knight and lover, the *Conte* takes up the conflict arising from the presence of two contradictory definitions of chivalric behavior. For Perceval to discover what it means to be a knight thus calls upon his capacity to choose the type of chivalric conduct that will facilitate his journey toward social preeminence. What is required, in other words, are such qualities as analytical intelligence, initiative, and cleverness. If Perceval's main characteristic is his *nicheté*, that is, his ignorance of the protocols of chivalry, he is clearly deprived of the very faculties that ensure, in Chrétien's previous romances, the hero's successful career in knightly society. For the majority of Chrétien's readers, therefore, Perceval's naivete serves to separate him from the realm of traditional prowess, signaling his significance as the agent of a new form of chivalric service.

To be sure, in the Vulgate Cycle, *engin* is no longer a prerequisite to success in the quest, nor is the quest, for that matter, a pursuit for pleasure and self-fulfillment. On the contrary, the quester's value is now proportional to his readiness to relinquish the self-serving type of pursuit that had characterized traditional chivalry and to adhere instead to a selfless use of prowess—hence the development of a notion of chivalric service (for example, in the *Queste del Saint Graal*) grounded in the commitment to obey and follow God's commands.[27] The rewriting and recycling of Chrétien's romance, which thus suggests an interpretation of the *Conte du Graal* that amplifies the distinction between Gauvain, viewed as the emblem of traditional chivalry, and Perceval, who appears to embody the promise of its regeneration, may well represent an adequate assessment of Chrétien's intention in composing his last romance. It is possible to see Chrétien's creation of a guileless protagonist, Perceval, as well as his introduction of the novel motif of the Grail quest as two indices of the author's desire to give romance a new, ethical direction, one that calls attention to the merit of purity and moral betterment. Seen in the light of the hermit's revelation that the *graal* contains the Host, Perceval's story in Chrétien's *Conte du Graal* seems to bespeak the emergence of a concept of heroic achievement wherein the true measure of growth and progress becomes spiritual. Yet the eucharistic interpretation of the dish in Chrétien's text, although consistent with the renewal of personal devotion during the period, does not entirely elucidate the significance of the romance either at the intratextual level, in reference to the *graal*'s function in both Perceval's and Gauvain's story, or at the extratextual level, in reference to the value of the *Conte* as the last of Chrétien's romances. As intimated in the Introduction, I propose a reading of the romance that assesses its innovative character as an indictment of the values that govern traditional chivalric society, values that are emblematized in the *graal* to the extent that the term refers metaphorically to a specific faction and encapsulates its dream of power and glory.

In elaborating a representation of the knightly realm that underscores the centrality of aggressive impulses rather than their domestication, Chrétien's *Conte du Graal* anticipates and thus may have influenced the pessimistic vision developed in the thirteenth-century Vulgate Cycle. But the condemnation of chivalry in Chrétien's *Conte*, unlike that articulated in those Grail texts, does not appear to invoke a higher, spiritually grounded definition of knightly service. First, in contrast to the Vulgate Cycle's vertically oriented, moralistic view of the Grail as a quest for inner perfection, the setting of the *Conte* is decidedly terrestrial, and so, I suggest, is Perceval's quest for the Grail in terms of a mission whose goal is the support and defense of lineal claims against Arthur's ambitions. Consequently, whereas Grail sequels develop a symbolic opposition between the Arthurian realm, representing earthly society, and the Grail realm, henceforth traditionally conceived of as the transcendent destination of the quest, in Chrétien's romance, this opposition brings to the fore the conflicts and tensions of chivalric society. Rather than elaborating a symbolic contrast between two vastly different systems of values, the conflation of Arthurian and Grail materials inaugurated in the *Conte* betokens a confrontation of two rival forces whose values are identical in terms of goals and ambitions. From this perspective, Chrétien's *Conte du Graal* does not mark the beginning of a new notion of chivalric quest, henceforth understood as a personal journey toward perfection, so much as it marks the end of the ideal and idealizing realm of traditional chivalric romance.

Proposing an interpretation of Chrétien's Grail story that focuses on the specific function of the quest in the romance rather than on its universal significance, I see Perceval's quest for the Grail not as a symbol or promise of the regeneration of chivalry, but as an emblem of the ubiquity of self-interested pursuits in knightly society and thus, inevitably, as a tale of ceaseless rivalry. In contrast to the Vulgate Cycle, which exalts the internal merit of adhering to the celestial chivalry of the Grail by underscoring the fractious character of Arthurian—that is, earthly—chivalry, Chrétien's *Conte* elaborates a strictly terrestrial depiction of knightly society that stresses the antagonistic character of chivalric interaction through a narration centering on two principal rival forces: the Grail faction and Arthur. The significance of Chrétien's introduction of the Grail material within the context of traditional Arthurian material consists in exposing—without solving—the unstable elements constitutive of knightly society as the locus of a clash between similar, hence competitive, desires to affirm one's autonomy and attain power.

Chrétien's introduction of a protagonist characterized by his ignorance of the protocols of traditional chivalry (an ignorance whose result is Perceval's lack of awareness of the motivations and modes of operation of the constituents of that society) contributes to the effect of the *Conte du Graal* as a romance demystifying the traditions of the genre. The focus of the *Conte* is not on Perceval as a "witty" hero, as in the case of traditional romance, but on his vulnerability in the face of characters endowed with superior knowledge. Considering that *engin* is a prerequisite to the success of a typical chivalric hero, Perceval's ignorance bespeaks a deactivation of the individualistic principles that empower knightly characters like Erec and Yvain to further their own interests and carve out for themselves a privileged position within the chivalric community. Read as a process of acculturation that effects his absorption by the divisive world of traditional chivalry, the story of Perceval the *niche* stands in striking contrast to that of the self-centered hero of classical romance. Instead of a biographical narration focusing on the hero's success in attaining social preeminence, as is the case of *Erec et Enide*, Perceval's adventures call attention to the disempowering effect of his entry in a society marked and marred by factionalism. Unlike the self-fulfilling quest of traditional romance, Perceval's journey in a realm that he does not understand and thus cannot control points forward to the progressive subjugation of his personal story to the unseen working out of a past history of lineal and clannish conflicts. Albeit elusive, allusions to the past are significantly abundant in the *Conte du Graal*; the story of Perceval (hence, ultimately, of the *Conte* itself) finds its full significance in the light of this "prediegetic history" (events that occurred before the temporal setting of the romance).

But this history, although its role is crucial to understanding both the story of Perceval and its significance in relation to that of Gauvain, is inaccessible to Chrétien's ignorant protagonist, whose journey in the chivalric realm is thus inscribed *in space* rather than in time. Herein lies the distinctive aspect of Perceval's quest in terms of a topographic displacement that stands equally at variance with the highly subjective value of the hero's journey in traditional romance, which demonstrates his capacity to "shape time,"[28] and with the fatalistic view of the quest in the Vulgate Cycle, which serves as a reminder that time rules man. To the extent that, for Perceval, the landscape of chivalry is *terra incognita*, it is in a literal sense that he qualifies as a wandering knight. In contrast with the narration of Yvain's story, which takes shape around a succession of critical moments (*kairoi*) in the hero's progress toward self-awareness,[29] the narration of Perceval's story takes place at a variety of isolated and, from the limited perspective of Chrétien's ignorant protagonist, apparently unconnected *places*. In the factional rather than biographical perspective characterizing the narration of Perceval's story, the prevalence of space over time is a powerful narrative device that discloses the disorienting and alienating effect of Perceval's peregrinations in the realm of traditional chivalry, seen as a locus (*stricto sensu*) of territorial conflicts and disputes.

Issues of allegiance and lineage are paramount for the knightly characters inhabiting the realm of the *Conte du Graal*, as they were for contemporary aristocratic society. But these blood ties and affiliations are also obfuscated in the *Conte*, consistent with the limited perspective of Perceval the *niche*, which the text reflects.[30] Thus he does not know that in joining Arthur's court he allies with a political force hostile to his own lineage, nor does he know, until the revelation provided him by the hermit, that he is related to a number of characters, including the wounded king of the Grail castle and the hermit himself. Lacking the knowledge necessary to identify the places and people he discovers along his way, Perceval errs on a path that is delineated by both accident and chance encounters. To "make sense" out of Perceval's enigmatic adventures thus requires that the places and people determining the direction of his itinerary be situated in their factional perspective, which is revealed only gradually in the course of the narration.

To summarize, a history of conflicts inscribes itself in both the spatial and social realm depicted in the *Conte*, and this history accounts for the significance of Chrétien's romance as a story of rivalry and vendetta. Although all the knights of the land are engaged in a similar quest for power, the circle of competition ultimately converges on the two principal contenders inferred from Chrétien's text (Arthur and the Grail lineage). This factional rivalry takes narrative form in the bipartite structure of the *Conte*, which at once emblematizes and testifies to the underlying divisiveness of a putatively military world of chivalry. The first issue that needs to be considered is thus how the meaning of the *Conte du Graal* as a tale of rivalry is embodied in the very bipartite nature of its narrative structure.

Bipartition and Factional Rivalry

Roughly divided into two parts,[31] the *Conte du Graal* narrates successively the adventures of Perceval the *niche* as he enters the realm of traditional chivalry and those of Gauvain, the paragon of Arthurian chivalry, in his traditional function as the king's most distinguished representative. Seen against Gauvain's experience in and knowledge of the mores and customs of chivalric society, Perceval begins in total ignorance of knightly culture, thus suggesting that his evolution in the realm of chivalry and education in its ways will enable him gradually to progress and mature into a worthy, responsible knight. Yet the contrast between the two protagonists does not invest Gauvain with exemplary value. To the contrary, the narration of Gauvain's adventures indicates that he too must progress and discover—or rediscover—what it means to be a knight. An effect of the romance's binary composition is thus the elaboration of an ironic contrast between two protagonists who face the same dilemma but whose respective situations are at the same time diametrically opposed.[32] One (Perceval) is characterized by a crude energy that conflicts with the normative standards of society, and the other (Gauvain) by a respect for conventional social ideals that is repeatedly undercut by both the superficial and futile nature of his chivalric performance. At the level of characterization, therefore, the *Conte*'s binary composition attests to Chrétien's intention "to provide a less than heroic view of both Perceval and Gauvain."[33]

Yet, while focusing on an equally unheroic set of protagonists, the poet invests their respective inadequacies with divergent significance. In contrast with Perceval's inability to conform to accepted norms, which has comic and even farcical effects, the presentation of Gauvain's inadequacies takes on a more serious, ironic tone. As Peter Haidu convincingly demonstrates in his detailed analysis of the *Conte*, in the narration of Gauvain's adventures, "the subject is no longer the fumbling imitation of certain social values, but those values themselves." The significance of Chrétien's romance lies in the juxtaposition of two stories whose respective protagonists undergo similar adventures and perform the same acts, but with vastly different results: "where Perceval is socially ludicrous but useful, Gauvain is polished but destructive."[34] From the parallelism thus obtained emerges a questioning of traditional chivalric behavior, as idealized by Gauvain, in its incongruous and ultimately lethal implications. In this connection, the narration of Gauvain's adventures, which exposes the negative consequences of conventional chivalry, implies that Perceval's future progress will lead him to adhere to a different set of values.

The Gauvain plot thus functions as a negative counterpart of the Perceval plot, illustrating Chrétien's mastery of such stylistic devices as the grammatical trope of *ironia* (to express something by its contrary) and the rhetorical figure known as *significatio per contrarium* (to produce meaning through the juxtaposition of two opposites).[35] In this light, Perceval's misguided attempt to conform to chivalric ideals, which wins him the glorious welcome awaiting him at Arthur's court, consists of attempting to imitate those whom he perceives as paragons of courtly conduct. Far from an eccentric or inconsequential supplement, the narration of Gauvain's adventures confirms that the ideals governing traditional chivalric society are both ineffective and unacceptable. That Chrétien's romance criticizes conventional knightly culture is in fact hardly in question. What remains obscure in the unfinished *Conte du Graal* is the direction that Perceval's story was to take. Although the text exposes the destructive potential in Perceval's transformation into Gauvain's double, it does not elaborate the positive side of the coin. The significance obtained per contra discloses the negative consequences of imitation, in reference to Gauvain as Perceval's temporary role model, but without providing any clear indication of how Perceval might establish himself as a different and distinct entity. What the text keeps tacit, in other words, are the positive principles of mimesis: which characters, if any, are likely to contribute to Perceval's progress toward maturity? Does the hermit, for example, induce Perceval to recognize Christ as the sole and true model? Or is Perceval, by virtue of his characterization as *niche*, the embodiment of a new notion of individuality, one that no longer entails conformity to established standards of conduct? In that case, what kind of new chivalric behavior might the character of Perceval introduce?

A partial answer to these questions may be found in Chrétien's previous works because they too rely on techniques of character doubling and narrative duplication. Chrétien's first four romances are also organized according to a bipartite pattern.[36] Although each work implements this pattern in its own unique way, the common effect of bipartition is to produce what Donald Maddox identifies as "a *textuality of crisis*" in reference to a narrative organization focusing on a climactic turning point. In each of Chrétien's first four romances, the crisis functions as a revelatory moment, bringing awareness of a need for change: "accordingly, structural and thematic details in the post-crisis phase frequently evoke those in the pre-crisis counterpart, so as to show, by contrast, how the protagonist's later development rectifies specifically the problematic aspect of his exploits prior to the crisis."[37] This is particularly so in the case of Erec, whose path toward regeneration entails his ability to act as husband without losing track of his knightly responsibilities, and of Yvain, who must learn not to let the realm of chivalry obfuscate that of amorous conquest. In *Cligés* (ca. 1176), as in *Lancelot* (between 1177 and 1181), the crisis calls upon the hero's capacity to overcome not so much an internal as an external type of obstacle, represented by Alis's or Meleagant's role in hindering, before unwillingly activating, the protagonist's realization of himself as knightly champion. Each of Chrétien's first four romances thus encompasses two phases, the first of which articulates a situation of tension that reaches its paroxysm midway in the narration, the second of which narrates the circumstances in which this tension is gradually resolved, either through the hero's victory over himself (as is the case of both Erec's and Yvain's success in coming to terms with the "split personality" aspect of their character) or through his triumphant combat over the forces of treachery (figured by Alis in the story of Cligés) or evil (figured by Meleagant in the story of Lancelot).

The twofold organization of Chrétien's *Conte du Graal*, which, as Donald Maddox notes, undertakes a double implementation of bipartition,[38] places a similar emphasis on the crisis as a turning point in its two protagonists' respective stories. Significantly, the revelation of each protagonist's chivalric inadequacy occurs during the same climactic scene, at the moment of Perceval's triumphant return to Arthur's court. In rapid succession, a Hideous Damsel arrives at court to blame Perceval for his behavior at the Grail castle; she is followed by one Guigambresil from the court of Escavalon, who accuses Gauvain of having caused the death of his lord. The core of the Hideous Damsel's excoriation of Perceval turns on his reprehensible passivity at the Grail castle, indicating that his dereliction of chivalric duty consists of a failure to assume his knightly responsibilities. At issue in Gauvain's case is the blameful character of his action in having caused in the past the death of Guigambresil's lord.[39]

From the standpoint of their respective accusers, Perceval's and Gauvain's past behavior has in common the contravention of a code of proper chivalric conduct. This scene of twin revelations, whose goal is in principle to provide the *Conte*'s two protagonists with an awareness of a need to change, echoes the climactic scenes of both *Erec* and *Yvain* insofar as the eponymous hero of each of Chrétien's two previous romances comes to recognize his inadequacy through the intervention of a messenger.

Voicing the discontent of Erec's barons, Enide's lament induces her husband to embark on a quest for prowess that will vindicate his seigneurial status.[40] In Yvain's case, this role is entrusted to one of Laudine's ladies in waiting, who blames the hero for having relinquished his responsibilities as faithful husband.[41] Like Laudine's messenger in the story of Yvain, Enide plays a crucial, "maieutic" function in that her lament brings to light the deficiencies in Erec's character. Because she appears to articulate a truth about his personality, Erec comes to acknowledge that truth, thus gaining the awareness necessary to correct in the future his past inadequate behavior.

The *Conte du Graal* at first appears to reproduce the pattern operative in the evolution of the respective protagonists of *Erec* and *Yvain* because here too a messenger's revelatory intervention marks the turning point in the respective stories of the romance's two protagonists. The Hideous Damsel, for example, plays a crucial part in prompting Perceval to recognize his imperfection and make amends for his behavior at the Grail castle.[42] Consistent with Perceval's characterization as *niche*, however, the nature of his imperfection also vastly differs from the type of chivalric imbalance that compromises Erec's or Yvain's status in chivalric society during the precrisis phase of their respective stories. If the Hideous Damsel is to be believed, the problematic aspect of Perceval's past conduct does not involve an excessive predilection for amorous or for martial activities; rather, it lies in his silence in the face of the wonders of the Grail castle.[43] From the Hideous Damsel's viewpoint, Perceval's reprehensible passivity during his brief stay at the castle calls into question the wisdom of his welcome at Arthur's court as a full-fledged member of the chivalric community. Although the Hideous Damsel's evocation of Perceval's silence is consistent with Chrétien's narration of this particular adventure, her interpretation of Perceval's behavior as a failure to act is neither necessarily correct nor impartial.

As I discuss in Chapter 3, the issue here is the degree to which the Hideous Damsel's message is reliable. A noteworthy aspect of her accusation is that she focuses on Perceval's conduct at the Grail castle as if it were emblematic of his behavior during the entire precrisis phase of his story. But if Perceval is now being acclaimed as one of the most worthy members of Arthur's knightly community, this is because he has accomplished a number of chivalric exploits.[44] Thus, the way the Hideous Damsel ignores Perceval's past feats of arms indicates that her rendition of the precrisis phase of Perceval's story is not accurate. That she focuses on Perceval's stay at the Grail castle, while making no mention of his other adventures in the precrisis phase of his story, also throws doubt upon the impartial character of her accusation. Why does she dwell exclusively on Perceval's adventure at the Grail castle, at the expense of any other events in Perceval's story prior to her arrival? Why does her evocation of his past behavior excise the feats of arms that justify the welcome he now receives at Arthur's court? Because Perceval's martial activities are the reason for this welcome, I suggest her silence bespeaks a tacit indictment of Arthurian chivalry. In this connection, Perceval's dereliction of chivalric duty would consist in having served the wrong party; and the way to atone for his past behavior would be henceforth to devote himself to the cause of the Grail.

From Perceval's standpoint, however, the Hideous Damsel appears to disclose a truth about his character. After hearing her excoriation, he decides to leave Arthur's court and promises never to rest until he finds the Grail castle and makes amends for his past behavior. But Perceval as *niche* is also not in a position to understand the Hideous Damsel's accusation beyond its literal meaning. He thus literally obeys her implicit injunction to return to the Grail in order to protect the castle from its predicted doom.[45] Oblivious of the motivations that inspire the Hideous Damsel to capitalize on the Grail episode as a testimony of his unworthiness, Perceval consequently fails to read her indictment as an attempt to disparage his value as an Arthurian knight. That she accuses Perceval in the presence of Arthur's court is, indeed, not gratuitous, indicating that the true target of her indictment is not Perceval the *niche* as much as it is Arthur, because the king's appropriation of Perceval's prowess directly affects the power of the Grail lineage. If the Hideous Damsel's rendition of the precrisis phase of Perceval's story takes no account of the protagonist's demonstrated prowess, and if her accusation aims at depriving Arthur of one of his most worthy knights, then her excoriation assumes a factional significance, a parti pris on behalf of a particular lineage—the Grail—whose survival is at stake.[46] The result of her excoriation corroborates this argument because it succeeds in inducing Perceval both to sever his association with Arthur's court and to initiate a journey intended to bring him back to the seat of his own lineage, that is, the Grail castle. In contrast with the "maieutic" value of Enide's lament, which enables Erec to gain awareness of his true self and thus empowers him to govern his destiny, the Hideous Damsel's excoriation seeks not to help Perceval gain control over his life but to control him in a manner that will both further the interests of the Grail lineage and undermine those of Arthur.

In this perspective, the median crisis that marks the turning point of Perceval's story radically differs in terms of its meaning and function from the climactic moment of revelation that allows both Erec and Yvain to come to terms with the "split personality" of their respective characters. A principal difference lies in the distance in terms of affection or allegiance that here separates accuser and accused. Unlike Enide and Laudine as represented by her messenger, the Hideous Damsel is not intimately related to Perceval, signaling that her excoriation is designed to affect his public persona rather than his private self. A corollary distinction, mentioned previously, is the apparently reduced importance of love in contributing to Perceval's maturation,[47] confirming that the primary puzzle arises not from the presence of conflicting codes of behavior in matters of love and chivalry, but from that of two contradictory definitions of proper chivalric conduct. For Perceval, who is faced with a choice between serving Arthur and serving the Grail cause, yet who is also unaware that he is being asked to choose, the climactic moment marked by the Hideous Damsel's arrival at court affects not the inner but the outer circumstances of his story. Although her "revelation" does change the course of Perceval's destiny, it fails to provide him either with clarification regarding the nature of his failure at the Grail castle or with information concerning the proper mode of chivalric behavior. In other words, the Hideous Damsel's excoriation does not address Perceval at a personal level; rather, her concern focuses on his potential utility as a reinforcement for the Grail lineage.

Although she speaks of Perceval's future only vis-à-vis the Grail castle, the fact that she does so in the presence of Arthur's court, while the king and his men celebrate Perceval as a new Arthurian champion, suggests that her accusation has factional motives. At the heart of her indictment of Perceval is an argument that might be formulated as follows: Perceval's failure consists of having served the wrong (Arthurian) party; he must now rectify his behavior by serving the right one (the Grail lineage). Implicit in her argument is a binary opposition between "right" and "wrong" that is neither ethical (as in the case of the opposition between Christians and pagans in the *Chanson de Roland*) nor social (in reference to the problematic combination of love and prowess in the story of Erec or Yvain). Indeed, the Hideous Damsel expresses not *the* truth about the matter at hand, but *her* truth; and it may stand at the opposite of Arthur's. This situation is still another example of what Peter Haidu describes as an ironic contrast between two identical while diametrically opposed narrative "objects." The object here is chivalry, inspiring two vastly divergent viewpoints on what it means to be a knight or, more specifically, what constitutes a "good" (proper) chivalric conduct. In the absence of an impartial referee (like the divine figure who authorizes the distinction between Christian right and pagan wrong in *Roland*), the antagonistic yet symmetrical conception of chivalry invoked in this scene discloses the irreconcilable, unsolvable character of the dispute that sets at odds the two principal contenders inferred from Chrétien's text. Perceval's dilemma is not that he must choose between right and wrong, but that his choice will inevitably be deemed wrong by one of the two contending forces. If we consider the naivete that is integral to his character, Perceval's decision to comply with the Hideous Damsel's injunction is not a conscious one, nor does it mark the emergence of awareness. Although he remains the focal point of the first part of the *Conte*, Perceval is never its agency; he is the uninformed register of the tension between reciprocally hostile *actants*.[48]

A second ironic contrast in the *Conte* is the juxtaposition of two protagonists whose situations are both similar and diametrically opposed. Perceval the *niche* and Gauvain as the paragon of Arthurian chivalry stand at the antipodes of one another, but find themselves the target of a parallel indictment during the same climactic episode. Guigambresil, who charges Gauvain with homicide, alludes in so doing to an event that occurred before the opening of the *Conte*. This complicates the task of determining which of the two disputants tells the truth. Whereas textual evidence (that is, the narration of Perceval's actual stay at the Grail castle) allows for an alternative reading of the Hideous Damsel's excoriation, no such means is here provided to test the validity of Guigambresil's accusation. However, the difference in terms of characterization between Gauvain, versed in the mores and customs of chivalric society, and Perceval the *niche* constitutes in itself an important clue. Naive Perceval believes in what proves to be an inaccurate and unreliable account of history; Gauvain, the expert in matters of chivalry, refutes Guigambresil's negative assessment of his action in the past. Regardless of the merit of Guigambresil's case, which I further explore in Chapter 2, the parallelism in these twin scenes of accusation suggests that, just as Perceval the guileless is probably innocent of the Hideous Damsel's accusation of reprehensible passivity, wily Gau-

vain is probably guilty as charged. But Chrétien provides no basis for
certainty on either point. With respect to the factional significance of
the *Conte*'s bipartition, there is a striking similarity between each ac-
cuser's arguments. Like the Hideous Damsel, Guigambresil establishes
Gauvain's "wrong" on the basis of the "right" of Gauvain's victim. But
Gauvain, who, unlike Perceval, possesses sufficient discursive mastery
to turn this argument around, proceeds to defend his "right" against
the dead man's "wrong." At issue here is not the right or wrong of the
dead man as an individual entity, but the crime allegedly committed
by Arthur's nephew against the lord of Escavalon. As in the case of
the Hideous Damsel's excoriation, the goal of Guigambresil's charge,
which forces Gauvain to leave Arthur and present himself to the court
of Escavalon, is to undermine Arthur's power. Because Gauvain intends
to demonstrate the legitimacy of his action—hence, of Arthur's rule—
by proving the wrong of the Escavalon faction, each disputant shows an
equal concern for furthering his own interests and those of the specific
chivalric community he represents.

The society depicted in the *Conte* is thus at a standstill by virtue of
the tendency among its knightly constituents to defend their "right"
against another's "wrong." As I examine in Chapter 2, lack of an im-
partial or at least stable system of arbitration is part of the instability
characterizing that society. Another crucial element is the resemblance
of its constituents in terms of goals and strategies. As Fredric Jameson
notes, the central problem of twelfth-century romance is "the perplex-
ing question of how my enemy can be thought of as being *evil* (that is,
as other than myself and marked by some absolute difference), when
what is responsible for his being so characterized is quite simply the
identity of his own conduct with mine, the which—points of honor,
challenges, tests of strength—he reflects as in a mirror image." [49] Tra-
ditional chivalric romance solves this dilemma at the moment when,
defeated and unmasked by the hero, the enemy "asks for mercy by
telling his name" (and Jameson cites the case of Yder in *Erec*),[50] "at
which point, reinserted into the unity of the social class, he becomes
one more knight among others and loses all his sinister" alterity.[51] This
imaginary solution appears impossible in the context of a society, like
that depicted in the *Conte*, that lacks solidarity and is the locus of re-
ciprocal animosity. As mutual mirror images, the knights of the realm
are for one another both equally familiar and equally alien. In addition,
this last of Chrétien's romances no longer focuses on a single hero, but

introduces two protagonists who, taken together, embody the divisive character of a society presented via two antagonistic systems of allegiance. One (Perceval) appears to be destined to reinforce the Grail lineage; the other (Gauvain) is by tradition Arthur's right arm and the paragon of the king's chivalry. The climactic scene that takes place at Arthur's court thus creates the possibility of a denouement entailing a confrontation between the respective champions of the two principal contending factions.[52] At the same time, the scene also suggests that this denouement could prove lethal for one of the two protagonists, if not both,[53] thus leaving unsolved the problematic juxtaposition of two contradictory definitions of proper chivalric behavior.

What emerges from this brief analysis of the *Conte*'s median episode is the vastly different function the crisis has in the *Conte du Graal* than in Chrétien's four previous romances. An initial distinction is how the crisis fails to contribute to the protagonists' awareness. Because Perceval learns nothing about himself from the Hideous Damsel's excoriation, he leaves Arthur's court as guileless as when he arrived. Gauvain, who shows himself as wily as his opponent (Guigambresil), refuses to acknowledge what may be a true assessment of his inner deficiency. In both cases, the crisis marks a turning point in the protagonists' respective stories only to the extent that it literally changes their course. But there is no corresponding transformation, so neither protagonist is in a position to rectify the problematic aspect of his behavior prior to the crisis. A corollary distinction is the role of the crisis in underscoring the factional orientation of this last of Chrétien's romances. In contrast to the author's previous works, the *Conte du Graal* elaborates a depiction of chivalry that underscores the role of knightly society in both causing and perpetuating the state of crisis that paralyzes each of its members, including the narrative's two protagonists. Lacking the revelatory function it has in *Erec et Enide*, for example, in the *Conte*, the crisis provides neither protagonist with the kind of awareness that ensures, in Erec's case, the successful outcome of his quest for status and renown. In thus depriving the characters of Perceval and Gauvain of the means to achieve self-control and self-determination, Chrétien also seems to refuse to direct the narration of his last romance toward a happy ending similar to those of his previous works. The result is a social landscape bereft of heroic figures and a reinscription of romance that demystifies the traditional characteristic of the genre as a "problem-solving" narrative.[54]

The unsolvable nature of the predicament affecting the *Conte*'s chivalric society does not only constitute an implicit acknowledgment of the mendacious and artificial character of the happy endings that conclude the story of Erec or Yvain. The *Conte* is also a forceful illustration of the social rather than individual values that govern the knightly realm of conventional romance, thus linking this literary production to the tradition of what Fredric Jameson designates as "preindividualistic narratives," that is, texts that "emerge from a social world in which the psychological subject has not yet been constituted as such, and therefore in which later categories of the subject, such as the 'character,' are not relevant." On the one hand, the significance of the happy endings of Chrétien's previous romances lies at the level of a social praxis whose goal here is to bring, in Jameson's words, "a symbolic [in the sense of fictional] resolution to a concrete historical situation."[55] On the other hand, the inconclusive character of Chrétien's *Conte du Graal* has as its symbolic (in the sense, this time, of representational) significance to implicate a concrete situation in the last decades of the twelfth century that anticipates the decline of feudalism in the face of the rising power of monarchic governments. The dilemma is whether one (Perceval) should ally with Arthur or join the forces of aristocratic resistance, which include the Grail lineage.

Gauvain's experience, illustrated by the fact that his story is rooted in prediegetic history, suggests that he sides and, if he so decides, will continue to side with Arthur. Perceval the *niche* represents a different case, and he is faced with a choice in terms of allegiance. The crisis in Arthur's court attests to the problem inherent in Perceval's public persona because it is as a newly dubbed Arthurian knight that he is indicted and thus induced to sever his ties with the king's chivalric community. In contrast with Erec's journey in the forest, which is integral to the hero's successful journey toward self-determination, Perceval's quest for the Grail is a long and slow process during which he loses track, literally as well as metaphorically, of his intended destination. Far from a measure of his ability gradually to progress toward maturity, his wanderings result from the Hideous Damsel's accusation, which prompts him to leave Arthur's court and change course. Her intervention is crucial in redirecting his journey, but fails to provide him with the information necessary to locate himself in the spatial and social realm of traditional chivalry. As a result, in both the precrisis and postcrisis phases of his story, Perceval's displacement is governed by the contingencies of accident and chance encounters. In other words, the median episode of his story merely confirms Perceval's inability to locate, hence control, the places and people he encounters along his way. To understand the meaning of his and Gauvain's wanderings therefore requires that we explore further the network of alliances and rivalries that inscribes itself in the topographical setting of the *Conte*.

A Land of "Ogres"

There is no question of accurate geographical description in the world of verse romance and, consequently, no question here of a definitive identification of the sites and names provided in Chrétien's *Conte*. Nor do I intend to present an exhaustive list of all the locations and characters cited in the romance. Instead, I propose a possible interpretation of Perceval's journey as a voyage that does not educate Chrétien's uninformed protagonist so much as it contributes to his disorientation.

Even at its most conventional, as Rosemary Morris remarks, the landscape of Arthurian fiction "is not simply a neutral decor: it is a cunning literary device."[56] An illustration of the strategic function of topography in traditional romances is the place occupied by the "Other World," that is, the supernatural world inherited from classical mythology and Celtic lore ("matière de Bretagne"). Often located in the wilderness (forest, island), this world is in part inhabited by dwarfs, giants, and fairies and in part by characters identified only through imprecise and mystifying epithets. Lack of cartographic consistency and stability also contributes to the apparently magical quality of the Other World in traditional romance. This does not mean, however, that this enigmatic realm serves as a fictional counterpart to the "reality" of the human, chivalric realm that is the central concern of Arthurian fiction. Nor is the Other World, despite its apparently marginal location, necessarily distant from the sphere of chivalric society. Indeed, the forest of traditional romance is never far away from court. An example in Béroul's *Tristan* (ca. 1160) is the proximity of the forest of Morrois that serves as shelter for the two lovers in relation to the city where Marc holds court.[57] Also noteworthy is the function of the sylvan site in which Erec chooses to prove anew his prowess. In the context of Erec's particular predicament, which requires that he confront and defeat worthy knightly opponents, it is clear that the forest is not an isolated, "wild" location, but an environment amply traversed by the constituents of chivalric society.

That the protagonist's adventures in the postcrisis phase of his story generally take place in the forest also confirms the value of this locus in the hero's progress toward self-realization. Although tourneying in the presence of Arthur's court serves similarly to test the knight's martial expertise, its primary effect is to strengthen the king's authority insofar as knights are thus prevented from using their prowess to their own advantage. In this connection, the forest has two widely different functions. As a setting removed from, albeit contiguous with, the sphere of royal authority, the forest is for Arthur a potential source of disempowerment. From the perspective of knights who, like Yvain, seek to affirm their personal knightly value, the forest offers an irresistible opportunity to achieve distinction in a manner that will allow the blossoming of their own public persona outside an Arthurian identity imposed on them at court.

Thus Yvain departs on a solitary quest for the mysterious fountain of the Brocéliande forest, only to meet with an anonymous knight (later identified as Esclados, Laudine's first husband), whom Yvain fights long and hard until he strikes him with a fatal blow. If their duel drags on, it is because the two fighters show equal prowess and expertise. But this equation ends when Yvain triumphs over his opponent, enabling the eponymous hero of Chrétien's romance to acquire an identity of his own in the face of the defeated knight's lesser value. The median crisis in this scene is Yvain's victory: whereas in the precrisis stage Yvain sees in Esclados a mirror image of himself, in the postcrisis stage he emerges as a distinct individual by virtue of his demonstrated chivalric superiority. Characteristically, therefore, the Other World of chivalric romance is where the protagonist comes face to face with the Other, that is, the embodiment of what the protagonist most fears in himself (inferior prowess, defeat, disempowerment). In that sense the Other is "evil," not because he is different but because he is governed by the same modes of operation (points of honor, challenges, and tests) as the hero. Unlike the effect of the binary opposition between court and forest in *Lancelot*, which develops into a conceptual *antinomy* ("good" and "evil"), at stake here is a *contradiction*, hence *confrontation*, between two identical objects. In the context of Yvain's story, Esclados is "good" (better) as long as he defeats each of the successive challengers who come to claim possession of the fountain; he becomes "bad" when he finally meets with his master, Yvain, whose chivalric superiority will eventually induce Laudine to marry her husband's killer. Esclados's ultimate disempowerment—his death—recenters the story on Yvain in his new persona as superlative knight and protector.[58]

The key word in the realm of romance is power, generating between the principal forces of chivalric society a tension that may either have an ethical character (as in the case of the opposition developed in *Lancelot* between Arthur's right and Meleagant's wrong) or may invoke, in the case of both *Erec* and *Yvain*, a more openly political form of confrontation. What emerges from my brief analysis of the Esclados episode in *Yvain* is thus the conflictual, rather than dialectical, significance of the opposition between court and forest and, within the latter locus, between the questing knights who seek to prove themselves the best of all knights. Chrétien's last romance develops even further the political significance of the tension between court and forest. The empowering effect of the forest upon worthy knights makes Arthur defend the value of his centripetal ideals by claiming that the marginal loci of the realm are potential sites of anarchy. As I show in Chapter 2, Arthur's discourse on law and order is grounded on a desire to disempower, by disparaging, any knightly forces that might rival his own. From Arthur's standpoint, "what is really meant by 'the good' is simply my own [Arthur's] position as an unassailable power center, in terms of which the position of the Other . . . is repudiated and marginalized in practices which are then ultimately themselves formalized in the concept of evil." [59] The manipulative character of Arthur's rule in the *Conte du Graal*, disclosed here through the cause-and-effect relationship between practices and ideology, constitutes a logical outcome of the problematic aspects—inefficiency and weakness—of Arthur's kingship in Chrétien's four previous romances.

Indeed, not only Chrétien's works but many verse and prose Arthurian romances thereafter provide a less than heroic portrayal of the legendary king to the extent that Arthur often appears "uncommonly depressed, lethargic, hesitant, powerless, concupiscent, incestuous, short-sighted, or even apparently senile." [60] This reinscription of King Arthur in vernacular romance represents a profound modification of his energetic, dynamic portrayal in the pseudohistorical chronicles that mark Arthur's entry as a full-fledged kingly figure in early-twelfth-century literature. At the core of Arthur's heroic quality in Geoffrey of Monmouth's *Historia regum Britanniae*, as in Wace's *Roman de Brut*,[61] are his actions as defender of the people of Britain and conqueror of historical conquerors such as Frollo in France, Lucius in Rome, and the Saxons in Loegria (that is, northern and eastern England).[62] For both chroniclers, one of King Arthur's merits is the right of his rule in the face of the wrong of the Other, as in the case of the Saxons of Loegria,[63] justifying Arthur's crusadelike aggression of the enemies of Britain. A similarly oppositional structure is at the core of Chrétien's *Lancelot*, in reference to the epiclike conflict that pits Meleagant's kingdom (Gorre,[64] a realm of evil aggression) against Arthur's, traditionally designated as Logres in vernacular romance.[65] Although the weakness of Arthur's rule,[66] which accounts for the state of crisis affecting Logres in the opening episode of the romance, creates the possibility of a negative denouement, it is compensated for by the prowess of his champion, Lancelot, who eventually succeeds in effecting Meleagant's demise. The focal point of the plot is therefore not Arthur's weakness so much as the presence of a character, Meleagant, whose power is inherently evil. By virtue of his significance in embodying the absolute opposite of the "good," Meleagant does not here function as a mirror image of either Arthur or his substitute, Lancelot. Consequently, Lancelot's actions are governed not by Arthur's desire to protect his position as a power center, but by the ethically grounded urgency to ensure the victory of "the good" by eliminating the forces of evil. The resolution of tension as effected either by Arthur himself in the Arthurian chronicles or by his substitute in *Lancelot* establishes an unambiguous distinction between the realm of right and the realm of wrong, embodied in Chrétien's romance in the two diametrically opposed kingdoms of Gorre and Logres.

Logres as a place name takes on a remarkably different significance and function in Chrétien's *Conte du Graal* when compared to *Lancelot*. The name first occurs during Gauvain's judgment at the court of Escavalon, where a nobleman mentions "li roiames de Logres, / Qui jadis fu la terre as ogres" (the kingdom of Logres, which once was the land of ogres; ed. Roach, ll. 6169–70). Logres reappears in the episode of Gauvain's story that describes his adventures in Galvoie. This section of the narrative begins with the encounter of Gauvain and Greoreas, a wounded knight, who warns Gauvain not to go further beyond, for, in the version of Ms. A,

> Ce est la bone de Galvoie;
> *Mout dure et mout est felenesse,*
> *Et s'i est la genz mout perversse.*

> Einz chevaliers n'i pot passer
> Qui vis an poïst retorner.
> (Ed. Lecoy, ll. 6362–66; my emphasis)

This is the boundary of Galloway; *it is a land highly hostile and evil, and its people are extremely perverse.* Never did a knight cross the boundary who was able to come out alive.[67]

Greoreas's wound results from his having gone beyond the boundary. But his warning only arouses in Gauvain the desire to enter this dangerous territory. Having crossed the boundary, he soon encounters an evil-tempered and wicked maiden (the "male pucele"; ed. Roach, l. 7145), who, Gauvain eventually learns from Guiromelant, happens to be the friend of "li Orguelleus / Del Passage a l'Estroite Voie / Qui garde les pors de Galvoie" (the Proud [knight] of the Strait of the Narrow Way, who watches over the passes of Galloway; ed. Roach, ll. 8646–48).[68] According to Guiromelant, one should stay away from Orgueilleux's friend, the "male pucele,"

> Que trop est male et desdaigneuse;
> Por che si a non l'Orgueilleuse
> De Nogres, ou ele fu nee.
> (Ed. Roach, ll. 8637–39)

for she is extremely wicked and disdainful; this is why her name is the Proud (maiden) of Nogres, where she was born.

The name of Orgueilleuse's birthplace varies in the manuscript tradition. Along with Ms. T in Roach's edition, three other manuscripts (E, M, and Q) designate this location as Nogres; two others (B and R) refer to it as Norgres. In the eight remaining manuscripts that preserve the "complete" or extensive, as opposed to fragmentary, text of the *Conte*, however, Orgueilleuse's birthplace receives the name of Logres.[69] I think the latter designation constitutes a better reading of Chrétien's original text,[70] one that links the aggressive origin of Logres as "a land of ogres" with the wicked character of one of its members, Orgueilleuse, whose evil nature is underscored by Chrétien's own description of the maiden as the "damoisele aniouse."[71]

Her friend (hereafter designated as Orgueilleux de Galvoie) shows an identically aggressive disposition in assuming his role as guardian of the strait. Embarking on a relentless pursuit of Gauvain once the latter has crossed the passes, Orgueilleux de Galvoie shows great pleasure when his path appears to be bringing him near that of the transgressor, for

> Paor ai eüe molt grant
> Que il ne me fust eschapez,
> Que chevaliers de mere nez
> Ne passe les pors de Galvoie,
> Se tant avient que je l'i voie
> Et que je devant moi le truisse,
> Que ja aillors vanter se puisse
> Qu'il soit de cest païs venus.
> Cist iert bien pris et retenus,
> Des que Diex venir le me laisse.
>
> (Ed. Roach, ll. 8382–91)

I greatly feared that he had escaped me, for no knight born of woman may cross the boundary of Galloway, should I happen to cross path with him and find him before me, and be able to leave and boast in some other place that he has come back from this land. This knight (Gauvain) will be captured and held prisoner, as soon as God leads his path toward me.

Like many of the characters whom Gauvain encounters in Galloway (for example, the guardian of the strait),[72] the people of Logres (including Orgueilleuse) share a similar inclination toward hostility and aggression. Also noteworthy in that connection is the ubiquity of the name "Orgueilleux"[73] and similarly belligerent individuals (like the Red Knight in Perceval's story or Greoreas in Gauvain's story) with whom Chrétien's two protagonists cross paths.

That knighthood tends on occasion to be contentious is corroborated in Chrétien's previous romances by the appearance of a number of "proud" characters, each determined to prove himself a superior knight. An example occurs during the tournament that King Arthur organizes some time after the wedding of Erec and Enide. As Erec enters the field where the joust is taking place,

> encontre lui,
> Point li Orguelleus de la Lande,
> Et sist sor un cheval d'Irlande
> Qui le porte de grant ravine.
>
> (*Erec*, ll. 2120–23)

the Proud (knight) of the Heath spurs against him, riding an Irish horse that carries him at a high speed.

Although the name of Erec's opponent alludes to the existence of an inherent aggression, the festive circumstances here diffuse the potential danger contained in Orgueilleux's challenge. By unhorsing his opponent, Erec also contributes to the reaffirmation of Arthur's presence, thus implying that his court as a locus of harmony deactivates any impulses to act aggressively. The hero's encounter with the guardian who protects the border that separates Logres from Gorre in Chrétien's *Lancelot* provides a contrasting illustration of the lethal character of chivalric pride when it manifests itself outside the Arthurian sphere:

> vint uns presanz
> D'un chevalier a l'uis defors,
> Plus orguelleus que n'est uns tors,
> Que c'est molt orguilleuse beste.
> (*Le Chevalier de la Charrete*, ll. 2566–69)

There arrived a present in the form of a knight outside the gate, more arrogant than a bull, which is an extremely arrogant animal.

In contrast with the festive atmosphere in which Erec's joust against Orgueilleux de la Lande takes place, the scene is here the stage of an adversarial encounter between Lancelot as the efficient, albeit involuntary,[74] agent of the Arthurian order and a representative of the evil realm of Gorre. Away from the civilized realm of Logres, the duty of the king's champion is to fight and, if need be, kill—as Lancelot does—this and other "Orgueilleux" who might endanger the peace of the kingdom.

In the *Conte du Graal* aggressive behavior seems neither contained, as is the case of Erec's "Arthurized" opponent, nor, in the case of *Lancelot*, situated at both a geographic and symbolic distance from Logres. The ubiquity of Orgueilleux and equally belligerent characters suggests that in this last of Chrétien's romances "Logres" is not a specific location so much as an indigenous disposition pervading the entire realm of the romance. Logres, as such, has no territorial boundaries but epitomizes onomastically the general tendency of each member of the chivalric realm to view "the Other" as rival. It is noteworthy in that context that there are no monsters or giants in the *Conte*, such as appear in Chrétien's *Yvain*. Aggression here takes an exclusively human form, whence the conspicuous presence of traits of temperament that evoke the vices (pride and covetousness) recorded in twelfth- and thirteenth-century sermons as endemic to human nature in general[75] and to the nobility in particular. The thirst for power and dominance that, the Church believed, governed the nobility could not be more eloquently exposed than through the denomination (Logres) designating the entire social map of the romance as a "land of ogres" inhabited by "Orgueilleux."

The immediate consequence of this endogenous threat is that no character in Chrétien's narrative, not even Arthur, is free from aggression, that is, from becoming an ogre himself. Evidence of the king's territorial ambitions is provided by the various locations at which he sets court. In the course of the narrative, Arthur resides at Cardoeil (Carlisle; ed. Roach, l. 336), then at Dinasdaron-en-Gales (l. 2753), later on at Carlion (Caerleon-on-Usle; l. 4003), and finally at the city of Orquenie (l. 8889; perhaps the Orkney Isles).[76] From the north (Orquenie) to the south (Carlion), the king appears to be attempting to establish himself as the sole ruler of the coastal part of the Welsh territory, which constitutes the landscape of traditional romance. At the same time, several incidents indicate that Arthur's rule is not yet universally accepted. One is the king's recent combat against Rion, the "king of the Isles" (l. 852). Although this and other allusions to the "Isles" in Chrétien's text lack geographical specificity, intratextual as well as extratextual evidence tends to imply a northern location. In the Vulgate Cycle, for example, Rion is identified as the king of Ireland, of Denmark, or of "Norgales."[77] That Perceval's mother in Chrétien's Conte is also from the Isles[78] indicates, in Madeleine Blaess's view, that both her lineage and Rion's kingdom were part of the same clan. Because Rion is Arthur's enemy, it follows that the lineage of Perceval's mother also numbered among Arthur's adversaries.[79]

The northern British origin of the clan of the Isles invokes a prediegetic history that might have its roots in Arthur's military campaign in Scotland, as recounted in the Arthurian chronicles.[80] The narration of this campaign occurs in the midst of Arthur's battles against invading forces, including the Irish. Arthur's victory over the latter, Geoffrey tells us, "uacauit iterum uastare gentem Scotorum atque Pictorum incommutabili seuicie indulgens" (freed Arthur's way, enabling him to attack the Scots and the Picts with incontrovertible severity).[81] However, the bishops of the sieged Scots and Picts begged pity of the king, and Arthur eventually granted a pardon to their people. In his rendition of the same episode, Wace expands the scene and endows it with a highly melodramatic character. In their plea to Arthur, which is here couched in direct discourse, the bishops question the fairness of the king's attack:

> Por coi as cest païs destruit?
> Aies merci des antrepris
> Que tu, sire, de fain ocis.
> Se tu nen as merci des peres,

> Voies ces anfanz et ces meres,
> Voies lor filz, voies lor filles,
> Voies lor gent que tu essilles!
> Lor peres rant as petit fiz,
> Et as dames rant lor mariz,
> Et les freres rant as serors,
> Rant a ces dames lor seignors![82]

Why did you destroy this land? Have pity for the unfortunate people that you, king, reduce to death by hunger. If you have no pity for the fathers, consider those children and those mothers, consider their sons, their daughters, consider their people whom you annihilate! Give fathers back to their young sons, and husbands to their wives, and sisters to their brothers, and lords to these ladies!

After having been victimized by the pagan Saxon invaders, the people of Scotland, who like Arthur are Christian, must now endure his lethal aggression. Wace's account of the event thus amplifies Geoffrey's text in a way that underscores the innocence of the besieged Picts and Scots, an innocence confirmed by the bishops' argument that their treatment by the king is both unwarranted and unfair: "Mal nos ont fet, tu noz fez pis" (they [the Saxons] did us ill, you do worse; l. 969). In the conclusion of the episode, however, Wace follows his model quite faithfully: here, too, Arthur is so moved by the bishops' plea that he grants his "pardon" to their people (ll. 983–86).

According to Madeleine Blaess, these pseudohistorical narrations of Arthur's campaign in Scotland imply that Perceval's father was one of the Scots defeated by Arthur, although not one of those to whom Arthur granted his pardon.[83] This would explain why Perceval's father fled Scotland and took refuge in "cest manoir," "Ichi en ceste forest gaste" (in this manor, here in this waste forest; ed. Roach, ll. 450, 451). Although I concur with Blaess's interpretation of Arthur's campaign as the cause that forced Perceval's father to seek exile in Welsh territory, I take issue with her conclusion that Perceval's father was a Scot. I suggest that he was not born in Scotland, but became allied with the clan of the Isles once he had married Perceval's mother. According to the latter,

> N'ot chevalier de si haut pris,
> Tant redouté ne tant cremu,
> Biax fix, com vostre peres fu
> En toutes les illes de mer.
> (Ed. Roach, ll. 416–19)

There was no worthier knight, no knight more feared or dreaded, fair son, than your father in all the isles of the sea.

In my view, the fear Perceval's father inspired among the knights of the Isles tends to indicate that his relationships with the people of Scotland were hostile until he married a member of one of the most noble lineages of the clan. But allusions to the "illes" in Chrétien's text, which, as Rupert Pickens remarks, tend to be used in conjunction with a superlative (as in "all the isles of the sea"; see l. 419, quoted previously), may thus have an idiomatic character.[84] Still, Pickens adds, "one should not ignore the fact that two adversaries are likewise associated with 'the islands.'" One is Rion ("li rois des illes," recently defeated by Arthur; ed. Roach, ll. 851–52) and the second is Clamadeu des Isles, whom Perceval sends as hostage to the king (ll. 2693–94). In this connection, Rion, Clamadeu, and Perceval's father after his alliance to the clan of the Isles would share similarly hostile feelings toward Arthur; and the origin of their resentment may well be the king's unfair aggression against the Scots as recounted in Wace's pseudohistorical chronicle.

Wace's perspective on this event appears to be echoed in the account that Perceval's mother provides her son regarding the circumstances that precipitated the demise of the people of the Isles. As she tells Perceval,

> Vostre peres, si nel savez,
> Fu parmi la jambe navrez[85]
> Si que il mehaigna del cors.
> Sa grant terre, ses grans tresors,
> Que il avoit come preudom,
> Ala tot a perdition,
> Si chaï en grant povreté.
> Apovri et deshireté
> *Et escillié furent a tort*
> Li gentil hom aprés la mort
> Uterpandragon qui rois fu
> Et peres *le bon roi Artu*.[86]
> Les terres furent escillies
> Et les povres gens avillies,
> Si s'en fuï qui fuïr pot.
> (Ed. Roach, ll. 435–49; my emphasis)

Your father, although you do not know this, was wounded in the leg, in such a way that his entire body was incapacitated. His vast land, his great treasures, which he held as a nobleman, were all ruined, and he fell into great poverty.

All the nobles were impoverished, disinherited, *cast into exile—and wrongly so*—after the death of Utherpendragon, who was king and father of *good King Arthur*. Lands were devastated, impoverished people were degraded, and those who could flee fled.

Here in her account Perceval's mother mentions the manor her husband possessed in the Welsh "forest gaste" (ll. 450–51). Thus, whether or not Perceval's father was originally from Scotland, what emerges from his wife's chronicle is her identification of two distinct residences, rooting this history in southwest Scotland and, after the downfall of the clan of the Isles, in Wales.

In this context, it is noteworthy that in Arthurian literature Rion is also linked with the same dual sets of locations. Not only does the Vulgate Cycle refer to Rion as the king of Ireland, Denmark, or Norgales; in Geoffrey's *Historia*, he also appears as a giant (Rithon), whom Arthur claims to have killed on Mount Aravius,[87] a place name traditionally designating the whole Snowdon region in northwest Wales.[88] An episode in the story of Utherpendragon reinforces the significance of Snowdon as a possible site of resistance not only to Arthur's rule but also, before him, to that of his father, Utherpendragon. Geoffrey thus narrates how Vortigern, after the assassination of Constantius, the king of Britain, sought by various means to take the throne away from Constantius's legitimate heirs (his three sons, Constans, Aurelius Ambrosius, and Utherpendragon), but was eventually forced to flee to Wales: "Afterward, having summoned his magicians, he consulted them and ordered them to tell him what to do. They told him to build for himself the strongest tower possible, which would ensure his safety should he lose all his other fortresses. After having inspected a vast number of places in order to identify the most suitable site for this purpose, in time he came to Mount Erith."[89] Yet Vortigern's efforts to build a tower on Mount Erith fail until Merlin reveals that a subterranean pool holding two fighting dragons, one white, one red, is what obstructs the foundations of the tower. Merlin also reveals that the end of the Red Dragon, representing Vortigern, is near. Aurelius Ambrosius (the legitimate heir to the throne after the death of his elder brother, Constans) marches to Vortigern's tower and sets a fire that burns up the tower and Vortigern in it.

Arthurian literature thus implies the existence of two areas of resistance to Arthur's lineage, one in southwest Scotland and the other in northwest Wales. These dual sites of hostility are also present in Chrétien's *Conte du Graal*, because Perceval appears to be linked not only to the clan of the Isles (his maternal kin), but also, through his father, to a part of Welsh territory that may be Snowdon. However, the specific location of the manor where Perceval's father sought refuge after the demise of the Isles, and where the opening episode of the romance takes place, is still the subject of scholarly debates. The only information is provided by Perceval himself, when he tells a group of knights-errant who happen to cross this area of the forest

> Or esgardez
> Le plus haut bois que vos veez,
> Qui cele montaigne avironne.
> La sont li destroit de Valbone.
> (Ed. Roach, ll. 295–98)

Now look at these elevated woodlands that you can see, encircling the top of that mountain. There are located the passes of Valbone.

Some scholars locate the passes Perceval mentions (hereafter designated as Valbone) in Snowdon; others associate them with Galloway.[90] Yet neither suggestion takes into account, as Lenora Wolfgang remarks, "the fact that Perceval is associated with two locations: the place where he was born [Galloway, in southwest Scotland], and the waste forest to which the family fled [Snowdon, in northwest Wales]."[91] Implying a chronicle of defeats at the hands of Arthur, the dual character of Perceval's territorial origins predicates that his mission will or should be the prosecution of Arthur as the cause of the demise of the clan of the Isles, of the impoverishment of Perceval's parents, and of their life of exile in Snowdon. That this mission belongs to Perceval is confirmed by the fact that, we learn from his mother, both his father and his two elder brothers are dead. A corollary reason is provided in the two maimed Grail kings. They, too, are members of the clan of the Isles because, Perceval learns eventually, the wounded king happens to be his mother's brother. In this connection, Perceval's stay at the Grail castle provides two of the surviving representatives of the Isles with the opportunity to direct, or redirect, Perceval's journey in such a way as to ensure that he pursues his mission as prosecutor of his lineage's avowed enemy: Arthur.

The rivalrous social landscape depicted in Chrétien's last romance is a clear indication of the lineal and factional, rather than biographical, character of the narration of Perceval's story. In contrast to the hero of traditional romance (for example, Yvain) whose journey is not only the vehicle of adventures but, in fact, *the* adventure of his story,[92] Perceval's displacement does not appear to be inspired by a desire to undertake adventures that would enable him to test his control over his environment. Whereas Yvain initiates his journey (and his adventure) to show himself a knight superior in terms of prowess and honor,[93] what motivates Perceval's departure from the natural shelter of his childhood is his eagerness to go to "the king who makes knights."[94] Perceval's inaugural journey is therefore a quest not for self-identification, but for identity, to be achieved by means of an allegiance with the king that awaits him at his intended destination (Arthur's court). In the postcrisis phase of his story, after the Hideous Damsel's excoriation, Perceval's attempt to return to the Grail castle is similarly a quest for social identity, but one whose achievement implicates his alignment with a force hostile to Arthur.

A second element distinguishes Perceval's displacement from that of the knights-errant of traditional chivalry. Consider Gauvain in the *Conte*: as Rosemary Morris notes, whereas the paragon of Arthurian chivalry, whose story is rooted in the inaugural period of Arthurian history, finds himself at ease in a realm where he knows virtually everyone or is known by everyone, Perceval, who "is a stranger to knighthood and to the Arthurian world, meets with ultimate strangeness."[95] The climactic moment of Perceval's peregrination in the realm of strangeness is his experience of and at the Grail castle, whose inhabitants have the bewildering capacity to appear and disappear at will.[96] Because the scene is narrated from Perceval's standpoint, the castle's peculiarity informs not the site itself, but the perspective of the *niche*. The experience of strangeness here results from Perceval's unfamiliarity with the *Conte*'s chivalric realm, which is in reality the claustrophobic landscape typical of verse romance, inscribing Perceval's and Gauvain's respective journeys "up and down the west coasts" of mainland Britain.[97]

The course of Perceval's route is northward. He departs from south Wales (Gales) to seek Arthur, whom he finds at an unnamed seaside castle. He then stops at Gornemant's castle (which stands by the sea; ed. Roach, ll. 1321–24) and then at Blancheflor's (Biaurepaire, also at a coastal location; ed. Roach, ll. 1707–9). At that point in the story, Arthur's seat is "Disnadaron en Gales" (l. 2753), a three-day journey from Biaurepaire; and no more than a four-day ride separates Disnadaron from the Grail castle, the site of Perceval's next adventure. Gauvain's route, which takes him from Tintagueil (extreme south Wales) to Escavalon (extreme north Wales), inscribes itself in the same territory: "he hugs the west coast, travelling both further south and further north than Perceval, but missing the one really important thing—the grail castle—in the middle."[98] That Gauvain's journey ranges more widely than Perceval's attests to the importance of his familiarity with the locus of chivalric culture in enabling him to cover more territory than his ignorant counterpart. At the same time, however, Gauvain's wanderings also take on a circular character, considering that his journey brings him back close to his starting point, that is, to Arthur's court.[99] That Arthur remains the focal point of Gauvain's journey, to all appearances at least,[100] is consistent with his traditional value as representative of Arthur's centripetal ideal. In this connection, Gauvain's "failure" to find the Grail castle is not fortuitous; on the contrary, it testifies to the site's insignificance for the furtherance of Arthur's ambitions. At the sociopolitical level, both the castle's apparent isolation and the weakness of its royal inhabitants underscore the marginal nature of the site.

It is in the context of Perceval's adventures, rather, that the Grail castle occupies a central position. In contrast to Gauvain, who "misses" the site in a strictly spatial sense, Perceval "misses" it in a symbolic sense. Gauvain travels up and down the coast without ever encountering the castle and without ever being reprimanded for failing to do so, whereas Perceval comes upon it, only to be repeatedly accused of having "failed" the test. The Grail castle thus performs an inverse function in the two protagonists' respective stories, consistent with the contrary type of allegiance that each is expected to contract. The median location of the Grail castle in the landscape of the *Conte* is, in that respect, far from gratuitous, for it implies that Arthur's centralizing ideals might find themselves challenged by a rival center of authority. In the temporal setting of the romance, however, the weakened Grail site does not constitute a threat as long as Perceval persists in serving Arthur's authority. Thus, if the castle is the one really important thing, it is so exclusively for Perceval, who must confront his role as both heir and champion of the Grail lineage. In this light, the centrality of the Grail castle in Perceval's story, together with its minimal importance in Gauvain's, serves as additional evidence of the factional setting of the *Conte*.

The inverted function of the Grail site in the narration of each of the two protagonists' adventures provides still another example of

Chrétien's ability to deploy the rhetorical figure of *significatio per contrarium*. Just as significant, in that connection, is the contrast between the Grail castle and Blancheflor's nearby castle (Biaurepaire) as two median locations within both the topography of the romance and the story of Perceval. Like the Grail castle, Biaurepaire lies in the most desolate part of the coastal setting of the romance. In Rosemary Morris's view, "the growing desolation of the landscape traversed by Perceval has a narrative and symbolic function: it is in this desolation (of the soul?) that he must encounter his, perhaps *the*, ultimate adventure," [101] the discovery of the Grail castle. That Perceval comes upon the castle after his adventure at Biaurepaire links the two, making the latter a negative mirror image of the former. A crucial element in my argument, which I articulate fully in Chapter 4, is the "symbolic" or evanescent character of the Grail castle in comparison with the highly concrete depiction of Biaurepaire. Indeed, as Rosemary Morris notes, "there is nothing unrealistic or mysterious about Blancheflor's castle." [102] This is why Perceval has no difficulty understanding its predicament and hence assuming its defense.

But Biaurepaire stands as an exception in Perceval's adventures, which take him progressively deeper into what remains for him the strange and unfamiliar realm of chivalry. Insofar as this realm is strange only from the standpoint of Chrétien's uninformed *niche*, its mysterious elements (such as curse and enchantment, magic and spells, ritual desolation) do not involve "the substitution of some more ideal realm for ordinary reality," to quote Fredric Jameson, "but rather a process of *transforming* ordinary reality." [103] Thus one could argue that "the strangely active and pulsating reality" of chivalric culture in Chrétien's *Conte* is in large part a product of Perceval's perception. Chrétien's uninformed protagonist, who endows the realm of chivalric culture with ideal significance, functions as a sort of "registering apparatus" for the transformed reality of that realm. The true *actant* in Perceval's story is therefore the "world," that is, "the ultimate perceptual horizon" within which Perceval's experience takes place. Like a number of similarly naive heroes (along with Perceval, Jameson cites Yvain, Fabrice del Dongo, and the "grand Meaulnes" of Alain-Fournier), Perceval shows a bewilderment that marks him not as a self-determined hero, but as a spectator destined to a task that he will accomplish "without ever having been aware of what was at stake in the first place." [104] To play on the title of Jameson's work, the "political unconscious" operative in the narration of Perceval's story refers, on the one hand, to the history inscribed in the spatial and social realm of the *Conte*, thus constituting its "ultimate perceptual horizon," and, on the other, to the distance in terms of knowledge and familiarity that induces Perceval repeatedly to misread, misjudge, and misunderstand that history. Presented with Perceval's distorting perception of traditional chivalry, listeners and readers of the romance are in their turn induced to translate that perception so as to recognize, hidden behind the mysterious or mystical aura of Perceval's adventures, the raw forces of knightly rivalry.

Perceval's "failed" adventure at the Grail castle (that is, his inability to understand the lineal significance of the affliction striking its royal inhabitants) puts his predestined mission in jeopardy while predicting Arthur's success as the sole, absolute ruler of the realm. At the same time, however, the king's hold over the land is far from secure. After their triumphant battle against Rion, Arthur's companions in arms have left him to return to their respective domains. As a coalman tells Perceval,

> Li rois Artus et toute s'ost
> S'est au roi Rion combatus;
> Li rois des illes fu vencus,
> Et de c'est li rois Artus liez,
> Et de ses compaignons iriez
> Qui as chastiax se departirent,
> La ou le meillor sejor virent,
> N'il ne set coment il lor va;
> Ce est li doels que li rois a.
> (Ed. Roach, ll. 850–58)

King Arthur and his entire army have fought against King Rion; the king of the Isles was defeated, and about this King Arthur is happy, but he is angry at his companions, who have returned to their respective castles, where it pleases them more to be, and he does not know what they are doing; this is the reason for the king's sorrow.

Indeed, none of Arthur's companions presents himself to fight the Red Knight, who, shortly before Perceval's first arrival at Arthur's court, defied Arthur by openly demanding his land and by stealing the symbolic cup of his kingship. The Red Knight's recent aggression betokens an ongoing strife between him and Arthur, as the king reveals when he explains to Perceval the reason for his being downcast and silent:

Je vos pri qu'a mal ne teigniez
Che qu'a vostre salu me teuc;
D'ire respondre ne vos peuc,
Que li pire anemis que j'aie,
Qui plus me het et plus m'esmaie,
M'a chi ma terre contredite;
E tant est fols que tote quite
Dist qu'il l'avra, ou weille ou non.
Li Vermax Chevaliers a non
De la forest de Quinqueroi.
(Ed. Roach, ll. 942–51)

I beg of you not to take ill that I did not respond to your greeting. Anger prevented me from replying, for the greatest enemy I have, who hates me and troubles me the most, has just laid claim to my land; and he is so possessed as to assert openly that he will have it, whether I like it or not. His name is the Red Knight from the forest of Quinqueroi.

Arthur's allusion to the history of rivalry that accounts for the Red Knight's aggression is yet another indication that the king's rule still encounters opposition in the temporal setting of the romance. If the Red Knight is Arthur's worst enemy, that is probably because of the power disparity between the two adversaries. Unlike many of Arthur's opponents, including the wounded Grail kings, the Red Knight is strong, hence, dangerous and fearless. In the face of the Red Knight's challenge, which undermines Arthur's position as an unassailable center of power, the king reacts by disparaging his adversary (calling him "fols," l. 948), thus characterizing the Red Knight's defiance as "foolhardy" and illegal aggression. In that context, the Quinqueroi forest appears to be one of those locations not yet marked by the royal seal. If Quinqueroi, as Rupert Pickens suggests,[105] corresponds to Coniston in Westmorland (south of Carlisle), this would locate the Red Knight in the middle of the territory (Galloway in southwest Scotland and Snowdon in northwest Wales) in which Perceval's dual lineal origins inscribe themselves.

Whether the Red Knight is allied with Perceval's maternal or paternal lineage, or whether he embodies an isolated form of resistance to Arthur, the fact remains that Perceval kills him, thus unwittingly reinforcing Arthur's rule by eliminating the king's worst enemy. At the same time, Arthur's position remains precarious, as the alternation of royal victory (over Rion), defeat (at the hands of the Red Knight), and temporary recovery (through the unintentional agency of Perceval when he slays the Red Knight) illustrates. Therein lies the reason for the king's mixed feelings: he is, simultaneously or successively, happy (having defeated Rion with his companions' help), angry (because of his companions' departure), distressed (on account of the Red Knight's defiance), glad (when he learns about Perceval's victory over his own worst enemy), and sad (because of Perceval's and/or Gauvain's absence from court). Arthur's variable moods, which fluctuate along those reversals of fortune, disclose the profound instability at the heart of the chivalric society depicted in this last of Chrétien's romances. Neither Arthur nor any of the representatives of the Isles lineage (including the wounded Grail kings) possess sufficient strength or vitality to realize their respective desires to rule over the land. For this reason, the two principal political forces implied in the text (Arthur and the Grail lineage) resort to discourse rather than to force to justify their claims to power.

At the core of this dual discourse is a similar determination to enlist the best knights of the land, particularly Perceval because his innate prowess, demonstrated early on in the narrative by his victory over the fearsome Red Knight, represents a highly desirable asset. Indeed, this spectacular feat of arms has a crucial importance in the social context of the *Conte*, for it signals the possibility of a reversal of fortune to the advantage of whichever party Perceval might eventually join. The last episode in the narration of Perceval's story indicates that he will in time side with the Grail and act in support of his own lineage against Arthur. But because Gauvain may in time resume his role as champion of Arthur's cause, this predicts an ultimate confrontation between him and Perceval as the respective champions of the two principal factions figured in the romance. Emblematizing the unsolvable character of the conflicts and tensions besetting feudal society at the end of the twelfth century, the parallel quest for power at the heart of the *Conte du Graal* suggests that, if Chrétien did not end his story, this is because the history of rivalry has no end.

Chapter 2

Arthur's Law

Only with the rise of a ruler possessing sufficient legal acumen to develop a fair and impartial system of adjudication can the chivalric community depicted in the *Conte du Graal* hope to break loose from the cycle of disputes in which it is embedded. At the base of Arthur's justification of his right to govern lies the claim that, as a selfless arbitrator committed to ensuring order and peace in the realm, he alone embodies a principle of justice capable of settling the conflicts and tensions inherited from prediegetic history. Yet the contending factions implied in Chrétien's text, particularly the Grail lineage, challenge Arthur's claim with a countervailing discourse that acquires its full significance only in light of the royal discourse on law and order. Thus, although the Grail myth, and consequently its meaning, is intricately connected with the section of the *Conte du Graal* devoted to Perceval, and although his story comes first in Chrétien's twofold romance, I begin my analysis by examining in Gauvain's story the function of Arthur's nephew as both spokesman and agent of the king's legal system.

Several factors account for the centrality of law as developed in the *Conte*. First, at the intratextual level, the highly litigious character of the society introduced in this last of Chrétien's romances underscores the urgency of renovating traditional juridical protocols in a manner conducive to social harmony and unity. Thus one of the central questions posed by the *Conte* is whether Arthur's judicial function contributes to the resolution of long-standing disputes, as the royal discourse argues, or whether it only exacerbates the climate of contention by being itself a subject of litigation. This chapter explores this question through a detailed examination of Gauvain's adventures, especially those elements in his story that appear at times to confirm and at times to undercut the peacemaking value of Arthur's rule. A second factor is the significance of Chrétien's romances in cumulatively elaborating a chronicle of Arthurian history whose narration points forward to the increasing ineffectiveness of the king's legal institutions in upholding justice and stability.

Although the *Conte* will forever preserve its enigmatic character as both an innovative and unfinished narrative, the remarkable resonance of this last of Chrétien's romances in echoing and amplifying many of the legal themes and motifs introduced and developed in the poet's four previous works suggests that its meaning might in part be retrieved in terms of the transtextual coherence of the poet's entire opus. That the legality of Gauvain's actions (that is, of Arthur's juridical system) becomes in the *Conte* the subject of open contest is a conspicuous index of the erosion of royal authority by the time the story of Perceval begins. If, as I suggest in Chapter 1, the key word in traditional chivalric romance is power, if, consequently, the key word for Arthur's success in maintaining his preeminence as overlord and sole adjudicator is containment of rival power, the gradual weakening of his rule, which reaches its paroxysm in the temporal setting of the *Conte*, indicates that, while the sole means of rescuing the Land of Logres from its heritage of contention is through a system of centralized justice, this solution is not a possible alternative in the social context of Chrétien's narrative.

Neither was it a conceivable option in contemporary society. When Chrétien was writing his romance, around 1181–90, notions such as public sovereignty and statehood were still at a nascent stage. As an illustration of what Donald Maddox calls "the common ground between fiction and history,"[1] the currency of the *Conte*'s chivalric community in mirroring the legal predicament of the nobility of northern Europe in the late twelfth century thus points to the interest of situating Chrétien's last romance in the sociohistorical circumstances that led to the development of a new concept and implementation of law and order during the following century.

In France, for example, the emergence of royal law as a central governmental institution began with Philip Augustus, but, as Harold J. Berman shows in his seminal work on the formation of the Western legal tradition, it was "brought to fruition by his son Louis VIII (1223–1226) and especially by his grandson Louis IX (1226–1270)." An important reason for the judicial ascendancy of thirteenth-century French monarchy was Philip's introduction in 1190 of a system of judicial administration (the bailiffs) that played a key part in enhancing "royal power by its support of a new territorial concept of kingship."[2] What also contributed to the growing authority of royal law in the course of the thirteenth century was in part the fact that traditional feudal law, which had achieved a high degree of coherence by the last decades of the twelfth century, was nonetheless far from being a systematic legal corpus. Like other competing systems of secular law (including mercantile and urban law) rooted in custom, feudal law was "treated more critically and more skeptically than the laws enacted by popes and kings"[3] by virtue of its customary component, which entailed diversity and regionalism. The effectiveness of thirteenth-century French monarchy as a central governmental institution thus rested on its capacity to regulate and regularize local customs in a manner confirming the sovereignty of royal law. By the late thirteenth century, French kings had assumed the authority to reject all customs that were "bad" and to accept only those that were "reasonable," hence, the authority to interpret customs so as to make them conform to reason. Thus, as Harold Berman notes, "One can speak of a common *customary law* of France as a whole, consisting of the diverse customs that prevailed in diverse places as interpreted and shaped by the royal courts."[4] Not only was royal law now in a position to control all the systems of secular law; by reaching down to all the people, this central legal system also "succeeded in confining the special interests of the feudal aristocracy."[5]

A precondition to the success of royal law in superseding traditional feudal law was therefore the king's capacity to affirm himself as both a territorial and judicial sovereign. In this connection, lack of resources in terms of wealth and land constituted a primary obstacle for the emergence of a feudal overlord, such as Philip Augustus, as supreme ruler of a given geographical area. Not only was Philip Augustus's authority initially limited by the smallness of his domain of Ile-de-France; his rule was also restricted by virtue of the contractual nature of feudal kingship, which compelled the ruler to uphold local usages and respect his vassals' privileges. Because *lex* made them *rex*,[6] twelfth-century princes were traditionally passive figures whose function was to maintain the status quo rather than extend their land and power.

The increasingly lethargic figure of Arthur in Chrétien's romances provides, in that sense, a more accurate, albeit fictional, account of the problems confronting contemporary feudal lords than does the dynamic royal hero introduced in both Geoffrey's and Wace's pseudohistorical chronicles,[7] revealing the part played by traditional feudal law in contributing to the disempowerment of the nobility in the last decades of the twelfth century. To quote Donald Maddox, "The age of Chrétien's Arthur is captured as the tension between a backward-looking king wedded to the anterior ideal of a thriving feudal community, and a far more complex contemporaneous world in which the pluralism of values and individual demands demonstrate in myriad ways the obsolescence of the early feudal mode."[8] Conventional standards of conduct and modes of operation appear no longer to provide the knightly constituents of the realm with an adequate means of settling their disputes, as underscored, in each of Chrétien's legal fictions, by the role of custom in aggravating and perpetuating conflicts and tensions. The effect of customary protocols in maintaining and at times even provoking a state of crisis in the Arthurian society depicted in Chrétien's romances is a testimony to the ineffectiveness of the king's legal system "either as a satisfactory basis for litigation or as an adequate guarantor of collective stability."[9] As the terminal stage of a chronicle that focuses on the gradual erosion of the Arthurian ideal, the *Conte* elaborates a remarkably suggestive account of the inadequacy of traditional legal procedures in rescuing chivalric society from its heritage of strife and contention.

Chrétien's Arthurian chronicle begins with a presentation of the potential vulnerability of the king's rule in the context of Arthur's adherence to legal protocols that were once operative, "in the bygone world of Uther[pendragon],"[10] but are already beginning to lose their effectiveness in the temporal setting of *Erec et Enide*. The romance thus opens with an episode that evokes the presence of two parallel customs, in reference, first, to the Arthurian Custom of the White Stag and, second, to the Custom of the Sparrow Hawk, a custom observed by the people inhabiting the uncultivated part of the forest.[11] In contrast with the latter custom, which involves the designation (and appropriation) of the fairest maiden and thus serves as a vehicle of personal distinction, the Custom of the White Stag as once observed by Utherpendragon and now revived by Arthur aims in principle at celebrating the collective solidarity of his court. Yet in clinging to a practice whose Pendragonian origin confirms his hereditary right to govern, Arthur fails to satisfy his knights' personal aspirations, thus incurring the risk that they seek elsewhere, as does Erec, the means of obtaining precisely the kind of chivalric valorization and self-determination that is proscribed by the Custom of the White Stag.

This inability to keep his knights at court accounts for the decline of Arthur's power at the time of the incident. What Arthur also fails to perceive is the fact that the proscriptive value of the Pendragonian custom is no longer operative, by virtue of a clause, hereafter described by Gauvain, that is predisposed to turn the volatile knights of his court into rivals:

> Nos savomes bien tuit piece a
> Quel costume li blans cers a:
> Qui le blanc cerf ocirre puet
> *Par reison* beisier li estuet
> Des puceles de vostre cort
> La plus bele, a que que il tort.
> Maus an puet avenir molt granz,
> Qu'ancor a il ceanz .v^c.
> Dameiseles de hauz paraiges,
> Filles de rois, gentes et sages;
> N'i a nule qui n'ait *ami*
> *Chevalier* vaillant et hardi,
> Don chascuns desresnier voldroit,
> *Ou fust a tort ou fust a droit,*
> Que cele qui li atalante
> Est la plus bele et la plus gente.
>
> (*Erec*, ll. 43–58; my emphasis)

We all know, and have known for quite a long time, what the Custom of the White Stag entails: whoever succeeds in killing the white stag must *by right* kiss the fairest of the maidens in your court, whatever might be the result. This could lead to very great trouble, for there are here at least five hundred high-born maidens, daughters of kings, noble and wise; each of them has as a *friend* a *knight* valiant and bold, who would want to claim, *rightly or wrongly*, that the one he prefers is the fairest and noblest of all.

What was *right* in the age of Utherpendragon, when the king was strong enough to ensure harmony at court, is destined in the present to become *wrong*, that is, an issue of dispute and contention. Arthur's court is not the locus of a happy gathering of knights and ladies. Hidden beneath Gauvain's description of Arthur's men as *ami chevalier* (knights as lovers) lies the reality of chivalric aggression: Arthur's "bold" companions are rivals in love as much as, and because, they are rivals in knighthood.[12]

The sequence of events that follows the killing of the stag tends at first to vindicate Gauvain's warning because each of Arthur's companions "vialt par chevalerie / Desresnier que la soe amie / Est la plus bele de la sale" (shows himself disposed to demonstrate by deeds of arms that his own beloved is the fairest of all in the hall; *Erec*, ll. 295–97). Turning the court's *ami chevalier* into enemies, the Custom of the White Stag discloses the presence of internecine violence, a violence heretofore contained but that now threatens to consume both the knights of Arthur's court and Arthur himself. Whereas the custom was once paramount for the confirmation of the *right* of the king's rule, in both the legal and political sense of the term, its enactment in the temporal setting of the romance serves primarily to confirm the fragility of Arthur's kingship in the face of his knights' contentious dispositions. That any claim regarding the superior beauty of a given lady friend can be either right or wrong—the *tort* or *droit* Gauvain mentions at line 56 in the previous quotation—is a measure of the inability of Arthur's legal system to maintain the cohesion of his court. Not only is the king no longer the guarantor and orchestrator of justice (any one of his knights can now arrogate the privilege of determining what is right and what is wrong), but the determination of right is itself exclusively based on one's capacity to claim, that is, to contest by means of force (*desresnier*, l. 55) [13] one's prerogative over and above any other member of the court, including Arthur. If right was ever the source of the king's might, as was allegedly the case in the bygone world of Utherpendragon, this equation now appears to be reversed: in the age of Arthur, might makes right.

However, because in this first of Chrétien's romances Arthur still possesses some of the martial energy that accounts for his legendary status as both hero and king in Geoffrey's and Wace's chronicles, the ritual ends to his advantage, insofar as he emerges as the winner of the hunt. The king's decision to revive the Custom of the White Stag inaugurated by his father thus proves to be a strategic move on the part of the ruler, enabling him to reaffirm his authority by showing himself the strongest of all. Nonetheless, Arthur must still confront the delicate task of selecting the fairest maiden in his court without sowing seeds of rivalry among the *ami chevalier*. In view of the knights' readiness to take arms should their respective ladies not be chosen, there seems to be no solution to the king's dilemma. Chrétien solves the problem, thereby deproblematizing, in effect, the legal predicament presented in the opening episode of the romance, through a narrative strategy that eradicates the threat of internecine violence, much in the same way that war against a common enemy is, in *Yvain*, a tactical expedient enabling Arthur to mollify the martial disposition of the chivalric community. [14]

The successful termination of the Custom of the White Stag involves the intrusion of a foreign element into the court. Although not hostile by nature, it provides the court with an essential outlet for its tensions. It is not accidental that Enide, whom both Arthur ("la plus bele," the most beautiful maiden; l. 1740) and Chrétien ("si bele criature / Ne fu veüe an tot le monde," one never saw such a beautiful creature anywhere in the world; ll. 422–23) describe in hyperbolic terms, is from a remote part of the forest. The king's selection of a lady who is a newcomer to the court prevents the latent rivalry among the *ami chevalier* from materializing into open struggle. Because Guìnevere (l. 1727) concurs with Arthur's and his knights' verdict,[15] it is clear that the entire court, both men and women, accepts Arthur's choice as a compromise that poses no threat to the self-image of any of its members. Ultimately, therefore, the king's court grants Arthur the right (the *par droit* of l. 1779) to designate Enide as the fairest of all. Chrétien's hyperbolic assessment of Arthur's and Enide's value also situates both characters outside the realm of mimetic rivalry that characterizes the king's chivalric followers: just as Enide is the fairest, Arthur is the strongest. Chrétien's use of an apparently "absolute superlative" (the fairest, the strongest) suggests that Enide and Arthur stand above and beyond the sphere of ordinary humanity. Yet the king's superlative value is, of course, not absolute but relative to the inferior prowess of the members of the community: he is the *strongest at court* because he has proved himself to be *stronger* than any of his men. Beneath this hyperbolic language, which supports Arthur's claim that he is entitled to rule the land, lurks his desire to attain and maintain absolute power.

It is significant that, in renewing the Custom of the White Stag, Arthur revives a ritual ordained by his father, as he asserts in his oration during the concluding sequence of the episode:[16]

> Je ne voldroie an nule guise
> Fere deslëauté ne tort,
> Ne plus au foible que au fort;
> N'est *droiz* que nus de moi se plaingne.
> Et je ne voel pas que remaigne
> La costume ne li usages
> Que siaut maintenir mes lignages.
> De ce vos devroit il peser,
> Se ge vos voloie alever
> Autre costume et autres lois

> Que ne tint mes peres li rois.
> L'usage Pandragon, mon pere,
> Qui rois estoit et emperere,
> Voel je garder et maintenir,
> Que que il m'an doie avenir.
>
> (*Erec*, ll. 1756–70; my emphasis)

I would not wish in any way to commit disloyalty or wrong any more against
the weak than the strong; it is not *right* that anyone could have a complaint
because of my behavior. And I do not wish to see disappear the custom and the
usage that my lineage is used to maintain. It would undoubtedly worry you if I
decided to establish other customs and other laws than those held by my father
the king. I want to preserve and maintain the usage of Pendragon, my father,
who was king and emperor, regardless of how this may affect me.

Despite Arthur's vow to respect and uphold local usages, in reality he
appropriates custom in order to legitimize his rule. His right is deter-
mined by his might, which enables him to control both the weak and
the strong members of his chivalric community. That the usage under
consideration dates back only a generation also calls into question the
status of the stag hunt as "custom." [17] The relatively recent origin of the
Custom of the White Stag, together with its Pendragonian roots, indi-
cates that its revival by Arthur constitutes not so much an appropriation
of custom as an imposition of royal rule.

The outcome of the ritual reaffirms Arthur's control over his knights.
Having rescued them from the danger posed by their own propensity to
violence and rivalry, the king succeeds in presenting himself as a strong
and indispensable judge, thereby obfuscating the absolutist character of
his rule. Yet Chrétien's comment at the end of the opening scene of *Erec
et Enide* favors an optimistic assessment of Arthur's legal practices:

> Li rois, par itele avanture,
> Randi l'usage et la droiture
> Qu'a sa cort devoit li blans cers:
> Ici fenist li premiers vers.
>
> (*Erec*, ll. 1793–96)

It is in the above-described circumstances that the king restored the usage and
justice that the [Custom of the] White Stag imposed at his court: here ends the
initial section of the story.

However, the episode proper ironically undermines the happy ending of
the Custom of the White Stag by hiding, without suppressing, the cen-

trality of rivalry as the primary mode of interaction at Arthur's court. The king's manipulative language [18] and the self-interested nature of his adherence to justice emblematize the competitive impulses that govern chivalric society. Relationships between Arthur and his men as well as between his knights and damsels inscribe themselves as a skein of aggression and resentment. In the masculine realm of Arthurian chivalry, love between a *chevalier* and his *amie* is not a central concern; moreover, love and prowess frequently prove to be mutually exclusive. Erec's predicament is symptomatic: although both he and Enide eventually recognize that they are equally worthy of one another, their reconciliation poses anew the problem that had provoked their dispute. In the end, Erec's dilemma remains unchanged: if he remains in Enide's company, he risks incurring yet again shame and public blame; but if he decides to show his prowess in chivalric pursuits designed to increase her self-image and his own, he must renounce the pleasures of amorous exchange.

Just as fictitious as the optimistic ending of the white stag episode, *Erec*'s happy resolution, which implies a compatibility between love and chivalry, thus stands in open contradiction to the romance proper.[19] Erec qua knight jeopardizes the blossoming of Erec qua lover. Erec as the new king of Nantes also poses an implicit threat to Arthur's hegemony, for the peaceful coexistence of two rulers of apparently equal power is problematic. Despite its seemingly positive resolution, Chrétien's first extant romance nonetheless exposes quite vividly the violent character of chivalric society by disclosing the centrality of might as the precondition for the attainment of political ascendency. Arthur's physical strength as successful deerslayer in the opening episode of *Erec et Enide* enables him to claim his status as sole ruler of the realm,[20] thereby deactivating the potentially rival force of Erec as winner of the hawk chase, liberator of the lethal Brandigan custom,[21] and newly elected king.

What emerges from the initial stage of Chrétien's Arthurian chronicle as described in *Erec et Enide* is the crucial importance of the king's might in asserting and confirming his right to govern. In contrast to this demonstration of royal strength in the early stage of Arthur's reign, the king's gradual transformation into a passive figure in Chrétien's subsequent romances contributes to the increasing ineffectiveness of his legal system in containing the destructive force of his knightly community. Lacking the strength to impose himself as sole ruler and central judge, Arthur ends by adhering exclusively to traditions and rituals that fail to accommodate his knights' eagerness for self-realization. This is why Yvain, for example, seeks elsewhere the means of satisfying his personal aspirations as both knight and lover. In this perspective, the Custom of the Fountain, in the course of which Yvain both demonstrates his superior prowess and obtains a bride, parallels the Custom of the Sparrow Hawk in *Erec*, at least to the degree that, like the hawk ritual with respect to the eponymous hero of Chrétien's first extant romance, the fountain provides Yvain with the opportunity to develop into an autonomous political ruler.

As in the case of *Erec*, however, the episode concluding the narration of *Yvain* neutralizes the legal issue raised by the existence of the non-Arthurian Custom of the Fountain because this ritual is associated with what appears to be the remote realm of Laudine's domain. Signaling the end of his chivalric career, Yvain's ultimate reconciliation with Laudine has the effect of marginalizing him at a safe distance from the center of power. Yet both Erec's and Yvain's careers are indicators of an increasing danger regarding Arthur's centripetal ideal, betokening his court's gradual attrition. This danger accounts for the vulnerability of Arthur's rule in the last of what Donald Maddox aptly describes as Chrétien's "customal romances." Indeed, in the *Conte du Graal*, the king finds himself singularly deprived of his companions, either because they have preferred the comfort of their own domains or because they are called, like Perceval and Gauvain, to present themselves to other courts. What was still latent in Chrétien's previous romances becomes flagrant in the *Conte*. Considering the state of virtually total dispersion of Arthur's Round Table, it appears, as Donald Maddox notes, that "crisis has become a way of life within the Arthurian community," whence the significance of Chrétien's last romance as "his own version of the beginning of the end of Arthur's reign." [22]

Gauvain's story takes on special interest in the context of the imminent collapse of the king's rule as depicted in the *Conte*'s crepuscular account of Arthurian history. In contrast to such heroes as Yvain or even Lancelot, Gauvain appears, at least at the level of discourse, to support the principles of the Arthurian order. For example, he describes Arthur's justice as a system of "loial justise, / Qui est establie et assise / Par toute la terre le roi" (of lawful justice, which is established and founded throughout the king's land; ed. Roach, ll. 7129–31).[23] Also noteworthy in this connection is the preponderance of legal terms in the section of the *Conte* devoted to Gauvain's story. In the course of his adventures, Arthur's nephew promises successively to show whose claim is right ("ara droit"; l. 4796), to defend the cause of right ("droit faire"; l. 5364), and to act according to the fair and impartial principles of Arthur's law ("loial/leal justise"; l. 7129).

The section dealing with Perceval contains only infrequent legal allusions. The most significant occurs during the arrival at the vale near Valbone of the group of Arthurian knights whose appearance leads to Perceval's discovery of the chivalric world. Perceval's ignorance of the code and equipment of chivalry prompts the knights to mock the Welsh boy:

> "Sire, que vos dist cist Galois?"
> "Il ne set pas totes les lois,"
> Fait li sire, "se Diex m'amant,
> C'a rien nule que li demant
> Ne me respont il ainc a droit,
> Ains demande de quanqu'il voit
> Coment a non et c'on en fait."
> (Ed. Roach, ll. 235–41)

"Sir, what does this Welshman tell you?" "He does not know all the rules," the lord replies, "so help me God, for he does not give me a straight answer to anything I ask him, but asks me instead about what he sees, how it is called, and how one uses it." [24]

Although Perceval's lack of knowledge here refers to his ignorance of the name and function of knightly armor, the rhyming pair of *Galois* and *lois* at lines 235–36 also indicates a distance between Perceval's literal understanding of the chivalric world and its institutional significance. [25] Not knowing the custom and code of social behavior entails, in Perceval's case, an inability to act properly, that is, to participate in the Arthurian system of righteous defense and legal justice. And if Perceval strays from the path of right (*ainc a droit*, according to the knight quoted previously), this implies that his acts are wrong. Terms denoting aggression and violence indeed prevail in the episodes that narrate Perceval's adventures, [26] suggesting that, prior to his formal induction into Arthurian chivalry by Gornemant, his feats of arms occur outside the scope of royal law. Compared to Perceval, whose utter lack of familiarity with Arthurian custom causes him to speak and act contrary to norms, Gauvain is the paragon of gallant and fair-minded chivalry and seems to possess all the qualities expected of a royal deputy, thus justifying his function as the primary emissary entrusted with the charge of propagating the principles of Arthur's law throughout the land. A number of Gauvain's adventures underscore his pivotal role in confirming the peacemaking value of Arthurian justice.

A Discourse of Reconciliation

In the *Conte du Graal*, Gauvain is rarely seen in action and is more often occupied by travel and talk than by actual feats of arms. Gauvain's peregrinations, together with his tendency to use words rather than force, is integral to Arthur's strategy, for these two characteristics of Chrétien's second protagonist contribute both to the promotion of the king's cause and to the presentation of Arthurian rule as a model of nonviolent, hence beneficent, kingship.

Several episodes in the story of Gauvain illustrate his role as the spokesman of Arthur's law in terms of a call for reconciliation and mutual assistance. An example, in the Tintagueil episode, is Gauvain's adjudicative action in a dispute opposing Meliant de Lis and his vassal Tibaut de Tintagueil. When Gauvain meets Meliant and his knights (ll. 4816–26), they are on their way to Tintagueil in order to tourney with Tibaut and his men. However, Tibaut's companions have convinced him not to engage in the tourney with Meliant,

> Car il avoient grant paor
> Qu'il les volsist del tot destruire,
> S'ot bien fait murer et enduire
> Del chastel totes les entrees.
> (Ed. Roach, ll. 4894–97)

For they greatly feared that [Meliant] had in mind to destroy them utterly, in view of which Tibaut had ordered that all the entrances to the castle be walled and mortared.

These fears suggest that Meliant's challenge has a combative rather than a festive significance.[27] To prevent Meliant from ruining their domain, they prepare themselves for a siege, thus revealing that they are not duped by Meliant's offer to engage in an allegedly playful contest. The mistrust of Tibaut's faction discloses in Meliant the presence of a gap between word and intention because his use of the term *tournament* contradicts the normally festive activities of a mock combat in traditional Arthurian romance. In hiding the aggressive nature of his challenge, Meliant violates the rules of proper communication while violating Arthur's call for peaceful and convivial interaction among knights.

Many Arthurian romances place the king at the center of public spectacles, among which tournaments play an important part. An example is the celebration that concludes Erec and Enide's wedding ceremony:

> Un mois aprés la Pantecoste
> Li tornoiz assanble et ajoste
> Desoz Teneboc an la plaigne.
> La ot tante vermoille ansaigne,
> Et tante guinple et tante manche,
> Et tante bloe, et tante blanche,
> Qui par amors furent donees;
> Tant i ot lances aportees
> D'azur et de sinople taintes,
> D'or et d'argent en i ot maintes,
> Maintes en i ot d'autre afeire,
> Mainte bandee, et tante veire;
> Iluec vit an le jor lacier
> Maint hiaume, de fer et d'acier;
> Tant vert, tant giaune, tant vermoil,
> Reluire contre le soloil;
> Tant blazon, et tant hauberc blanc,
> Tante espee a senestre flanc,
> Tanz boens escuz fres et noviax,
> D'azur et de sinople biax,
> Et tant d'argent a bocles d'or;
> Tant boen cheval, baucent et sor,
> Fauves, et blans, et noirs et bais,
> Tuit s'antre vienent a eslais.
> D'armes est toz coverz li chans.
>
> (*Erec*, ll. 2081–105)

A month after Pentecost the tournament assembles and opens in the plain below Tenebroc. Many a vermilion pennon and many a wimple and sleeve, some blue and some white, had been given as love tokens; many lances were brought there, painted in blue and red, many made of gold and silver, and many others with different appearances, some banded, some spotted; that day one could see there many a helmet being laced, made of iron and steel, some of which were green, some golden, some vermilion, all shining in the sun; many a blazon, white hauberk, sword carried on the left side, good shield fresh and new, some beautified with blue and red, many others with silver and gold bosses; many a good horse, some bay and some chestnut, some sorrel, some white, some black, and some bay, all coming together at full speed. The field is completely covered with arms.

This is not a battlefield, but the deployment of pageantry; these are not arms in the martial sense, but objects of art displayed to stimulate public awe. Under royal eyes, but also under the eyes of admiring damsels, knights are given the opportunity to shine by unseating the greatest number of opponents possible. By the end of the first day, Erec emerges as "li miaudres . . . de l'estor" (the best of the tournament; l. 2198), thus proving himself worthy of belonging to the most brilliant of all courts. It is no wonder that, in *Cligés*, Alexandre wants to join so famed a court (ll. 66–75) nor that, in the *Conte du Graal*, Perceval is eager to become "Ausi luisanz et ausi fais" (as shining and handsomely equipped; ed. Roach, l. 181) as the five dazzling Arthurian knights who happen to cross the vale near Valbone in the opening episode of the romance.

In sharp contrast to this festive atmosphere of tournaments at Arthur's court, Meliant's offer to tourney creates a context of abuse and aggression. Not only does Meliant disregard the principle of peaceful interaction that accounts for the prestige of Arthur's court as it is still operative in *Cligés*; he also contravenes the verbal oath that defines the reciprocal obligations between lord and vassal. As a son of the lord who held his vassal Tibaut in great esteem (so much so that, on his deathbed, he urged Tibaut to raise his son; ll. 4842–45), Meliant betrays both his feudal and affective bonds vis-à-vis Tibaut. The latter had carried out his pledge to the dying father by welcoming Meliant and caring for him "au plus chierement que il pot" (with as much affection as he could; l. 4847). But neither feudal loyalty nor sentimental investment is here repaid. Realizing that Meliant intends to penetrate their castle and turn it into a battlefield, Tibaut's men resort to a defensive strategy—the siege—that indicates a prolongation of strife, thus jeopardizing, or at least postponing, a resolution of the conflict through decisive military victory.[28] As they defend the castle against Meliant and his knights, Tibaut's counselor suddenly advises the men of Tintagueil to accept Meliant's challenge. This change of heart results from Gauvain's appearance on the scene:

> Sire, se Diex me saut,
> Je ai, mien escïent, veü
> Des compaignons le roi Artu

Deus chevaliers qui çaiens vienent.[29]
Dui preudome molt grant liu tienent,
Que neïs uns vaint un tornoi.
Et je loëraie endroit moi
Que nos vers le tornoiement
Alissons tot seürement,
Que vos avez bons chevaliers
Et bons serjans et bons archiers
Qui lor chevax lor ocirront.
(Ed. Roach, ll. 4932–43)

Sir, so help me God, I have seen, I believe, two knights coming here, who number among Arthur's companions. Two valiant knights are of great worth, for either one can win a tourney. Thus I for my part hold the opinion that we can enter the tournament at no risk because you have good knights, good men-at-arms, and good archers who will kill their horses.

That the counselor interprets the Arthurian knight's arrival at Tintagueil as a promise of victory reveals that he assesses Gauvain's value primarily in terms of military expertise.[30] Indeed, Gauvain diffuses the tension between lord and vassal through sheer physical force:

Et mesire Gavains s'esmuet
Tant com chevax porter le puet
Vers celui qui pas nel redoute,
Ainz met sa lance en pieces tote.
Et mesire Gavains fiert lui
Si qu'il li fait molt grant anui,
Que tot envers l'en porte al plain.
(Ed. Roach, ll. 5513–19)

And my lord Gauvain charges as fast as his horse can carry him toward the knight, who does not fear [Gauvain], but shatters his lance in pieces. And my lord Gauvain strikes him with such force that he causes him great trouble, throwing him headfirst to the ground.

The effect of Arthur's champion in halting the feud, which renders possible Meliant's plan to marry Tibaut's elder daughter, brings forth the value of Arthur's rule in controlling private warfare and vendettas. Inducing the two former opponents henceforth to exchange civil words and women rather than blows, royal adjudication as carried out by Gauvain succeeds insofar as Arthur's deputy here appears to act as a third party not personally involved in the strife and therefore impartial.

Yet Gauvain's intervention is in reality not a disinterested effort to settle the conflict merely for the sake of the two former opponents. Although his mediation prevents the "tournament" from turning into warfare, the first beneficiary of the reconciliation thus achieved is Arthur because Gauvain's victory enables the king to regulate all social transactions at Tintagueil and to impose his plenary presence in this remote part of the realm. Not only does Gauvain's triumph over Meliant ensure the protection of Tibaut and his men against an abusive lord, but Meliant's spectacular demise at the hands of Arthur's nephew also compels him to submit to royal rule and recognize the king as his overlord.[31] Because Gauvain's deed restores Tibaut's rights, the latter is prompted to acknowledge his obligation to Arthur. Also noteworthy is the reliance on force as Gauvain's means of proving the peacemaking value of Arthur's rule. Confirming that Arthur's champion, the jewel of the knights of the Round Table, "Qui sont li plus proisié del monde" (who are the best knights in the world; l. 8126), is indeed the strongest of all, his triumph over Meliant demonstrates the role of might in securing Arthur's "right" to govern. Beneath the claim that the king is selflessly committed to the support of the common good, the royal discourse of reconciliation aims in reality at promoting the king's ambitions.

The Greoreas episode provides additional evidence that the Arthurian discourse of reconciliation is grounded in manipulation, precisely because this particular adventure at first appears to sustain the beneficent value of Arthur's rule through that of his deputy's action. The episode begins when Gauvain sees a grieving damsel and, lying nearby, a wounded knight, Greoreas (ll. 6541–56). Gauvain, who knows "plus que nus hom de garir plaie" (more than any man how to heal a wound; l. 6911), goes in search of the singular herb that will cure Greoreas. As he returns to the wounded knight, he describes to the latter's female companion the power of that herb:

> Qu'il ne covient sor plaie metre
> Meillor herbe, tesmoinz la letre,
> Qui dist que ele a si grant force,
> Qui la l'ieroit sor [l']escorce
> Dun arbre qui fust entechiez,
> Mais que del tot ne fust sechiez,
> Que la rachine reprendroit
> Et li arbres teus devendroit
> Qu'il porroit foillir et florir.
> N'avra puis garde de mourir,

> Ma demoiselle, vostre amis,
> Que de l'erbe li arons mis
> Sor ses plaies et bien liie.
>   (Ed. Roach, ll. 6935–47)

That one could not place a better herb upon a wound is testified by a writing asserting that the herb has such power that, should it be tied over the bark of a tree that had been infected but had not yet completely withered, the root would recover, and the tree would thus be restored such that it would resume leafing and flowering. My lady, your friend will be in no danger of dying once we place this herb on his wounds and bind it tightly.

Gauvain's unique talent as healer is remarkable on several counts. First, in contrast to other healers who figure in Chrétien's earlier romances,[32] the power to heal here belongs to a male rather than to a female character, resulting in a distancing of the *Conte*'s chivalric realm from the magical realm inherited from the Celtic tradition, where manifestations of supernatural power often imply a matriarchal substratum.[33] Second, the hyperbolic quality of the herb, which is "better" than any other, mirrors that of Gauvain as the paragon of Arthurian chivalry: what is now evoked, parallel to the martial strength of the king's nephew, is a nonmuscular form of power. Finally, Gauvain's medicinal expertise is not black magic because it is based on written documents, that is, on white science. To all appearances, his healing gift thus functions as a spectacular confirmation of the legitimate character of Arthur's rule as well as of its beneficent role in ensuring the well-being of his people.

Arthurian Custom and the Containment of Aggression

Before exploring further the Greoreas episode, I consider the significance of Gauvain's curative power in the larger context of both Chrétien's oeuvre and other texts of the Arthurian tradition. The persistent attribution of healing skill to Arthur's nephew in medieval romance indicates, in Jessie Weston's view,[34] that Gauvain derives from a Celtic tradition where his role was that of a medicine man, capable of restoring the dead or wounded to life and health. An example is the reference in the *Triads* to Gwalchmai (the Welsh Gauvain) as one of the three men of whom it is said that "there was nothing of which they did not know its material essence, and its property, whether of kind, part, quality, compound, coincidence, tendency, nature, or of essence, whatever it might be."[35] Chrétien's *Conte* appears to retain and even amplify Gwalchmai's distinction because Arthur's nephew, whose medical competence has no equal (according to l. 6911, cited previously), is also the sole character in the narrative who puts this particular talent to use:

> Et voit une herbe en une haie,
> Trop bone por dolur tolir
> De plaies; il le va queillir.
>
> (Ed. Roach, ll. 6912–14)

And in a hedge he sees an herb of superior value for the relieving of pain caused by wounds; he goes to pick it.

Although most manuscripts concur with version T of this scene as edited by Roach, two among them (Mss. B and C) expand line 6912 with the following sequence:

> Une herbe voit an une haie
> Qu'il quennoissoit, lonc tens avoit,
> Et sa mere apris li avoit
> Et enseingniee et bien mostree
> Et il l'a molt bien esgardee
> Si l'a molt bien reconeüe.
>
> (Ed. Hilka, note to l. 6912)

In a hedge he sees an herb that was known to him long before, for his mother had told him and taught him about it and frequently shown it to him, such that, examining it carefully, he was able to recognize it.

That Gauvain owes his skill to his mother (whose own mother, Ygerne, also engendered Morgan le Fay, according to tradition) brings forward the often female property of magical power in Celtic lore.[36] According to Ms. S, Gauvain's instructor is not his mother, but "son mestre" (his master), a variant that appears to adhere more faithfully to Chrétien's first version insofar as it roots the transmission of power in a masculine context, thereby suggesting a parallel between Gauvain's power over nature and his power over men. Indeed, the circumstances in which Gauvain activates his talent as healer tend to underscore the value of this singular skill in confirming his preeminence in the *Conte*'s chivalric society. In that sense, the added lines quoted previously constitute an unwarranted interpolation because, even in version S, they present the talent of Arthur's nephew as acquired rather than innate. This does not cohere with the uniqueness of Gauvain as a *knight* (as opposed to the female and male medical practitioners mentioned in Chrétien's romances) exceptionally endowed with wondrous power.

Although Gauvain represents in that sense an exceptional case within the *Conte du Graal*, Arthurian literature contains other characters deriving from Celtic mythology who appear to have once possessed comparable privileges. One example is Keu, Arthur's seneschal, to whom legend assigns the ability to hold his breath under water for nine nights and nine days, become as high as the highest tree, master rain and fire alike, and inflict wounds that no doctor can heal.[37] Translated into psychological terms within the courtly tradition, Keu's consistently belligerent behavior derives from an animosity toward the king whose origins are embedded in the circumstances that forced him to become Arthur's foster brother. As recounted in the prose rendition of Robert de Boron's verse *Merlin*, this history begins when Utherpendragon endeavors to seduce Ygerne, the wife of the Duke of Tintagueil. With the help of Merlin, Utherpendragon assumes the appearance of Ygerne's husband and is thus able to satisfy his desire. As a reward for his service, Merlin is given the fruit of their union, Arthur, whom Merlin entrusts to Keu's blood father (Eutor), ordering him to have Arthur nursed by his wife and to confide his own son to a wet nurse. Later on, when Keu attempts to take the sword of sovereignty away from Arthur, Eutor begs the young king to forgive Keu:

Je ne vos demenderai mie vostre terre, mais tant vos dis je bien et requier que vos Qex vostre frere, se vos estes roi, façoiz seneschal de vostre terre en tel maniere que por forfet que il face ne a vos ne a home ne a femme de vostre terre ne puisse perdre sa senechalcie, que il touz jorz tant comme il vivra seneschaus ne soit. Et se il est fols et vilains et fel, vos le devez bien soufrir, que ces mauvaises tesches a il eues por vos et prises en la garce que il alaita, et por vos norrir est il desnaturez: por quoi vos le devez mielz soufrir que li autre. (*Merlin*, p. 278, ll. 13–23)

I will make absolutely no claim on your land, but I ask of you and request that, if you become king, you make of Keu your brother the seneschal of your land, such that, regardless of the wrong he might commit against either you or any of the men or women in your land, he will never lose his stewardship, but will remain your seneschal as long as he lives. For if he is vile and uncourteous and cruel, you must endure it, considering that he inherited these bad stains from the lowly woman who suckled him and thus lost his true nature because of you, who were fed [his mother's milk] in his stead: this is why you must show more patience with him than with any other.

The prose *Merlin*'s account provides a retrospective explanation of Keu's persistently discourteous behavior in many of Chrétien's romances, including the *Conte du Graal*, where the first mention of Arthur's seneschal occurs during the episode that narrates Perceval's initial arrival at court. Angrily reacting to Perceval's request that Arthur give him the Red Knight's armor, Keu (whom Chrétien describes as being "correciez"; ed. Roach, l. 1002) challenges the boy to "lui tolir orendroit / Les armes, car eles sont vos" (go and snatch his arms at once, for they are yours to take; ll. 1004–5).

That Keu's interaction with others often combines anger and sarcasm is corroborated by an incident that takes place during Perceval's second encounter with Arthur's court. The episode begins with the scene of the blood drops on the snow, which marks Perceval's growing awareness of the Other insofar as the bicolor tenor of the sight awakens in him the memory of Blancheflor.[38] Absorbed by the contemplation of his beloved, Perceval does not realize that Arthur and his court have set up camp nearby in the same meadow. While Arthur still lies asleep in his tent, the king's squires tell his knights that they just saw outside the camp "un chevalier / Qui someille sor son destrier" (a knight sleeping on his warhorse; ll. 4225–26). First Sagremor and in time Keu proceed to attack the unknown knight, only to find themselves unhorsed; and Keu is thrown down so hard on a rock that his right arm is broken. Feeling compassion for Keu, a companion whom he loves dearly ("molt l'amoit en son corage"; l. 4339), Arthur sends him his best healer along with three maidens trained in the art of setting broken bones. Gauvain's reaction to Arthur's gesture, however, indicates that he does not approve of the king's tender touch:

> Sire, sire, se Diex m'aït,
> Il n'est raison, bien le savez,
> Si com vos meïsmes l'avez
> Tos jors dit et jugié a droit,
> Que chevaliers autre ne doit
> Oster, si com cist dui ont fait,
> De son penser, quel que il l'ait.
>
> (Ed. Roach, ll. 4350–56)

Sire, sire, so help me God, it is not fair—as you know well because you yourself have always stated and proclaimed this by right—for a knight to interrupt another's thoughts, regardless of their nature, as these two knights have done.

Remarkably, it appears from Gauvain's reproach to the king that the latter ignores the royal custom according to which one cannot challenge in combat a knight who shows no such disposition.[39] It is thus left to Gauvain to "awaken," in both the literal and figurative sense, Arthur's attention to the code of behavior that guarantees order and peace in his realm. Acting as both spokesman and agent of that code, Gauvain offers to go to the unknown knight to invite him, whenever he emerges from his meditation, to come and present himself at court. Here in the episode Keu, giving way to his anger, derides Arthur's nephew for his tendency to resort to words rather than deeds and to conquer through "beles paroles" rather than feats of arms (l. 4371–403).[40] As in the previously mentioned example, Keu's angry sarcasm calls into question the prowess of the one he derides; and because the subject of Keu's verbal attacks is, in Perceval's case, a prospective Arthurian knight and, in Gauvain's case, the king's very own champion, the true target of Keu's belligerent attitude is clearly Arthur himself.

The fact that Keu can vent his aggressive impulses with impunity, although consistent with Arthur's obligation to show indulgence toward his foster brother in the name of the wrong he caused him, attests not only to the existence of conflict and rivalry within the king's circle, but also to the presence of forces that represent a threat to Arthur's sovereign status. Sagremor, who like Keu transgresses the code of courteous behavior by attacking Perceval irrespective of the latter's meditative stance, similarly endangers Arthur's preeminence at court. In this context, it is noteworthy that Sagremor, like Arthur's seneschal, invokes a tradition that endows him with singular power. The character is mentioned in both *Erec et Enide* (l. 1701) and *Cligés* (l. 4612) with a qualifier, "li Desreez," that recurs in the *Conte du Graal*: upon their return to camp with the news that they just saw nearby a knight on his horse, Arthur's squires first meet "Devant le paveillon le roi / Saigremor, qui par son desroi / Estoit Desreez apelez" (in front of the king's tent, Sagremor, who was known as the Unruly because of his hot temper; ed. Roach, ll. 4219–21). As Alice Planche notes, the character's name echoes that of the sycamore (*sagremor*), a tree mentioned in Chrétien's *Lancelot* during the narration of the hero's combat against Meleagant, which takes place in a heath in the midst of which stands a "sagremor gent et bel / Qui fuz plantez del tans Abel" (a tall and beautiful sycamore, which had been planted in the age of Abel; *Le Chevalier de la Charrete*, ll. 6989–90).[41]

That the prehistoric *sagremor* (a word whose pseudo-etymological roots link the tree to the combined concepts of sacredness—*sagre*—and death)[42] possesses extraordinary power is confirmed in *Erec et Enide* by its association with the Brandigan custom, which condemns Maboagrain, a knight of gigantic proportion, to remain in the garden of his beloved

lady until a challenger comes and vanquishes him in armed combat.[43]
Located outside the castle of Brandigan (whose king, Evrain, is Maboa-
grain's uncle), the lady's garden is protected in such a way that nothing
can enter it "Ne que s'il fust toz clos de fer" (any more than if it were
fenced in by iron; *Erec*, l. 5695). Apparently her talent as a practitioner
of black magic ("Par nigromance"; l. 5692) enables Maboagrain's lady
friend to enjoy the safety of her orchard, where she rests, sitting on a bed
"Desoz l'onbre d'un siquamor" (in the shade of a sycamore; l. 5832).
Significantly, her expertise in necromancy is both supplemented and
activated by Maboagrain's prowess, as testified by the presence in her
garden of a row of stakes bearing the severed heads of his previous vic-
tims. Necromancy (the art of predicting the future through invocation
of the dead—*nekros* in Greek) here refers to the lethal implications of
a prowess turned aggressive. Chrétien's use of the prehistoric *sagremor*
thus transforms what was traditionally a symbol of wondrous control
over the natural elements into an emblem of the violence inherent in
chivalric society. As embodied here by Maboagrain, as well as by Keu
and Sagremor li Desreez, the dark side of chivalry in terms of "black
magic"[44] consists of a propensity to use martial expertise for purposes of
destroying one's rivals.

Whereas the Brandigan episode situates chivalric aggression outside
the realm of Arthur's court, in the *Conte du Graal*, the manifestation
of anarchic and lawless forces emerges within the king's own circle,
thereby endangering the stability of the Arthurian realm as well as royal
authority. At the same time, the inclusion of both Keu and Sagremor
within the king's retinue lessens the possibility that they might act
as his enemies. Moreover, because neither Keu nor Sagremor succeeds
in defeating Perceval, the raw power assigned to them in Arthurian
literature is proportionally reduced. That Arthur is asleep in his tent
when Sagremor and Keu attack Perceval suggests the king's lack of vigi-
lance over the behavior of his closest companions. The sleeping king
motif also elaborates a significant contrast between Arthur's lethargy
and the alertness of his knights in acting on their contentious impulses.
Although Perceval, for example, is to all appearances "sleeping on his
horse," the speed and efficiency with which he reacts to Sagremor's and
Keu's successive attacks indicate a degree of awareness awakened by
the pugnacious temperament of his two aggressors. In the previously
cited reproach he addresses to Arthur, Gauvain thus reminds the king
of the latter's custom regarding the principle of courteous behavior that

forbids one to attack a knight who shows no belligerent disposition. Implicit in that custom is a positive corollary prescribing that one assist a fellow knight. At the heart of the Arthurian discourse on law and order is thus a twofold principle of proper chivalric conduct: not only does royal law claim to rescue chivalric society from its own violence by implementing a custom whose effect is the containment of aggression; it also induces each member of the knightly community to observe and practice the rule of mutual assistance.

Arthurian Custom and the Rule of Mutual Assistance

Gauvain activates this corollary clause in the Greoreas episode. Compared to the tradition that assigns to Keu the deadly ability to inflict wounds that no doctor can heal, Gauvain's healing of Greoreas displays a benevolent control over the natural elements, thereby confirming Arthur's claim that royal rule represents the establishment of a realm of physical and social well-being.

This claim invokes a familiar motif in the history of medieval kingship, that is, the exaltation of kings as miracle workers. French kings, for example, had long claimed the power to cure scrofula (a tuberculous condition of the lymphatic glands characterized by abscesses and skin disease).[45] The exaltation of the thaumaturgical powers of the "king's touch," which gained significance in the context of the rivalry between Capetians and Plantagenets[46] in the late twelfth century, sought to demonstrate the holiness, and consequently the superiority, of their respective realms. Gauvain's healing talent in Chrétien's romance appears to have a comparable function. Unlike the king's touch, however, Gauvain's healing power does not ratify Arthur's authority on the basis of its divine foundation.[47] Rather, its function is to exalt the superior character of Arthur's rule in protecting the order of the realm and, in the context of the Greoreas episode, in restoring the order of nature.

Yet Greoreas's reaction after regaining his health,[48] a recovery that enables him to steal Gauvain's horse, belies the apparently disinterested character of Gauvain's healing abilities. To Arthur's nephew, who wonders about Greoreas's ungrateful behavior, the latter replies:

> Ne te sovient il de celui
> Cui tu feïs si grant anui
> Que tu le feïs sor son pois
> Avec les chiens mengier un mois,
> Les mains liies triers le dos?

Saches que tu feïs que fols,
Que orendroit grant honte i as.
(Ed. Roach, ll. 7111–17)

Do you not remember the man to whom you caused great harm by forcing him against his will to eat with the dogs for a month, his hands tied behind his back? Know that you acted foolishly, and this is why you now endure this great shame.

Greoreas's allusion to the past triggers Gauvain's memory. Recognizing his interlocutor, Arthur's nephew presents his own version of the incident:

Es tu dont che, Greoreas,
Qui la demoisele preïs
A force et ton buen en feïs?
Neporquant bien savoies tu
Qu'en la terre le roi Artu
Sont puceles asseürees;
Li rois lor a triues donees,
Si les garde, si les conduit.
(Ed. Roach, ll. 7118–25)

Are you, then, Greoreas, who took the damsel by force and used her for your pleasure? Yet you knew perfectly well that in the land of King Arthur maidens are protected; the king has granted them a truce, and thus guards and defends them.

Gauvain reminds Greoreas that under Arthur's rule, infractions of social and moral decency are to be punished, thus presenting his treatment of the offender in the past as being integral to his duty as an impartial agent of the common good. In Gauvain's perspective, Greoreas is guilty on two counts: first, for having in the past transgressed the Arthurian edict regarding the protection of women and, second, for disregarding in the present the royal custom prescribing courteous interaction among knights. From Greoreas's viewpoint, however, the second part of Gauvain's accusation is moot inasmuch as the first part is untrue: his action in forcing Gauvain to mount a vulgar packhorse is thus a justified retaliation for the shameful and unwarranted treatment the latter once imposed on him.

The opening sequence of the episode does support Greoreas's account of the past. Contrary to his accuser's assertion, the request Greoreas addresses to Gauvain when the latter first approaches him indicates that he firmly adheres to his chivalric duty as protector of women:

                        por charité
        Et por la sainte trinité,
        De ceste pucele vos pri
        Que vos prenez garde de li,
        Qu'ele n'ait honte ne mesaisse;
        Et por ç'a faire le vos plaise
        C'ainc Diex ne fist ne ne volt faire
        Plus france ne plus debonaire,
        Plus cortoise, plus afeitiee.
        Or me sanble que desheitiee
        Est mout por moi, si n'a pas tort,
        Que ele me voit pres de mort.
        (Ed. Roach, ll. 6639–46; ed. Pickens, ll. 6607–10)[49]

In the name of charity and of the Holy Trinity, I implore you to watch over
this maiden, that she suffer no shame or abuse; and may it please you to do so,
for God never created nor intended to create one more noble, more refined,
more courteous, or more gracious. I sense that she is deeply afflicted by my
condition, and with good reasons, because she sees me near to death.

Greoreas's concern for his female companion at the hour of his death
calls into question the possibility that he ever was a rapist.[50] In view of
the growing number of landless knights who were, in Chrétien's time,
seeking to acquire territory through marriage,[51] it may be that Greo-
reas attempted to find a lover, if not a bride, capable of enhancing his
status. In that case, his transgression would have consisted of thwart-
ing Arthur's control over all social transactions, including matrimonial
alliances.[52] Considering the allusive character of this evocation of the
past, however, whether Greoreas, like the eponymous hero of Chré-
tien's *Yvain*, had in the past sought the love of a lady in order to obtain
her domain and thus assert his own autonomy remains unclear. His
request to Gauvain nonetheless provides evidence that he contests in the
present, as he probably did in the past, the sovereignty of Arthur's rule.
Although dictated by the dying man's dire condition, the religious tenor
of his plea, which invokes God as the sole source of authority regarding
proper chivalric behavior, implicitly devalues any royally regulated cus-
toms such as the edict prescribing the protection of women. Ignoring by
anticipation Gauvain's praise of Arthur's legal system, Greoreas instead
grounds his own principle of conduct on Christian ethics. Not only does
he contest Arthur's claim that royal law is right and true; Greoreas also
glosses Arthur's silence regarding the moral value of royally regulated
customs by implying that this law is *not* good. In Greoreas's perspec-

tive, Gauvain's action as healer is neither compassionate nor disinterested. Although Gauvain restores the order of nature, his intention is to impose Arthur's self-serving view of order—whence Greoreas's resentment against a system of justice that circumscribes his own autonomy for the benefit of Arthur's quest for power.

Greoreas's case proves that, despite Arthur's claim, royal law does not necessarily promote peaceful interaction among knights because it often exacerbates their determination to contest the absolutist character of his rule. Gauvain's function as peacemaker (in the Tintagueil episode) and healer (in the Greoreas episode), although proof of his capacity to perform "good" deeds, is also salient testimony to the king's desire to control all forms of social transactions. At Tintagueil, Arthur's nephew sides with Tibaut against his lord Meliant and with Tibaut's daughter against her older sibling, Meliant's lover. Reconciliation occurs in contradiction to the customary rights of both primogeniture and feudal dependence, a departure from tradition that favors Arthur's totalizing ambitions. Protection of the oppressed, in this case, Tibaut, turns out to be the most effective method to undermine powerful lords such as Meliant. The history of Gauvain's relationship with Greoreas betokens a similarly centralizing intention on the king's part because Greoreas's past "transgression" may have consisted of a claim to autonomy deemed guilty insofar as it defied Arthur's regulation of alliances, including marriage. Although under the king's rule amorous interaction is supposed to be a consensual rather than contractual bond—one that takes into account the wishes of two partners, as is inferred from the custom prescribing the respect and protection of maidens—*consensus* must first be ratified by royal *consent*. Evidence of the absolutist significance of Arthur's call for reconciliation and mutual assistance as activated by Gauvain is the fact that its main, if not sole, beneficiary is the king himself.

Arthurian Justice Prosecuted

The relative strength displayed by Arthur as deerslayer in Chrétien's first extant romance, *Erec et Enide*, is integral to the king's claim that royal adjudication is both impartial and disinterested. But the Arthurian discourse on law and order obfuscates the paramount role of force in the king's emergence as absolute ruler. In the oration that concludes the white stag episode, Arthur thus justifies his preeminence at court on the ground that his goal is the preservation and protection of right:

> Je sui rois, si ne doi mantir,
> Ne vilenie consantir,
> Ne fauseté ne desmesure;
> Reison doi garder et droiture,
> Qu'il apartient a leal roi,
> Que il doit maintenir la loi,
> Verité, et foi, et justise.
>
> (*Erec*, ll. 1749–55)

I am the king; thus I must not lie, nor accept wickedness, deception, or unruliness. I must safeguard reason and right, for the duty of a loyal king is to maintain the law, truth, integrity, and justice.

Under Arthur's leadership, everyone in the Land of Logres is both assured of receiving and asked to provide fair treatment, for no one, not even the king,[53] is above the law. But Arthur's claim that his is an impartial system of arbitration is jeopardized by his gradual weakening throughout Chrétien's oeuvre, culminating with the *Conte*'s crepuscular account of his realm. Keu's persistently aggressive behavior, which is already manifest in *Erec et Enide*,[54] attests to the centrality of physical strength as a prerequisite to the attainment of power while demonstrating the ineffectiveness of Arthur's law in guarding his own court from wickedness. By the time in which the narration of the *Conte* takes place, the king seems no longer able to maintain *reison* and *droiture* (right and reason; l. 1752) at court, as is confirmed by the conduct of either Sagremor "the Unruly" or Keu, whose "vilonnie" Arthur deplores (l. 1017) all the more as it contributes directly to the attrition of his Round Table.

In that context, Gauvain's prowess becomes Arthur's ultimate means of compensating for both the dispersion of his companions, who are now enjoying the comfort of their respective domains, and his own weakness. Demonstrating, at least verbally, a relentless dedication to Arthur's cause, the king's nephew appears to have realized, well before the time in which the romance is set, the importance of his mission as royal deputy. An example of Gauvain's long-standing commitment to royal law is Greoreas's allusion to the event in the past that inspires him in the present to seek retaliation. At issue here is whether Gauvain's past treatment of Greoreas was consistent with the Arthurian discourse on justice and fairness or whether, as Greoreas argues, it represented an abuse of force in support of the king's totalizing ambitions. On the basis

of the transtextual narration of Arthurian history from Chrétien's *Erec*
to the *Conte du Graal*, Greoreas's reasoning may be presented as follows:
because Gauvain's conduct proved to be governed by the principle that
might alone makes right, Arthur's claim to disinterested adjudication
is grounded on manipulation; and because the king's principal deputy
acted contrary to Arthur's promise to maintain *verité*, *foi*, and *justise* in
the land (truth, integrity, and justice), royal law itself is the locus of
vilenie and *fauseté* (wickedness and deception).

The Indictment of Arthur's Nephew

Such is in essence the counterclaim advanced by Arthur's opponents
as they attempt to halt the king's drive to hegemony by contesting the
legal character of Gauvain's actions. This is why Gauvain is the most
often challenged of all the characters introduced in Chrétien's *Conte du
Graal* and why the section of the romance devoted to Arthur's nephew
focuses on him as the target of repeated accusations.

His story proper thus begins with the arrival at court of Guigambre-
sil, who, as shown in Chapter 1, enters Arthur's hall almost immediately
after the Hideous Damsel's departure from Carlion:

> Guigambresils le roi conut,
> Sel salua si come il dut;
> Mais Gavain ne salua mie,
> Ains l'apele de felonnie
> Et dist: "Gavains, tu océis
> Mon seignor, et si le féis
> Issi que tu nel desfïas.
> Honte et reproce et blasme i as,
> Si t'en apel de traïson;
> Et sachent bien tuit cist baron
> Que je n'i ai de mot menti."
>
> (Ed. Roach, ll. 4755–65)

Guigambresil recognized the king and greeted him as was proper, but he
did not greet Gauvain; on the contrary, he charged him with felony, saying:
"Gauvain, you killed my lord, and you struck him such that not once did you
challenge him first. For this you deserve shame, reproach, and blame, and I
therefore accuse you of treachery; and may all these barons here acknowledge
that I have not said one untrue word."

In greeting the king with a gesture that acknowledges his vassalic alle-
giance, Guigambresil seems to indicate his intention to challenge not

the principle of Arthurian law, but Gauvain as transgressor of that law. However, several elements in Guigambresil's address to Gauvain cumulatively disclose that the ultimate target of his accusation is Arthur himself, insofar as royal practices as implemented by Gauvain do not cohere and even clash with the king's claim to impartial adjudication. What is noteworthy in Guigambresil's account of the past is the transtextual connection it establishes between Gauvain's conduct in the *Conte*'s prediegetic history and that of Keu in *Erec et Enide*. Like Arthur's seneschal in Chrétien's first romance, Gauvain assaulted Guigambresil's lord without challenging him first; and if Gauvain showed himself to be Keu's mirror double by attacking his victim "sanz desfïance," this implies that his action was similarly an abuse of prowess (the "par force" Erec mentioned against Keu). That there appears to exist no essential difference between Gauvain, the alleged champion of justice and fairness, and Keu, the emblem of discourteous behavior, calls into question the motivations governing the actions of Arthur's favorite deputy.

At the core of Guigambresil's argument, therefore, lies an assessment of Arthurian law that contradicts point by point the claim advanced in the royal oration quoted from Chrétien's first romance: Gauvain is an embodiment of wrongdoing (*felonnie*; l. 4758 in Guigambresil's address) rather than integrity (*foi*; l. 1755 in Arthur's oration), of deception rather than right (*fauseté/droiture*; ll. 1751 and 1752 in Arthur's oration), and of unruliness rather than reason (*desmesure/reison*; ll. 1751 and 1752 in Arthur's oration). Moreover, by calling upon Arthur's barons as his witnesses, rather than on the king himself as guarantor of justice, Guigambresil appears to contest the truth of Arthur's discourse (*verité*; l. 1755 in Arthur's oration) as well as the trustworthiness of the king's claim that "Je sui rois, si ne doi mantir" (I am the king, thus I must not lie; l. 1749 in Arthur's oration). Guigambresil's claim that every word he pronounces is true elaborates an interpretation of Arthur's oration that converges on the manipulative character of royal rule. Because the sole guarantee of the truth of Arthur's word is his word, this creates the possibility that both Arthur's claim and his kingship are abusive. Guigambresil's argument discloses, retrospectively, the priority of might as the foundation of Arthur's sovereign status at the time during which the narration of *Erec et Enide* takes place. Guigambresil's indictment of Gauvain also confirms the king's considerable weakening in the temporal setting of the *Conte du Graal*, considering that Arthur now relies on his principal deputy as a means of imposing royal law throughout the realm.

Two factors point to Guigambresil's awareness of the effect of time in gradually undermining Arthur's former preeminence. That he has not presented himself at court sooner suggests, first, that he feels now sufficiently secure to come and challenge the king at his own court. Second, Guigambresil's appeal to Arthur's barons indicates that they can *now* act as his witnesses, in a legal sense, because they were *then* witnesses to the event of his lord's death, in reference to the past during which Gauvain endeavored—for political reasons, as becomes clear later in the text—to murder his victim. The reason and right on which Arthur's law is allegedly grounded (*reison* and *droiture*; l. 1752 in Arthur's oration) here take their full significance in relation to the absolutist direction of Arthur's rule. "Reason" does not refer to the rational grounds that ensure the fair settlement of a dispute, but to the motivation governing the Arthurian discourse on law and order. Hidden behind the king's praise of truth, integrity, and justice lie the centripetal ideals of his realm, according to the true law of the "land of ogres," that is, that the "reason" (argument) of the stronger is also the better. In the context of Guigambresil's accusation, Gauvain's strength in the past is the sole reason he and, through him, Arthur triumphed over Guigambresil's lord. But raw force does not make right; and because Gauvain also transgressed custom as it applies to combat,[55] *felonnie* (l. 4758 in Guigambresil's address) has apparently become a way of life at Arthur's court, infecting everyone down to the king's closest and most reliable companion. Against the royal order of the day, a fabric of lies and manipulation, Guigambresil lays claim to verbal truth.

But nothing guarantees that Guigambresil's word is true, whence the ever-present possibility that one contests another's word and the resulting impossibility of terminating a dispute.[56] Indeed, Gauvain's questioning the validity of Guigambresil's charge attests to the unsolvable aspect of verbal exchanges as a means of settling conflicts because, like his accuser, Gauvain appears determined to contest Guigambresil's claim rather than to arrive at truth. Thus, consistent with the traditional distinction between murder and homicide in customary law,[57] Gauvain vehemently refutes his accuser's allegation that he committed a murder:

> Mais se je rien mesfait eüsse
> Au chevalier et jel seüsse,
> Molt volentiers pais en queïsse
> Et tele amende li feïsse
> Que tot si ami et li mien
> Le deüssent tenir a bien.

> Et se il a dit son outrage,
> Je m'en desfent et tent mon gage
> Ou chi ou la ou lui plaira.
> (Ed. Roach, ll. 4779–87)

But if I had committed any wrong against this knight, and I learned of it, I would eagerly seek to make peace by offering such amends that all his friends and mine would declare it equitable. And if he has uttered his outrage to insult me, I wage that I will defend myself either here or wherever he wants.

This part of Gauvain's reply to Guigambresil contains two parallel hypotheses: were my accuser right, I would react according to custom and redress the wrong I committed; contrarily, if he is wrong, I will defend my right before this or any other court. Gauvain's use of the imperfect and pluperfect subjunctive in the first part of his reply relegates this hypothesis to the realm of the improbable: if it could ever have happened that I had unknowingly committed a wrong, once I were to become aware of that fact, I would at once provide the wronged party with appropriate compensations. In this perspective, ignorance means innocence. Considering Gauvain's long-standing devotion to Arthur's cause, however, the chance of his being unaware of his own actions in the past is highly unlikely. The improbable tenor of Gauvain's first hypothesis, signaled by a *but* (*mais*, l. 4779), implying that the witnesses at court should reject it as contrary to fact, confirms that he favors the second one: *and* (*et*, l. 4785) if Guigambresil's charge is a fabrication, which happens to be the case, then he will pay dearly in retaliation for the shame he has caused me. Gauvain's use of the present and future tenses supports his implicit claim that this second hypothesis is not only more probable than the first, but in reality the sole correct one. Words of conciliation (I would have provided my accuser with adequate compensatory goods) now turn into threat: in the near future, here or elsewhere, I will prove Guigambresil wrong by defending my right on the battlefield.[58]

That *might* remains the sole means of determining *right*, in the political and legal sense of the term, is integral to the state of crisis that characterizes the Arthurian realm in the temporal setting of the *Conte*. According to Gauvain's own admission, it is now conceivable that an Arthurian knight might commit a wrong unknowingly; and although Gauvain rejects the hypothesis of his ignorance as highly improbable, he also appears to consider as highly probable, hence normal, the possibility that a knight of lesser status than he (that is, any other member of Arthur's court) could be unaware of his own violence. If violence is neutral unless a knight finds himself accused, and if the accused knight resorts to violence in order to defend his name, then the reliance upon force for settling a dispute, although confirming one's status at the level of prowess, brings about a form of resolution whose grounds are neither impartial nor, consequently, legal.

Yet it is obviously not in Gauvain's interest to acknowledge the lack of fairness inherent in any resolution obtained through sheer human force. For this reason, he keeps clearly separate and distinct the cases of violence respectively developed in his two hypotheses. The first invokes a violent act committed unknowingly, to be redressed, once the accused learns of it, by means of a nonviolent, compensatory form of resolution. In the second, the emphasis is on awareness: that of the accuser, whose "outrageous" charge seeks to insult the accused, and that of the accused, who understands the true motivation of his accuser. Just as Gauvain, as shown previously, presents this second hypothesis as the only correct one, he also presents as the sole means of adequate resolution his offer to defend himself through fighting. By assigning to Guigambresil the role of verbal aggressor (in reference to the outrage of his charge), Gauvain appropriates the role of the victim, thereby justifying his recourse to force as a proper means of punishing his accuser's unwarranted aggression. Indeed, the gesture (*tent mon gage*; l. 4786) implied from Gauvain's verbal challenge suggests that he is not waging his intention to defend his name in an abstract manner so much as he is throwing down the gage of combat. In contrast to the compensatory form of settlement mentioned in the first hypothesis as an adequate means of appeasing the wronged party, the second bespeaks a martial type of resolution, that is, the judicial duel.[59]

Gauvain's offer to settle the dispute through trial by combat provides indirect evidence that, despite the Church's repeated condemnation of forms of conflict favored by the nobility (including feuding, warfare, duel, and the latter's "sporting equivalent,"[60] the tournament), these practices retained their currency, the result of which was that judgment in a disputation, for example, was frequently obtained by martial rather than verbal means. At issue in the judicial duel was the abuse of a system in which judgment was increasingly determined on the basis of physical strength alone, instead of involving a transcendental decision (the *judicium Dei*).

Two examples in Chrétien's *Yvain* underscore not only the negative effect of this legal procedure in the hands of unscrupulous knights, but also its inadequacy in distinguishing right from wrong. The first occurs in the episode that narrates Yvain's actions as defender of Lunete, once the latter finds herself accused by three of Laudine's barons for having beguiled their lady into marrying someone who proved to be an unfaithful knight. Because of Lunete's vow to find a protector who will defend her against all three of her accusers, the judicial duel is no longer a single combat, as ordained by custom, but a conspicuously unequal fight. In the second example, in which Yvain engages in a judicial combat with Gauvain to solve a case of disputed inheritance between two sisters, the problem is, first, that Gauvain defends the party of the wrongdoer and, primarily, that both Yvain and Gauvain are here the recognized champions of the land in terms of prowess. That each of the two sisters selects her defender on the exclusive basis of his chivalric expertise represents a corruption of the legal procedure insofar as the outcome of the judgment rests on human might rather than divine force.[61] Not only does the martial reputation of the two champions contradict the principle of fairness that guarantees the carrying out of justice through trial by combat; the fact that Yvain and Gauvain are of equal force also creates the possibility that neither will emerge as a clear-cut winner or, worse still, that their fight will conclude with the champions' mutual destruction.[62]

In the last of his romances, Chrétien amplifies even further the ineffectiveness and corruption of the judicial duel as a means of settling a conflict insofar as the ground of the dispute between Gauvain and Guigambresil is factional rather than personal. In contrast to the still protective character of the judicial duel, which in *Yvain* assigns to Gauvain and the protagonist the task of fighting on behalf of women, the two contestants are here to act as the respective champions of two rival systems of authority. A first indication that Guigambresil intends to put Arthur's rule on trial is the effect of his indictment in shaming the king's nephew before the latter's own court. Another is how the accuser reinscribes Gauvain's offer to settle the matter "here" or wherever he, Guigambresil, considers an appropriate site ("Ou chi ou la ou lui plaira"; l. 4787). Although Guigambresil makes no explicit mention of the ties linking Gauvain to Arthur, these ties appear to play a part in inducing him to reject Arthur's court (*chi*) as a possible option, revealing his awareness that the king's arbitration is not disinterested. To Gauvain's manipulative identification of *chi* as a possible terrain, Guigambresil thus responds with another stratagem by selecting, as a second alternative, a site prone to tip the balance of justice in his favor:

> Et cil dist qu'il l'en provera
> De traïson laide et vilaine
> Dusqu'al chief de la quarentaine
> Devant le roi d'Escavalon
> Qui plus biax est que Absalon.
>   (Ed. Roach, ll. 4788–92)

And [Guigambresil] replie[s] that he will prove [Gauvain] guilty of foul and vile treachery at the end of 40 days before the king of Escavalon, who is more handsome than Absalon.

Guigambresil's selection of the court of Escavalon as an alternate site is far from innocuous because, as we learn later, the murdered lord mentioned in his charge against Gauvain ("mon seignor"; l. 4760) was the king of Escavalon.[63] Although the deferral of 40 days is consistent with custom,[64] Guigambresil's choice of site nonetheless discloses that his intention, in all respects comparable to that of Gauvain, is to subvert the procedure in a manner ensuring a judgment advantageous to the accusing party.

Gauvain's reaction to Guigambresil's charge reveals that, although he denies his accuser's allegation that he acted as a common murderer, he does not contest Guigambresil's account of the fate of the king of Escavalon. His response thus implies his acknowledgment that he was involved in a violent encounter with his accuser's lord and that this encounter led to the latter's death. But Gauvain also insists that he behaved properly, either because it was a case of *legitimate defense* or because Guigambresil's lord was guilty of unlawful conduct vis-à-vis a third party. Gauvain's avowed intention here is to appeal to the legal integrity of his action in the past, which he proposes to demonstrate anew in the near future. Yet the vehemence with which he refutes the charge of having killed the king contrary to custom, together with his virtual indifference toward the latter's fate, discloses the political rather than the legal grounds of his defense.

At the heart of his counterclaim is a twofold definition of proper chivalric behavior the significance of which is its exclusive attention to what constitutes a case not of legitimate defense but of *legitimate aggression*: if a knight is forbidden to attack another knight without challenging him first, attacking a knight *after* challenging him is permissible. Gauvain's denial focuses on the first clause, for it is paramount for his renown as the deputy of a fair and impartial system of justice that he prove himself innocent of the charge of homicide. The fact that Guigambresil also pays exclusive attention to the first clause confirms the factional significance of a debate with a central issue not of the determination of truth, but of the desire to impair the political authority of the rival party by accusing its champion of aggressive behavior. Against Gauvain, who defends the probity of his past action by invoking his steadfast adherence to custom, Guigambresil casts doubt upon the value of Arthur's law by charging his nephew with criminal behavior. If Arthur's preeminence in the present results from the unlawful conduct of his champion in effecting, for example, the demise of the king of Escavalon, then the royal discourse on law and order is grounded in abuse and deception. In this perspective, Guigambresil's offer to settle the dispute before the court of Escavalon bespeaks an attempt to undermine Arthur's preeminence by depriving the king of his most effective and devoted champion. From the standpoint of the rival Escavalon faction, Arthur's present dominance elicits a history of violent appropriation of power, and it is in the name of this past that, through Guigambresil as his representative, the son of the murdered king of Escavalon now summons Gauvain to his court of justice.

Gauvain's Sentence at Escavalon

Compared to the long-standing hostility between Arthur and the Escavalon faction implied in the narration of the *Conte du Graal*, other texts of the Arthurian tradition tend to assign to the site of Escavalon a proroyal significance. The best-known instance remains Avalon (which the word *Escavalon* duplicates to the extent that the prefix *es-* here functions as an intensifier),[65] the name of the famed island of King Arthur's "dormition." According to tradition, Arthur settled on this island after his defeat at the hands of his nephew Mordred, and he will sojourn here until his triumphant return.[66] Celtic lore confirms that, like Morgan le Fay, the site of Arthur's dormition is endowed with a supernatural quality, as testified by the connection between Avalon (the name of Morgan's island), Avallach (the name of Morgan's father, who rules over a magical island), and Ablach (that is, the "Apple Island"), the name of an island associated with the Irish god Manannan, who regulates the seasonal cycle.[67] At the core of the island motif in Celtic mythology is a principle of power understood in magical terms: it is said, for instance, that Manannan's island of Ablach, known by the Welsh as Ynys Wydrin, the "Glass Island," is a site of eternal youth.

Traces of this mythical interpretation of rulership subsist in medieval romance. An example is the representation of power in the guise of formidable giants, as in the case of the Green Knight depicted in the fourteenth-century alliterative poem that bears his name, *Sir Gawain and the Green Knight*. The text is based in part on a folktale motif, the "beheading game," whose purpose is to identify a warrior worthy of becoming the Green Knight's successor.[68] Gawain takes up the giant's challenge to fight him, thus proving that he deserves his renown as the best knight of the Round Table. Of particular interest is the effect of the champion's prowess, in this poem as in other similar narratives,[69] in connection with the establishment of Arthur's sovereignty. Although these stories retain some of the magical components characterizing the representation of power in Celtic mythology, they also elicit a human rather than supernatural understanding of rulership. In inheriting the power of such figures as the Green Knight, Arthur demonstrates the incontrovertible character of his authority.

In their pro-Arthurian reinscriptions, therefore, the founding myths of the Celtic tradition take on a political significance and testify to the superiority of Arthur's rule. Avalon is a salient illustration of this rewriting process insofar as the name designating the island of Arthur's dormition represents a conflation of various legends—from the "Apple Island" of the Irish tradition to the "Glass Island" of the Welsh tradition—out of which there gradually emerged an homonymy between "apple" (*ablach* in Irish, *aval* in Welsh), "glass," and the origin of Arthur's power. The fusion of the fabulous islands of Celtic lore into the single mythical site of Avalon identified Arthur as possessor of the fruit of eternal youth, as master of an island of endless spring, in short, as a figure guaranteeing the preservation of order. Not only was the atemporal quality of Avalon proof that the "once and future king" would return in an eschatological apotheosis. The name of Arthur's island became an emblem of his triumph as sole ruler of the Britons during his lifetime, as the homophonic and topographic correlations between Avalon/Escavalon and such variants as Cavalon, Carlion, and Camelot indicate.[70] Further evidence of the king's territorial dominance is the connection, grounded in pseudoetymology, between Glastonbury (now in Somerset) and the "Glass Island" invoked by the legend and site of Arthur's dormition. In the twelfth century, Welshmen still designated the town of Glastonbury under the name Ynys Wydrin (or Ynys Gutrin) because of the resemblance between the first syllable of Glas/tonbury and the famous "Glass Island" of eternal youth.[71] The gradual metamorphosis of Celtic mythology into Arthurian mythology thus played a crucial part in ensuring the dominant place of Arthur's kingship in medieval romance.

In contrast to this textual tradition, Chrétien's *Conte du Graal*, which undercuts Arthur's mythical figure as once and future king, narrates an aspect of Arthurian history wherein the king's rule is still, and more than ever before in the context of Chrétien's Arthurian chronicle, subject to open contention. Escavalon remains a site of keen opposition to Arthur's regime, all the more so in view of the ties that appear to link the Escavalon and the Grail factions,[72] as suggested from the mention of Perceval's mother that her eldest son was sent to the court of the king of Escavalon to be trained in the art of chivalry and dubbed (ed. Roach, ll. 463–65). Of equal significance within the history of factional contention alluded to in her chronicle is the fact that her younger son went to King Ban de Gomorret (ll. 466–67), considering that Arthurian literature after Chrétien identifies Ban as the grandfather of Galahad, the ultimate hero of a quest that will prove fatal to Arthur's kingship.[73] That Perceval's father chose not to send his elder sons to Arthur, the legendary source of chivalric expertise, suggests that both Ban de Gomorret and the king of Escavalon were leaders of factions hostile to the king. Perceval's brothers were apparently to be trained as members of the resistance to Arthur's territorial ambitions and specifically as agents destined to avenge their father's downfall at the hands of Arthur. Perhaps their deaths, which prevented the exaction of vengeance, occurred concomitantly with that of the former king of Escavalon, thus pointing to Gauvain as the possible perpetrator of all three murders.

Although the *Conte*'s allusions to this past are too evasive to provide a clear answer regarding the fate of Perceval's elder brothers, the narration of Guigambresil's indictment of Gauvain unambiguously designates the latter as directly involved in the death or "murder" of the king of Escavalon. It is this charge, which endangers Arthur's status as absolute ruler and undermines his claim to provide a fair and impartial system of adjudication, that compels Gauvain to depart from Carlion and present himself before his accusers' court. As he approaches the kingdom of Escavalon,

> Le siege del chastel esgarde,
> Qui sor un bras de mer seoit,
> Et les murs et la tor veoit
> Tant fors que nule rien ne doute.
> Et esgarde la vile toute

Pueplee de molt bele gent,
Et les changes d'or et d'argent
Trestoz covers et de monoies,
Et voit les places et les voies
Toutes plaines de bons ovriers
Qui faisoient divers mestiers.

. . .

Bien poïst l'en cuidier et croire
Qu'en la vile eüst toz jors foire.
(Ed. Roach, ll. 5754–64, 5777–78)

He contemplates the site of the castle, which stood on an arm of the sea, and sees that its walls and tower are so strong that it fears no attack. He looks over the town, inhabited by very handsome people, and the booths of the money changers covered with gold, silver, and other coins, and sees the squares and streets filled with fine workmen skilled in many crafts. . . . One could easily conclude and believe that every day was fair day in the town.

The court of so rich and potent a stronghold should in principle possess sufficient might to win over Gauvain as the champion of the rival party, thus predicating a reversal of fortune that would initiate Arthur's downfall and the ensuing emergence of the young king of Escavalon as new ruler of the realm. In anticipation of this possible outcome, the impregnable character of the site suggests that Arthur has still not attempted to impose his rule in this part of the realm, as confirmed by the fact that the king's champion, whose reputation usually precedes him such that he is virtually "known to everyone,"[74] had never before been seen at Escavalon ("onques mais n'i fu veüs"; l. 5752). This is why the young king of Escavalon does not recognize Gauvain in the knight with whom he crosses paths as he is going out for a hunting party and why he invites him to lodge at his manor and await his return in the company of his own sister.

The young king's courteous attitude, together with Gauvain's "ill-timed amorous dalliance" with the former's sister,[75] situate the opening sequence of the episode in a context forecasting that the judgment of Arthur's nephew will not take place. However, the text also underscores the latent danger that awaits Gauvain at Escavalon by specifying that the knight who now leads him to the chamber of the young king's sister is bringing him to "La ou de mort le heent tuit" (the place where everyone bears him a mortal hatred; l. 5750). That revenge is the primary motivation governing Guigambresil's indictment of Arthur's nephew becomes manifest through the reaction of the townspeople once one of the young king's knights (who had apparently witnessed Gauvain's action when the event occurred at a site other than Escavalon) recognizes in him the murderer of their lord. The townspeople immediately launch an attack and assault the tower where Gauvain is courting the young king's sister, and only the return of the king's hunting party saves Gauvain from fatal harm, for, unlike the townspeople, the king and his nobles are obliged to guarantee Gauvain's safety. The law of hospitality must prevail regardless of the treacherous nature of their guest, as Guigambresil himself reminds the young king:

> J'avoie Gavain apelé
> De traïson, bien le savez,
> Et ce est il que vos avez
> Fait hebergier en vos maisons,
> Si fust molt bien drois et raisons,
> Des que vostre hoste en avez fait,
> Qu'il n'i eüst honte ne lait.
> (Ed. Roach, ll. 6064–70)

I charged Gauvain with treason, as you well know, and thus it is the very same Gauvain whom you invited to lodge at your manor; right and reason would dictate that, because you have made him your guest, he should endure neither shame nor dishonor.

Should they allow the townspeople to kill Gauvain, the king and his men would leave themselves open to accusations of improper procedure, engendering a new prosecution, this time against them, that would cancel out their own suit against Arthur's nephew. In protecting Gauvain from the townspeople's attacks, the king and his men also ensure that the judicial duel will take place, thus honoring the legal contract made earlier in Arthur's presence that, in Gauvain's words, right will be served ("Et la verrons qui ara droit"; l. 4796). Yet the conspicuous inequality between the now identified Gauvain, famed throughout the land as the paragon of chivalry, and Guigambresil, who is at best an unknown quantity at the level of prowess, also predicts that Gauvain will triumph over his adversary. But if the Escavalon faction disregards Gauvain's offer to solve the dispute through a trial by combat, they will appear to refuse legal means in favor of traditional vendetta. It is thus urgent that the king and his men concoct, within the limits of legality, an alternative strategy enabling them to remove Gauvain's dangerous presence from their domain without offsetting Guigambresil's successful maneuver in compelling Gauvain to depart from Arthur's court.

The circumstances that have caused the townspeople to attack Gauvain, now besieged and mortally threatened, help the king and his men solve their dilemma by providing them with a ready argument to postpone the trial. In Gauvain's presence, the king's counselor proposes to Guigambresil a form of settlement designed to satisfy both litigants:

> il ert fait a la devise
> Mon seignor le roi qui est chi:
> Il me comande et je le di,
> Mais qu'il n'en poist ne vos ne lui,
> Que vos respitiez ambedui
> Dusqu'a un an ceste bataille,
> Et mesire Gavains s'en aille,
> Mais c'un sairement en prendra
> Me sire: que il li rendra
> Jusqu'a un an, sanz plus de terme,
> La lance dont la pointe lerme
> Le sanc tot cler que ele plore:
> Et s'est escrit qu'il ert une hore
> Que toz li roiames de Logres,
> Qui jadis fu la terre as ogres,
> Sera destruis par cele lance.
> De che sairement et fiance
> Velt avoir me sire li rois.
>
> (Ed. Roach, ll. 6156–73)

Let [the case] be settled according to the wishes of my lord the king here present: he orders me to propose to you that, should neither of you object, you both postpone this battle for a year and that my lord Gauvain be allowed to depart, but not without first swearing an oath to my lord, promising to deliver to him within a year and no more the lance whose point sheds a tear of the brightest blood; and it is written that the time will come when the entire kingdom of Logres, which was once the land of ogres, will be destroyed by this lance. My lord the king wants to have this oath and promise.

Echoing the Arthurian discourse of reconciliation, the proposed settlement betokens a determination to diffuse aggression and effect a peaceful resolution to the dispute at hand. Despite the conciliatory tenor of this proposal, which appears to guarantee Gauvain's safety by means of a task that will both protect him from the townspeople's violence and contribute to his renown, it is nonetheless obvious that the goal here is to empower the king of Escavalon by undermining Arthur's authority. Considering the effect of the settlement in postponing the judicial duel between Guigambresil and Gauvain, its terms might be read as an implicit acknowledgment of the lesser martial expertise of the Escavalon champion as compared to that of Arthur's champion. Moreover, because Logres is the territorial space over which King Arthur attempts to impose his rule, finding the lance that is destined to destroy the entire Land of Logres is a sentence clearly detrimental to the eventual triumph of Arthur's hegemony. At the core of the settlement is thus an effort to distance Gauvain from his uncle's circle by imposing on him a task that signifies a temporary abandonment of his Arthurian mission.[76]

Showing that he is not duped by the amicable appearance of the proposed settlement, Arthur's nephew declares that he would rather die or languish at Escavalon for seven years than swear and "vivre a honte et parjurer" (live in shame and perjure myself; l. 6182). The most famous knight of the Round Table does not question his capacity to find the lance and undertake a dangerous task. At issue is the effect of agreeing to a task that would annihilate the traditional realm on which his reputation is grounded and consequently terminate his preeminent status within that realm. In response, the counselor of the young king of Escavalon devises a compromise whereby the terms of the settlement are emended in a manner apparently designed to satisfy Gauvain's eagerness to fulfill both his obligations to Arthur and his legal contract vis-à-vis the Escavalon faction:

> "Biax sire," fait li vavasors,
> "Il ne vos iert ja deshonors
> En un sen que je vos weil dire,
> Ne ja, ce quit, n'en serez pire:
> Vos jüerrez que de la lance
> Querre ferez vostre puissance;
> Se vos la lance n'aportez,
> En ceste tor vos remetrez,
> Si serez del sairement quites."
>   (Ed. Roach, ll. 6183–91)

"Fair sir," says the vavasor, "it will not ever bring you shame in a sense that I will now tell you, nor will you suffer dishonor, I know: you will swear that you will do everything possible to find the lance; if you do not bring it here, you will return to this tower, and you will thus be absolved of your oath."

Gauvain accepts the compromise to the extent that the emphasis is now on the merit of the quester in doing his best to find the lance, rather than on the success of his quest. He thus swears to undertake a task that presents him with an opportunity to increase his renown, ratifying by the same token the corollary clauses of the settlement, that is, to return within a year and resume his imprisonment in the tower of Escavalon. However, Gauvain does not seem to realize that the revised settlement is really a truncated version of the original, given that it no longer contains any reference to the judicial duel that was to take place a year hence. Compared to the temporary effect of Guigambresil's challenge to a trial by combat, which in all likelihood would have resulted in Gauvain's triumphant return to Arthur's court, the counselor's sentence creates the possibility of deferring indefinitely his mission as royal deputy.

Gauvain's endorsing of a compromise that deprives him of an opportunity to reaffirm Arthur's power over his rival constitutes a decisive moment in the history of the king's reign, confirming the crepuscular character of that history in the temporal setting of the *Conte*. Although the Arthurian chronicle elaborated throughout Chrétien's romances fails to obtain closure in his last, unfinished work, the narration of Gauvain's adventures after the Escavalon episode tends to corroborate the crucial importance of the counselor's sentence in depriving Arthur of his most devoted and efficient agent, indicating that the ensuing course of events will inexorably tip the balance of power in favor of the king's rivals. Indeed, Gauvain's increasing absorption in tasks that not only prevent him from serving Arthur's cause but also work against the centripetal ideals of Arthur's realm predicts the disintegration of Arthur's sovereignty. What emerges from my analysis of the section of the *Conte* devoted to Gauvain's story is the ineffective and ultimately counterproductive character of his actions in maintaining the preeminence of Arthurian rule. Belying Arthur's hope that his nephew will help him restore the glorious years of his reign, Gauvain's increasing propensity not only to neglect his task in propagating the principles of Arthurian justice but also to use his prowess exclusively for self-serving purposes contributes in the end to the collapse of Arthur's kingship.

The Call of the Road: Gauvain's Absenteeism and the Collapse of Arthur's Round Table

The significance of the section of the *Conte* devoted to Gauvain's story lies in the notable discrepancy between the character's preestablished image as the paragon of Arthurian chivalry and the dubious and at times negative value of his actions as royal deputy that it discloses. In contradistinction to the unswerving fidelity to Arthur that is Gauvain's trademark in many Arthurian romances,[77] the *Conte du Graal* proffers important evidence that Arthur's nephew, like many of the king's companions, is inclined to use his prowess in the service of his own, centrifugal ideals. It is noteworthy, for example, that Gauvain's primary motivation for leaving court in response to Guigambresil's challenge is not the determination to defend the legitimacy of Arthur's rule so much as his desire to defend his own name. He will allow no one, not even his brother, Agravain, to undertake the task of restoring his honor:

> Et il dist: "Frere, ja nus hom
> Ne m'en desfendra se je non;
> Et por che desfendre m'en doi
> Qu'il n'en apele autre que moi."
> (Ed. Roach, ll. 4775–78)

And he answers: "Brother, no man but myself will assume my defense; and if I alone must defend myself, this is because he accuses no one but me personally."

Although Gauvain's eagerness to prove that he never committed a homicide is bound to demonstrate the value of royal law in containing aggression, the stress on personal vindication here undermines Gauvain's role as voluntary agent of Arthur's principle of justice. Typical of the narrative errancies of romance, his route to Escavalon is not direct, leading him to a chance encounter with Meliant and his knights that sets in motion his involvement in the Tintagueil dispute. Gauvain's behavior in the opening sequence of the episode indicates that clearing his name is for him a priority. Thus, despite the inherent appeal of a dispute that provides him with the opportunity of showing his prowess, Gauvain at first resists the temptation to join in the tournament:

> Il pense, si a raison,
> C'on l'apele de traïson,
> S'estuet que desfendre s'en aille;
> Que s'il n'estoit a le bataille
> Ensi come il l'a en covent,
> Il aroit lui honi avant
> Et puis son lignage trestout.
> Et por che qu'il ert en redout
> Qu'il n'i fust affolez ou pris,

Ne s'est del tornoi entremis
Et si'n a il molt grant talent,
Car il voit le tornoiement
Qui toz jors efforce et amende.
(Ed. Roach, ll. 5095–107)

He recalls, rightly so, that he has been accused of treachery and must thus go
defend his honor, for if he failed to engage in a trial by combat, as he promised
under oath, he would shame himself first of all, and his lineage with him. And
because he feared being injured or captured, he did not join in the tourney,
although great is his desire to do so, when he sees that the tournament becomes
each passing minute greater and mightier.

The personal reason that keeps Gauvain from participating in the tour-
nament augurs well for his eventual contribution to the support of
Arthur's *raison d'état*, for were he to prove himself innocent of the charge
of treacherous homicide, he would also confirm the value of the royal
distinction between proper and improper uses of prowess.

But Gauvain's self-control does not endure. Interestingly, it is not
so much the men of Tintagueil who provoke Gauvain into action as re-
marks made by the ladies of the domain when they notice his suspicious
inactivity. From the vantage point of the tower, whence they observe the
preparations for the oncoming tournament, the ladies comment on the
respective value of each challenger (ll. 4991–5090). Seeing Meliant, her
lover, Tibaut's older daughter marvels at his commanding appearance
and boasts:

"Dames, veez merveilles;
Ainc ne veïstes les pareilles
Ne mais n'en oïstes parler.
Veez le meillor bacheler
C'ainc mais veïssiez de vos oeix,
Qu'il est plus biax et sel fait miex
Que tot cil qui sont el tornoi."
Et la petite dist: "Je voi
Plus bel et meillor, se devient."
(Ed. Roach, ll. 5031–39)

"My ladies, look at these wonders; you never saw nor heard tell of any compa-
rable ones. Behold the best young knight whom it was ever given you to see
with your own eyes, for he is the finest, and indeed does better than any one of
those who participate in the tourney." To which [her] younger [sister] replied:
"I see one finer and worthier, I believe."

The elder sister praises Meliant in a series of comparisons designed to stress her own preeminence (she is the first born, courted by her father's lord) on the basis of her lover's superior beauty and martial expertise. From the standpoint of the noble ladies atop the tower as well as in the perspective of the knightly characters of the realm, individual value is not internal, but exists to the extent that it is demonstrated before witnesses. The physical challenge pitting Meliant against Tibaut and the verbal confrontation between the two sisters are therefore of exactly the same nature. But if age and status have so far forced the younger sister silently to endure her sibling's pride, Gauvain's presence now gives her the opportunity to take her revenge. Just as the men of Tintagueil welcome his arrival as a guarantee of their future victory against Meliant, so does it prompt the younger daughter to see in Gauvain the promise that her sister's ostentatious behavior is about to be assailed. Appraising Gauvain's excellence exclusively in concrete terms, she relishes by anticipation the pleasure of retaliation.

Yet Gauvain's behavior discredits her assessment of his value. His chivalric equipment lies about, unused; he has dismounted beneath a tree, hung up his two shields, and sits idly by while the tournament takes place. As they wonder about the knight's inactivity, one of the ladies sarcastically remarks that "cist a le pais juree" (this knight must have sworn to observe the law of peace; l. 5058).[78] For another lady, this man is a merchant intent on selling his horses.[79] For yet another, he is a "changieres" (money changer), who has no "talent que il departe / As povres bachelers anqui / Cel avoir qu'il porte avec l[u]i" (no desire to share with the poor young knights of today the goods that he carries with him; ed. Roach, ll. 5064–66). The younger daughter attempts in vain to come to the stranger's defense:

> "Il samble molt miex tornior
> Que marcheans ne changeor;
> Chevaliers est il, bien le samble."
> Et les dames totes ensamble
> Li dïent: "Por che, bele amie,
> S'i[l] le samble, ne l'est il mie.
> Mais il le se fait resambler
> Por che que ensi quide embler
> Les costumes et les paages.
> Fols est et si quide estre sages,
> Que de cesti sera il pris

> Come lerre atains et repris
> De larrecin vilain et fol,
> Si en ara le hart el col."
>
> (Ed. Roach, ll. 5077–90)

"He looks far more like a jouster than a merchant or money changer; he is a knight, by all appearances." But the ladies all replied together: "On that matter, fair friend, he may look the part, but he is not a knight. But he has assumed that appearance because he sought thus to evade paying customs and tolls. He is a fool, although he thinks himself clever, for he will be caught for this like a thief and accused and charged with vile and foolish larceny, for which he will deserve a rope around his neck."

Appearances alone do not a knight make: does the fact that the man owns knightly equipment signify that he belongs to the chivalric order, or is it a mask behind which an unidentified merchant intends to escape paying the dues of his trade? From Gauvain's standpoint, joining in the tournament, hence risking injury and capture, create the danger that he might break his pledge to go before the court at Escavalon. However, a different shame awaits him in the ladies' eyes if he does not.

Gauvain's predicament reveals that an overwhelming concern for fame and a corresponding fear of shame govern the chivalric society of the *Conte du Graal*. As the elder sister's treatment of her lover, Meliant, indicates, everything, including love, has a price and requires public demonstration. This is why she has decided to test Meliant's value, pledging that she will not reciprocate his feeling

> Tant que vos aiez devant moi
> Tant d'armes fait et tant josté
> Que m'amours vos avra costé;
> Que les choses c'on a en bades
> Ne sont si dolces ne si sades
> Com[e] celes que l'en compere.
> Prenez un tornoi a mon pere,
> Se vos volez m'amor avoir;
> Que je weil sanz faille savoir
> Se m'amors seroit bien assise,
> Se je en vos l'avoie mise.
>
> (Ed. Roach, ll. 4858–68)

until you have fought and jousted before me frequently enough to have earned my love, for things that one gets free of charge are never so sweet and enjoyable as those that one purchases. Challenge my father to a tourney, if you want to have my love, for I want to ascertain without a doubt that my love would be well placed, were I to invest it in you.

In the court of love, as in the court of justice (the assizes invoked in the word *assise,* l. 4867), the truth of a case must be verified through feats of arms. If the chivalric society depicted in the *Conte du Graal* lacks unity, the cause lies in a generalized tendency to use social transactions for personal advantage. The other's value is a matter of personal investment because each individual, ladies and knights alike, entertains alliances only to promote his or her own interests.

The ladies' assessment of Gauvain as a tradesman, although designed to deride Tibaut's younger daughter, nonetheless reveals the ambiguous character of chivalry as an order identified by visible signs (the armor) rather than by internal qualities. If in the temporal setting of the *Conte* knighthood is no longer the measure of intrinsic merit but a matter of appearance—worse still, if distinction can now be acquired by money—any common man may look like a noble, or vice versa. The frequent mercantile similes throughout Chrétien's romance are not innocent images, for they express a real danger threatening an aristocratic class in the process of losing its primacy.[80] Arthur's nephew cannot accept the verdict that he is a "common" thief any more than he could earlier accept Guigambresil's treatment as a "common" criminal. In both instances, his reaction is motivated by wounded pride, inducing him to relinquish his mission as Arthurian deputy in favor of the more urgent call to defend his own good name before the court of Escavalon, but first, before the "assizes" held by the Tintagueil ladies.

Pride is the vulnerable point not only of Arthur's nephew, but of the king's entire chivalric community, as most eloquently disclosed in the circumstances, provoked by the Hideous Damsel's arrival at Carlion, that prompt the Round Table to leave Arthur's court. We learn from the Hideous Damsel that she is on her way to the Chastel Orgueilleus (the "Proud Castle"; l. 4689), a site inhabited by 566 worthy knights, each accompanied by a fair and noble lady:

> Por che vos en di la novele
> Que la ne faut nus qui i aille
> Qu'il ne truisse joste ou bataille.
> Qui velt faire chevalerie,
> S'il la le quiert, n'i faldra mie.
> Mais qui voldroit le pris avoir

De tot le mont, je quit savoir
Le liu et le piece de terre
Ou l'en le porroit mix conquerre,
Se il estoit qui l'ossast faire.
Au pui qui est soz Montesclaire
A une damoisele assise;
Molt grant honor aroit conquise
Qui le siege en porroit oster
Et la pucele delivrer.
(Ed. Roach, ll. 4696–710)

I can thus tell you about this site that anyone who goes there will not fail to find occasions of jousting and fighting. Anyone who seeks to perform deeds of chivalry, if he looks for them at this site, will undoubtedly be satisfied. But for anyone who wished to prove himself the worthiest in the world, I believe I know the site and the specific spot where one could achieve that goal, if he were bold enough to dare. On a peak below Montesclaire, there is a damsel under siege. Whoever would succeed in lifting the siege and deliver the damsel would thus acquire great honor.

The Hideous Damsel's description of the challenges provided by the Chastel Orgueilleus resonates powerfully in the transtextual chivalric paradigm developed in Chrétien's oeuvre, for it reproduces the predicament endangering Arthur's sovereignty in the opening sequence of *Erec et Enide.* As in the case of the 500 maidens at Arthur's court, each of whom has as "ami / Chevalier vaillant et hardi" (as a friend a knight valiant and noble; *Erec*, ll. 53–54), the 566 knights at the Chastel Orgueilleus have each a lady friend "cortoise et bele" (ed. Roach, l. 4695). The "proud" character of the knightly inhabitants of the Chastel Orgueilleus signals that, like Arthur's companions in *Erec*, they, too, are rivals in love because they are rivals in knighthood. In view of this danger of internecine violence, the challenge offered at the Chastel Orgueilleus represents a means of transforming the contentious community of the *ami chevalier* inhabiting the castle into a united front against any newcomer bold enough to defy them. Echoing the royal strategy that confirms in *Erec* the value of Arthur's plenary presence in containing his knights' aggressive impulses, the challenge of the Chastel Orgueilleus has a similar effect insofar as it cements the cohesiveness of its knightly community. Coming from outside rather than from within, the source of aggression here consolidates the bonds of the castle's inhabitants in gathering them together against a common enemy.

The resemblance between the knightly community of the Chastel Orgueilleus and Arthur's court in *Erec* is a striking index of the erosion of the king's authority by the time in which the *Conte* is set. No longer the center and source of all chivalry, Arthur now finds himself threatened by the existence of courts, like that of the Chastel Orgueilleus, rivaling or even surpassing his own in power and prestige. Of particular interest in the Hideous Damsel's implicit devaluation of the Arthurian order is her assessment of chivalry as a demonstration (*"faire* chevalerie"; (ed. Roach, l. 4699) rather than an identity, revealing that *to be* a knight (that is, to belong to Arthur's court) is not, or not any more, sufficient proof of one's prowess. In the crepuscular account of Arthurian history as chronicled in the *Conte*, the king is no longer the powerful figure of the anterior order (the *rex quondam* of Geoffrey of Monmouth) any more than he is the embodiment of an order to be (the *rex futurus*). As his silent and passive reaction to the challenges described by the Hideous Damsel suggests, Arthur is aware that the glorious years of his realm have forever disappeared. That the Hideous Damsel so easily disrupts the festive celebration of Perceval's arrival at Carlion is another testimony to the illusory character of Arthur's court as a center of communal revelry. Many of Arthur's men have left court to return to their respective domains, and his remaining companions are experiencing the progressive degradation of royal might in a manner that predisposes them to turn into errant knights.

The Hideous Damsel's speech inspires in them an immediate desire to accept her challenges and prove their individual valor by outdoing one another. While Gifflet, for example, declares that he will brave the trial awaiting any newcomer at the Chastel Orgueilleus,[81] Gauvain vows to undertake what the Hideous Damsel has presented as the most difficult, hence worthiest, of all tests: the delivery of the besieged damsel near Montesclaire. At the heart of Gauvain's motivation is apparently not his concern for the fate of the damsel so much as the value of his success in the most praiseworthy demonstration of prowess. His boast discloses that he gives priority to the chivalric rather than amorous merit of this future exploit: in the spectacular setting where his liberation of the damsel *assise* atop the peak of a mountain is to take place, he will prove his martial superiority and thus turn the knightly inhabitants of this remote locus into a court (assizes) of admiring witnesses. Although consistent with Gauvain's renown as the paragon of chivalry, however, this display of self-assurance does not seem to cohere with his decision, later at Tintagueil, not to join in the tournament for fear of being "affolez ou pris" (injured or captured; ed. Roach, l. 5103). In the context of the Tintagueil episode, however, reason ("a raison"; l. 5095) rather than fear of defeat motivates Gauvain's restraint as he considers the dishonoring consequences that his failure to present himself at the Escavalon court would generate. But because a greater shame awaits him at the assizes of the ladies of Tintagueil should he fail to prove his knightly status, Gauvain abandons *raison* in favor of what qualifies as a wrong impulse to respond to the demands of the *hic et nunc*.

Gauvain's erratic conduct in the *Conte du Graal* constitutes the most blatant evidence of the collapse of Arthur's reign in the temporal setting of this last stage of Chrétien's Arthurian chronicle. Dominated by an obsessive determination to protect his self-image at all costs, an obsession that prevents him from entertaining long-term commitments, the Gauvain of the *Conte* shows an increasing incapacity to control his whereabouts, the result of which is a journey governed by the caprice of fortune and, ultimately, by the dictates of self-promoting impulses that take Arthur's nephew farther away from the king's court. As we saw in Chapter 1, this journey begins at Carlion (when Gauvain leaves court to present himself at Escavalon) and ends at La Roche Canguin, near Orquenie, where Arthur is holding court in the final episode of Chrétien's unfinished romance.

That the last of Gauvain's adventures brings him closer to Arthur's court, however, is not in itself proof that his actions necessarily contribute to the reinforcement of royal authority or that they necessarily reflect Gauvain's willingness to support his uncle's system of governance. Arthur's court remains in topographical terms the focal point of his route. Nonetheless, even when they concur with his assigned mission as Arthurian deputy, Gauvain's actions take on a character of formality, disclosing that the sole deep-seated conviction now governing Arthur's nephew is the urgency of protecting the prestige of his public persona. In view of the centrality of personal vindication as the primary factor in each of Gauvain's displacements, his journey appears to qualify as circular only insofar as it transforms him into a perdurably errant knight, thus deferring indefinitely both his return to Arthur's court and his resumption of his mission as royal deputy. Moreover, the peripatetic character of Arthurian governance, far from enabling the king to impose his rule on the remotest parts of the land, signals Arthur's gradual ineffectiveness in maintaining his authority over the areas and sites—including Carlion—that used to be part of his kingdom during the glorious years of his reign. In that sense, both the king's and Gauvain's locations at the end of the *Conte's* unfinished narration illustrate the increasingly marginal, insignificant, and irrelevant role of Arthurian kingship. We last see Gauvain awaiting his uncle's arrival in the distant realm of La Roche Canguin while Arthur, "mornes et pensis" (forlorn and downcast; ed. Roach, 1. 9220) at Orquenie, laments the absence of both his nephew and his own "grant baronie" (l. 9221).

The increasingly farcical aspect of Gauvain's adventures up to the episode of La Roche Canguin confirms the irrelevance of Arthur's rule in the temporal setting of the narration. As Peter Haidu shows in his detailed analysis of the section of the *Conte* devoted to Arthur's nephew,[82] two principal factors account for the transformation of Chrétien's second protagonist into the epitome of polished but destructive chivalry. The first is Gauvain's obsessive concern for his reputation, which induces him to go to clear his name at Escavalon, participate in the Tintagueil tournament, cross the boundary of Galloway, confront the enchantments of La Roche Canguin, and accept Guiromelant's challenge to a trial by combat. The second is Gauvain's equally obsessive desire to succeed with the ladies, which prompts him to pledge a lifelong service to Tibaut's *niche* younger daughter, court at Escavalon the daughter of a king whom he is accused of having murdered, seek to impress the *male* Orgueilleuse de Logres, and engage in a seemingly amorous exchange with his own sister at La Roche Canguin. To a degree, however, in this last of his adventures Arthur's nephew shows his capacity to use prowess in the service of others. Surviving the test of the Bed of Marvels, he liberates the castle from the spell that had held it in isolation and proceeds to land its widows, marry off its maidens, and dub its 500 squires. At the same time, Gauvain reacts with remarkable indifference to the news that the three ladies of the castle are his grandmother, Ygerne, his mother, and his sister, Clarissant, while not revealing to them his own identity.

Gauvain's lack of interest in the fate of his lineage points to the mechanical aspect of his chivalric performance, which manifests a strictly literal application of the normative standards of conduct in traditional chivalric society. Eager to adhere to ideals that were operative in the bygone glorious time of Arthur's early reign, Gauvain fails to realize their inadequacy in the temporal setting of Chrétien's last romance. In contrast to Perceval, whose silence at the Grail castle results in part from his ignorance of custom, Gauvain's egotism causes him not to ask questions that would have revealed to him the origin of the misfortune of La Roche Canguin. It is noteworthy, as we learn from Guiromelant's account (ed. Roach, ll. 8740–53), that Ygerne took refuge ("si frema"; l. 8744) in this remote part of the realm at the time of Utherpendragon's death, that is, of Arthur's accession to the throne. Of equal interest is the identification, in many texts of the Arthurian tradition, of the nearby city of Orquenie (the last location of Arthur's court in the *Conte*) as part of the kingdom of Loth, Gauvain's father.[83]

This combined intra- and extratextual evidence suggests that Arthur's hold at Orquenie resulted from a violent appropriation of a land that used to belong to his late brother-in-law and should now belong to Loth's rightful heir, Gauvain. In this perspective, the "spell" that had turned La Roche Canguin into a wasteland might have a political significance, invoking the violent origins of Arthur's rule in prediegetic history. The king's ambitions would have induced him, during the inaugural moment of his reign, to eliminate a rival (Loth) and ensure the disempowerment of his kingdom by depriving it of its titular heir (Loth's oldest son, Gauvain). Gauvain's role as savior of the people of La Roche Canguin therefore creates the possibility that he will redress this past of abuse, regenerate and revive Loth's former kingdom, and become the new ruler of the land. Yet this chance disappears in the face of Gauvain's lack of concern for the paternal branch of his lineage. Although he breaks the spell that had heretofore maintained the marginal status of La Roche Canguin, he also rejects the opportunity presented him of assuming the leadership of Loth's kingdom. Instead, he opts to resume the wandering mode of life that holds for him the promise of endless and, ultimately, aimless adventures. At the heart of Gauvain's behavior as he is depicted in Chrétien's *Conte* is a relentless devotion to prowess for the sake of prowess, inducing him to refuse a life-style that would terminate his quest for self-gratifying chivalric deeds.[84] In the end, the call of the road proves irresistible. Beyond the river encircling the castle of La Roche Canguin, there exists a cohort of knights-errant (for example, Orgueilleux de Galvoie and Guiromelant) who await their defeat at the hands of the best knight in the world.

That Guiromelant accuses Gauvain of having murdered his first cousin is an ultimate illustration of the circular character of Gauvain's journey. Just as his story begins with his indictment by Guigambresil and their ensuing agreement to solve the dispute by means of a trial by combat, it ends with his indictment by Guiromelant and a similar promise to settle their conflict through a judicial duel. In the context of Arthur's authority, however, a major difference distinguishes these twin scenes of accusation, considering the fact that, on Guiromelant's suggestion, their duel is to take place in Arthur's presence:

> Que jusqu'a set jors atendrons
> Et al septisme jor vendrons
> En ceste place tot armé,
> Et tu aies le roi mandé
> Et la roïne et sa gent toute,
> Et je ravrai la moie route
> Par tot mon roialme assamblee,
> Si n'iert mie faite a emblee
> Nostre bataille, ainz le verront
> Tuit cil qui venu i seront.
> (Ed. Roach, ll. 8851–60)

Let us defer our combat for a week, and on the seventh day let us return here fully armed, by which time you will have summoned the king, as well as the queen and their entire community, as I will have summoned my own people from throughout my kingdom, such that our battle will not occur in secret, but will be witnessed by all those who will have gathered here.

This is why Gauvain orders a squire to go to Orquenie and announce to Arthur that he must come with his court,

> Que j'a[i] une bataille prise
> Vers un chevalier qui ne prise
> Ne moi ne lui qui gaires vaille.
> (Ed. Roach, ll. 9121–23)

for I have engaged to do battle against a knight who feels very little respect either for myself or for [Arthur].

Because Guiromelant's animosity toward Gauvain as Arthur's nephew roots their upcoming combat in a factional rather than a personal context, Gauvain's eagerness to defend his name should in the end enable the king to resume his preeminence as the focal point of Gauvain's story. This suggests that Chrétien's second protagonist is on his way to resuming, albeit unwittingly, his traditional role as Arthur's most reliable agent. Running counter to this possible interpretation of Gauvain's final adventure is the fact that nothing guarantees that he will not encounter another challenger, forgetting in the process his vow to fight Guiromelant, as he seems to have forgotten his successive promises to deliver the damsel besieged near Montesclaire, seek the Bleeding Lance, and return to La Roche Canguin. Boasting has become Gauvain's way of life, hence his increasing incapacity to make good on his vows and Arthur's ensuing lament at Orquenie as he hopelessly waits for the return of his nephew and of his once brilliant and grand baronage.

My examination of the section of the *Conte* devoted to Gauvain points to the significance of this part of Chrétien's narrative as an account of the imminent collapse of Arthur's reign. Once the paragon of Arthurian chivalry and the king's most efficient and devoted deputy, Gauvain now shows, in the terminal stage of Chrétien's Arthurian chronicle, a growing indifference toward the fate of his uncle's kingship. It is in the context of the attrition of Arthur's court as aggravated by the prolonged absence of the king's former champion that the story of Perceval retrospectively finds its meaning. The weakened state characterizing not only the king but also most of his contenders in the temporal setting of Chrétien's last romance focuses attention on Perceval as a potential reinforcement of whichever party he might eventually join. From the perspective of each of the rival factions inferred from Chrétien's text, the *niche*'s demonstrated prowess as he enters the realm of traditional chivalry represents a renewed hope of victory. That Arthur is fully aware of Perceval's knightly potential is illustrated by the king's concern over the fate of the boy after his departure from Carlion: "Puis m'a si bien a gre servi [que] . . . Ains movrai ja por aler querre" (He has since served me so well [that] . . . I shall at once go and seek him; ed. Roach, ll. 4133, 4140). Parallel to Arthur's desire to direct the boy's prowess in support of his rule, representatives of the Grail faction manifest a similar intention to use Perceval for the prosecution of his own lineage's causes. The presence of those two parallel, hence conflicting, systems of allegiance is a crucial element for the understanding of Perceval's story, indicating that Chrétien's uninformed character is the target of a dual discourse whose goal, from the standpoint of the Grail faction as well as Arthur, is not the education of the *niche* so much as his transformation into a warrior assigned the mission of securing the triumph of their respective systems of governance. Focusing on the first part of Chrétien's twofold romance, the analysis developed in the following chapter proposes to explore successively the Arthurian episodes and the Grail episodes of Perceval's story as evidence that the knightly ideal articulated in the discourse of both rival factions, which shares the same totalizing character, discloses the failure of traditional values to inhibit factionalism and rescue chivalric society from its own violence.

Chapter 3

The World According to the Grail

I propose to explicate retrospectively the narration of Perceval's story in the context of the diminishing value of Arthur's nephew as champion of the royal cause. At the core of my reading is the striking resemblance between Chrétien's two protagonists with respect to their involvement in adventures that first support, but ultimately jeopardize, the principle of Arthurian leadership. Like Gauvain's story, Perceval's takes on a progressively anti-Arthurian destination. Although its narration focuses first on the *niche*'s initiation into the Arthurian chivalric ideal, it converges in the end on the Grail as a supreme center and source of chivalric excellence, over and above the type of knightly service encouraged at the king's court. The parallel effect of the Escavalon episode in imposing on Gauvain the search for the Bleeding Lance and of the hermit episode in persuading Perceval to abandon the sphere of secular (that is, Arthurian) chivalry underscores the significance of these two adventures as decisive moments in the fortune of Arthur's kingship. Taken together, these adventures predict the collapse of the king's rule as he finds himself successively deprived of his formerly most faithful deputy and of his newly acquired champion. Running counter to Arthur's centripetal ideals, the dual displacement from court that takes Gauvain to the remote locus of La Roche Canguin and, in the present state of the text, seems to lead Perceval to the Grail castle results in a transformation of the configuration of the social landscape as traditionally charted under the king's rule. During the particular moment of Arthurian history in which the narration of the *Conte* is set, the prestige and ascendancy of the formerly marginal sites of the realm (including the Chastel Orgueilleus evoked by the Hideous Damsel) appear to have grown and continue to grow steadily while those of Arthur's court proportionally decline.

This shift of emphasis away from Arthur's court calls attention to the significance of the motif of the remote locus in providing each of the protagonists of Chrétien's romance with the opportunity to fulfill his dynastic duties. Like Perceval's eventual return to the Grail castle as the seat of his matrilineal heritage, Gauvain's arrival at La Roche Canguin places Chrétien's second protagonist in a position to assume sovereignty within the context of his matrilineal kin. The blood relation linking this branch of Gauvain's family to Arthur suggests, in Donald Maddox's view, that Gauvain's destiny is to inherit the throne of Logres, thus signaling his role in inaugurating, as potential *rex futurus*, "the beginning of a new phase for [Arthur's] anterior order."[1] According to Maddox, therefore, the two mirror loci of La Roche Canguin and the Grail castle are indicators that the unfinished *Conte* implies a conclusion leading its two protagonists to ensure the regeneration of chivalry by substituting a new system of governance for the outmoded Arthurian order. From the sites where the Arthurian and the Grail lineages are to survive will emerge, however, a vastly different representation of the chivalric ideal: whereas Gauvain's task at La Roche Canguin is to revive the brilliance of Arthur's now tarnished kingdom as a viable alternative *within* the world, at the Grail castle, where Perceval is called to assume a spiritual form of leadership, exile itself will become "an alternative kingdom permanently *apart from* the world and its ways, in anticipation of the end of time, the ultimate closure."[2]

In this chapter I interpret the *Conte*'s remote loci in a manner that calls into question their significance as a promise of a regenerated chivalry, either in terrestrial or transcendent terms. For example, Donald Maddox's assessment of Gauvain's future role appears not to cohere with the circular and aimless character of the protagonist's journey in the latter part of his story. Amplifying Maddox's argument that the gradual erosion of Arthur's power lies in a legal system that proves no longer adequate for the maintenance of order, I situate this system at the heart of the collapse that threatens to engulf not only Arthur's court, but the entire chivalric realm (including the Grail society) depicted in the romance as the final stage of the poet's chronicle.

The centrality of might in the customary enactment of justice, which accounts for the decline of that society in the temporal setting of the *Conte*, also accounts for the renewed hope that Perceval's arrival on stage inspires in each of the principal rival forces figuring in the romance. The chivalric ideal articulated in both Arthur's discourse and that of the Grail representatives bespeaks, in that sense, a similar investment in prowess as a prerequisite for the success of either faction in recovering its past power and prestige. If this last romance elaborates a crepuscular account of Chrétien's fictional chronicle, this is because the society whose history it narrates fails to solve the problems of its own aggression by clinging to protocols that perpetuate factionalism and the violence that is its ever-present companion.

Making (New) Knights: Perceval and the Restoration of Arthurian Order

Whereas the renown of Arthurian chivalry in the glorious years of the king's reign was such that it prompted individuals like Cligés's father, Alexandre, to seek his court and request induction as his knight, this prestige appears to have virtually disappeared by the time in which the *Conte* is set. What was once the most illustrious court in the land is threatened by the existence of rival courts that ineluctably draw Arthur's knights away from service to the king, thus depriving him of the military force on which depends, now more than ever before, the demonstration of his authority. In the face of the numerous "kings" figuring in the romance, Arthur's kingship is on its way to becoming an empty word. This explains in part the volatile and disenchanted disposition of the remaining members of his court. For Arthur to recover his previous preeminence therefore depends entirely on the king's ability to convince his companions of the value for them of belonging to his chivalry.

But because the attrition of the king's court results precisely from Arthur's failure to attract new adherents, the argument that his order of chivalry represents an enticing alternative holds little persuasive power over its current participants. If the desire to prove oneself superior in prowess had in the past inspired Arthur's knights to live at the grandest of all courts, the same desire is now propelling them one by one to respond to the call of the road and seek elsewhere the means of demonstrating their value. The competitive impulses that used to be one of the constitutive elements in the success of Arthur's court have become the very grounds of its depletion in the temporal setting of the romance. What Arthur perceives as his knights' desertion is, from their standpoint, necessitated by the deterioration of his court as a locus that no longer provides them with the means to achieve their quests for honor and glory.

Enter Perceval, and with him the promise of a reversal in the fortune of Arthur's rule. Indeed, the arrival at court of a character who displays so irrepressible an eagerness to go "Au roi qui fait les chevaliers" (to the king who makes knights; ed. Roach, l. 494), combined with so un-adulterated a deference for the Arthurian order of chivalry, potentially represents a pivotal moment in the king's history, presenting him with the opportunity to claim that his court has lost none of its prestige. What is noteworthy here is the value of the *niche* in invoking, by his very request to Arthur, the former brilliance of the king's reign. Perceval's ignorance of the past, which accounts for his unawareness in the present of the problems besetting Arthur's court, predisposes the protagonist to pay tribute to the king as the sole center and source of chivalry, thus substituting the former figure of Arthur as *rex sublimis* for his present one as *rex inutilis*. That the king's companions witness the (unexpected) arrival of a new aspirant creates the possibility that they will recognize both the superiority of the king as a producer of chivalry and that of his court as a locus gathering together the worthiest knights in the land.

Yet Perceval's potential role in reactivating the prestige of Arthur's time-honored Round Table is held in check by the *niche*'s behavior as he fails, first, to recognize Arthur amid the members of his court and then proceeds to bring his horse so close to the king that he knocks down the latter's cap. Perceval's ignorance and clumsiness provoke a reaction marked by unanimous indifference, for "Nus qui le voit nel tient a sage" (none of the witnesses thinks him wise, l. 976), except for Keu, who expresses his outright contempt toward the boy. While admonishing his seneschal for his wickedness, Arthur shows little interest in Perceval, whose greeting he does not initially acknowledge.[3] Realizing finally that the king will not satisfy his request soon enough, Perceval decides to leave court. Thus, instead of capitalizing on Perceval's petition as a means of demonstrating anew his preeminence as the producer of the most prestigious order of chivalry, Arthur lets this opportunity go by and, with it, one last hope of retaining his knights at court.

However, what seems to be here a lack of strategic acumen on Arthur's part is instead dictated by the urgency, from the king's view-point, of inducting into his ranks only those individuals whose martial value augurs well for their agency as reinforcement of his rule. To everyone's assent, the boorish boy who presents himself at Carodoeil is handsome and noble ("bel" and "gent"; l. 978); but is he a worthy warrior? Only a dimwit (the damsel who had not laughed in over six full years; l. 1046) or a fool (the court's jester, who had predicted that the damsel would laugh upon seeing "Celui qui de chevalerie / Avra toute la seignorie"; he who will surpass everyone in chivalry, ll. 1061–62) could be so naive as to place their trust in the prowess of a *niche* wearing a coarse jacket and rawhide buskins on his feet. As for the rest of the court, with the exception of Keu, they answer the rhetorical question of Perceval's value with a polite silence.

The *niche*'s success in defeating the Red Knight, whom he had met prior to entering Arthur's hall, represents, in this sense, a dramatic turn of events because this victory transforms what Arthur's companions had perceived as an insignificant halfwit into an individual of unquestionable martial talent. Evidence of the centrality of physical strength in ensuring one's status at Arthur's court is provided by Yvonet, the court's habitual messenger and sole witness to Perceval's deed, who returns to court with the cup that the Red Knight had snatched away from the king:

> Si li dist: "Sire, or faites joie,
> Que vostre colpe vos renvoie
> Vostre chevaliers qui chi fu."
> "De quel chevalier me dis tu?"
>   (Ed. Roach, ll. 1211–14)

And [Yvonet] tells the king: "Sire, rejoice, for your knight who was here sends back your cup to you." "What knight are you talking about?"

Yvonet's reference to Perceval as "Arthur's knight" points to the value of the boy's killing of the Red Knight as sufficient proof that he deserves immediate admission into the king's order of chivalry. Arthur should *faire joie* (l. 1211), for his "knight" has just eradicated one of the king's most powerful rivals while restoring to him the symbolic cup of his kingship. Echoing the concluding episode of *Erec et Enide*, the "joie de la cort" evoked in Yvonet's message thus alludes to the renewal of Arthur's hold both on his court and on the land, as generated by the selfless agency of his new "knight." So unexpected is this potential turn of events that Arthur urges his messenger to reveal the identity of this putative new champion: is Yvonet really talking of the "vallet galois" who requested the armor of him who "hontes maintes /

M'a faites" (shamed me so deeply; ll. 1222–23)? If so, how did the boy succeed in retrieving the cup? Did the Red Knight like and respect him so much that he gave it to him willingly? Yvonet replies to the king's inquiries by narrating in detail how the boy threw a javelin through the eye-slit of the Red Knight's helmet

> si qu'il li fist par de derriere
> Le sanc et le cervele esp[a]ndre,
> Si qu'il le fist a terre estandre.
> (Ed. Roach, ll. 1236–38)

so that blood and brains spilled out from beneath, causing him to fall dead on the ground.

Recognizing through Yvonet's narration the boy's exceptional combative talent, Arthur realizes at the same time the extent of his loss in the face of this new champion's departure. What should have been an occasion of "joy" thus turns into a cause of renewed worries, inducing Arthur to vent his anger toward Keu:

> Ha! Keu, com avez hui fait mal!
> Par vostre lange, l'enuiouse,
> Qui avra dite mainte oisouse,
> M'avez vos le *valet* tolu
> Qui molt m'a hui cest jor valu.
> (Ed. Roach, ll. 1240–44; my emphasis)

Alas! Keu, what grave harm you have done today! Because of your venomous tongue, which has spoken many an idle word, you have driven away from me the *boy* who has achieved today a deed of extreme value for me.

Despite his boorish appearance, the *valet* who presented himself at court has revealed himself to be a worthy warrior, justifying Yvonet's evocation of Perceval as "Arthur's knight." In his turn, Arthur acknowledges belatedly the boy's military value, for he now begins to refer to Perceval not as the *valet* mentioned at line 1243, but as a *chevalier*.[4] If Arthur no longer doubts that the *valet* is a knight, it is because Perceval's feat has eradicated the most recent challenger to the king's rule.

Rex quondam: Arthur's Institution of the Round Table

The notably martial definition of Arthurian chivalry here discloses the deterioration of what was once the king's ideal knightly brotherhood into a "crack regiment" now assigned the task of restoring the preeminence of his rule. Gone is the inspired ruler immortalized in Geoffrey's chronicle, gone, too, his capacity to induce the forces of the realm into joining together and forming a chivalric fraternity. First mentioned in Wace's account, Arthur's celebrated Round Table remains the most often cited example of the beneficence of the king's rule in encouraging the knights of the land to relinquish their tradition of rivalry. Wace situates this event at a time when Arthur's prestige is such that his court has attracted the most eminent nobles in the realm,

> Don chascuns miaudre estre cuidot,
> Chascuns se tenoit au meillor,
> Ne nus ne savoit le peior.
> *(Brut,* ll. 1208–10)[5]

each of whom thought himself to be worthier than the others, each of whom considered himself the best, and none of whom accounted himself the worst.

Determined not only to gather around him the knightly elite of the land, but also to assuage the competitive impulses of his companions, Arthur decides then to create "la Reonde Table,"

> Dont Breton dient mainte fable.
> Iluec seoient li vasal,
> Tuit chevelmant et tuit igal;
> A la table igalmant seoient,
> Et igalmant servi estoient;
> Nus d'aus ne se pooit vanter
> Qu'il seïst plus haut de son per;
> Tuit estoient asis mayen
> Ne n'i avoit nul de forien.
> *(Brut,* ll. 1212–20)

about which Britons tell many a tale. There the vassals sat, each knight equal in chivalry; all were seated equally, and each equally served; none among them could boast of sitting higher than his peer; for all were seated around the table in such a way that no one was farther away from its center.

In Wace's perspective, the value of the king's Round Table lies in its effect in promoting equity and fairness through a system of parity wherein the function of the king—*primus inter pares*—is not to impose, but to guarantee order in the realm. It is in the name of the unifying quality of Arthur's leadership that both Geoffrey and Wace grant to their hero his symbolic immortality as the "once and future king."

In sharp contrast to this eulogistic tradition, a profoundly different destiny appears to await the weakened and ineffective figure portrayed in the *Conte*. In this twilight of Arthurian history, the inspired ruler immortalized by Chrétien's predecessors has forever disappeared, never to return. The final stage of Chrétien's chronicle thus develops a pessimistic account of the passing of time, of the ineluctable decline that is the fate of even the most prestigious of all courts. Not only does Chrétien's romance question the status of the *rex futurus* as a model exemplar for all generations to come. Also at issue is the glorious status of the *rex quondam* in the hands of Arthur's previous chroniclers: was Arthur ever the ideal monarch celebrated by tradition?

A preliminary response to this question can be found in Wace's recounting of Arthur's creation of the Round Table insofar as the episode discloses the significance of the chronicler's narration as a biased and idealizing reconstruction of this legendary past. When Arthur institutes his fraternity, his hold on the realm has reached such proportions that, in Wace's words, "nus guerroier ne l'osa, / Ne il autre ne guerrea" (no one dared wage war against him, nor did he fight any one; *Brut*, ll. 1193–94). While drawing to his court the greatest barons in the land, Arthur's power also elicits alarm in "li roi estrange" (foreign kings),

> Car molt cremoient et dotoient
> Que tot le monde conqueïst
> Et lor dignetez lor tolsist.
>   (*Brut*, ll. 1242–44)

for they greatly dreaded and feared him in his capacity to conquer the world and deprive them of their power.

Arthur's ensuing actions confirm the validity of these fears inasmuch as the king's Round Table supplies him with the means of engaging in expansionist politics:

> Et par la grant chevalerie
> Qu'il ot afeitiee et norrie,
> Dist Artus que mer passeroit
> Et tote France conquerroit.
>   (*Brut*, ll. 1261–64)

Taking into account the chivalric force that he had formed and trained, Arthur declared that he would go beyond the sea and conquer the whole of France.

If Arthur's creation of the Round Table is a critical moment in the king's history, this is because it inaugurates the transformation of the *primus into pares* into a leader governed by imperialistic ambitions. However, Wace's emphasis is not on Arthur's personal motivation, but on the value of the Round Table in strengthening his kingly status. While unwittingly revealing the centrality of might in authorizing the emergence of Arthur the conqueror, his chronicle's primary goal remains the idealization of its royal figure: this is why Wace assigns to fate, and not to imperialistic ambitions, the tragic outcome of Arthur's reign. That Arthur's military expedition on the Continent ultimately leads to his demise at the hands of Mordred becomes part of the king's mythical status as both the *rex quondam* and *rex futurus*.

By focusing on the destabilizing effect of political ambition, Chrétien's *Conte* provides a demystifying perspective on the origin of Arthur's sovereignty. If loss of power accounts for the failure of his leadership in the *Conte*, this reveals that in the past power played a key part in Arthur's success in imposing his rule. The *Conte*'s implicit reinscription of the legend thus ascribes the emergence of Arthur's sovereignty not to the king's disinterested commitment to order and peace, but to his self-promoting actions as an inspired strategist. Behind Arthur's invention of a chivalric order allegedly assigned the "mission" of protecting the weak and containing the strong lay the king's desire to channel prowess in support of royal ambitions. Apparently Arthur's strategy in concocting his ideal brotherhood was not to suppress so much as to utilize chivalric rivalry, which survived in the form of an emulation among the king's *ami chevalier* as they strove to outdo one another in fulfilling their "mission." Because Arthur's sovereign status rested entirely on his superior strength at court, the king's strategy also contained the inherent danger that, should Arthur fail to control his companions' competitive impulses, they might bear arms against each other or, worse still, against Arthur himself.

This is the danger that stands at the heart of the problems besetting chivalric society in the period of Arthur's reign narrated in Chrétien's chronicle. From the outset, in the opening episode of *Erec et Enide*, the main predicament of Chrétien's Arthur is the inadequacy of a leadership system that relies on might alone when the power of the king's barons now rivals his own. An example is Arthur's misguided revival of the Custom of the White Stag, an initiative that undermines his value as an astute strategist because, rather than reaffirming the king's preeminence at court, it turns the community of his *ami chevalier* into a horde of mutually hostile individuals. Not only does Arthur's action testify to the failure of his rule in containing aggression; it also arouses his knights' competitive impulses in a manner that discloses the inherently divisive and combative character of chivalric society. Despite the optimistic out-come of Chrétien's first narrative, this initial stage of the poet's own Arthurian chronicle points to the vulnerability of the knightly realm of romance in terms of a community threatened by internecine strife and tension. Still latent in *Erec et Enide*, this danger becomes widespread by the time in which the *Conte* is set, as illustrated by the antagonis-tic character of knightly interaction, both within and outside Arthur's court. In this last stage of Chrétien's Arthurian chronicle, Arthur is not a mythical monarch, but a waning noble ruler; his court is not a center of cultural and social enlightenment, but the locus of irreconcilable differ-ences; and chivalry is not an ideal, but a means of self-aggrandizement that exacerbates aggression.

The result is a meditation on the obsolescence of the chivalric ideal in the last decades of the twelfth century, when the nobility who sponsored the writing of romance was experiencing a decline in prestige and status. An indication that the *Conte* tends to reflect, more forcefully than any of Chrétien's previous works, the current political and social problems of contemporary nobility is provided in a prologue highlighting the author's intention to liberate himself from the inherited literary tradi-tion. Whereas allusions to an "authoritative" model in twelfth-century French literature serve, as David Fein notes, primarily to respond "to the audience's desire to participate in the illusion of the story's truth, aiding it to momentarily suspend disbelief,"[6] the reduced role of the "livre" in the *Conte*'s prologue situates the significance of Chrétien's last romance within the story itself. Rather than playfully grounding his narration on a literary model, or pre-text, Chrétien roots it in a subject matter—the Arthurian legend—that is here reinscribed in a manner undercutting the tradition of the genre. What emerges is a fatalistic revision of Arthurian history the effect of which is to demystify the legendary material by acknowledging that chivalric society is not only a fabrication, but also an idealizing representation of the nobility that patronized the writing of such narratives. In minimizing the role of the alleged "livre" on which the *Conte* is based, Chrétien amplifies his own creative role in elaborating a new, unadorned version of the Arthurian legend, one that distances itself from the escapist and utopian world of romance.

Although the world of the *Conte* is grounded on the imaginary, it reflects the problems besetting contemporary aristocracy through a pro-cess of defamiliarization that renders them "all the more conspicuous."[7]

The self-contained "truth" of fiction here lies in a prosaic depiction of chivalry as a collectivity incapable of coming to terms with its own self-destructive impulses, hence the vulnerability of that society in a period of its history that witnessed the degradation and obsolescence of its protocols. Although Chrétien's unfinished *Conte* will retain its enigmatic character, the unflattering assessment of chivalry developed in the poet's last romance suggests that its significance is embedded in that moment when the balance of power between monarchy and aristocracy was shifting in favor of the king, as it did decisively at the battle of Bouvines.[8] Instead of deproblematizing, as does traditional romance, the issues confronting a feudal community both marred by internecine rivalry and threatened by competing forms of power, the *Conte* underscores the instability marking that community as it clings to values and customs that paradoxically contribute to its marginalized social status. The presentation of Arthurian society in Chrétien's last romance in this sense emblematizes the predicament of the feudal order in witnessing the gradual erosion of its traditional prerogatives as effected by an emerging system of royal centralization.

The *Conte*'s demystifying assessment of the codes and mores of Arthurian society is all the more noteworthy when one considers the effect of chivalric ideology in contributing to the ethical reinscription of romance during the thirteenth century. Chrétien's last work owes its singularity to the fact that it destabilizes the ideal realm of traditional romance without adopting the transcendent vision of chivalry that subsequently becomes the trademark of the genre. This reinscription of chivalry as a fictitious and fraudulent ideal stands in striking contrast to the mystique of the perfect knight developed both before and after Chrétien.

At the origin of this mystique, as Jean Flori has shown, was the ecclesiastical notion of a just war assigning to the king, the leader of the "bellatores," the mission of ensuring the protection of the weak and the poor.[9] By the second third of the twelfth century, the nobility had begun to appropriate the mystique of the *ordo militaris* as a means of demonstrating the ethical basis of its social function.[10] This appropriation by princes and lords of a mission heretofore entrusted to kings alone formed part of the strife between aristocracy and monarchy, helping the nobility protect its autonomy and privileges against royal ambitions. What was initially a moral ideal thus turned into an ideology of sociopolitical significance, leading to the valorization of chivalry by poets and panegyrists as an order promoting prowess in feats of arms, cultural refinement, and courteous manners.[11] Not only did the mystique of chivalry in courtly literature seek to demonstrate the nobility's interest in the realm of ideas, thus elevating the *ordo militaris* to a status comparable to that long enjoyed by the clergy. It also demonstrated its dedication to a selfless and legitimate use of arms, as opposed to the interested and violent character of military force at the hands of mercenary soldiers (from the Latin *merces*, "salary") willing to sell their service to the highest bidder. It is not accidental, as Flori remarks, that the ideal of the noble, courteous, and generous knight developed in those areas (England and Normandy) that first resorted, and with increasing frequency, to the practice of hired military companies.[12] Neither is it accidental that this ideal flourished in writings sponsored by noble courts (including that of the Plantagenets, of the county of Champagne, and of that of Flanders), which found themselves increasingly challenged by the combined threat posed by royal centralization and the rising power of money.

Behind the glorification in twelfth- and thirteenth-century romances of such chivalric attributes as honor, loyalty, and generosity lies, therefore, the reality of an impoverished and enfeebled aristocracy, leading to the emergence of an increasing number of poor knights—the "poor young knights of today" mentioned by one of the ladies at Tintagueil ("povres bachelers anqui"; l. 5065)—who went in search of opportunities to improve their social status. The mystique of the chivalrous knight as a defender of country, Church, widow, and orphan in courtly narratives also contradicts the often sordid reality of knighthood, which, in Tony Hunt's view, was nothing more than "self-interested adventurism" encouraging rapine, cruelty, and free-booting.[13] In the context of the nobility's declining prestige and wealth by the end of the twelfth century, tourneying, for example, represented an important means of survival and probably the only opportunity for poor knights to acquire wealth as rapidly as merchants: the goal of participation in tournaments was thus "to win" in terms of both glory and money.[14] This is one of the reasons the heroes of romance are often engaged in seemingly "amorous" or "moral" quests in the course of which they gain status, worth, and renown, as does Yvain by winning Laudine, the lady of a rich and hence highly desirable domain.[15] Despite the mystique of courtly love and the glorification of the knight's internal value, traditional chivalric romance is grounded in a transaction ("my love for your kingdom") that tends to favor the receiver at the expense of the giver. Yet the Arthurian literary tradition also tends to hide the self-promoting character of the chivalric quest through an idealizing assessment of its effect in ensuring the peacemaking value of Arthur's reign. In traditional chivalric romance, service to the king is thus supposed to promote a disinterested use of prowess, one in which the king directs his knights' martial talent in support of harmonious legal and social transactions.

Arthur's Order of Chivalry

This tradition is the target of Chrétien's entire opus, leading to the *Conte*'s patent demystification of the chivalric ideal as a mendacious glorification of what is, in reality, an order essentially occupied in warlike activities. Throughout Chrétien's Arthurian chronicle, part of the king's strategy consists of hiding his self-interested use of knightly force under the veil of a discourse that asserts that his order of chivalry promotes between the king and his knights an exchange in which both parties give and receive equally. As illustrated in the concluding episode of *Erec et Enide*, for example, induction into Arthur's chivalric order guarantees that service to the king will bring honor and wealth to the newly dubbed knight.[16] In the *Conte du Graal*, Gauvain's reference (l. 7129) to the *loial* (or *leal*) character of the Arthurian system of exchange between ruler and ruled similarly contributes to the glorification of royal chivalry as an order devoted to disinterested and altruistic activities. Yet a close analysis of Arthurian chivalry unmasks the presence of an opposite function, revealing that the service expected of the knights of the Round Table is in reality not free, either in the time of Arthurian history invoked in *Erec* or in that of the *Conte*.

Perceval's first encounter with Arthur in Chrétien's last romance confirms the martial rather than moral character of Arthurian chivalric service. To Perceval's request to be made a knight, Arthur responds: "Chevaliers serez jusqu'a peu / A m'onor et a vostre preu" (You will soon become a knight, to my honor and your profit; ed. Roach, ll. 983–84). Behind the king's claim that Arthurian knighthood represents a fair and equitable exchange between the king, whom the knight promises to "honor," and the knight, who is assured of a reward ("preu"; l. 984), lies a unilateral investment of prowess. Derived from the Latin *prodis* (in the general sense of "price"), prowess as invoked in the Old French *preu* designates alternately a qualitative kind of merit (chivalric deeds) and a quantitative one (material advantages). In the context of Arthur's reply to Perceval, chivalric *preu* refers to the second type of merit, as is confirmed by Keu's sarcastic suggestion that Perceval go at once and take the Red Knight's arms, "car eles sont vos" (for they are yours to take; l. 1005). But Arthur is prompt to correct his seneschal's realistic assessment of chivalry:

> Et dist a Keu: "Grant tort avez
> Qui le vallet chi ramprosnez;
> A preudome est [che] trop grans visces.
> Por che, se li vallés est niches,
> S'est il, puet c'estre, gentix hom,
> Que il li vient d'aprision,
> Qu'il a esté a malvais mestre;
> Encore puet preus vassax estre."
>
> (Ed. Roach, ll. 1009–16) [17]

And he says to Keu: "You are gravely wrong in thus mocking this boy; this is a wicked vice in a noble man. For, although the boy is naive, he may well be of a noble lineage, and the cause of his behavior may well be poor teaching, suggesting that he was taught by a lowly master; but he may yet become a worthy vassal."

Arthur's idealizing revision of Keu's assessment posits a definition of the Arthurian knight as a worthy man (*preudome*), in reference to a notion of worth ("preus vassax") grounded in distinguished lineage and proper courtly training. Arthur thus seeks to exalt the honorific rather than tangible nature of the reward (*preu* as "price") awaiting any knight who promises to use his prowess for moral and altruistic purposes.

Perceval's killing of the Red Knight is consistent with this definition of a just and good use of military talent because his feat as *bellatoris* contributes to the eradication of the forces that threaten and endanger social order. However, the fact that Perceval earns the attributes of *gentix* (l. 1013) and *preus* (l. 1016) only after he proves his martial ability undercuts the ethical value of chivalry as exalted in Arthur's discourse. Perceval's abrupt transformation into an Arthurian knight shows that the king is not concerned with distributing aristocratic or courtly titles, but that he capitalizes on manifest physical prowess as a necessary and sufficient quality entitling an individual to be granted access to the king's order of chivalry. Arthur's belated recognition of Perceval's martial value also proves that Keu's comment is not a *grant tort* (l. 1009), as the king claims, but a correct assessment of the self-interested motives governing Arthur's praise of his chivalric order. Heretofore on his way to becoming a *rex inutilis*, Arthur now finds himself in a position not only to resume his role as a producer of chivalry, but also to turn back the course of history that anticipated the ineluctable collapse of his reign.

The significance of Perceval's initiation as a sensational turn of events from the standpoint of Arthurian history seems, however, not to cohere with the affirmation, made by one of the five knights who earlier in the text come across the vale of Perceval's childhood, that he (and possibly his four companions) owes his chivalric equipment to "Li rois Artus qui m'adouba" (l. 290). The question here is the value of the knight's use of the grammatical past in asserting that Arthur "m'adouba." Does he allude to a recent past, as may be inferred from a manuscript tradition wherein the event of his dubbing occurred five *days* ago, or to a more remote past (five *years* ago), according to another manuscript tradition?[18] The first alternative, which would indicate that Arthur never lost his capacity to "make knights" (that is, to attract new adherents to his chivalric order) is inconsistent with the *Conte*'s unadorned depiction of a crumbling Arthurian realm.[19] The second alternative reflects more convincingly the state of crisis resulting from the erosion of Arthur's sovereignty over the past five years.

Confirmation of the spectacular effect of Perceval's induction in Arthur's resumption of his knight-producing leadership is Gornemant de Gohort's reaction when he hears from Perceval the news that the king has just knighted him ("chevalier m'a fait"; l. 1369):

> "Chevalier! Se Dex bien me doint,
> Ne quidoie c'or en cest point
> De tel chose li sovenist;
> D'el quidoie qu'il li tenist
> Ore que de chevaliers faire.
> Or me di, frere debonaire,
> Ces armes, qui te les bailla?"
> "Li rois," fait il, "[le mes] dona."
> (Ed. Roach, ll. 1371–78)

"A knight? So help me God, I did not think that he had still this in mind in the present circumstances; I thought that he was too preoccupied with different concerns than making knights. Now tell me, my good brother, who provided you with this armor?" "The king," the boy replies, "gave it to me."

Chrétien's public knows, of course, that Perceval obtained his armor by force and not through Arthur's generosity. For his part, Gornemant guesses from seeing the *niche* and *sot* (l. 1365) that the latter has no experience with shield, horse, and lance; indeed, Perceval unseated and killed the Red Knight by resorting to his javelin. But raw force and rustic equipment do not ensure that Perceval will prevail in the future over more seasoned and skilled opponents. This is why, earlier in the narration, Arthur laments the premature departure of his new champion, who left before receiving adequate instruction in the use of weaponry to ensure his maturation into a fine knight ("Bons chevaliers"; l. 1288):

> Or siet armez sor son cheval,
> S'enconterra alcun vassal
> Qui por son cheval gaaignier
> Nel redoutera mehaignier.
> Tost mort ou mehaignié l'ara,
> Que desfendre ne se sara;
> Tant est niches et bestïax,
> Tost ara fait ses envïax.
> (Ed. Roach, ll. 1293–300)

Now that he is sitting, fully armed, on his horse, he will encounter some vassal who will not hesitate to maim him in order to win his horse. He will find himself dead or wounded before long, for he will not know how to defend himself; he is so simpleminded and uncouth that he will soon meet his master.

As Gornemant is given to realize, however, the *niche*'s innate martial talent belies Arthur's fears. Responding to Gornemant's request that he test himself in a practice combat, Perceval proves to the nobleman his ability to carry the lance and the shield

> Com s'il eüst toz jors veschu
> En tornoiements et en guerres
> Et alé par toutes les terres
> Querant bataille et aventure;
> Car il li venoit de nature.
> (Ed. Roach, ll. 1476–80)

as easily as if he had spent his entire life in tournaments and wars, and ridden through every land in search of battle and adventure; for it came naturally to him.

Perceval's dubbing by Gornemant is thus merely a ratification after the fact of his physical valor. Beneath the appearance of a ritual revealing to the neophyte the symbolic significance of Arthurian chivalry, the goal of the ceremony is to induce Perceval to use his prowess to reinforce the king's authority. Although supposedly a service that includes such tasks as the defense of the weak and the maintenance of order, bearing arms in Arthur's name in reality condones recourse to violence, provided that violence proves favorable to the king.

Under the pretext of turning his pupil's natural military talents to a defensive rather than aggressive use, Perceval's master thus proceeds

> D'armes ensaignier et aprendre
> Que il se sache bien desfendre
> A l'espee, s'on le requiert,
> Et envaïr quant lius en iert;
> Puis a main a l'espee mise.
> "Amis," fait il, "en itel guise
> Vos desfendez, s'on vos assaut."
> (Ed. Roach, ll. 1523–29)

to teach and instruct the boy in the art of arms so that he could defend himself with the sword, if he were challenged, and go on the offensive when need arose. Then he took hold of the sword: "Friend," he said, "this is the way to defend yourself, if anyone attacks you."

Having deserved to become an Arthurian knight because of his victory over the Red Knight, Perceval is now told that he will maintain his new identity on condition that he perform similar deeds on behalf of the king. In this perspective, any other use of prowess (including, for example, service to the Grail king) is bound to bring about Perceval's loss of his newly acquired status. That Gornemant's instruction runs counter to the teaching that Perceval is about to receive from the spokesmen of the Grail is nowhere better evinced than in the parting words with which the master closes the ceremony of dubbing:

> "Or ne dites jamais, biax frere,"
> Fait li preudom, "que vostre mere
> Vos ait apris rien."
>
> . . .
>
> "Coment dirai dont, biax dols sire?"
> "Li vavasors, ce porrez dire,
> Qui vostre esperon vos caucha,
> Le vos aprist et ensaigna."
> (Ed. Roach, ll. 1675–77, 1685–88)

"Never say, dear brother," the nobleman says, "that your mother taught you this or that." . . . "Then what shall I say, fair sir?" "You can say that the vavasor who attached your spur taught and instructed you."

Perceval's maintenance of his Arthurian identity requires that he sever his ties with his mother. From the nobleman's standpoint, these ties do not refer to the affective bonds between son and mother,[20] but to the lineal connections that both entertain with the Grail faction.

Gornemant masks the political significance of Arthur's order of chivalry by impressing upon Perceval the fact that he now belongs to a prestigious caste:

> Et li preudom l'espee a prise,
> Si li çainst et si le baisa,
> Et dist que donee li a
> Le plus haute ordene avec l'espee
> Que Diex ait faite et comandee:
> C'est l'ordre de chevalerie,
> Qui doit estre sanz vilonnie.
>
> (Ed. Roach, ll. 1632–38)

And the nobleman took the sword and girded it on the boy and kissed him and said that with the sword he had given him the highest order that God had created and ordained: that is, the order of chivalry, which must be maintained without wickedness.

Because Gornemant is a knight, and not a cleric or a priest, the ceremony has a political rather than religious significance.[21] Perceval's chivalric deeds after his induction[22] serve as a warning to all those who endeavor to transgress the king's law by using their martial power without his consent. Under Arthur's rule, to bear arms is not a right, but a privilege granted by the king[23] to knights who promise to defend the weak— beginning with Arthur himself—against their aggressors. Hiding the self-centered character of the Arthurian chivalric ideal, the royal discourse as articulated by the king's representatives stresses its moral and social value, insisting, for example, on the merit of clemency in combat. Thus Gornemant tells Perceval that a knight worthy of belonging to Arthur's order of chivalry must show mercy toward those he defeats.[24] As demonstrated by the large number of hostages Perceval eventually sends to the king's court, "mercy" is both integral to Arthur's strategy to turn his rivals into allies and the most effective means of subduing Arthur's opponents.[25] It is noteworthy in this sense that Perceval's victory over the Red Knight earns for him induction into Arthurian chivalry, despite—indeed, because of— the fact that he has killed the most recent challenger to the king's authority. Ostensibly presented as an ethical code of conduct, the Arthurian order of chivalry reveals itself to be a warlike function in the service of Arthur's rule.

~~~~~

This reading of Perceval's chivalric induction belies Arthur's claim that prowess brings profit to his knights. Neither Arthur nor Gornemant is apparently able or willing to participate actively in establishing peace and order, imposing instead this dangerous task on the members of the royal order of chivalry. This is revealed by Gornemant's indifference to the plight of his brother's daughter, Blancheflor. While she is besieged by Clamadeu and his faction, Gornemant wanders nonchalantly about his domain. When Perceval encounters him, the *preudom* (l. 1353) is strolling on a bridge, dressed in a fur coat and holding "Par contenance un bastonet" (a cane; l. 1357). If the wealthiest members of Arthurian society value elegance over action, it is all the more imperative that they find substitutes who will assume the task of defending their leisurely mode of life. Perceval's inability to see beyond words makes him a likely candidate to adopt at face value the king's idealizing discourse on chivalry: as the number of hostages he sends to Arthur demonstrates, his exploits as an Arthurian knight prove that he fulfills his part of the contract. But no exchange takes place, and Perceval's only reward is to be granted the "right" to fight and, if need be, die in support of Arthur's ambitions. Gornemant's emphasis on the duties of Arthurian knights regarding the defense of orphans and ladies[26] is another indication of the self-interested character of the Arthurian order of chivalry, given that Perceval as a fatherless adolescent should himself receive protection, instead of being induced to protect the interests of the king.

The Arthurian adventures incurred by Perceval in the section of the *Conte* devoted to his story are thus embedded in a rhetoric of sacrifice that threatens to consume the protagonist by imposing on him a course of action adverse to the blossoming of his personal history.[27] Far from initiating a realm of order and harmony, the expansion of Arthur's rule entails the victimization of those who live within its compass, chief among them Perceval, his new champion. Against this totalizing thrust of Arthurian law, the world according to the Grail purports to introduce a radically different understanding of order, one grounded in divine justice. Yet the mystique of the Grail as exalted by the spokesmen of Arthur's principal contending party does not have a divine significance;

nor is it disinterested. Rather, the Grail discourse betokens the desire of the rival faction to effect Arthur's demise and ensure its own political hegemony.

Perceval's Grail "Educators": A Discourse of Accusation

The series of episodes narrating Perceval's gradual discovery of the Grail ideal is generally understood in the light of the obvious failure of Arthurian chivalry to eradicate aggression. According to Donald Maddox, for example, this ideal leads Perceval to realize that "the essence of his quest is not primarily a tangible object or a spatial place, but above all a cognitive discovery." [28] This is fully revealed to him during the episode of the hermitage, where he finally recognizes that the ritual in the Grail castle (that is, the procession of the *graal* as bearing the Host) involves "service to a static transcendence," as opposed to the type of service that, under the king's rule, compels the knight to act in support of Arthur's ambitions. [29]

Although consistent with the hermit's eucharistic perspective on the ritual in the Grail castle, however, this interpretation does not explain the centrality of lineage in the sermon that the hermit delivers to his nephew. Nor does it elucidate the role that Perceval was destined to play at the Grail castle upon his eventual return to the site. The clue to the significance of Perceval's story lies in the antithetical contrast between the non-Grail (that is, Arthurian) episodes and the Grail (or anti-Arthurian) episodes in the section of the *Conte du Graal* devoted to Perceval's adventures. Emerging from this contrast are two conflicting judgments regarding Chrétien's *niche*, inviting listeners and readers of the romance to determine which one of these intratextual assessments represents that of the author or, more important, whether either one reflects Chrétien's intention in narrating the story of the *niche*'s entry into chivalric culture.

Considering the general tendency, generated by the hermitage episode, to view Perceval's behavior at the Grail castle in terms of a selfish indifference toward the plight of his hosts (a view leading to the hypothesis that his quest for the Grail was to have a regenerative or redemptive function), it is noteworthy that the protagonist does not inspire exclusively negative comments on the part of the various individuals he encounters. At the intratextual level, therefore, Perceval appears to have a certain number of supporters (particularly Arthur once the king becomes aware of the *niche*'s innate martial talent). Also re-markable is the fact that no member of Arthurian society ever mentions the Grail incident and, consequently, that none ever views Perceval as a sinner. Gornemant is the only one who alludes to the ethics of chivalry or, more precisely, to the Arthurian protocols of chivalric behavior when he advises Perceval to refrain from excessive loquacity:

> Ne ne parlez trop volentiers:
> Nus ne puet estre trop parliers
> Qui sovent tel chose ne die
> Qui torné li est affolie,
> Car li sages dit et retrait:
> "Qui trop parole, il se mesfait."
> Por che, biax amis, vos chastoi
> De trop parler.
> (Ed. Roach, ll. 1649–56)

And be careful not to talk too much: anyone who is too talkative is bound often to say things that make him look a fool, for, as the wise man says and asserts, "He sins who speaks too much." Thus, dear friend, I warn you against talking too much.

Perceval's relentless questioning concerning chivalric equipment in the opening scene of his story, which motivated the five Arthurian knights to dismiss him as a half-witted Welsh ruffian ("Galois . . . sont plus fol que beste en pasture"; ll. 243–44), proves Gornemant right in advo-cating moderation. Yet Gornemant's warning against *excessive loquacity* [30] also articulates a view of proper conduct diametrically opposed to that enunciated by those individuals, particularly the hermit, who urge Perceval to repent for the sin of *excessive silence* he committed during his stay at the Grail castle. Is Perceval, then, a hero, as suggested by Arthur and his men once the *niche* demonstrates his prowess? Or is he a culprit, as the perspective of three of his educators implies?

Perceval's Cousin: Sin of Matricide

Perceval's silence at the Grail castle, which provokes three of the characters he encounters in the course of his adventures to reveal to him the nature of his sin, is most often cited in support of the peniten-tial significance of Perceval's story. The first in this series of mentors is Perceval's cousin, with whom he meets immediately after his departure from the now deserted Grail castle (ll. 3422–33). When Perceval comes upon his as yet unidentified cousin, she is holding a knight "Qui avoit trenchie la teste" (whose head had been cut off; l. 3455) and whose death she grieves:

> "Lasse!" fait el, "maleürouse!
> Con de pute heure je fui nee!
> L'eure que je fui engendree
> Soit maldite et que je nasqui,
> Qu'ainc mais voir tant ne m'irasqui
> De rien qui poïst avenir.
> Je ne deüsse pas tenir
> Mon ami mort, se Dieu pleüst,
> Qu'assez miex esploitié eüst,
> S'il fust vis et je fuisse morte.
> La mors qui si me desconforte,
> Por coi prist s'ame ainz que la moie?
> Quant la rien que je plus amoie
> Voi morte, vie que me vaut?
> Aprés lui certes ne me chaut
> De ma vie ne de mon cors.
> Mors, cor en giete l'ame fors!"
>   (Ed. Roach, ll. 3434–50)

"Alas!" she says, "How unfortunate I am! How evil the hour I was born! Cursed be the hour I was begotten and born, for nothing ever afflicted me as much as what has now happened to me. May God help me, I should not be thus holding my dead lover, and it would be far better for him to be alive and for me to be dead. Why did death, who causes me thus to suffer, take his soul rather than mine? When I see dead the one I most loved, what is life to me? With him gone, I have no care for my life or body. Death, come and take my soul out of my body!"

Human violence has caused her present loss, yet she reacts here by incriminating death as the cause of her present misery. Untrained in the art of rhetoric, Perceval does not listen to his cousin's invocation of death, but focuses his attention on the dead man whom he sees her holding. Their ensuing dialogue rouses his cousin to a more realistic perception of her predicament:

> "Damoisele, qui a ocis
> Cel chevalier qui sor vos gist?"
> "Biax sire, uns chevalier l'ocist,"
> Fait la pucele, "hui cest matin.
> Mais molt me merveil de grant fin
> D'une chose que je esgart,

Que l'en porroit, se Diex me gart,
Chevalchier, ce tesmoigne l'en,
Quarante liues en cest sen
Tot droit, einsi com vos venez,
C'uns hosteus n'i seroit trovez
Qui fust bons ne leaus ne sains,
Et vostre chevax a toz plains
Les flans, le poil aplanoié.

. . .

De vos meïsme m'est avis
Que vos aiez anuit estez
Bien aesiez et repossez."
(Ed. Roach, ll. 3462–75, 3480–82)

"My lady, who killed this knight who is lying in your lap?" "Good sir," the maiden replies, "a knight killed him, this very morning. But there is something about you that quite amazes me: God help me, one could ride, so they say, 40 leagues in the direction whence you come without finding a good, honest, and proper lodging, yet your horse's belly is quite full, and his coat, quite smooth. . . . And it appears to me that you yourself have had a comfortable and restful night."

Although Perceval's cousin now identifies her lover's killer in human rather than fatalistic terms, she does not elaborate on this event, opting instead to question Perceval on his whereabouts. The reason for her inquiry soon is explained. As she induces Perceval to describe the lodging where he was welcomed, his hosts, and finally the mysterious procession he observed at their domain, her questioning becomes increasingly intense:

"Or me dites se vos veïstes
La lance dont la pointe saine,
Et si n'i a ne char ne vaine."
"Se je le vi? Oïl, ma foi."
"Et demandastes vos por coi
Ele sainoit?" "Ne parlai onques,
Si m'aït Diex." "Or sachiez donques
Que molt avez esploitié mal."
(Ed. Roach, ll. 3548–55)

"Tell me now whether you saw the lance whose tip bleeds, although it has neither flesh nor veins." "Did I see it? Yes, in faith!" "And did you ask why it bled?" "I did not utter a single word, so help me God." "Then know now that you have done great ill."

Although Perceval acknowledges that he did not pose one single question during his stay at the castle ("ne parlai *onques*"; l. 3553), he still remembers quite vividly his eagerness to ask why the lance bled (ll. 3204–12) and whom the *graal* served (ll. 3244–45 and ll. 3292–94).[31] That he refrained from satisfying his curiosity is, in his view then as now, an index of his success in containing his impulses, for he had recalled the admonishment of his mentor, Gornemant,

> Qui li ensaigna et aprist
> Que de trop parler se gardast.
> Et crient, se il le demandast,
> Qu'en le tenist a vilonie.
> (Ed. Roach, ll. 3208–11)

who taught and instructed him to guard himself against talking too much. Hence he [had] feared that his inquiring would make him look uncouth.

In Perceval's view, his behavior at the Grail castle was consistent with Gornemant's advice. He acted as a mature individual and remained silent, "Si m'aït Diex" (with the help of God; l. 3554).

Interestingly, both Hilka and Pickens assign the formula of line 3554 in Roach's edition—"Si m'aït Diex"—not to Perceval, but to his cousin's reply. It may be that she calls upon God, even in an idiomatic formulation, as a means of amplifying the gravity of Perceval's wrong ("mal," l. 3555). Roach's interpretation underscores more significantly the contrast between Perceval's and his cousin's assessment of his behavior at the castle. Certain that he behaved in compliance with the code of proper chivalric conduct, Perceval does not notice his cousin's growing discontent. The accelerated tempo of her interrogation ("Who was holding the grail?" "Where did she come from?" "Where did she go?" "Who came after the grail?" "What was she holding?") nonetheless recasts her questioning into the form of a trial. Her inquiry also provides Chrétien's audience with a number of important clues: it seems that she knows everything there is to know about the Grail, that Perceval knows nothing and has only a literal understanding of the event, that she knows that he does not know anything about his lineal ties with the Grail kings, and that she intends to disclose these ties and to set her revelation in an accusatory context.

Her "revelation" is notably incomplete. Although she informs Perceval that they are cousins, she does not disclose the fact that a familial relationship also links his mother to the two royal characters living at the Grail castle.[32] She thus gives priority to Perceval's responsibilities toward his mother, stating that he failed to ask the question that would have healed the king "Por le pechié, ce saches tu, / De ta mere," who died "del doel de toi" ("because of the sin" he committed against his mother, who died "of grief on [his] account"; ll. 3593–95). Perceval's negligence in abandoning his mother and his indifference toward the plight of the Grail king here coalesce in a manner designed to convince the boy of the urgency for him to make amends for his filial indifference. Because his mother is dead, taking action in the present will allow Perceval to redress the wrong he committed in the past, as suggested by the causal link his cousin posits between the death of his mother, the plight of the Grail king, and the loss of her own lover:

> Ne ne me poise mie mains
> De che que si t'est mescheü
> Que tu n'as del graal seü
> Qu'en en faisoit, n'u on le porte,
> Que de ta mere qui est morte,
> Et qu'il fait de cest chevalier
> Que j'amoie et tenoie chier
> Molt por che que il me clamoit
> S'amie chiere, et qu'il m'amoit
> Come frans chevaliers loiaus.
>
> (Ed. Roach, ll. 3602–11)

I grieve no less because of your misfortune in failing to learn what was done with the grail and where it was taken than for your mother who has died or for the death of this knight whom I loved and held dear because he called me his dear friend and loved me like a noble, loyal knight.

A "noble" and "loyal" knight would not have failed at the Grail castle because he would not have caused the death of a loved one. In his cousin's reasoning, Perceval must redeem his indifference to his mother by acting as her protector because she is virtually his sister:

> Ensamble od toi norrie fui
> Chiez ta mere molt lonc termine:
> Je suis ta germaine cousine.
>
> (Ed. Roach, ll. 3598–600)

I was brought up with you at your mother's house for a very long time: for I am a first cousin of yours.

Curiously, however, Perceval neither recognizes his cousin nor remembers a common past, a "lapse of memory" that calls into question the truthfulness of his cousin's claim that they were raised together.

Just as her evocation of a common past seems to be contradicted by Perceval's reaction, so is her charge of matricide not entirely consistent with the narration of his departure from the vale near Valbone. The concluding scene of this episode relates how, riding his hunting horse away from the vale of his childhood, Perceval looks back and sees his mother lying "pasmee en tel maniere / *Come s'ele fust cheüe morte*" (in a faint *as though* she had fallen dead; ll. 624–25). The interpretation of Perceval as a *niche*, an unformed and uninformed boy, does not establish his mother's death with this observation, but it reflects the realistic character of his perception of the scene.[33] He assumes that her fainting is the predictable response of a mother forced to witness the departure of her last surviving son. Although Perceval could be accused of insensitivity toward his mother's feelings, the narration of this episode does not indicate that his mother died at the moment of his departure. Yet his cousin's dramatic rendition of the incident deludes Perceval into believing he is a matricide and must repay his filial indifference through service to others, as he could and should have at the Grail castle:

> Que tant eüsses amendé
> Le buen roi qui est mehaigniez
> Que toz eüst regaaigniez
> Ses membres et terre tenist,
> Et si grans biens t'en avenist!
> Ma[i]s or saches que maint anui
> En avenront toi et autrui.
> (Ed. Roach, ll. 3586–92)

For you would have healed the good king who is crippled, such that he would have regained use of his limbs and ruled his land, and much good would have happened to you! But know now that many ills will befall both you and others.

Her use of the past conditional in alluding to the misfortune of the Grail suggests that it is too late for Perceval to make amends for his insensitivity to the plight of the king, thus too late for him to effect the latter's healing and resumption of his kingship.

Dismissing his sojourn at the castle as a failed adventure, his cousin also suggests that future good is still within his grasp: if he follows her advice and redresses the wrong done her, ills *will not* befall him. In the context of his cousin's necrologic retrospection, this "future" clearly refers to Perceval's immediate participation in the revenge of her lover's death, as Perceval ultimately acknowledges:

De vos grant folie me samble,
Qu'isi seule gaitiez cest mort;
Mais sivons celui qui l'a mort,
Et je vos pramet et creant:
Ou il me fera recreant
Ou je lui, se jel puis ataindre.
                    (Ed. Roach, ll. 3632–37)

It seems foolish to me for you to watch alone over this body; instead, let us both pursue his killer, and I promise and swear to you that either he will make me yield or I him, if I can find him.

Perceval's resolve to find his mother, which had inspired him to leave Blancheflor despite her pleas and his love for her, is here cut short, and his promise to return to Blancheflor is momentarily forgotten. His cousin has thus succeeded in diverting Perceval from his personal journey and in persuading him that the sole duty of the living is the cult of the dead, specifically, the prosecution of her lover's killer. Matricide is therefore a key argument in his cousin's attempt to co-opt Perceval. Her strategy consists of convincing him of his guilt for his mother's death in order to force upon him the role of avenger. Her definition of Perceval's "penitential" quest bespeaks a personal vendetta. With the appearance of the Hideous Damsel, however, the duty of avenging the dead takes on a more collective significance, which directly focuses on the restoration of the Grail faction.

The Hideous Damsel: Perceval as the Perpetrator of Universal Doom

Perceval's cousin is successful, to a degree, in persuading him to assume the role of gallant protector that she prescribes. In the episode immediately following their encounter, he sides with a distressed damsel against the tyrannical Orgueilleux de la Lande (ll. 3691–932), a violent knight who, within this sequence of events, appears to be the killer of his cousin's lover. By defeating Orgueilleux, Perceval honors both his cousin's request and the memory of her dead lover while demonstrating his progress toward "altruistic" chivalry. Yet his cousin's message does not have a lasting influence on Perceval. After his victory over Orgueilleux, he no longer mentions her and is instead occupied with amorous rather than martial thoughts, as indicated in his renewed longing for Blancheflor (ll. 4164–210).

Perceval's new relative autonomy, however, is jeopardized by the appearance of the Hideous Damsel in the midst of the festivities that cele-

brate Perceval's arrival at Arthur's court (ll. 4603–13). As the Hideous
Damsel approaches the court,

> Le roi et ses barons salue
> Tos ensamble comunement,
> Fors que Percheval solement.
> (Ed. Roach, ll. 4642–44)

She greets the king and his barons all together, with the sole exception of
Perceval.

Her attitude indicates that she does not share the court's high esteem for
Perceval, as the contemptuous tone of the first words she addresses to
him confirms:

> Ha! Perchevax, Fortune [est] cauve
> Detriers et devant chavelue.
> Et dehais ait qui te salue
> Ne qui nul bien t'ore ne prie,
> Que tu ne la recheüs mie
> Fortune quant tu l'encontras.
> (Ed. Roach, ll. 4646–51)

Ah, Perceval! Fortune is bald behind and hairy in front. A curse on anyone who
greets you or wishes you well, for you did not catch Fortune when you met her.

The Hideous Damsel invokes Fortune to symbolize that Perceval is
not the champion he appears to be. If Perceval is unworthy of praise,
then he should not be the object of the court's joyful welcome (another
allusion to Arthur's "joie de la cort" as generated by manifest martial
value), hence her curse on the entire company. Implicit in the Hideous
Damsel's blame of Perceval is a derogatory assessment of Arthurian
chivalry. Her statement that Perceval failed to grasp Fortune impugns
not his prowess, but his role as reinforcement of the wrong party.

The factional grounds of her accusation become clear when she cites
Perceval's behavior at the Grail castle as both the reason for and the
prime exhibit of his unworthiness as a knight:

> Chiez le Roi Pescheor entras,
> Si veïs la lance qui saine,
> Et si te fu si tres grant paine
> D'ovrir ta bouche et de parler
> Que tu ne poïs demander
> Por coi cele goute de sanc
> Saut par la pointe del fer blanc;

> Ne del graal que tu veïs
> Ne demandas ne n'enqueïs
> Quel preudome l'en en servoit.
>   (Ed. Roach, ll. 4652–61)

You entered the castle of the Fisher King and saw the lance that bleeds, but it was so much effort for you to open your mouth and speak that you did not ask why that drop of blood springs from the tip of the white head; nor did you ask and inquire what worthy man was served from the grail that you saw.

Unlike Perceval's cousin, the Hideous Damsel does not accuse him of matricide, but of sinful indifference, which she interprets as a conscious decision not to engage in altruistic activities. The significance of her initial allusion to the rhetorical figure of Fortune is now fully revealed: Perceval's failure to take hold of Fortune refers specifically and exclusively to his unwillingness to rescue the Grail king, whom the Hideous Damsel thus identifies as Perceval's victim. Yet, significantly, she does not mention the lineal ties that link Perceval with his ill-treated host, thereby giving his sin an allegedly universal rather than factional significance:

> Che iez tu, li maleüreus,[34]
> Qui veïs qu'i[l] fu tans et leus
> De parler et si te teüs;
> Assez grant loisir en eüs.
> A mal eür tu [te] teüsses,
> Que se tu demandé l'eüsses,
> Li riches rois, qui or s'esmaie,
> Fust ja toz garis de sa plaie
> Et si tenist sa terre en pais,
> Dont il ne tendra point jamais.
>   (Ed. Roach, ll. 4665–74)

You deserve, indeed, to be called the wretched one, you who saw that it was the time and place to speak, yet stayed silent; you had nonetheless ample opportunity to speak. Cursed be the hour you kept silent, for if you had asked, the rich king who is greatly suffering would have by now been healed of his wound and would be holding his land in peace, which he will never do.

Her use of grammatical tenses amplifies the collective character of the doom precipitated by Perceval's crime. She combines past conditional ("Fust ja toz garis de sa plaie"; l. 4672) and future ("il ne tendra point jamais [sa terre]"; l. 4674) in a manner that associates Perceval's destiny with that of the Grail. Because Perceval failed to grasp the "opportunity" offered him in the past, he must now devote his life to a redemptive mission. The Hideous Damsel confronts him with two diametrically opposed options: either he will remain a pariah, in reference to his responsibilities in precipitating doom, or he will become a messiah, saving himself and "the world" in an eschatological apotheosis.

Yet the Hideous Damsel never specifies how Perceval is to undertake his redemptive mission or indicates how asking a question could have cured the Maimed King of the Grail, what profit Perceval would have gained from the king's recovery, and how he will change the course of Fortune. She does not address these issues because her principal concern is to extract Perceval from the service of the king and to induce him to side with the Grail faction.[35]

The Hideous Damsel concludes her address to Perceval with the following prophecy:

> Et ses tu qu'il en avendra
> Del roi qui terre ne tendra
> Ne n'iert de ses plaies garis?
> Dames en perdront lor maris,
> Terres en seront escillies
> Et puceles desconseillies,
> Qui orfenines remandront,
> Et maint chevalier en morront;
> Tot cist mal esteront par toi.
> (Ed. Roach, ll. 4675–83)

And do you know what will happen to that king who will not rule his land or be healed of his wounds? Ladies will lose their husbands, lands will be laid waste, maidens in distress will be left orphans, and many a knight will die; all these evils will occur because of you.

Her prediction, although a powerful argument in support of the charge she makes against Perceval, also openly contradicts the facts at hand. If there is an apparatus of cause and effect between the Maimed King's wound and the doom of the domain, then doom should have begun some fifteen years ago, soon after the event that provoked the king's injury. Lack of logic in the Hideous Damsel's discourse bespeaks manipulation, as eloquently revealed in the intended effect of her prophecy in attempting to ensure Perceval's commitment to the restoration of the Grail.

The Hermit: Perceval as the Emblem of Imperfect Chivalry

Persuaded by the Hideous Damsel that the Grail is the site where he will become a full-fledged knight, Perceval vows not to lodge in the same place "deus nuis en trestot son eage" (for two nights together as long as he lives; l. 4729) until he knows who is served from the grail vessel, finds the Bleeding Lance, and learns the certain truth about why it bleeds.

At this point in his romance, Chrétien leaves his first protagonist and focuses on Gauvain in a narration that comprises the Tintagueil and Escavalon episodes. Then, some 1,500 lines later, the author declares his intention not to speak further of Gauvain.

> De monseignor Gavain se taist
> Ichi li contes a estal,
> Si comenche de Percheval.
> Perchevax, ce nos dist l'estoire,
> Ot si perdue la miemoire
> Que de Dieu ne li sovient mais.
> (Ed. Roach, ll. 6214–19)

The narration here ceases to tell about my lord Gauvain and begins to speak of Perceval. Perceval, the story tells us, had lost his memory to such a degree that he no longer remembers God.

Marked by an initial at line 6217 of Roach's edition (an initial illuminated in gold in Guiot's copy), the return to Perceval indicates the author's intention to highlight a major narrative moment, as corroborated at the intratextual level by the repetition of Perceval's name in both ending the first section of Gauvain's story (l. 6216) and opening the final section of Perceval's (l. 6217). Why does Chrétien interrupt his recounting of Gauvain's adventures? Why does he situate a scene that in the present state of the text constitutes Perceval's last appearance between Gauvain's adventure at Escavalon and his peregrinations in Galloway up to the remote locus of La Roche Canguin?

A preliminary response to these questions exists in the way Chrétien stresses, intentionally, it appears, the hermitage episode's lack of temporal relationship with the whole of Gauvain's story. As Rupert Pickens observes, the author "overstates this temporal disjointment by repeating six times in about twenty lines" the fact that Perceval encounters his eremitic uncle "five years after leaving Arthur [ll. 6220–38], which, in the time of the Gauvain plot, is only a few days before."[36] Echoing the value of the Grail castle as "a locus marked by tranquility and ambient silence," the hermitage, according to Donald Maddox, is itself a symbolic retreat "from a flawed and decadent courtly world."[37] In both Maddox's and Pickens's views, this last episode of Perceval's story implicitly articulates a derogatory assessment of the protocols that govern the realm of Arthurian chivalry, against which the hermit recommends to Perceval a mode of conduct to restore "his mental and spiritual condition to what it was *before* [his] sin," that is, to recover "the essence of his *gallois* nature."[38] Interestingly, Chrétien never refers to Perceval as *chevalier* after the protagonist guesses that he is "Perchevax li Galois" (l. 3575), indicating that the author links the gradual maturation of his protagonist to his ability to transcend his identity as an Arthurian knight. Also noteworthy in the transitional passage cited previously is the contrast it establishes between *li contes* (l. 6215) and *l'estoire* (l. 6217), that is, between Chrétien's own poem ("Li *Contes* del Graal," l. 66) and its fictive source. In Rupert Pickens's analysis, "it is Chrétien's work of art that is structured with the intrusive Hermitage episode, not (necessarily) the source *estoire*."[39] The temporal incoherence of the episode thus draws attention to its significance in substituting the values of Christian ethics for the codes and mores of traditional chivalry. Evidence of the episode's function in offering Perceval the opportunity to redeem himself, according to Pickens, is the hermit's emphasis on Christian charity, which not only resonates with the prologue's repeated references to that particular virtue (ll. 42–59), but also contrasts suggestively with Gauvain's uncharitable behavior, narrated in the next scene when the protagonist "ignores the wounded Greoreas in his haste to meet the guardian of Galloway."[40]

Perceval's arrival at his uncle's cell seems to cohere with the interpretation of the hermitage episode in introducing Christian ethics. Stimulating his moral awareness, it enables the protagonist to understand the working of cause and effect that links his selfish attitude at the Grail castle to his neglect of God:

> Sire, chiez le Roi Pescheor
> Fui une fois et vi la lance
> Dont li fers saine sanz dotance,
> Et de cele goute de sanc
> Que a le pointe de fer blanc
> Vi pendre, rien n'en demandai.
> Onques puis, certes, n'amendai.

Et del graal que je i vi
Ne sai pas cui on en servi,
Si ai puis eü si grant doel
Que mors eüsse esté mon wel,
Que Damedieu en oblïai,
Ne puis merchi ne li crïai
Ne ne fis rien, que je seüsse,
Por coi jamais merchi eüsse.
(Ed. Roach, ll. 6372–86)

Sir, I was once at the house of the Fisher King, and I saw the lance whose blade undoubtedly bleeds, and I saw the drop of blood hanging from the tip of that white head, but I asked nothing about it. And truly, I have done nothing since then to make amends. Nor do I know who was served from the grail I saw there, and I have since suffered such grief that I would rather have died, for I forgot our Lord God because of it, and I did nothing, to my knowledge, that would deserve me His mercy.

Perceval's statement, which repeats, almost verbatim, the Hideous Damsel's accusation, inspires the hermit to reveal that

Pechie[z] la langue te trencha,
Quant le fer qui onc n'estancha
De sainier devant toi veïs,
Ne la raison n'en enqueïs.
Et quant del graal ne seüs
Cui l'en en sert, fol sens eüs.[41]
(Ed. Roach, ll. 6409–14)

It was sin that cut off your tongue when you saw with your own eyes the lance whose blade never stops bleeding, but failed to ask the reason. And madness seized you when you failed to learn who was served from the grail.

Curiously, however, Chrétien places in the hermit's mouth a new inter-pretation of the sequence of events that caused Perceval's sinful state. Why does the hermit link Perceval's alienation from God to his fail-ure at the Grail castle rather than to the time of his encounter with the Hideous Damsel, as suggested in Chrétien's remark that five years passed "Ains que il entrast en mostier / Ne Dieu ne sa crois n'aora" (without him entering a church to adore God and His cross; ll. 6222–23)? Could his five-year wandering have resulted not from his failure to find the Grail, but from his active participation in a different cause?

Perceval's neglect of God during the past five years did not prevent him from

> requerre chevalerie;
> Et les estranges aventures,
> Les felenesses et les plus dures,
> Aloit querant, et s'en trova
> Tant que molt bien s'i esprova.
> Soissante chevaliers de pris
> A la cort le roi Artu pris
> Dedens cinc ans i envoia.
>   (Ed. Roach, ll. 6226–33)

seeking deeds of chivalry; and he went in search of the most unusual, challenging, and difficult adventures and found enough of them to prove his valor. Within five years, he sent 60 worthy knights as prisoners to King Arthur's court.

Just as Perceval has performed one of the tasks expected of an Arthurian knight by defeating a large number of challengers, he has also obeyed Gornemant's injunction never to kill a defeated opponent. Yet the hermit instructs Perceval in a manner that suggests his chivalric failure:

> Se che te vient a volenté,
> Encor porras monter en pris,
> S'avras honor et paradis.
> Dieu aime, Dieu croi, Dieu aeure,
> *Preudome* et preudefeme honeure.
>
>   . . .
>
> Se puecele aïde te quiert,
> Aiue li, que miex t'en iert,
> Ou veve dame ou orfenine.
>   (Ed. Roach, ll. 6456–60, 6465–67; my emphasis)

If you place your heart to it, you will improve yourself and win honor and paradise. Love God, believe in God, worship God, honor *worthy men* and women. . . . If a maiden or a widow or an orphan requests your help, help her; you will be the better for it.

Devotion to God, respect for worthy men and women (*preudome* and *preudefeme*, l. 6460), and protection of the weak are, according to the hermit, the three principal aspects of proper chivalric behavior. As I analyze in Chapter 4, Perceval's defensive action at Biaurepaire, in addition to his deferential attitude toward the hermit (qualified as a *preudom*, for example, at l. 6368), testify that, on two counts at least, his conduct is consistent with the hermit's views on proper chivalry. But Perceval has failed to assume what the hermit considers the most important of all three duties, apparently as a result of a course of action (service to Arthur) that has led him to neglect his service to God.

A comparison between the hermit's and Gornemant's teaching confirms the anti-Arthurian direction of the former's criticism of chivalry. While drawing a similarly tripartite list of chivalric duties, Perceval's two male instructors list the priority of these duties in a reverse order. Gornemant first mentions the code regulating relationships between knights (ll. 1640–56) before evoking, second, proper chivalric conduct regarding women (ll. 1656–61), then adherence to God's commands as regulated by institutionalized religion (ll. 1666–70). What counts most in his perspective are the Arthurian customs regarding the proper use of prowess, which prohibit the killing of a defeated opponent and prescribe courteous behavior between knights (ll. 1639–47). The hermit minimizes the importance of companionship ("preudome . . . honeure"; l. 6460), amplifying instead the knight's duty of submission to the Church's institutions (ll. 6440–59), which comes first in his list. The emphasis here is on gestures and external attitudes rather than on spiritual virtues: Perceval will atone for his sin by going to church "quant sonera la closche" (when the bells ring; l. 6448), by attending the service of the mass until the priest "Avra tot dit et tot chanté" (has said and sung it all; l. 6455), by rising in the presence of priests ("Contre les provoires te lieve"; l. 6461), and, presently, by staying two full days at the hermitage, taking "Tel viande com est la moie" (what is my habitual nourishment; l. 6479) and memorizing a prayer listing many of God's holiest names (ll. 6481–88).[42] In light of the tendency to value practice over meditation in contemporary didactic works composed for the edification of the laity,[43] the hermit's insistence on behavior as a means of attaining salvation is not in itself remarkable. His injunction that Perceval go to church "each morning" and attend mass echoes the Church's repeated warning against religious apathy.[44]

What is remarkable in the hermit's emphasis on behavior rather than intention is that his teaching is only a repetition of Gornemant's. Despite an inversion in their ordering of duties, both instructors provide their pupil with a view of chivalry that promises honor and glory to its adherent. In conferring on Perceval the sword of knighthood, Gornemant thus glorifies the value of his entry into "Le plus haute ordene," that is "l'ordre de chevalerie" (ll. 1635, 1637). The hermit mentions the social promotion ("monter en pris"; l. 6457) and "honor" (l. 6458) awaiting Perceval if he follows his advice. In the perspective of both educators, a proper use of prowess is, for example, the protection of widows and orphans because, in the hermit's words, "Iceste almosne est enterine" (this kind of service is most worthy; l. 6468).[45] Particularly noteworthy is the hermit's statement that, if Perceval assumes his protective mission, he will recover "totes tes graces / Issi com tu avoir les seus" (all the virtues that used to be yours; ll. 6472–73). According to Rupert Pickens, this recovery entails a return to the state of innocence he enjoyed in the Welsh vale, except that Perceval's innocence henceforth should have a childlike, rather than childish, quality.[46] In this light, the hermit's anticipatory praise suggests that Perceval will be honored to the extent that he forswears the Arthurian order of chivalry and devotes himself instead to the "virtuous" order of the Grail. An opportunity had presented itself at the Grail castle, but Perceval failed to seize it. Now is the time to redeem himself by undertaking the quest that will bring him back to the site, offering him full understanding of his knightly mission. As interpreted by the hermit, therefore, Perceval's future journey will lead to a reenactment of the Grail event.

Tracing the genesis of this event, the hermit contends that Perceval's mother died of grief at his departure (ll. 6392–98), hence his silence at the Grail (ll. 6399–401) and his sinful five-year wandering (l. 6402). Interestingly, unlike Perceval's cousin, the hermit does not charge him with matricide:

> Frere, molt t'a neü
> *Uns pechiez dont tu ne sez mot*:
> Ce fu li doels que ta mere ot
> De toi quant departis de li.
> (Ed. Roach, ll. 6392–95; my emphasis)

My brother, *a sin of which you know nothing* has caused you great harm: it is the grief your mother endured on your behalf when you left her.

In Jean-Charles Payen's view, the hermit's apparent disregard for intentional ethics reflects a still archaic understanding of sin.[47] Man is judged here not on the basis of his motivations, but his acts. Perceval's inaction at the Grail castle represents a failure to pursue the regeneration of a postlapsarian world, a ritual transgression the effect of which is universal rather than personal. That the hermit absolves Perceval because of his lack of awareness at the time of his departure from Valbone indicates that he wants to emphasize the seriousness of Perceval's failure at the Grail castle.

At the same time, the hermit's presentation of the Grail as the sole site that can effect Perceval's regeneration is not altogether justified, indicating the presence of ulterior motives that cast suspicion on the "universal" implications of his assessment of Perceval's failure. Before elaborating his definition of proper chivalry, the hermit reveals to Perceval that the Grail site is the root of both Perceval's familial tree and his own. By a stroke of highly charged "coincidence," the hermit is the brother of the Grail king and of Perceval's mother (ll. 6415–16). In this lineal context, the hermit's exaltation of good chivalry as a service to *preudome* and *veve dame* becomes an argument on behalf of factionalism. Because Perceval's mother is dead, his duty lies in the first type of service, inducing him to help, protect, and if need be die in defending the frail king of the Grail. "Making amends" or, from the hermit's perspective, "being converted" requires that Perceval return to the scene of his crime, that is, to the Grail domain, where he will accomplish his destiny as champion of his lineage.

The familial ties that link Perceval to the royal character inhabiting the Grail castle are paramount for the factional interpretation of the *Conte* that I am proposing. Curiously, however, the identification of the Grail king greatly varies throughout the narration, leading to an even greater confusion in Grail literature after Chrétien. What are the possible reasons for the confused and confusing identity that the Grail king acquires in the course of Perceval's story?

The King(s) of the Grail

Four episodes successively provide the reader with information on the royal character who lives in the castle. The first is the Grail episode proper (that is, the narration of Perceval's adventure), which begins with his arrival near a river, where he sees a boat with two men in it. The version of Ms. T in Roach's edition is as follows:

> Atant vit aval l'eve aler
> Une nef qui d'amont venoit;
> Deus homes en la nef avoit.
> Et il s'areste, si atent.
> (Ed. Roach, ll. 2998–3001)

Then he saw a boat coming down the water; there were two men in the boat. He stops and waits.

Ms. A in Pickens's edition proposes a similar rendition of the scene:

> Atant vit par l'eve avaler
> Une nef qui d'amont venoit,
> Deus homes an la nef avoit.
> Il s'areste, si les atant.
> (Ed. Pickens, ll. 2964–67)

Then he saw a boat coming down the river; there were two men in the boat. He stops and waits for them.

In Lecoy's edition of Ms. A, two more lines appear in between lines 2966 and 2967 of Pickens's edition:

> Et il vit par l'eve avalant
> une nef qui d'amont venoit;
> .ii. homes an la nef avoit.
> *Li un des .ii. homes najoit,*
> *li altre a l'esmeçon peschoit.*
> Il s'areste, si les atant.
> (Ed. Lecoy, ll. 2990–95; my emphasis)

And he saw a boat coming down the river; there were two men in the boat. *One of the two men was rowing; the other was fishing with a hook.* He stops and waits for them.

The two added lines here specify that one of the men is rowing and the other, fishing. Rupert Pickens, however, rejects this reading as an unnecessary addition. Yet the specification it provides is noteworthy, for it distinguishes between rower and fisher in a manner that anticipates the hermit's explanation of the Grail adventure.

Once the two men have anchored their boat in midstream, Perceval asks them first about possible means of crossing the river, only to be told there is no ford or ferry or bridge, and then about a possible lodging. In Ms. A, as in the entire manuscript tradition, the fisher responds to Perceval's inquiries:

> Et cil respont: "De che et d'el
> Avriiez vos mestier, je quit.
> Je vos hebergerai anuit."
> (Ed. Roach, ll. 3026–28)

And he replies: "You would need this [a lodging] and more, I believe. It is I who will give you lodging tonight."

Later in the episode Perceval is led to the hall of what is later revealed to be the Grail castle:

> Ens enmi la sale en un lit
> Un bel preudome seoir vit,
> Qui estoit de *chaines mellés*.
> (Ed. Roach, ll. 3085–87; my emphasis)

In the middle of the hall he saw, seated upon a bed, a handsome nobleman with *graying hair*.

Not only old age (evoked in the graying character of the nobleman's hair), but also illness prevent Perceval's host from rising to greet him, for, as he tells the boy, "je n'en sui mie aesiez" (it is far from easy for me; ed. Roach, l. 3109). And when it is time to retire for the night: "Jou n'ai nul pooir de mon cors, / Si covenra que on m'en port" (I have no power over my body, thus I will have to be carried; ed. Roach, ll. 3342–43). The "fisher" who had promised earlier in the narration to lodge Perceval that night appears to be aged and ill.

The episode of Perceval's encounter with his cousin tends to confirm the identification of Perceval's host as the "fisher." Once his cousin guesses from Perceval's praise of his lodging that he spent the night "Chiez le riche Roi Peschor" (ed. Roach, l. 3495), Perceval proceeds to narrate how he came upon two men in a boat:

> Li uns des deus homes nagoit,
> Li autre a l'ameçon peschoit,
> Et *cil* sa maison m'ensaigna
> Ersoir, et si me heberga.
> (Ed. Roach, ll. 3503–6; my emphasis)

One of these two men was rowing; the other was fishing with a hook, and *this latter* told me about his house last night and thus sheltered me.

As in both Pickens's and Méla's, Roach's edition of lines 3503–4 repeats verbatim the previously cited passage of Ms. A, which occurs early on in the Grail episode. Perceval's narration prompts his cousin to reveal to him that the fisher was "mehaigniez" (wounded; ed. Roach, l. 3510) in a battle,[40] the result of which is that he can neither ride nor hunt, but is reduced to entertaining himself by fishing: "Por che li Rois Peschiere a non" (hence his name, the Fisher King; ed. Roach, l. 3520). Revelation of the king's misfortune in turn induces Perceval to identify as the Fisher King the host who welcomed him the preceding night, considering that the latter could hardly move and entreated Perceval "que je venisse / Les lui seoir" (that I come and sit beside him; ed. Roach, ll. 3539–40).

The third reference to the Fisher King occurs during the Hideous

Damsel's excoriation of Perceval, which corroborates his cousin's mention of the illness that afflicts the royal character. The Hideous Damsel blames Perceval's behavior toward the *Roi Pescheor* on two counts: first, he saw the *graal* but failed to ask "Quel *preudome* l'en en servoit" (which *nobleman* was served thus; ed. Roach, 1. 4661; my emphasis); second, if he had asked the question, "Li riches rois, qui or s'esmaie, / Fust ja toz garis de sa plaie" (the rich king, who greatly suffers, would have at once been cured of his wound; ed. Roach, ll. 4671–72). As is confirmed by a manuscript tradition that consistently refers to the character served by the grail as the *riche home*[49] (against the previously cited *preudome* of Ms. T, l. 4661), the Hideous Damsel's emphasis is on the power and wealth of both the wounded king and his realm.

Yet the equation, elaborated in both the cousin episode and the Hideous Damsel episode, between the fisher, Perceval's host, the Fisher King, and the rich king is in question when we consider the last intratextual reference to the Grail adventure. As he begins his confession to the hermit, Perceval mentions his unfortunate silence "chiez le Roi Pescheor" (ed. Roach, 1. 6372). In the course of his admonition, as we saw, the hermit reveals to Perceval that the royal figure served by the grail is both the brother of Perceval's mother and his own:

> Et del riche Pescheor croi
> Qu'il est fix a icelui roi
> Qu'en cel gr[a]al servir se fait.
> (Ed. Roach, ll. 6417–19)

And know that the rich Fisher is the son of the king who is served by the grail.

Whereas both Perceval's cousin and the Hideous Damsel focus on a single Grail king (characterized by the fact that he fishes, is wounded, and is rich), the hermit evokes two different characters, reserving for the son the qualification of wealthy. The hermit's distinction echoes Perceval's when he tells his cousin about the two men he saw in a boat. Only because she talks exclusively of the wounded Fisher King is Perceval led to associate the latter with the lame character who offered him food and lodging. The hermit's mention of two distinct characters also coheres with the scene that describes Perceval's coming upon two men in a boat, suggesting that the fisher is the son (the Fisher King) and the rower, his father (the *rois mehaigniez* or wounded king).[50] The narration of the event that occurs while Perceval and his host share their evening meal appears to confirm the hermit's identification of two distinct Grail kings. As

Perceval and his host are eating, a procession of squires and maidens, one of whom carries a *graal* (ed. Roach, l. 3220), arrives in the hall, files before the bed where the two diners are seated, and "d'une chambre en autre entrerent" (left the hall to enter the room; ed. Roach, l. 3242). That the grail is not brought to Perceval's host indicates that, as the hermit says, it is not the son but his father who is served by it.

The four episodes that provide information on the royal character(s) of the Grail castle are significant proof of the complexities inherent in Chrétien's narrative. In the manuscript tradition, these passages vary, for example, in the nature of the wound afflicting the wounded king. Yet this tradition is also remarkably consistent with respect to the information that Perceval receives from his cousin, then the Hideous Damsel, and finally the hermit. At the same time, this information lacks coherence because it mentions here a single, there two Grail kings. If all the manuscript versions share the same confusion regarding both the identity of the Fisher King as opposed to the wounded king *and* his identification as wounded king, then this places the origin of the confusion back in the first version of the *Conte*. Instead of correcting what could have been construed as narrative inconsistencies, the scribes faithfully reproduced these inconsistencies, suggesting that they recognized their significance in the overall design of Chrétien's romance. This apparent lack of coherence is integral to the author's presentation of an ignorant *niche* easily confused by the contradictory information provided him, thus easily persuaded to adopt his interlocutor's point of view at any given moment in the course of the narrative. In that context, the reading, peculiar to Ms. A, yet generally rejected by its editors, of the two lines that describe Perceval's first sighting of the two men in a boat is remarkable indeed, for it anticipates both Perceval's mention of this sighting (in the cousin episode) and the hermit's distinction between father and son. The result is a constant, and intentional, clash between two kinds of perspective in reference, first, to Perceval's prosaic view of the chivalric realm and, second, to the biased views enunciated by his interlocutors as they each attempt not to enlighten so much as to control Chrétien's ignorant protagonist.

Perceval's ignorance as *niche* thus plays a critical part in the unfolding of his story to the extent that it allows each of the more experienced characters he encounters to pose as an omniscient messenger and as a purveyor of the "truth" about proper chivalry. In the factional setting of the *Conte*, truth is not absolute, but varies according to the speaker's specific allegiance. As in the case of the Arthurian discourse on law and order, the message conveyed by each of the Grail representatives, including Perceval's eremitic uncle, seeks not to generate but to obfuscate meaning in an attempt to manipulate truth, this time to the advantage of the Grail faction.

The argument presented here that the hermit is a pro-Grail representative and that his sermon is a discourse on behalf of factionalism has focused on the lineal perspective introduced by Perceval's uncle. The information he provides to the protagonist does not, however, exclusively take the form of a familial chronicle. Central to the hermit's teaching, indeed, paramount for scholarly assessments of its religious, hence, impartial value, is his revelation that the *graal* contains the Host. The task thus remains to determine whether the hermit's message focuses on the promotion of lineage or whether Perceval's final adventure—in the present state of the text—indicates that he will embark on a journey toward what most commentators describe as the spiritual order of the Grail.[51]

The "Holy" Grail: Exegesis as Manipulation

Borrowing their notion of textual truth from scriptural exegesis, twelfth-century authors of verse romances call attention to the deep significance of their narratives, inviting their listeners to act as interpreters. Clearly, "exegesis" evokes here a type of interpretive activity that differs widely from that of the monastic tradition. This difference is integral to the status of vernacular romance as a production grounded in "literate orality,"[52] in reference to a culture granting equal importance to the written and spoken word. Although based on a text, the "exegesis" in question took place orally. More important, this reliance on the hermeneutics of scriptural exegesis did not aim at investing fiction with religious significance, but sought to praise the intellectual value of vernacular writings. One of the goals was to demonstrate that chivalric (that is, aristocratic) society was a social order concerned not only with fighting, for protective purposes, but with learning as well.

Chrétien's *Yvain* provides eloquent testimony to the value of vernacular creation as an interpretive exercise prompting the characters within the narrative, as well as the listeners to whom it was addressed, to decipher the signs, or signifiers, in which the signified is contained. Particularly noteworthy is the role of Calogrenant in emblematizing an art of storytelling that produces meaning.[53] At the core of Calogrenant's story is his unsuccessful duel against Esclados, a failure that he endeavors to recount in a truthful and straightforward manner, "Car ne vuel pas parler de songe, / Ne de fable, ne de mançonge" (for I do not intend to speak of a dream, a fiction, or a lie; *Le Chevalier au Lion*, ll. 171–72). Calogrenant, and through him, Chrétien himself, thus stresses the value of speech over action. Seen against the surface meaning of the story (that is, military defeat), a deeper meaning arises, focusing on the protagonist's ability to translate action into words. What emerges both from Calogrenant's story and from the story of Calogrenant by Chrétien is a praise of prowess understood as a verbal rather than martial exploit. Calogrenant here epitomizes the value of Chrétien as the agent of an idealized and ideal representation of courtly society. In defining truth in terms of a speech act, the author equates chivalry with eloquence. The true hero of the romance in that sense is Chrétien, to the extent that he guarantees, by speaking, the nobles' claim that life at court is the locus of intellectual debates rather than combats.

Additional testimony to the value of the author in developing the exegetical expertise of his noble audiences is the opaque character of the signs that make up their universe. As Joan Tasker Grimbert notes, "the discrepancy between reality and the signs used to represent it is one of the most pervasive themes" in Chrétien's romances.[54] The inability to decipher verbal and nonverbal data leads to misunderstanding, as in the case of the amorous protagonists of *Erec et Enide*, or even to warfare. Chrétien's protagonists thus illustrate that the world is not what it seems to be and that sensory perceptions can be deceptive. The heroes' progress is, in that connection, a mental process, entailing, to cite Grimbert, "their ability to interpret their experiences."[55] Intellectual development, by trial and error, gradually enables them to control their impulses and to consider, before reacting, the motivations that prompt their opponents to behave aggressively. Chrétien's romances therefore insist on the importance of distinguishing between appearance and reality as a prerequisite for the elaboration of harmonious and refined exchanges among the members of courtly society. In contributing to the exegetic proficiency of his listeners, Chrétien empowers them to avoid violence (the trademark of a society of warriors such as that depicted in the *Chanson de Roland*), thereby confirming the peaceful, indeed, peacemaking, quality of aristocratic society.

Yet the fact remains that Yvain, not Calogrenant, emerges as the true hero of the story. In the last analysis, and despite Chrétien's self-exaltation as a producer of meaning, meaning derives from chivalric prowess in its martial manifestation. If appearance belies reality, it is because fiction, courtly romance itself, praises and defines "truth" in terms of a verbal rather than military exploit, yet at the same time concludes with an apotheosis of the hero as the best of all knightly combatants of the realm. Speech acts, then, are replaced by martial prowess, indicating that the "truth" of fiction lies in a realistic assessment of chivalric—aristocratic—society as an order in quest of a military rather than intellectual type of empowerment.

Although critics do not necessarily concur with this assessment of Chrétien's romances in articulating an essentially military representation of knighthood, most agree that his last work elaborates a definition of chivalry radically different from that found in his four previous romances. An essential component of this difference is the *Conte*'s use of exegetic techniques in a manner that seems to stress its Christian, rather than secular, import. Along with the ritual in the Grail castle, the hermitage episode is the most frequently cited exhibit in support of this argument, due primarily to the scriptural references contained in it. The first occurs in the narration of Perceval's "chance" encounter with a group of penitent characters (ll. 6242–46), which precedes and leads to his meeting with the hermit (ll. 6338–50). Noting that Perceval is carrying arms on the day when Jesus Christ died, one of the penitents wonders aloud:

> Biax amis chiers,
> Dont ne creez vos Jhesucrist
> Qui la novele loi escrist,
> Si le dona as crestïens?
> (Ed. Roach, ll. 6254–57)

Fair and dear friend, do you not believe in Jesus Christ, who laid down the new law and gave it to the Christians?

At the core of the penitent's excoriation is the claim that Christ's new law calls for an end to customary chivalric behavior, that is, aggression. Because the penitents' Christian wisdom results from their encounter with the hermit, whom they praise in a manner that inspires Perceval to seek his spiritual guidance, their allusion to Christ's new law suggests that the hermit's teaching has a religious value. Is Perceval's story a parable illustrating the nonviolent significance of Christ's message?

The hermit's interpretation of Perceval's experience at the Grail castle, which thus constitutes a critical clue to the meaning of Perceval's story, has "considerably exercised critics for twenty-five years," [56] beginning with Albert Pauphilet in 1950. According to Pauphilet, the hermit's claim that Perceval's indifference toward his mother caused his failure at the Grail is both "artificial" and "absurd," for his mother accepts, if she does not approve, her son's departure. Focusing on the link between Perceval's departure from his mother, his silence at the Grail castle, and the hermit's penitential interpretation of both events, many critics argue against Pauphilet that Perceval is guilty. For Myrrha Lot-Borodine, his guilt is unconscious, and his silence at the castle indicates that he has not yet attained adequate awareness of man's postlapsarian condition. But most critics underscore the conscious character of Perceval's guilt, which results from his willful refusal of faith, represented by his mother.[57] According to David G. Hoggan, this indicates a deliberate neglect of the principles of religion, which Jean Frappier emblematized in his still selfish attitude at the castle.[58] In this light, Perceval's encounter with the hermit marks the final stage in his maturation and initiation into an altruistic kind of chivalry.[59] In Alexandre Micha's view, for example, Perceval's story is the locus of a successive initiation into chivalry (through Gornemant), into love (through Blancheflor), and into religion (through the hermit).[60]

Invoking the hermit's eucharistic interpretation of the *graal* (a "sainte chose," he tells Perceval, because it carries the Host; ll. 6422–25), proponents of the moral import of his message thus tend to interpret Perceval's story in terms of a religious allegory. For Amelia Klenke, who sees in the wounded king of the Grail a symbol of the prophet Elijah,[61] Perceval's encounter with the hermit represents a substitution of the Church (the Grail) for the synagogue (the Bleeding Lance), signaling the emergence of spiritual chivalry. Helen Adolf[62] establishes a parallel between the wounded king (who, in the hermit's words, never left his room and has led an ascetic existence for the past fifteen years)[63] and King Hezekiah, Jerusalem's savior, who was granted fifteen years to repent and lead a perfect life. For Adolf, the hermit's mention of the fifteen-year period that marks the recluse's ascetic existence may be interpreted as a warning—addressed to Perceval and, through him, to Philippe of Alsace—that the time has come to restore the Grail domain, that is, the kingdom of Jerusalem. Thus, Adolf proposes to read the *Conte du Graal* as an invitation to the nobility (in particular, Chrétien's current patron) to take up the cross and fight for the defense of the holy city.

That Philippe did join the Third Crusade, however, does not prove that Chrétien's romance inspired him to do so or that the author intended to connect the Grail with the kingdom of Jerusalem. Other scholars deny any spiritual significance to the hermit's interpretation of Perceval's stay at the Grail castle, arguing that it lacks coherence. According to Jean Marx, Chrétien misunderstood the original meaning of the Grail as an initiation rite grounded in ancient Celtic traditions.[64] In Leo Pollmann's view, the poet's moral assessment of Perceval's failure contradicts contemporary theological beliefs about the intentional nature of sin. By contrast, a number of critics maintain that Chrétien's talent resides precisely in his ability to introduce characters, particularly the hermit, who provide a retrospective justification to Perceval's story. Michelle Freeman, for example, argues that, thanks to the hermit's historical knowledge, Perceval's apparently chaotic wanderings are finally linked in a coherent chronology.[65]

Whether they confirm or question the coherence of the episode, critics in the main assume that Chrétien's and the hermit's voices are one and the same,[66] promoting a reading of the episode that takes at face value the hermit's sanctification of the *graal*. However, the question is whether the hermit's singular interpretation of the serving dish is trustworthy: is his revelation consistent with the accusatory discourse of both Perceval's cousin and the Hideous Damsel? First, to what extent does it represent a fair account of Perceval's experience at the Grail castle?

Central to the last episode of Perceval's story is the reliability of his uncle's eucharistic exegesis, which focuses on the scene that occurred while Perceval was dining with his host, the Fisher King. The scene includes the following sequence of events: soon after they begin their meal, a procession crosses the room, led by a young man carrying a lance from whose tip blood drops down to his hand (ll. 3191–212). Two other boys follow him, each with a golden candlestick; then a maiden (*damoisele*), holding a golden dish (*un graal*) set with precious stones; followed by another damsel, holding a silver trencher. With each change of course, the procession files by Perceval and his host and disappears into an adjoining chamber.

The hermit is emphatic: the golden dish contains the Host and is brought to the father of the Fisher King. As he tells Perceval,

ne quidiez pas que il ait
Lus ne lamproie ne salmon;
D'une sole oiste le sert on,
Que l'en en cel graal li porte;
Sa vie sostient et conforte,
Tant sainte chose est li graals.
Et il, qui est esperitax
Qu'a se vie plus ne covient
Fors l'oiste qui el graal vient,
Douze ans i a esté issi
Que for[s] de la chambre n'issi
Ou le graal veïs entrer.
Or te weil enjoindre et doner
Penitance de ton pechié.
(Ed. Roach, ll. 6420–33)

Do not think that he is given pike, lamprey, or salmon; he is served a single Host, which is brought to him in that grail; such a holy thing is the grail that it sustains and comforts his life. And he, who is so spiritual that he does not need, to survive, more than the Host carried to him in the grail, has lived thus for twelve years without ever leaving the room where you saw the grail enter. Now I want to impose and bestow on you penance for your sin.

The hermit's assessment of the spiritual value of the *graal* (implying that of the old king, of the site, and hence, of Perceval's quest for the Grail) is all the more interesting because it departs from the emphasis that Perceval's cousin places on the wealth and power of the castle[67] and contrasts with the splendor of the place as it is described during Perceval's adventure. For example, the narration specifies that one could not find from there to Beirut a tower "Si bele ne si bien assise" (finer or better situated; ed. Roach, l. 3053). The lodges of the castle are so refined that "jusqu'a Limoges / Ne trovast on ne ne veïst / Si beles, qui les i queïst" (one could search as far as Limoges without finding or seeing any so handsome; ll. 3076–78). Torches light up the hall with the brightest light, and "Bien poïst l'en quatre cens homes / Asseoir environ le feu" (400 men could easily sit around the fire; ll. 3096–97). The dinner table, made of a single solid piece of ivory, is covered with a cloth of such quality that "Liegaus ne cardonax ne pape / Ne menga onques sor si blanche" (no legate or cardinal or pope ever dined at one so white; ll. 3278–79). Both Perceval and his host are served with dishes "que rois ne quens / Ne empereres doive avoir" (befitting a king or a count or an emperor; ll. 3316–17) and presented with fruit and drinks of the dearest kind. It is the richness of the Grail domain, and not the solemnity of the procession, that strikes the Welsh boy: 'De tot che se merveille trop / Li vallés qui ne l'ot apris" (he is filled with wonder, for he had never experienced anything like this; ll. 3334–35).

In remarkable contrast to this presentation of the site, the hermit equates the recluse's value with religious worth rather than wealth: in the course of an unspecified event that appears to have occurred approximately at the time of Perceval's birth ("fifteen" years ago), the old king was inspired to become a spiritual man, so blessed that he has no need for terrestrial nourishment. Also noteworthy is the fact that, unlike Perceval's cousin, the hermit never designates the recluse as the *roi mehaigniez*, any more than he mentions the original blow that, according to her, caused his wound. The hermit thus emphasizes the king's ascetic quality by presenting a nonviolent account of the circumstances that inspired him to renounce the world and become a holy recluse. Moreover, before exalting the sacramental function of the *graal*, the hermit makes a point of telling Perceval what the dish is not (a recipient carrying pike, lamprey, or salmon), thus clearly distinguishing the sacred container both from the common serving dish mentioned in vernacular literature[68] and from the mythical food-producing platter so abundantly present in Celtic lore.[69] The result of the hermit's reinscription of the Grail incident is a dematerialization of the dish, the domain, as well as the old king, suggesting that Perceval's quest for the Grail has a strictly personal and redemptive significance and is in no way linked to the revival of his lineage.

The issue remains, nonetheless, to determine whether the hermit's interpretation enunciates the author's main or even sole intention and, more broadly, whether the pervasive religiosity marking the hermitage episode articulates in and of itself a spiritual kind of teaching. Indeed, the presence of biblical references here and in other episodes of the *Conte du Graal* does not necessarily imply that these are an essential part of the plot. Why does Chrétien's prologue attribute to Paul ("Diex est caritez," God is charity; l. 47) a quote from John (First Epistle 4:16)? This erroneous identification may indicate, as has been suggested,[70] that the author was a convert from the Jewish community of Champagne (hence a neophyte in catechistic matters) or, more likely, may reflect a level of knowledge and understanding of the gospel typical of what could be expected of a twelfth-century secular cleric. The allusion to

Christ's "novele loi" made by the penitents whom Perceval encounters in the opening scene of the episode would articulate, in that sense, a quite conventional approach to the Scriptures, that is, a reading of the Old Testament as a foreshadowing of the New.[71] In view of Chrétien's rhetorical expertise, which testifies to his acquaintance with the interpretative techniques of both the religious and classical traditions available in the schools of his time, an even more likely possibility is that the Conte's biblical references, including the prologue's praise of charity, indicate not a questionable or limited knowledge of the Scriptures so much as the author's ironic use of exegetic practices. In Roger Dragonetti's view, Chrétien's "mistake" in the prologue is intentional, acknowledging that the language of romance lacks meaning.[72]

Against this exclusively ludic assessment of the language of fiction, however, I contend that Chrétien's romance does have meaning, but it stands an ironic distance from the various semantic fields, including that of religious allegory, cumulatively employed in the narration.[73] Amplifying Peter Haidu's analysis of Yvain, I suggest that in the Conte du Graal as well Chrétien's use of symbolism is antisymbolic,[74] inducing readers and listeners to seek the meaning of the story at the level of events and phenomena.

The perplexing character of the hermitage episode as Perceval's last adventure in the present state of the text derives in part from the presence in it of multiple layers of signification. The apparently symbolic character of the hermit's exegesis of the graal induces Perceval to discover that his literal perception of the dish was inadequate, its true value being sacramental. In criticizing Perceval's fetishistic fascination with traditional knighthood (as illustrated by the seductive effect upon him of shining armors and objects made of gold and silver, as well as by his desire to join an order that guarantees social promotion and material advancement to its adherents), the hermit seems to provide the protagonist with a definition of chivalry now grounded on transcendence. In this perspective, Perceval's final educator articulates an impartial sermon whose goal is to warn the protagonist against the violent and self-serving use of prowess in traditional chivalry. A good knight does not "sell" his service as a means of consolidating a lord's hold over his land, thereby increasing his own wealth and status. Neither does his "payment" come in the form of arms, money, land, or marriage, for what is promised to all those who endeavor to defend the poor from their oppressors is an intangible, immaterial kind of reward: honor in paradise. The hermit's warning against a lucrative and aggressive use of prowess implies, then, that he does not intend for Perceval to abandon chivalry altogether. Rather, his goal seems to be to direct the protagonist's martial energy in a manner consistent with the crusading missions recommended by the Church.[75] His revelation would thus introduce Perceval to a definition of chivalry understood as an altruistic and disinterested kind of service, one that calls upon the protagonist to relinquish self-gratifying adventurism in favor of the only worthy chivalric pursuit: the quest for the Holy Grail. In Donald Maddox's analysis, Perceval's task is to restore the kingdom of the Grail, a kingdom that will differ radically from Arthur's because of its adherence to the mandate of Christ's *novele loi*, rather than to the obsolescent protocols maintained under Arthurian rule.[76]

However, because the hermit does not specify what kind of mission Perceval is supposed to assume, the assessment of the Grail as a kingdom symbolizing "spiritual exile" remains hypothetical, for, as Donald Maddox acknowledges, "it obviously cannot be known precisely how Perceval's inquiry was to have been salutary to the [wounded] king."[77] Furthermore, why venerate the Host at the Grail castle, rather than at other and more truly consecrated sites? A proper way to calm Perceval's agitated soul would be to talk of the divine King and encourage the penitent to avoid tourneys, lucrative pursuits, and quests for honor, as clerical *rigoristi* sought to do. Yet the hermit insists on the Grail in a manner designed to perpetuate Perceval's obsession, indicating that his sermon is not impartial, nor its goal disinterested.

A noteworthy aspect of his "revelation" is that it either distorts or eliminates certain elements provided in the accounts of both Perceval's cousin and the Hideous Damsel and in the Grail episode itself. For example, the hermit's claim that the king has lived for "fifteen" years without ever leaving his room contradicts the fact that he is outside, rowing, when Perceval first meets him. It is also significant that the hermit mentions the Bleeding Lance only in passing and, even more significant, that he makes no allusion to the sword his Grail host offers Perceval. The hermit thus tends to obfuscate two of the main attributes of chivalric equipment, the lance and the sword, suggesting that his goal is to encourage Perceval to relinquish the self-serving, violent pursuits that make up traditional chivalry.

The bestowal of the Grail sword by Perceval's host, however, is an important event in the narration of the protagonist's adventure at the castle. Just before the appearance of the procession of the *graal*, a young man enters the hall and brings the Fisher King a sword sent to him by his niece:

> Vos le donrez cui vos plaira,
> Mais ma dame seroit molt lie
> Se ele estoit bien emploïe
> La ou ele sera donee.
>
> (Ed. Roach, ll. 3150–53)

You may give it to whomever you like, but my lady would be most happy if it were put to good use where it is bestowed.

Perceval's host girds his guest with the sword, telling him "Biax frere, ceste espee / Vos fu voëe et destinee, / Et je *weil* molt que vos l'aiez" (Fair brother, this sword was ordained and destined for you, and I very much *want* you to have it; ed. Roach, ll. 3167–69). Considering that the sword was "intended and destined" for Perceval, the scene is, to cite Jean Gouttebroze, "a rite of transmission of power." [78] Specifically, the bestowal of this piece of chivalric equipment on Perceval has a factional significance. That Perceval is on three occasions given access to a sword may indicate Chrétien's expertise in symbolic numerology. [79] More likely, this redundancy signals the presence of competing factions as each seeks to appropriate Perceval's prowess. Representatives of the two rival parties manipulate the rite of chivalric initiation [80] in order to delude Perceval into believing that the sword he receives marks his entry into the realm of perfect chivalry. But, as Perceval's violent acquisition of the Red Knight's armor demonstrates, in the Land of Logres, chivalric equipment has not a symbolic but an aggressive function. After having received from Gornemant a sword that turned him into an Arthurian warrior, Perceval receives from his Grail host a sword that seeks to induce him to shift his allegiance. Far from "a symbol of goodness," [81] the sword is here a concrete manifestation of the plans concocted by the Grail faction regarding Arthur's defeat. The "gift" [82] of the Grail sword thus represents a first effort to extract Perceval from his service to Arthur. That Perceval uses it to fight Orgueilleux de la Lande, [83] whom he proceeds to send as hostage to Arthur, indicates that he has yet to fulfill the task expected of the heir to the Grail, hence the key role played by the hermit as a final attempt to co-opt Perceval.

The hermit's dematerialization of the Grail site and the nonviolent character of his rendition of Perceval's adventure at the castle constitute a testimony to the partial and partisan significance of his teaching. Rather than inducing his penitent to discover the deep meaning of chivalry, his reliance on exegetic techniques redirects Perceval's prowess in support of lineage by persuading him that the quest for the Grail has a redemptive value. Several elements in the ritual as observed at the castle belie the hermit's eucharistic interpretation of the *graal*. First, the serving dish is not held by religious hands, but by a maiden. Second, the fact that the grail is brought to the royal recluse several times implies that he receives communion more than once a day. Third, no mention is made of a priest, indicating that the king did not confess before receiving the Host.

In light of the Church's prescriptions regarding communion by the laity, the hermit's rendition of the scene would appear to border on sacrilege. In the last decades of the twelfth century, when the sacrament of communion was the subject of considerable discussion,[84] these prescriptions represented an attempt to foster the participation of the laity in the celebration of the Eucharist, turning communion and the relatively new sacrament of penance into mandatory practices.[85] The Church's views on communion by the laity suggest that receiving the sacrament was an exceptional, possibly only annual, event requiring proper preparation and, consequently, that this sacrament was not recommended on a daily basis. In the hermit's account, therefore, the king displays a rather eccentric piety, contradicting not only ordinary devotional behavior, but also the Church's regulation forbidding communion more than once a day. More important, the nonsacerdotal character of the procession, combined with the fact that the *graal* is carried by a maiden, runs counter to both contemporary clerical thought and devotional practices, thus casting suspicion on the hermit's eucharistic exegesis of the ceremony. Considering also that the setting of the Grail ritual is not a great church but "the hall of a feudal castle," it is not surprising that "the church authorities were consistently cautious in their approach to the story of the Holy Grail."[86]

The hermit's sanctification of the site thus does not signal that the final episode of Perceval's story introduces a new, spiritual understanding of chivalry. Nor does the fact that the episode occurs during Holy Week prove, pace Bonnie Buettner,[87] that the hermit seeks to effect Perceval's reconciliation with God. His use of religious symbolism and exegetic techniques has a strategic function, situating the meaning of his discourse at the level of events and phenomena. Hidden beneath the hermit's idealizing view of the *graal* as a "tant sainte chose"[88] lies the reality of a lineage intent on recovering its lost power and glory. In this light, the "decidedly anti-Arthurian"[89] perspective developed in the hermitage episode is an index of the decidedly conventional character of the hermit's definition of chivalry. What he presents to Perceval in terms of a "penitential" and "redemptive" journey seeks to redirect his nephew's martial energy in support of the Grail faction.

The factional character of the role played by Chrétien's hermit in Perceval's story becomes all the more evident in light of Robert de Boron's reinscription of the episode (as preserved in the prose rendition of the Didot Perceval). In his account of Perceval's encounter with his eremitic uncle, the author of the Didot Perceval interpolates his own interpretation—and denigration—of Chrétien's rendition of the scene:

> Et se dist li contes que ensi com Dex volt asena a le maison le sien oncle l'ermite, la u se suer l'avoit mené confesser. Et se confessa a lui et prist penitance tele com il li encarja, et demoura avuec lui deus mois.
>
> Mais de çou ne parole pas Crestiens de Troies ne li autre troveor qui en ont trové por faire lor rimes plaisans, mais nos n'en disons fors tant com au conte en monte et que Merlins en fist escrire a Blayse son maistre. . . . Or saciés que nous trovons en l'escrit que B[l]ayses nos raconte, si com Merlins li fist escrire et metre en auctorité, que Percevaus demoura a le maison son oncle deus mois.
> (*Didot Perceval*, ll. 1467–74, 1477–80)

And the tale says that, by God's will, [Perceval] came upon the lodging of his eremitic uncle, where he had been led by his sister for him to confess. And he confessed to him and accepted the penance as the hermit ordained him, and stayed with him for two months.

But Chrétien de Troyes failed to mention this, as did all the other versifiers who endeavored to retell the episode on a pleasant mode, but as for us, we relate nothing but what is pertinent to the tale and that Merlin had his master Blaise put into writing. . . . Know, then, that we find in the writing that Blaise tells us, consistent with what Merlin told him to write and record, that Perceval stayed for two months at his uncle's.

These two months give the hermit of Robert's text an opportunity to persuade his pupil to go "veoir le vostre repair, qui fu Alain le Gros vostre pere et le mien frere" (see your domain, which belonged to Alain the Fat, your father and my brother; ll. 1496–98). Fearing to find the familial domain empty, Perceval at first refuses to undertake that journey, "qui me donroit le roiaume au rice roi Artu" (even if I were offered the rich king Arthur's kingdom; l. 1500). Once his uncle assures him that the domain is not empty, Perceval promises to go, vowing never to stop until he finds "le maison mon taion, le vostre pere" (the house of my grandfather, your father; l. 1505). The author's corrective view of the episode criticizes Chrétien's narrative for being reductive and for lacking moral amplification. Against Chrétien's and others' entertaining renditions of the legend, the author proposes his own edifying version. However, in stressing the genealogical import of the Grail castle, he unwittingly reveals the aggressive direction of the quest. That Perceval's recovery of the Grail, in the unfolding of the Didot Perceval, coincides with Arthur's demise emphasizes, on the one hand, the author's misguided exaltation of the hermit as a spiritual messenger while unmasking, on the other hand, the political function of Perceval's eremitic uncle in Chrétien's narrative.

In contrast to the allegedly scriptural import of the Grail in the Didot Perceval, as in many other Grail sequels,[90] Chrétien's romance introduces the serving dish in a context indicating that the object has an eminently dynastic connotation. This is all the more remarkable in view of the popularity of the cult of the precious blood in twelfth-century Flanders. While in the Holy Land in 1146, Thierry of Alsace (the father of Philippe of Flanders, Chrétien's patron) received from the patriarch of Jerusalem a crystal flask that contained a small amount of Christ's blood, which the patriarch had taken from Joseph of Arimathea's vessel. Thierry's return to Flanders generated great devotion for the relic, culminating with the flask's official transfer to Bruges in 1150 and, soon after, the erection of a chapel to house it.[91] The cult of the precious blood, which spread to Normandy and insular Britain, also played a symbolic part in the dispute opposing territorial princes (who in 1181 had formed an alliance including the Count of Flanders and the Plantagenet king) against Philip Augustus.[92] Rival political powers attempted to emulate the saintly character of French kingship by claiming, as did the Plantagenets, that they also possessed the ability to cure scrofula or, as did the German emperor during the ceremony of his coronation, by carrying the holy lance that was supposed to contain a nail from Christ's cross.[93]

Considering the popularity of the cult of the precious blood and the association of the relic with Bruges and Philippe of Flanders, together with the fact that the cult spread over territories hostile to the Capetians, it is noteworthy that the grail dish is given a sacred significance not in the *Conte du Graal* but in its sequels, beginning with Robert de Boron's account, where the vessel becomes the receptacle of Christ's blood and a major factor in the evangelization of insular Britain. Jean Marx concludes that Chrétien and Robert de Boron worked from different sources.[94] More likely, it is because the hermit's eucharistic interpretation of the Grail was not consistent with Perceval's story that Robert invested Chrétien's *graal* with a meaning radically different from that intended by the author of the *Conte*. Lack of coherence in the interpretation of the Grail incident by Chrétien's hermit is probably neither accidental nor unintentional, but bears the mark of an ideological argument. Presented in the guise of an ideal, the hermit's account seeks to persuade Perceval that the quest for the "Holy" Grail is superior to any other type of chivalric pursuits, thus legitimizing through a false sanctification his enlistment on the side of the Grail faction.[95]

The hermit's interest in Perceval's confession, his ability to understand Perceval's rather confused narration of the Grail incident, and his expertise as chronicler of the Grail family demonstrate that, in his perspective, Perceval is not meant to become a recluse but to resume his chivalric activities—this time for the benefit of the rivals to Arthurian rule. This is why Perceval stays at the hermit's cell for only two days (rather than the two months mentioned in Robert's revisionist narrative) while his horse is given "de l'estrain / Et de l'orge un bachin tot plain" (straw and a full trough of barley; ed. Roach, ll. 6505–6). The hermit's mystique of the Grail and his presentation of the quest as a redemptive course for Perceval appear to have succeeded in transforming the protagonist into a de facto avenger of the Grail faction.

Perceval's Mission: The Revenge of the Grail Faction

The circumstances leading to Perceval's encounter with the hermit, which results from Perceval's "chance" encounter with a group of penitent characters, provide significant allusions to the anti-Arthurian tenor of the hermitage episode. Seeing that Perceval wears his armor, one of the penitents blames him, for

> Certes, il n'est raisons ne biens
> D'armes porter, ainz est grans tors,
> Au jor que Jhesucris fu mors.
> (Ed. Roach, ll. 6258–60)

it is assuredly neither right nor good, but on the contrary, immensely wrong, to bear arms on the day when Jesus Christ died.

Just as in the first episode of Perceval's story, a group of Arthurian knights inspired him to leave the vale near Valbone (as evoked in the two parts of his name, perce-val: to go beyond the vale) in order to acquire chivalric equipment, another group of knights now entices him to disarm.[96] In the first case, the five knights act as intruders to the extent that they disturb the quiet life in the "forest gaste" and cause Perceval to lose his former state of innocence by joining the ranks of Arthurian chivalry. In the second case, it is Perceval who is now "the intruding knight, incongruous in his armor on Good Friday [ll. 6247–48], for, as in the Waste Forest, weapons are out of place" in the "boschage" (l. 6337) where the hermitage is located.[97]

The penitent's blame questions the value of Perceval's use of arms during the past five years, which has enabled him to send 60 fearsome knights as hostages to Arthur. Considering the pro-Arthurian significance of Perceval's deeds, the penitent's blame may also articulate a resentment toward those rulers, like the French kings, who reserved for themselves the right to wage wars (then said to be "holy") even during the Truce of God, Good Friday included.[98] In this light, the penitent's argument that it is both immoral and illegal (justified neither by *bien* nor by *raison*, mentioned at l. 6258) for Perceval to be fully armed represents an implicit indictment of Arthur to the extent that his rule entrusts the king's agents, and only them, to bear arms and wage war—regardless, it appears, of such prohibitions as those invoked by the Truce of God.[99]

The hermit turns out to have played a crucial role in their present disposition, as the following exchange between Perceval and one of the penitents indicates:

> "Por Dieu, seignor, la que feïstes?
> Que demandastes? Que queïstes?"
> "Coi, sire?" fait une des dames,
> "De nos pechiez li demandames
> Conseil et confesse i preïsmes.
> La plus grant besoigne i feïsmes
> Que nus crestïens puisse faire
> Qui weille a Damedieu retraire."
> (Ed. Roach, ll. 6307–14)

"In God's name, my lords, what were you doing there? What were you asking? What did you seek?" "What?" said one of the ladies, "we asked him advice for our sins, and made confession. We did the greatest thing any Christian can do who wants to return to God."

The lady penitent does not respond directly to Perceval's questions, but exalts the penitential value of their meeting with the hermit, inviting Perceval in his turn to seek out the hermit and beseech his advice. The path to the hermit's abode is not clear-cut, for his cell is situated in the midst of a "bos espés et menu" (thick and dense forest; l. 6324). Thus, the penitent knights have knotted branches and left such signs so that "nus n'i esgarast / Qui vers le saint hermite alast" (no one would lose his way while going to see the holy hermit; ll. 6329–30). A conventional topos in hagiographic and courtly literature, the forest can have a maleficent influence on the hero, effecting, as in Yvain's case,[100] his transformation into a "wild man," but can also be a beneficent locus, as appears to be the case for Perceval's eremitic uncle. In many narratives,[101] however, eremitic characters serve not as mediators but as obstacles hindering the relationship between man and nature and between humans as well. In this, vernacular literature reflects the ambivalence of contemporary clerical thinkers regarding a mode of life that could induce rather than subdue temptations, hence their tendency to restrict eremitic solitude to exceptionally devout monks.[102] The hermit's mode of life in the *Conte* is therefore not proof that he is an exceptionally devout individual.

Furthermore, the location of the hermit's cell in the thick of a forest, which invokes other anti-Arthurian sites, such as the Welsh forest, points to his still active involvement in the society depicted in the romance, rather than to his role as a contemplative recluse.[103] The hermit's apparent ability to orchestrate the whereabouts of passersby suggests that Perceval's arrival at his cell is not fortuitous. Beneath this "chance" encounter lies a strategy designed to convince the boy that he will remain a wandering (that is, imperfect) knight unless and until he achieves the restoration of the "Holy" Grail

The Hermit as Knight (Preudome)

That the eremitic characters of medieval romance, including Chrétien's hermit in the *Conte du Graal*, reflect not a clerical view on chivalry but the nobility's desire to legitimize its role and status in medieval society is confirmed by the Church's indifference or, in some cases, hostility toward Grail literature.[104] The nobles' effort, via romance, to glorify their function was in part, as often noted, a reaction to their decline in the emerging monetary society of the late twelfth century.[105] That the ladies of Tintagueil can mistake Gauvain for a merchant or a "changiere" is a measure of the urgency to stress anew the intrinsic, rather than visible, distinctions of true chivalric nobility (*preudomie*). For, as Erich Köhler notes, if all the *preudomes* of chivalric romance are knights by virtue of their inherited nobility, all knights are not necessarily *preudomes*, that is, endowed with internal, nonpurchasable qualities.[106]

Chrétien's *Conte du Graal* grants *preudomie* to a number of characters, including Perceval's father (ed. Roach, l. 439), Gornemant (from l. 1353), the Fisher King (l. 3086), the wounded king (l. 4661), Gauvain (l. 7480), and, most noteworthy, the hermit (l. 6303). The result is that within Chrétien's romance all members of the contending factions possess or claim to possess equal rights regarding their privileged status in society. Moreover, *preudomie* is often connected with wealth, thus associating true chivalric nobility with monetary worth and not merely with birth. For example, Perceval's mother links her husband's *preudomie* to his status as the ruler of a "grant terre" and "grans tresors" (great land and great treasures; l. 438). Another example occurs in the Grail episode: when Perceval joins his host in the dining hall, the Fisher King is sitting on a bed like a true *preudome*, wearing a cap

> D'un sebelin noir come meure,
> Vals d'une porpre par deseure,
> Et d'autel fu la roube toute.
> (Ed. Roach, ll. 3089–91)

of sable, black as mulberry, covered in a purple cloth on top, and his robe was of the same material.[107]

Together with nobility and wealth combined, what also distinguishes *preudomie* is prowess: Gauvain's arrival at Escavalon inspires the king's counselor to recommend that they accept Meliant's challenge because the presence of a worthy knight (*preudome*) is often sufficient to win a tourney (ll. 4936–37).

Thus, although true *preudomie* is supposedly set apart from wealth and aggression, nonetheless these two elements are conspicuously part of the chivalric realm of Chrétien's romance.[108] The *Conte's* demystifying depiction of chivalry thus points to the value of prowess[109] in the pursuit of personal ambitions. All the knightly characters of Chrétien's narrative hide the self-serving motivations impelling their chivalric activities, yet each intends to emerge as the best warrior in the realm. This is the context in which the respective discourses of the two principal contending factions acquire their full meaning, as an attempt to veil their true purpose under the pretext that chivalry is an order of high value, benefiting all its adherents. Such is the case, from the Arthurian perspective, when the king promises Perceval that he will soon be inducted into his order of chivalry, "A m'onor et a vostre preu" (for my honor and your profit; l. 984), and, from the perspective of Arthur's rival faction, when the hermit urges his nephew to become a knight according to *his* definition of chivalry, for "si i avras preu" and "Encore porras monter en pris" (you will reap great profit and you will gain in value; ll. 6444, 6457). It is as a hermit that he sermonizes Perceval and inspires him to recognize the gravity of his sin and to repent in order to earn access to paradise.

The way of life of Perceval's uncle, however, "is just about as divorced as may be from the world of the organised ecclesiastical hierarchy." As Maurice Keen observes, most of the numerous solitaries introduced in Grail literature after Chrétien "prove to be men who, until they felt the strength to bear arms ebbing from them in the autumn of life, had followed the vocation of knighthood." When they speak as guardians of the Grail, their message conveys essentially secular ideas about lineage; indeed, in Keen's view, "The whole Grail story is in one sense the history of a knightly lineage . . . of a line pre-elected by God to fulfil a special mission." [110] This is also the case of the *Conte*'s hermit, whose deceptively moralistic teaching hides a partisan determination to redirect Perceval's prowess on behalf of lineage. Thus, it is as a knight anxious to see his faction triumph over Arthur that he intervenes in Perceval's story and compels him to employ his chivalric talent for the regeneration of Grail kingship.

That Chrétien's hermit is not an impartial member of the Church but a noble *preudome* who voices the claim of his party is corroborated, at the extratextual level, by the fact that, in several sequels to Chrétien's *Conte*, he is openly described as a former knight. [111] These sequels also confirm the significance of Perceval's story as one of vendetta by emphasizing the military character of Grail chivalry. In Wolfram von Eschenbach's *Parzival*, the "Gral" is neither a chalice nor a paten, but a stone endowed with the power to bestow immorality. Acting as a source of sustenance, the "Gral" assures its adherents (the many formidable fighting men who dwell at Munsalvaesche) of remaining young and strong. The Welsh tale *Peredur*[112] reveals even more clearly the significance of the Grail as a symbol of violence and revenge. The hero witnesses a procession in the course of which a dish carrying a man's head swimming in blood is borne. Later in the text Peredur learns that it was the head of his cousin and undertakes to avenge his death.

Recognizing the centrality of vengeance in the legend, as in the case of these two sequels, some critics assert, nonetheless, that Chrétien's romance obfuscates rather than develops its basic premise. Citing the eucharistic interpretation of the content of the *graal* introduced in the hermit episode, Jean-Claude Lozachmeur sees the resulting substitution of a Host for the head of Peredur's cousin as the reason why revenge plays only a marginal role.[113] Such is the case in Gauvain's adventures at La Roche Canguin, which Lozachmeur sees as obscure echoes of the part played by Arthur's nephew in fighting the Grail king's enemies. According to Madeleine Blaess, Perceval's sin consists primarily of allying with a clan hostile to his own. But, she claims, Chrétien did not understand the dynastic elements of the original folktale, attempted to fuse it with Arthurian romance, and, in so doing, failed to give it coherence.[114]

Yet the ubiquity of rivalry in the *Conte du Graal* testifies to the coherence of Chrétien's narrative, which converges on the revenge of the Grail faction against Arthur as usurper. The knightly identity of Perceval's uncle, which places him squarely within the competitive ranks of chivalric society in Chrétien's romance rather than in the realm of religious reclusion, discloses his role as initiator effecting the boy's absorption by the history of violence and rivalry that marks the Land of Logres. The significance of Chrétien's romance lies not in an allegedly impartial use of scriptural motifs, but in the prevalence of an accusatory discourse that focuses on the respective champions of the two principal factions.[115] In view of the abundance of challenges and prosecutions that incriminate Arthur's nephew, Gawain's story is in that respect emblematic. Perceval's story is equally grounded in accusation, culminating with the hermit's portrayal of Perceval the *niche* as sinner. Moreover, Perceval's accusers intend not only to extract him from service to Arthur, but also to co-opt him in support of the Grail faction.[116] This is why the hermit's discourse combines blame and praise, persuading Perceval that the quest for the "Holy" Grail will effect his metamorphosis into the champion of spiritual chivalry.

Perceval's "Redemptive" Course

A result of the hermit's hagiographic exaltation of the old Grail king is the transformation of the decline of the Grail faction into a parable of Christ's Passion.[117] From this perspective, Perceval's indifference toward the plight of his uncle represents a sin committed against a Christlike figure. Thus, the first redemptive gesture for Perceval requires that he acknowledge his role as "persecutor" of the holy recluse of the Grail castle, his innocent "victim." Considering that the God of the Bible traditionally sides with the oppressed,[118] the hermit's exegesis is a powerful argument to convince Perceval that his redemptive pilgrimage has not only personal but also universal value. The hermit's exegesis also constitutes an effective strategy to transform Perceval the *sinner* into Perceval the *savior* of the Grail.

The other two Grail messengers similarly incriminate Perceval's behavior at the castle. From his prosecutors' standpoint, regardless of the particular argument on which they ground their accusation (Perceval's filial indifference, his selfishness, or his neglect of God), Perceval's silence *bespeaks* guilt and is the event from which the meaning of his story derives. The accusatory character of their discourse does not reflect a desire to reveal the truth in an impartial manner, thereby guiding Perceval on the road to maturity and acculturation; rather, it expresses their desire to convince him of his guilt. They succeed in convincing Perceval of his personal implication in the tragic familial history to the extent that they do not tell him everything and present him with only a partial chronicle of his forerunners. Because the boy's silence at the castle stems in part[119] from his ignorance of society's ways, the "truth" of the case lies not in his behavior during the Grail incident, but in the language of the prosecutors. The coherence engendered by Perceval's accusers as each articulates a sequential link between his attitude at the Grail castle and the present state of disorder is a fiction, inventing a cause for the sole purpose of forcing Perceval into the role of the accused. Their incrimination of Perceval consists of a retrospective fabrication of causality in the course of which the past becomes Perceval's past, a "primal scene" in which the principal actor is presented as both the source of the doom of the Grail domain and its future remedy. Perceval's adventure at the Grail castle becomes the locus of a narration in which "beginnings are chosen by and for ends,"[120] that is, by and for the Grail's spokesmen as they voice the parameters of their own cause and desire.

The Grail messengers' power of reasoning enables them to control Perceval as *niche*. Although Chrétien's verse romance, as already noted, is grounded in literate orality, the Grail messengers' superiority over the ignorant boy evokes the triumph of literate society over the illiterate (*rustici*) as it was developing when Chrétien was composing his romance, although the messengers employ oral speech. In R. I. Moore's analysis, the "dark side" of literacy at the turn of the twelfth century was its manipulative use by experts in the emerging "new technologies of government, [such as] the counting of money, the sealed writ, the legal tag,"[121] which sought to serve the interests of royal and papal government against the interests of the less educated members of society. An example is the progressive equivalence in both ecclesiastical and royal discourses of terms such as *rusticus, illiteratus*, and *idiotus* to describe "those accused of heresy, of leprosy, of Jewry," with the help of ancient texts in which clerical experts "found both their authority and their instruments for persecution."[122] Moore dates around the year 1180 the emergence of this coercive practice of law, which consisted of "imposing from above a pattern of guilt or innocence in accordance with codes promulgated by the central authority."[123]

In a manner strikingly similar to contemporary rulers,[124] Perceval's Grail educators exhibit a tendency to resort to persecution to ensure their faction's victory. To that effect, they base their indictment of Perceval on a "conspiracy theory" whereby Arthur is guilty of oppressing the innocent (such as Perceval's father), and Perceval is guilty of not having acted in support of the oppressed (the old Grail king). Central to the conspiracy theory is the accusers' argument that the ones they accuse committed their crimes for their own benefit.[125] Thus were conspiracy myths invented, which were all the more convincing because they were crafted by experts at interpretation in an attempt to manipulate public opinion against a "common enemy."[126] In the context of Perceval's story, the manipulative effect of the Grail messengers' discourse deludes him into believing that he caused the doom of the Grail and must therefore redeem himself by serving the Grail cause.[127]

Just as Perceval's *nicheté* facilitates Gornemant's task in convincing him to devote himself to Arthur, the putatively pacific and disinterested ruler, so does it facilitate the Grail messengers' task in launching him on what they maintain is a redemptive mission of both individual and universal value. Chrétien neither blames nor praises his protagonist, suggesting that the author does not endorse the viewpoint of either rival faction. His aside that "Qu'ausi se puet on bien trop taire / Com trop parler a la foie[e]" (one can be too silent as well as too talkative; ed. Roach, ll. 3250–51; this comment appears in the episode of Perceval's adventure at the castle) is particularly noteworthy, for it distances the author's perspective on his unformed protagonist both from the Grail messengers' accusatory exegesis of Perceval's "excessive" silence at the castle and from Gornemant's warning against "excessive" loquacity. On the basis of Chrétien's innovative creation of a *niche* character, Perceval's silence at the Grail castle is a natural result of his tendency to follow literally instruction provided him by the representatives of chivalric culture: Perceval did not speak because he was determined to obey Gornemant's command.

Seen against Chrétien's realistic appraisal of Perceval as *niche*, the hyperbolic language used by representatives of the two rival factions reveals itself as an abusive and, ultimately, victimizing discourse. The boy's entry into chivalric society places him in the midst of conflicting parties and presents him successively with conflicting models of behavior. Perceval's eagerness to be accepted and integrated into the realm of chivalry prompts him to trust the diverging assessments of his character as pronounced by each of his educators. In his desire to be perceived as an Arthurian knight, for example, he endeavors to eliminate all the external marks that distinguish him as a "foreigner," a Welshman.[128] But his new Arthurian identity causes, in turn, the Grail representatives to accuse him of neglecting his lineage.

Thus, the real *victim* of the plot is not the old Grail king, but Perceval. If the equally idealizing discourse of the two rival parties endangers Perceval's maturation, the reason is that his educators' exalted view of chivalry, although allegedly beneficial to the transformation of the simpleton into a paragon of virtue, actually encourages his natural aggression. As praised by Arthur as well as by the Grail messengers, the order of chivalry represents an invitation to join a tight-knit, elitist, martial fraternity. Access to this knightly brotherhood, whose members move in a rarefied world of privilege, endows the newly dubbed knight with the right to resort to armed violence. Whether Perceval obeys Arthur's rule or whether he sides with the Grail party, his entry into traditional chivalric culture does not provide him with the means to control his violent impulses, as illustrated in his slaying of the Red Knight. On the contrary, it jeopardizes his development as an autonomous individual while impressing on him the notion that society is made up exclusively of persecutors and victims. Beyond the binary vision of the world as articulated by the spokesmen of the two rival parties, Chrétien's text also alludes to a different form of acculturation, one that invites Perceval to a discovery of self and other no longer grounded in strife and competition.

Chapter 4

In Quest of a New Order

At the heart of my "social" reading of Chrétien's *Conte du Graal* is the centrality of bipartition as a narrative pattern underscoring, more openly than in any of the author's previous works, the divisive character of traditional chivalric society. In this last of Chrétien's romances, the narration focuses not on one hero, as is the case of *Yvain*, but on two knightly protagonists, each of whom undertakes adventures that appear to question the adequacy of his chivalric conduct. Each character finds himself the target of an indictment in the course of which an accuser criticizes his past behavior. The recounting of Perceval's as well as Gauvain's adventures is thus structured around a critical central scene of revelation that seems to provide each protagonist, as it does Erec and Yvain, with the opportunity to correct his past behavior and assume his heroic destiny in the postcrisis phase of his story.

Despite this structural homology, however, several elements also indicate that the function and hence the significance of the climactic episode in either section of Chrétien's last romance profoundly differ from those in his previous works. A notable distinction is, first, the nature of the relationship between accuser and accused. In *Erec* and *Yvain*, an affective tie links the plaintiff to the hero, whose inadequate behavior affects primarily, albeit not exclusively, the sphere of the private. In the *Conte du Graal*, by contrast, Perceval's and Gauvain's respective "crimes" consist of having affected the welfare of a specific community. A second distinction is, consequently, the social rather than individualistic tenor of the *Conte*'s twin scenes of accusation. It is not accidental that both Perceval's and Gauvain's indictments take place at Carlion in the presence of Arthur and his court. Nor is it coincidental that the protagonists' respective accusers (the Hideous Damsel in Perceval's case and Guigambresil in Gauvain's) turn out to represent factions hostile or rivalrous to Arthur. Far from a relevatory scene enabling the hero to gain awareness of (hence to correct) his past deficiency, the partisan character of the charges made against Perceval and Gauvain situates their respective stories within a history of strife and contention that inscribes itself in the social landscape of the *Conte*. If Perceval and Gauvain lack the heroic qualities of an Erec or Yvain, part of the reason is that the true subject matter of Chrétien's last romance is not the individual subject, but traditional chivalry as a social order governed by clan rivalry and competition.

As a result of the general weakening that affects chivalric society in this crepuscular account, the two principal contending factions implied in the *Conte*'s consistent use of bipartition find themselves compelled to rely on discourse in an attempt to regain the power and status they each used to enjoy in prediegetic history. At the core of the Arthurian discourse on law and order, as we saw in Chapter 2, is the king's desire to present his rule as the sole institution capable of ensuring individual maturation and communal harmony. Despite the deterioration of his authority in this last stage of Chrétien's Arthurian chronicle, Arthur's self-glorification of his rule is so entrenched that Gauvain himself persists, verbally if not actively, in claiming the beneficent effect of his kingship. Although the final phase of Gauvain's story is proof of his growing indifference toward Arthur's cause, Chrétien's second protagonist continues, from sheer force of habit perhaps, to praise the value of Arthur's court as a locus of refinement and enlightenment. To Ygerne's inquiry about the fate of King Arthur and his Round Table, for example, Gauvain responds by citing the king's wife as a paradigmatic exhibit of the excellence of his court:

> Dame, voir, ele est tant cortoise
> Et tant est bele et tant est sage
> C'ainc Diex ne fist *loi ne langage*
> Ou l'en trovast si bele dame.
> Des que Diex la premiere fame
> Ot de la coste Adan formee,
> Ne fu dame si renomee.
> Et ele doit molt bien estre:
> Tot ausi com li sages mestre
> Les petis enfans endoctrine,
> Ausi ma dame la roïne

Tot le mont ensaigne et aprent;
Que de li toz biens descent
Et de li vient et de li muet.
(Ed. Roach, ll. 8176–89; my emphasis)

My lady, truly, she is so courteous, so beautiful, and so wise that God never made a *realm or society* in which so fair a lady could be found. Since God formed the first woman from Adam's rib, there has never been a lady of such renown. And she deserves to be thus acclaimed: just as the wise master educates the little children, so my lady the queen teaches and instructs everyone; for every good thing comes and derives from her.

Parallel to the claim of the rival discourse that the Grail compels obedience to Christ's "novele loi" (new law; l. 6256), Gauvain's allusion to the superiority of Arthurian society over all others ("loi ne langage"; l. 8178) glorifies royal rule as a system of governance designed to promote wisdom and learning. By praising the queen as an exceptional embodiment of virtue, unique of her kind since the foundation of the world, Gauvain voices Arthur's claim that his rule is itself unique of its kind and exceptionally beneficent. From the royal perspective, any other form of governance is of lesser value; more specifically, any rival claims, such as that of the Grail faction, pose a threat to peace and order.

This implicit reference to Arthur's (oral) *loi* elaborates a significant contrast with Christ's written *loi* ("Qui la novele loi escrist"), suggesting an equally political use of exegetical techniques on the part of the two rival discourses. On the one hand, the connection established in the hermitage episode between the law of the Grail and Christ's "novele loi" bespeaks a desire to sanctify the Grail cause over and above Arthur's. Relying on the typically medieval approach to the Scriptures, the hermit's strategy would consist of claiming that, just as the message of the Gospel supplanted and replaced that of the Old Testament, the order of the Grail deserves to supplant and replace that of Arthur. Using a reverse argument, Arthur would attempt to belie the spiritual legitimacy implicit in the mystique of the Grail by denouncing the anarchic character of its proponents: as a strategy on behalf of factionalism, their claim to obey Christ's "novele loi" works against the king's disinterested attempt to rescue society from its tradition of violence and deserves to be condemned and prosecuted.

Although this suggested reading of the dual reference to Arthur's law and to Christ's law remains hypothetical, in both rival discourses *loi* refers to an exclusively oral system of protocols. In this duplicate quest for power, the dispute between the two contending factions becomes a war of words, wherein language seeks, in both cases, to politicize all aspects of life as a means of controlling the subjects of the realm on both the private and public levels. Whether *loi ne langage* refers to "any other place" (that is, other than Arthur's realm),[1] to "race or land,"[2] to "religion and nation,"[3] or to "institution and language,"[4] the all-encompassing character of the expression discloses its significance as an eloquent summary of Arthur's drive to rule over the body politic and organized religion. Hyperbole here as well as in the sanctifying discourse of the opposition therefore produces an equally totalizing view of world order. Despite their claim, neither Arthur's law nor the Grail law ("Christ's law") supports the establishment of a peaceful communal life, precisely because each contending party has a rivalrous and totalitarian understanding of order, and the victory of one therefore entails the vanquishing of the other.

The emergence of a truly novel understanding of order, one that would no longer reduce the land of Logres to an opposition between "victims" and "persecutors," calls for a third and radically different alternative. At issue is not only the dissolution of the factional aspect of chivalric society as depicted in Chrétien's last romance, but also the establishment of a system of exchange and interaction valorizing reciprocity rather than aggression and dominance. The harmonious co-existence of love and chivalry would require the *ami chevalier* of the realm to cease to be rivals in love as they are rivals in knighthood, to abandon their quest for preeminence, and to recognize the inherent danger of pursuits whose goal is to prove the superiority of one or another quester. Of equal importance is the need for the chivalric community to renounce what might be called "the law of the tombs," a reference to the tradition whereby the duty of the living is to avenge the death of their ancestors.

Calling into question the systematic exaltation of violence in traditional chivalric romance, Chrétien's last work proposes in the character of Perceval the possibility of knightly regeneration. However, the *Conte du Graal* does not suggest an idealized or spiritual type of regeneration, one that would valorize either Arthur's viewpoint or that of the Grail messengers. Rather, it invokes a realistic regeneration of chivalry by focusing on a nonheroic, ignorant boy who represents the promise of a mode of existence grounded on self-determination. Acknowledging that the realm of harmonious and peaceful interaction belongs to fiction, Chrétien's romance introduces in Perceval a protagonist marked by natural aggressive impulses that he needs to learn how to control out of respect for the needs of others. Perceval's maturation implies a capacity to recognize that communal life is, essentially, a realm of compromise.

Natural Law: Life in the Welsh Forest

Whereas Chrétien's previous romances exploit discord and conflict as given forces that the hero progressively controls and transcends, the *Conte du Graal* proceeds in an opposite manner and starts, so to speak, at the end. The opening scene of the narrative introduces a setting of natural and human juvenility:

> Ce fu au tans qu'arbre foillissent,
> Que glai et bois et pre verdissent,
> Et cil oisel en lor latin
> Cantent doucement au matin
> Et tote riens de joie aflamme,
> Que li fix a la veve [d]ame
> De la gaste forest soutaine
> Se leva, et ne li fu paine
> Que il sa sele ne meïst
> Sor son chacheor et preïst
> Trois gavelos, et tout issi
> Fors del manoir sa mere issi.
>
>   . . .
>
> Por la douçor del tans serain
> Osta au chaceor le frain,
> Si le laissa aler paissant
> Par l'erbe fresche verdoiant.
>   (Ed. Roach, ll. 69–80, 91–94)

It was in the season when trees burst into leaf, and fields and woods and meadows are green, and the birds in their Latin sing sweetly in the morning, and everything is aflame with joy, that the son of the widowed lady in the wild and lonely forest rose, and effortlessly set his saddle on his hunting horse, and took three javelins, and at once set out from his mother's house. . . . The weather was so sweet and calm that he took the bridle from his hunting horse and let it wander to graze among the fresh green grass.

Nothing in the vale constrains Perceval's frolicking, for, although the scene contains certain elements of dissonance (a widowed mother, a wild and lonely forest), those elements relate to a past about which the boy knows nothing. The sole *loi* and *langage* of his universe are those of nature, allowing him, by virtue of his age and ardor, to follow his impulses as he pleases and to enjoy the pleasant sound of birds that sing "in their Latin." This seasonal setting is a conventional *topos* in the vernacular lyrical tradition, wherein poets evoke the vernal awakening of nature either to celebrate the blossoming of love or, more frequently, to mourn its absence.[5] It is equally prevalent in courtly romance because spring ("Pentecost") usually inaugurates the festive gathering of Arthur's court.[6] In contrast to both the lyrical and narrative tradition, however, spring in the opening scene of the *Conte* serves neither to oppose man and nature, as is often the case in love songs, nor to emblematize Arthur's role as leader of chivalric society. Rather, spring reflects the presence of a harmonious relationship between man and nature, inducing Perceval to set aside his hunting horse and taste the sweetness of the season.

The opening scene of Chrétien's narrative also suggests a contrast between court and forest radically different from its usual function in Chrétien's earlier romances. Whereas Erec or Yvain emerges as the best knight by leaving Arthur's court and successfully confronting the dangers that lurk in the forest, Perceval's story bespeaks a reverse process, from forest to court, potentially leading to a loss of distinction. Far from representing the typical locus where the hero demonstrates his chivalric prowess, Perceval's forest constitutes a sanctuary against the threats posed to personal integrity by an imperfect knightly culture.[7] His mother apparently decided to raise Perceval in the natural surroundings near Valbone in order to protect him from the menace of absorption into the ranks of traditional chivalry. Although she is aware that Perceval, as heir to a noble family, is destined to enter chivalric society, she is also determined to prevent him from adhering to the self-destructive world of martial fraternity. But the vale near Valbone ceases to function as a sanctuary with the arrival of the five Arthurian knights (ll. 100–110) who make Perceval want to look like them,[8] prompting him to go in search of the king who makes knights. Perceval's encounter with representatives of traditional chivalry, which thus constitutes a pivotal moment in the story of his youth near Valbone, also effects a clear distinction between his mother's role as nurturer, prior to the intrusion of Arthurian knighthood, and as educator thereafter.

Perceval's Mother as Nurturer

A *veve dame* (according to version A, as opposed to *veve fame* of version T, l. 74), Perceval's mother is situated in a context of grievous personal experience (a widow) and aristocratic culture (a lady) at Chrétien's first mention of her. In the wild and lonely forest, Perceval and his mother are the only extant members of a once illustrious and strong family. Because Perceval knows nothing about his tragic familial history, his mother is also the only living witness to the series of events that caused the dispersion of the Isles faction in the north, the return of her wounded husband to a family manor in a remote Welsh vale, the death of their two sons, and, finally, the demise of her spouse. Her lack of protectors, loss of social status, and determination to protect Perceval from knowledge of the past indicate that it is not the forest that is "lonely," but, through a rhetorical hypallage, she herself. Her silence reflects a desire to nurture her last surviving son in an environment propitious for his development as an autonomous individual. In the opening lines of Chrétien's narrative, Perceval's originality thus consists of a capacity to act as "free lance," not in the medieval sense of the term, but in the sense that he is free to pursue individual goals, unconstrained by the need to prosecute family quarrels (free, in this respect, of the Bleeding Lance heritage).

However, the discovery of his difference from the five knights who cross the vale near Valbone fosters in the naive and ignorant boy a sense of inadequacy and alienation. His "difference" as an unrefined Welshman living in the reclusion of the forest induces Perceval to mistake chivalry for a locus of distinction and to assign to knightly equipment a discriminating value: "Car fuisse je ore autretiex, / Ausi luisanz et ausi fais" (how I wish I were like you, as shining and as handsomely formed; ll. 180–81). Perceval's admiration for the costume of chivalry provokes consternation among the harrowers of the manor:

> Et quant il virent lor seignor,
> Si tramblerent tot de paor.
> Et savez por coi il le firent?
> Por les chevaliers que il virent,
> Qui avec lui armé venoient,
> Que bien sevent, s'il li avoient
> Lor afaire dit et lor estre,
> Que il volroit chevaliers estre;

Et sa mere en istroit del sen,
Car destorner l'en quidoit l'en
Que ja chevalier ne veïst
Ne lor afaire n'apreïst.
(Ed. Roach, ll. 311–22)

When they saw their lord, they all trembled with fear. And do you know why they did? Because of the armed knights that they saw coming with him, for they knew well that if these knights had told him of their ways and mode of life, he would want to be a knight; and his mother would lose her mind, for she believed that he could be kept away from it so long as he never saw knights or learned of their ways.

The awareness of Perceval's mother concerning the deadly character of knightly pursuits is therefore the reason that she—and, at her request, her servants—have raised the adolescent in total ignorance of chivalric "afaire."

Not all critics concur with this positive assessment of the motivations of Perceval's mother in attempting to prevent her son from discovering traditional chivalric culture. Omer Jodogne, for example, argues that she is guilty of having robbed Perceval of his noble calling, thus preventing him from assuming his social responsibilities.[9] For Charles Méla, her fault is not having told her son his name, thereby impeding his access both to the Father (père)—echoed in the first syllable of his name (Per-ceval)—and to knowledge.[10] Other scholars, minimizing the moral or psychological aspect of Chrétien's maternal protagonist, stress instead her cultural significance. According to Sara Sturm-Maddox,[11] myths such as the Grail seek to redefine the proper modes of exchange and communication by reminding society of the disorderly effects produced by excessive silence and abstinence (emblematized by Perceval and his mother) and by excessive promiscuity (Gauvain).

Although it is valid to see, in agreement with Claude Lévi-Strauss,[12] a reverse similarity between myths of the "Oedipian" type (in which an unanswerable question is asked) and myths of the "Percevalian" type (which focus on an unasked question), and although the two types of myths are similarly concerned with the problem of communication, the question is whether Chrétien's Grail narrative qualifies as a myth according to Lévi-Strauss's definition. In my view, the Conte's bipartition is not a neutral structure used to delineate the conditions necessary for the emergence of a viable social order. Nor are the overly masculine realm of the Grail locus and the overly feminine realm of La Roche Canguin strictly opposite poles schematically illustrating the dangers of imperfect or interrupted communication. If Perceval's story has a universal significance, it is not because he serves as the emblem of defective communication, but because of traits of character (impulsiveness, curiosity, impressionability) evoking a typical adolescent. Like many of Chrétien's heroes,[13] Perceval is last born and fatherless, thus relatively sheltered from a past of family grievances and in a position to act in support of his personal interests, present and future. The sanctuary of the vale in the "wild" and "lonely" Welsh forest, which distances him from the site and history of dynastic vendetta, is also Perceval's best asset with respect to his development into a mature and responsible knight.

That the *Conte* is essentially a story of vendetta is confirmed, retrospectively, by Wolfram von Eschenbach's reinscription of Chrétien's narrative (*Parzival*, ca. 1200–1210). Unlike its French antecedent, the German text gives detailed information on the life and death of Parzival's father, Gahmuret, in a narration that constitutes the first two books of *Parzival*. The hero's story does not begin ex nihilo, as it does in Chrétien's text, but has its roots in an illustrious paternal lineage, that of Gahmuret, as well as that of Herzeloyde, Parzival's mother, whose motives for keeping her son ignorant about chivalry arise from possessive love:

> Si kunde wol getriuten
> Ir sun. Ê daz sich der versan,
> Ir volc si gar für sich gewan:
> Ez waere man oder wîp,
> Den gebôt si allen an den lîp,
> Daz se immer titters wurden lût.
> "Wan friesche daz mîns herzen trût,
> Welch ritters leben waere."
>
> (*Parzival*, sec. 117, ll. 18–25)

How she cosseted her son! Before he arrived at years of discretion she summoned her people, man and woman, and forbade them on pain of death ever to breathe the name of "knight"—"For if my darling were to learn of knighthood I should be very heavy-hearted." (Tr. Hatto, p. 70)

As the threat contained in her command indicates, Herzeloyde's control of her son's destiny courts abuse. Her course of action at the moment of Parzival's departure from the vale discloses the self-centered character of her relationship with her son. In contrast with Perceval's mother, who gives priority to her son's safety over her personal interest,[14] Herzeloyde

forces Parzival to wear fool's clothing: "Wirt er geroufet unt geslagn, /
Sô kumt er mir her wider wol" (sec. 126, ll. 28–29). ("Then, if he is
roughly handled, he will surely come back to me"; tr. Hatto, p. 75.)

At the same time, Herzeloyde, as queen of three kingdoms and the
widow of an illustrious noble, is not immune from the imperatives of re-
venge. Once Parzival manifests his determination to leave the forest and
become a knight, Herzeloyde reveals to him the origin of their tragic
familial history:

> "Du solt och wizzen, sun mîn,
> Der stolze küene Lähelîn
> Dînen fürsten ab ervaht zwei lant,
> Diu solten dienen dîner hant,
> Wâleis und Norgâls.
> Ein dîn fürste Turkentâls
> Den tôt von sîner hende enphienc:
> Dîn volc er sluoc unde vienc."
> "Diz rich ich, muoter, ruocht es got:
> In verwundet noch mîn gabylôt."
> (*Parzival*, sec. 128, ll. 3–12)

"You must learn another thing, my son. Arrogant bold Lähelin has wrested
two lands, Waleis and Norgals, from your Princes. By rights they should sub-
serve you. Turkentals, one of your Princes, was killed by him, and he killed
your people or took them prisoner." "I will avenge this, mother, if God pleases.
My javelin shall wound him yet!" (Tr. Hatto, p. 75)

Her desire to prosecute the enemies of their faction proves, in the final
analysis, stronger than her possessive love for Parzival. Maternal in-
struction, which predisposes Parzival to assume his role as avenger from
the very moment of his entry into chivalric culture, also enables him
to understand the full implications of the message conveyed by his suc-
cessive educators. When Parzival learns from his cousin, Sigune, that
the knight who slew her lover happens to be the murderer of his pater-
nal uncle, his response to her is unequivocal: "Swenne ich daz mac
gerechen, / Daz wil ich gerne zechen" (sec. 141, ll. 27–28). ("If ever I
have power to avenge it I will settle the account"; tr. Hatto, p. 82.)
Herzeloyde, as Parzival's first initiator into the modes of operation of
traditional chivalry, facilitates the task of the subsequent guides by
ensuring that the boy will follow the path of revenge to its end.

Wolfram's rewriting of Chrétien's maternal character, while placing
her squarely in the realm of chivalric aggression, contradicts her sin-

gular role in the *Conte du Graal*. The motives that induced Perceval's mother to raise her son in a remote locus of the Welsh forest are selfless. She differs from Herzeloyde in this way. Her fear of knighthood is all-encompassing, signaling her awareness of the equally violent and rivalrous effects of chivalry as idealized in both the Arthurian and Grail discourses. Hence her response when she hears Perceval talk of "knights":

> "ne vi je or
> Les plus beles choses qui sont,
> Qui par le gaste forest vont?
> Il sont plus bel, si com je quit,
> Que Diex ne que si angle tuit."
> La mere entre ses bras le prent
> Et dist: "Biax fix, a Dieu te rent,
> Que molt ai grant paor de toi.
> Tu as veü, si com je croi,
> Les angles dont la gent se plaignent,
> Qui ocïent quanqu'il ataignent."
> "Non ai, voir, mere, non ai, non!
> Chevalier dïent qu'il ont non."
> La mere se pasme a cest mot,
> Que chevalier nomer li ot.
> (Ed. Roach, ll. 390–404)

"Have I not just seen the most beautiful things that exist, passing through the waste forest? They are more beautiful, I think, than God and all his angels." His mother took him in her arms and said: "Fair son, I commend you to God, for I am deeply afraid for you. I believe that you have seen the angels everyone complains about, who kill whoever they come across." "I did not, truly, mother, I did not, absolutely not! They said that they are called knights." His mother fainted at this word, when she heard him utter it.

Perceval's mother shows greater fear of knights than of devils. Although the latter constitute a lethal danger, knights are apparently even more destructive. A testimony to the deadly effect of traditional chivalric protocols is the death of her husband and of their two elder sons. In view of the disastrous consequences of chivalric culture for the family's history, her silence up to that moment and now her anguished reaction appear fully justified. Once Arthurian chivalry intrudes and forever disturbs the tranquil site of Perceval's childhood, she knows her silence is no longer tenable and she must provide her son with adequate instruction to ensure his survival in the realm he is about to enter.

Perceval's Mother as Educator

Aware that Perceval is on the verge of discovering the world outside the Welsh vale, Perceval's mother reveals to him his illustrious origin:

> Chevaliers estre deüssiez,
> Biax fiz, se Damedieu pleüst,
> Qui vostre pere vos eüst
> Gardé et vos autres amis.
> N'ot chevalier de si haut pris,
> Tant redouté ne tant cremu,
> Biax fiz, com vostre peres fu
> En toutes les illes de mer.
> Biax fiz, bien vos poëz vanter
> Que vos ne dechaez de rien
> De son lignage ne del mien,
> Que je sui de chevaliers nee,
> Des meillors de ceste contree.
> Es illes de mer n'ot lignage
> Meillor del mien en mon eage.
> (Ed. Roach, ll. 412–26)

You were destined to be a knight, fair son, if it had pleased God to protect your father and others close to you. There was no knight of such high worth, more feared and more dreaded, fair son, as your father was in all the Isles of the Sea. Fair son, you may boast the fact that you fear no shame of your lineage, either on his side or mine, for I too was born of a line of knights, one of the best in that land. In all the Isles of the Sea there was no finer lineage than mine in my time.

The exalted nature of Perceval's paternal and maternal lineages (the finest in the land) in his mother's account suggests that she invites her son to show himself worthy of his heritage. She appears here to encourage her son to become, in imitation of his father, a knight of high worth, thereby empowered to restore the family to its previous splendor.[15]

But other aspects of his mother's account point to an opposite interpretation. To occupy an elevated position in society, as her husband did, invites the danger of conflict and tension, provoking both rivalrous desires on the part of the less powerful members of the Isles of the Sea and the eventual downfall of its leaders:

> Mais li meillor sont decheü,
> S'est bien en pluisors lius veü
> Que les mescheances avienent

> As preudomes qui se mai[n]tienent
> En grant honor et en proëce.
> Malvestiez, honte ne pereche,
> Ne dechiet pas, qu'ele ne puet,
> Mais les buens deschaoir estuet.
>
> (Ed. Roach, ll. 427–34)

But the greatest have fallen, for it has been demonstrated on numerous occasions that misfortunes befall the noblemen who adhere to a life of great honor and prowess. Wickedness, shame, or sloth never falls, for it cannot go lower, but the good must always fall.

Although the proverbial character of the last part of her chronicle invokes adversity as a universal occurrence, the first part focuses on the reason that aristocratic culture is particularly vulnerable to the wheel of fortune. Consistent with the homonymy between *preudomie* and prowess in their acquisitive significance, her statement that the "greatest" of her line fell while striving to demonstrate and confirm their superiority assigns the primary cause of the family's misfortune not to a particular individual or faction, but to chivalry itself. In contrast to Wolfram's Herzeloyde, Perceval's mother does not evoke the family's tragic history in the form of an accusatory discourse against the enemies of lineage and clan. Her use of the passive voice to describe the strife that initiated the family's downfall suggests, on the contrary, a desire not to cast the blame on any particular group or individual:

> Vostre peres, si nel savez,
> Fu parmi la jambe navrez
> Si que il mehaigna del cors.
> Sa grant terre, ses grans tresors,
> Que il avoit come preudom,
> Ala tot a perdition,
> Si chaï en grant povreté.
>
> (Ed. Roach, ll. 435–41)

Your father, although you do not know this, was wounded through the leg, so that he was maimed in body. His great land and his great treasures, which he held as a nobleman, went to perdition, and he fell into great poverty.

Far from serving as a justification for the resumption of vendetta, her chronicle is a warning against the violent outcomes that quests for *preudomie* and prowess are likely to engender.

Her reaction when Perceval mentions the word *knight* shows that she fully grasps the significance of her son's encounter with the five representatives of traditional chivalric culture. She knows that by wanting to go "to the king who makes knights," Perceval risks entering into an alliance against his own lineage. Remarkably, however, she chooses to disclose neither the history of rivalry between Arthur and Perceval's paternal bloodline nor the existence of the maternal branch of his family, the Grail lineage. If Perceval does not learn the identities of those who contributed to his father's demise, to the plight of the Grail kingdom, and to her own misfortune, a chance exists that he will not be absorbed into the history of vendetta. Thus, although she situates the origin of the family's misfortune at the moment of Utherpendragon's death (ll. 444–45), she also intentionally suppresses the connection between that event, King Arthur's access to power, and the ensuing chronicle of conflict and revenge—hence her reference to Arthur as the "good King Arthur" (l. 446).

Knowing from experience the tragic results of chivalric rivalry, she appears to be aware that none of the participants in the initial strife was entirely innocent or, more precisely, that everyone involved in the event shared equal responsibility. Her dating the event after Utherpendragon's death suggests that she is evoking Arthur's attack of British strongholds in northern England as narrated by Geoffrey of Monmouth. Unlike Geoffrey's idealizing account of Arthurian history, however, her chronicle has no hero, from which we may infer that Perceval's father played a part in the circumstances that led to the dispersion and destruction of her Isles lineage, to the death of their two elder sons, and to his own. Indeed, as she now reveals, the demise of Perceval's brothers was a direct result of his father's fanatic resolve to take his revenge against Arthur. Entrusting them to the care of Arthur's enemies, the king of Escavalon and Ban de Gomorret, he had imposed on them a preordained role as avengers of family and clan. This mission had rendered the two brothers highly vulnerable to royal prosecution, as suggested by the fact that they both died on the very day they were dubbed (ll. 469–75).

Implicit in the mother's brief recapitulation of the past is the argument that prowess should be employed for life-enhancing purposes, not for self-interested or vengeful *preudomie*. It is the realm of traditional chivalry that she criticizes, for its stark conception of a world made up of pursuers and prey. This contradicts Omer Jodogne's previously cited contention that Perceval's *nicheté* is the consequence of his parents' deliberate and guilty decision to extract him from his social and moral duties. As Lenora D. Wolfgang argues, the critical stance of Perceval's mother is neither pathetic nor misguided, but an accurate description of the realm of traditional chivalry. For Wolfgang, Perceval's mother refers to chivalry as it existed in the time of Utherpendragon because "she cannot know that the world she feared has changed since the coming of Arthur and the brotherhood of the Round Table." [16] Against this assessment of Arthur's accession to the throne, traditional chivalry in prediegetic history, as in the temporal setting of the *Conte*, is a culture obsessed with the cult of dead ancestors, which is employed either to justify or to contest royal authority. This is the legacy that Perceval's mother rejects in favor of a mode of chivalric behavior that should blossom outside the "law of the tombs." In concluding her chronicle, Perceval's mother establishes an eloquent contrast between the cult of the dead and true grief:

> Del doel del fil morut li pere,
> Et je ai vie molt amere
> Sofferte puis que il fu mors.
> Vos estïez toz li confors
> Que jou avoie et toz li biens,
> Car il n'i avoit plus des miens;
> Rien plus ne m'avoit Diex laissiee
> Dont je fuisse joians ne liee.
>
> (Ed. Roach, ll. 481–88)

Your father died of grief for his sons, and I have suffered a very bitter life since his death. You were the sole consolation that I had and all that I possessed, for all my loved ones had departed. God had left me nothing else to give me joy and happiness.

On the basis of the casualties evoked in her recollection of the past, Perceval's mother urges him to view chivalry not as a duty to redress past grievances, but as a call to care for the living.

Her recommendations at the moment of Perceval's departure from the vale near Valbone (ll. 527–72) specify more directly the line of conduct that will help him achieve chivalric maturity. She knows that Perceval will go to Arthur and eventually receive the arms of knighthood:

> Mais quant ce vennra a l'essai
> D'armes porter, coment ert donques?
> Ce que vos ne feïstes onques,
> Ne autrui nel veïstes faire,
> Coment en sarez a chief traire?
>
> (Ed. Roach, ll. 516–20)

But when the time comes to try out these arms, how will it turn out? Because you never used them before and never saw anyone use them, how will you know how to manage?

Her concern is directed not so much at Perceval's martial capability as at the way he will use it. It is urgent that she advise him against imitating the mode of chivalric aggression, and she does so by delineating a program of behavior grounded in responsibility and service. Like those of Gornemant and, later, the hermit, the instructive message of Perceval's mother defines the proper modes of communication between knights and God, between knights, and between knights and ladies. Yet she also differs from Perceval's other educators in two important ways: first, by giving priority to the relationship between men and women instead of valorizing, as does Gornemant, interaction among chivalric brothers and instead of stressing, like the hermit, the knight's subservience to the Church; second, by emphasizing the value of friendly and fruitful exchanges in all three types of interaction. As illustrated by Perceval's initial adventures in the world outside the Welsh vale, his behavior indicates that he has absorbed, if not fully understood, the essential message of his mother's instruction, hence the originality of Perceval's behavior as he enters the realm of predatory chivalry.

Beyond Predatory Pursuit

Before the arrival of the five Arthurian knights, Perceval's life in the Welsh forest entails a pastoral type of existence in which chasing birds and beasts serves primarily as a means of gathering nourishment. In the joyful opening of Chrétien's narrative, Perceval's chasing activities have a sportive character: wandering through the fresh green grass, he throws his javelins "Une eure [arriere,] l'autre avant, / Une eure bas et autre haus" (sometimes behind him, sometimes forward, sometimes low, sometimes high; ll. 98–99). The text emphasizes not Perceval's success in catching his prey, but the spirited and restless quality of his performance, thus presenting the chase as an outlet for the adolescent's natural impulses.

Precisely at this moment Perceval hears five armed knights coming through the woods:

> Et molt grant noise demenoient
> Les armes de ciax qui venoient,

Que sovent hurtelent as armes
Li rain des chaines et des carmes.
Les lances as escus hurtoient
Et tout li hauberc fresteloient;
Sonent li fust, sone li fers
Et des escus et des haubers.

                    (Ed. Roach, ll. 103–10)

And the arms of the approaching knights made a terrible din as the branches of oak and elm slapped against them. Their lances clashed upon their shields, their hauberks rang throughout; the wood and the iron of mail coats and shields resounded.

Sound prompts Perceval to believe that the loud creatures he hears coming are devils, "Les plus laides choses del mont" (the foulest things in the world; l. 116), just as sight leads him eventually to conclude that these creatures are angels:

Et quant il les vit en apert,
Que du bois furent descovert,
Et vit les haubers fremïans
Et les elmes clers et luisans,   130
Et vit le blanc et le vermeil   133
Reluire contre le soleil,
Et l'or et l'azur et l'argent,
Si li fu molt bel et molt gent,
Et dist: "Ha! sire Diex, merchi!
Ce sont angle que je voi chi."

                    (Ed. Roach, ll. 127–38) [17]

And when he saw them in the open, as they came out of the wood, and saw their hauberks glittering, and their helmets bright and shining, and saw the white and the vermilion shining brightly in the sun, and the gold, the blue, and the silver, he thought it most handsome and noble, and said: "Oh, Lord God, I thank you! These are angels that I see here!"

Although Perceval's doubly hyperbolic assessment, which relies on sensorial perceptions, is consistent with his naive and literal understanding of the world, it also discloses indirectly the ambiguous character of chivalry as depicted in the *Conte du Graal*. Belying the knights' appearance, the aesthetic quality of which seems to reflect the ethical value of chivalry, the "terrible din" of their armor indicates that knighthood is a source of dissonance and discord, as confirmed by the knights' explanation of their presence in the Welsh forest. In contrast with Perceval, they are here not to track down the "birds and beasts" of the woodland, but to pursue a "game" of a different kind: "Veïs tu hui par ceste lande / Cinc chevaliers et trois puceles?" (Have you seen five knights and three maidens pass this heath today?; ll. 184–85).

The encounter between Perceval and the five knights thus generates two opposite images of pursuit, designated in this chapter as the "chase" and the "hunt." Whereas the chase, which implies a distinction between humanity and fauna, has a nutritional function or is, in Perceval's case, a sportive outlet for the adolescent's natural impulses, the hunt takes the form of aggression, transforming the forest into a battleground and human interaction into warfare. Traditional chivalric culture as presented in the *Conte* reveals itself to be the locus of an obsessional vision of the Other as either pursuer or prey.

The Human Quarry

That knightly pursuits have a predatory character is abundantly illustrated in twelfth- and thirteenth-century chivalric romances, particularly in narratives (such as *Tristan*, the *Romance of the Rose*, and Chrétien's *Erec*) whose venatic imagery points to a specific target: the human quarry. In the legend of Tristan and Yseut, which provides particularly significant information on the function of venatic imagery as an emblem of the organizing principle of chivalric society, hunting motifs serve to assess Tristan's exalted status at the court of King Marc, his uncle— before Tristan's transgressive love for Marc's wife, Yseut.[18] In Gottfried von Strassburg's rendition of the legend (in the early thirteenth century), Tristan functions as a master hunstman.[19] At the end of a royal hunting party that concludes with the capture of a stag, Marc's nephew directs the parceling out of the carcass, which is then reassembled in the stag's shape.[20] Tristan follows a precise procedure, differentiating the lower morsels (which go to the poor) from the more noble portions, reserved for Marc and his men. The anatomization of the quarry thus establishes an equivalence between the body of the hunted animal and the body politic. Tristan's observance of venatic protocol indicates that he recognizes Marc as his lord, and his expertise as master huntsman signals that he occupies a high position in the king's court. As soon as he transgresses his vassalic fealty by loving his lord's wife, however, Tristan becomes a cause of social disorder, hence the hero's transformation from master huntsman to quarry.

Béroul's less courtly[21] version of the legend (ca. 1160) presents a vastly different interpretation of Tristan's amorous relationship with Yseut. Love, which Béroul does not present in terms of transgression, inspires the couple to take refuge in the forest of Morrois, where the fugitives are the objects of repeated manhunts.[22] To track down the outlaws, Marc's men release Tristan's dog, Husdent, whose arrival generates great fear in Tristan. Realizing that Marc has given orders to track them down ("nos fait li rois Marc *querre*"; l. 1530), he decides to teach Husdent how to hunt its prey in silence. In this episode as well as in Chrétien's description of the arrival of the five armed knights at the vale near Valbone, the hunt as chivalric pursuit is a "noisy" affair, signaling the intrusion of discordance into the midst of nature. As represented by both Marc's and Arthur's rule, social law, which imposes on the royal court the duty to prosecute any and all fugitives, endangers and disturbs the harmonious relationship between the two lovers or, in Perceval's case, between man and nature. The noncourtly character of Béroul's text contributes to a negative assessment of the chivalric order, leading the poet to exalt the lovers' consensual union and, implicitly, to question the contractual associations that lie at the core of aristocratic society.

Further evidence of the mission that impels Marc's men to act as huntsmen is provided by a subsequent episode in Béroul's narrative, which describes the lovers' discovery by a forester. Reading certain marks in the forest as indications of human presence, the forester tracks down the lovers until he finds their natural abode: "Vit les dormanz, bien les connut" (He saw them sleeping, and recognized them at once; l. 1817). The forester's fearful reaction results from his knowledge of Marc's edict ("Out fait li rois *crier* son ban"; l. 1405) whereby whoever finds the fugitives must immediately sound the alert ("le *cri* lever"; l. 1410). In compliance with the royal edict, the forester proceeds to cover, in haste, the two leagues that separate the lovers' abode from Marc's court: going down from the mountain ("du mont *avale*"; l. 1840), he enters the hall where King Marc is holding his court of justice. Although the verb *avaler* in Béroul's text has a concrete meaning, in reference to the forester's displacement from mountain to vale, it is not accidental that *avaler* (to swallow, to consume) in both Old and modern French also has a nutritional significance. In contrast to Tristan's reliance on venatic activities as a means of ensuring their survival in the woodlands, tracking down the fugitives emblematizes the voracious character of Marc's rule.[23] The distance from forest to court thus separates and distinguishes the realm of natural law from the realm of royal justice. Under Marc's rule, on the one hand, interaction takes the form of a reciprocal "devourment" consistent with a perception of the Other as either pursuer or prey. On the other hand, Tristan and Yseut find in the natural refuge of the forest an environment beneficial to the blossoming of life-enhancing interaction, in contrast to the court as a locus generating human antagonism. In Béroul's "vulgar" interpretation of the legend, therefore, court and forest acquire an antithetical significance, signaling that right is not located at Marc's court, but is on the lovers' side.

Not only does Béroul's ethical assessment of the lovers' asylum in the Morrois forest evoke, as Ulle E. Lewes observes,[24] the natural sanctuary of hermits such as Saint Giles; it also echoes numerous renditions of the Golden Age in both religious and secular literature. A well-known example, in Jean de Meun's *Romance of the Rose* (ca. 1268–78), is the idyllic depiction of life before the emergence of human interaction as warfare. According to Friend,[25] in a past Golden Age, humanity lived a natural existence, gathering acorns and heads of grain, making their homes in rocks and trees, and leading their lives in frank and joyous friendship. The weather was like an everlasting spring, inviting men and women to enjoy the songs of birds saluting dawn "in their Latin":

> N'encore n'avoit fet roi ne prince
> Meffez, qui l'autrui tost et pince.
> Trestuit pareill estre soloient
> Ne riens propre avoir ne voloient.
> Bien savoient cele parole,
> Qui n'est mençongiere ne fole,
> Qu'onques amor et seigneurie
> Ne s'entrefirent compaignie
> Ne ne demorerent ensemble:
> Cil qui mestroie les dessemble.
> (*Roman de la Rose*, ll. 8415–24)

Crime, who robs and despoils others' good, had not yet made a king or a prince. All were accustomed to being equal, and no one felt the desire to claim anything as one's own. People then believed in the saying that states, wisely and truthfully, that love and lordship never kept each other company nor dwelt together: the dominant one of the two keeps them separate.

But, according to Friend, Baraz (Greed) put an end to the simple, vegetarian mode of life of the Golden Age, when the desire to expand one's horizon precipitated the appearance of social evils such as avarice and possessiveness. No longer loving each other without "simony" (l. 9496), people, like Jason, undertook to go in quest (*querre*) of "golden fleeces" (l. 9477), traveling throughout the lands ("par toutes *terres*"; l. 9535) and sowing discord, dispute, and war (*guerres*; l. 9536). Rhyming words in Friend's discourse establish an equivalence between quest, conquest, and violent interaction, thus disclosing the self-interested character of chivalric pursuits. Friend's evocation of the Age of Iron confirms that his diatribe focuses on aristocratic society. Endeavoring to flay the earth and draw from her entrails "Metauz et pierres precieuses" (metals and precious stones; l. 9543), people used iron to forge arms, including swords and coats of mail, that empowered them to fight their neighbors and used stone to build forts and castles designed to shelter and protect their booty.

Aroused by man's thirst to prove himself superior, stronger, and richer than his fellow men, hunting is, in Friend's discourse, an invention that contributed to the transformation of the vegetarian community of the Golden Age into a society of "ogres." Friend's account thus posits a causal link between the disappearance of the Golden Age and the emergence of a notion of quest understood as aggressive and acquisitive pursuit ("La grant ardeur d'avoir aquerre"; l. 9547).[26] That hunting emblematizes the human desire to acquire superfluous possessions, above and beyond the sustenance required for survival, also reveals that the object the quester seeks functions as a status symbol. The goal in tracking down people or animals and in accumulating possessions is not to ensure humanity's survival or maintain order, but to establish one's preeminence in the social hierarchy. In that sense, Friend's account of the Iron Age foreshadows Walter Burkert's assessment of the symbolic value of hunting after the Neolithic revolution: "It was no longer a question of catching one's dinner, but purely a demonstration of the ruler's power to kill. Thus, the most prestigious quarry was the beast of prey."[27] In both Friend's and Burkert's views of history, the emergence of hunting in its aggressive dimension is concomitant with the human capacity to master the environment.

An important aspect of Friend's depiction of primitive society is its utopian character, reflected in Friend's lament for an age that owed its "golden" quality primarily to the fact that it was not stained by the evil invention of hunting. On that point, Jean de Meun's allegorical figure stands at odds not only with Burkert's "hunting hypothesis," but also with the view of many classical authors, such as Virgil, for whom hunting represents the condition of savage nature, a condition contained and limited by the emergence of a more advanced agrarian culture.[28] Virgil distinguishes between a regressive form of hunting (when people revert to techniques of primitive hunting or resort to the techniques of prehoplitic combat) and a positive form of hunting as a ritual reaffirming the cohesion of the community. This second use of venatic activities confirms the pacific value of the king's rule in many Arthurian romances. By directing chivalric forces to pursuit of an animal, the Custom of the White Stag in Chrétien's *Erec* originally prevented knights from acting as manhunters. As reinstated by Arthur, the ritual leads to the reaffirmation of the king's supremacy: by eliminating the danger of internecine violence generated by the Custom of the White Stag, Arthur demonstrates his capacity to control and manipulate to his own advantage his knights' competitive impulses.

The motif of the hunt is thus symbolic of the time-honored principle of dominance in Roman and post-Roman history (that is, to divide in order to rule), allowing Arthur, as the winner of the game, to prove himself the strongest of all. Royal hunting is therefore not an "art" of husbandry, but a strategy of appropriation. Beneath Arthur's claim that he alone is capable of orchestrating the stag ritual because he alone knows the "proper" techniques of husbandry lurks a "proprietary" gesture, as the conclusion of the ritual demonstrates. Just as Arthur claimed possession of the white stag at the end of the hunt, so does he now claim possession of Enide, "la pucele au cheinse blanc" (the maiden with the white garment; *Erec*, l. 1071): "Je di que droiz est antresait / Ceste l'enor del blanc cerf ait" (I say that it is right that this damsel receive the honor of the white stag; ll. 1743–44). *Droiz*, that is, Arthur's law, entitles him to bestow on Enide a form of "honor" that anticipates the sixteenth-century seigneurial tradition (*jus primae noctis*) granting to a lord the right to deflower his subject's betrothed.[29] Royal husbandry under Arthur's rule poses a direct threat to Erec as new conqueror of the white-cloaked Enide. The fact that Erec deliberately ignored Arthur's ritual of the stag and undertook instead to conquer a hawk indicates that, like Arthur, he intended to assume the role of pursuer.[30] The parallel between the master of the stag and the master of the hawk thus suggests a potential collision between the narrative's major male figures as two pursuers equally determined to become proprietor of a superlative prize, Enide. In this rivalrous quest for power, Enide's value is symbolic, for the real prize, the "most prestigious quarry," is in reality the rival himself.

As a counterpoint to a society occupied with pursuits that reveal themselves as manhunts, both Béroul and Jean de Meun conjure a realm protected from predatory interaction by invoking either a different site, like Béroul's Morrois forest, or a different time, as in the case of Friend's Golden Age. In contrast to those spatial or temporal representations of natural law, Chrétien's *Conte du Graal* contains a markedly distinct depiction of pristine life. Unlike Tristan and Yseut, Perceval and his mother are neither transgressors nor fugitives, but refugees who took shelter in a remote vale of the Welsh forest. Unlike Friend's bygone Golden Age, the vale near Valbone is a site that coexists with the realm of chivalric aggression, a site where hunting as "chase" is the accepted mode of food gathering. The opposition between the Welsh forest and the outside world is thus not between frugivore and carnivore culture, but between two vastly different uses of venatic expertise. Because hunting outside the Welsh vale fails to limit and contain violence, every knight in the land of Logres, regardless of his allegiance, qualifies as a "regressive" figure.

Proof of the regressive character of traditional chivalry is the crucial importance of Gauvain's horse by way of confirming his status as a worthy knightly "hunter." As he proceeds to Escavalon, Gauvain sees a herd of hinds grazing at the edge of a forest and endeavors to chase them:

> Et si lor fist tans tors et guiches
> Que une blanche en entreprist
> Lez un ronschoi et si li mist
> Sor le col sa lance en travers.
> Et la bische salt come cers,
> Si li estort, et il aprés.
> (Ed. Roach, ll. 5676–81)

And he hunted them with such cunning and guile that he caught a white one beside a thorn bush and laid his lance across its neck. And the hind leapt like a stag and escaped from him; and he leapt after her.

Like the pursuit of knights, the tracking down of wild animals represents for Gauvain an opportunity to prove his prowess.[31] When his mount fails him, as it does in this scene, or when it is stolen from him (by Greoreas; ll. 7072–74), Gauvain finds himself deprived of his mobility, hence of his capacity to show his excellence as the best of all knightly "pursuers."

That Gauvain undertakes to chase the white stag with his lance (a choice of weapon clearly inappropriate for deer hunting) points to what Norris J. Lacy calls "the trivialization of chivalry" under Arthur's rule.[32] According to Lacy, the crisis of chivalry in Chrétien's romance invokes a conflict between Arthurian culture and a non- or post-Arthurian culture, in connection with the role of the Grail myth in introducing a new ideal of chivalry. Inverting the terms of Lacy's contrast, Jean Markale opposes the primitive Grail culture and Arthur's more advanced, agrarian culture.[33] At the core of Markale's argument is his assertion, based on the fact that the hunt of a stag is a motif that appears in almost all the texts of the Grail corpus, that the Grail legend dates back to a civilization of hunters of cervidae when men survived adverse climatic conditions by chasing reindeer.

Despite their inherent contradiction, these interpretations concur in focusing on Chrétien's romance as the locus of a conflict between two types of culture. In view of the ubiquity of predatory pursuits in the land of Logres, however, the *Conte*'s social landscape seems marked not by distinction and conflict between two different cultures, but by cultural homogenization. It is precisely the homogeneous character of chivalry as exalted in both the Arthurian and the Grail discourses that increases the chance that Perceval will become an "ogre" and outdo, by imitating, the cruelest of the knights who inhabit the "savage" land of traditional chivalric culture. Thus the conflict between nature and culture articulated in the narrative has a political dimension. In contrast to Chrétien's previous narratives, where the "law of Camelot" allegedly eradicates the violence that lurks in the wilderness,[34] violence and hostility inhabit every site of the *Conte*'s landscape. Contradicting the king's claim that his court is testimony to the pacific quality of royal culture, his opponents glorify the superior value of those who find themselves forced to take refuge in nature. Center and periphery thus function as two emblems of the dispute over power that is at the core of Chrétien's romance, a dispute that deludes Perceval into believing that Arthur's court or, conversely, the hermit's natural shelter represents the ultimate site of acculturation.

Wolfram's *Parzival* discloses, forcefully if perhaps unwittingly, that the realm of traditional chivalry is the locus not of different cultural stages, but of an all-encompassing quest for power. Although Wolfram "did not wish to put too strongly the idea that the Grail could be the object—'quarry'—of a hunt with all of a hunt's frenetic haste,"[35] the simultaneously literal and metaphorical meaning of words such as *jagen* and *bejagen* ("to hunt down," to "quest for," "to win") contributes to an identification of Parzival's quest for the Grail as track (*slâ*),[36] in the cynegetic sense of the word (that of a trail fresh with blood). Parzival's gradual progress toward his preordained destiny is thus presented in hunting imagery, as when God's trail[37] leads him to Kahenis, who exhorts Parzival to follow the "scent,"[38] and to the hermit Trevrizent, whose guidance prods Parzival on the "sacred trail."[39] The legendary wild hunter (Hellequin in the French tradition, Ërlkönig in German, and Arlequin in Italian) provides further evidence of the political rather than otherworldly or Christian significance of the quest for the Grail in Chrétien's narrative. Obliterating the infernal origin of Hellequin,[40] the figure of the wild hunter is reinscribed in twelfth- and thirteenth-century fiction as an emblem of the drive to conquer characteristic of traditional chivalric culture. Hunting imagery ended in symbolizing the workings of royal authority, as invoked in the last syllable of the word *Hellequin* (when "quin" is read as "king").[41] In Chrétien's first extant romance as in his last one, royal discourse maintains that the forest is a refuge for anarchists and violent individuals: it is therefore just that "wolves" be tracked down and prosecuted. However, that Arthur is not a lamb but himself a "wolf" is indirectly revealed, in Jean de Meun's *Romance of the Rose*, by False Seeming's admission that "Dehors semblons aigneaus pitables, / Dedanz somes lous ravisables" (we look like pitiful lambs, but are, within, ravening wolves"; ll. 11687–88).[42]

The problem facing Perceval and his mother, therefore, is that the forest is not truly "wild and lonely" because it can easily be crossed by wandering knights, such as the five characters introduced in the first episode, as well as the fugitives they are pursuing. Knightly mobility, which reduces the distance between forest and court, is a crucial factor in imparting to the forest of chivalric romance an ambiguous significance, precluding any romantic or ecological interpretations. Far from being a site untouched by people, the forest in contemporary imaginative literature is a primary locus of chivalric encounters. Damsels in distress seek a protector, questing knights go in search of adventures, heroes demonstrate their prowess, and kings confirm their preeminence. The invasion of forest by court is the reason for the ubiquity of venatic imagery as a symbol of the organizing principles of traditional chivalric society. The fears of Perceval's mother, which focus on the regressive aspect of traditional chivalry—in either its Arthurian or Grail definition—justify and explain her attempt to propose to her son a more civilized form of knightly existence.

Nonsacrificial Interaction

The value of his mother's instruction is that it provides Perceval with a mode of behavior conducive to the development of the self on both the private and public level. In her view, chivalry is neither a privilege reserved for elitist brotherhoods nor a function in support of factional ambitions, but should be, instead, the agency of individual and social betterment. In questioning a definition of *loi* and *langage* that promotes rivalry rather than communication and reconciliation, she displays her understanding of the resemblance, in terms of goals and strategies, between Arthur's law and the law according to the Grail messengers. The advice she gives her son at the moment of his departure from the Welsh vale near Valbone thus focuses on the body politic and organized religion as two homologous concepts of social order, to the extent that both exacerbate a vision of the self as victim and of the other as persecutor.

The significance of the mother's instruction therefore lies in her assessment of the entire established institution. Social law (as represented by Arthur) and religious law (in the Grail messengers' discourse) are similar precisely because of the emphasis they place on "transgression" as the sole means of distinguishing the realm of right from the realm of wrong. But because the notion of transgression varies according to the perspective of each rival discourse, the resulting distinction between "victims" and "persecutors" reveals itself to be nothing other than a symmetrical, albeit inverted, vision of the other. In that sense, the established institution jeopardizes knowledge of the self by predisposing the individual to appraise his or her value strictly in reference to the value of others, thus contributing to a vision of society as essentially competitive.

Perceval's mother seeks to offer her son a different view of social order and of Perceval's place in the world. To become a responsible and worthy knight requires that he assist ladies and damsels in distress, associate with the good members of the chivalric realm, and conduct himself as God's faithful and obedient servant:

> "Sor tote rien vos weil proier
> Que a l'eglise et al mostier

> Alez proier nostre Seignor
> Qu'en cest siecle vos doinst honor,
> Et si vos laist si contenir
> Qu'a bone fin puissiez venir."
> "Mere," fait il, "que est eglise?"
>
> (Ed. Roach, ll. 567–73)

"Above all, I want to beg you to pray to our Lord in chapel and church to give you honor in this world and grant you that you so lead your life that you may come to a good end." "Mother," he said, "what is a church?"

Last but not least in the tripartite list of advice that Perceval's mother gives to her son is her appeal that he conduct himself like a good Christian. Although a number of scholars, such as Paul Imbs, praise the piety of Perceval's mother, others, on the basis of Perceval's reaction to her last counsel, criticize her for having neglected to teach her son the principles of religion.[43] A similar contradiction marks the interpretation of Perceval's religious disposition. According to Carlo Pellegrini, Perceval, and hence Chrétien himself, are profoundly devout Christians. But Margaret Hurley agrees with Per Nykrog's assertion that "in the world of Chrétien . . . the religious dimension is either absent or [in the *Conte du Graal*] conventional."[44] At issue is not only the religious value of maternal instruction, but also, in a broader sense, the role of Perceval's mother in ensuring or hindering his success as a knight. Why does she place last in her list the two counsels regarding proper communication between knights and between knights and God? Why does she reveal only in extremis the meaning of a church?

The answer to these questions lies in the institutional resemblance between secular chivalry and religious chivalry in the idealizing discourse of the two contending parties. The episode that narrates Perceval's meeting with a damsel in a pavilion, which marks his entry into traditional chivalric culture, illustrates this similarity. In the morning following his departure from the Welsh forest, he comes upon a pavilion pitched in a beautiful meadow:

> Li vallés vers le tref ala,
> Et dist ains que il venist la:
> "Diex, or voi je vostre maison.
> Or feroie jou mesprison,
> Se aorer ne vos aloie.
> Voir dist ma mere tote voie
> Qui me dist que mostiers estoit

> La plus bele chose qui soit,
> Et me dist que ja ne trovaisse
> Mostier qu'aorer n'i alaisse
> Le Creator en cui je croi.
> Je li irai priier par foi
> Qu'il me doinst anqui a mengier,
> Que j'en aroie grant mestier."
> (Ed. Roach, ll. 653–66)

The boy rode toward the pavilion and said before he reached it: "God, I see your house. I would do wrong if I did not go worship you. My mother told me the truth when she said that a chapel is the most beautiful thing on earth, and she told me also that whenever I came across a chapel, I should go worship the creator in whom I believe. I shall go and pray to Him, by my faith, that He may give me food today, for I am in dire need of it."

Inside the pavilion Perceval finds a young girl, sleeping. That he mistakes a pavilion for a church contributes to Chrétien's humorous portrayal of Perceval as *niche*. Perceval's confusion also reveals the existence of a disturbing resemblance between a typically secular site, the courtly pavilion, and a typically religious site, a consecrated church. If pavilions and churches look alike to Perceval, it is because he has never before seen either type of edifice. More important, this similarity discloses the homogeneous character of aristocratic culture (emblematized here by the courtly pavilion) and ecclesiastical culture. His mother's fear at the moment of Perceval's departure appears to take this similarity into account. Her response to Perceval's questions ("What is a church?" "What is a chapel?"; ll. 573, 577) indicates that, in her view, the institutional world outside the Welsh vale advances a sacrificial vision of order, one that fosters aggression and prosecution. Like a church, a chapel, she says, is

> Une maison bele et saintisme
> Ou il a cors sains et tresors,
> Si i sacrefion le cors
> Jhesucrist, le prophete sainte
> Cui juïf fisent honte mainte.
> Traïs fu et jugiez a tort,
> Et soffri angoisse de mort
> Por les homes et por les fames,
> Qu'en infer aloient les ames
> Quant eles partoient des cors,
> Et il les en regeta fors.

> Si fu a l'estache liiez,
> Batus et puis crucefiiez,
> Et porta corones d'espines.
> Por oïr messes et matines
> Et por cel Seignor aorer
> Vos lo jou al mostier aler.
> (Ed. Roach, ll. 578–94)

a beautiful and most holy house where there are holy relics and treasures, and where we sacrifice the body of Jesus Christ, the holy prophet, to whom the Jews did many a shame. He was betrayed and wrongfully judged and suffered death's anguish for all men and women, whose souls went to hell when they left their bodies, but He set them free. He was bound to a stake, beaten, and then nailed on a cross and made to wear a crown of thorns. To hear masses and matins and to worship this lord, I want you to go to chapels.

To all appearances, her depiction of organized religion anticipates the explanation provided in the hermitage episode.[45] Central to the devotional practices of a good Christian is the mass, celebrated in the house of worship, where believers commemorate the sacrifice of Christ's body. A major difference, however, distinguishes her account from the eremetic instruction articulated in the last episode of Perceval's story. Although Perceval's mother alludes to the Jews' involvement in Christ's Passion ("juïf fisent honte mainte"), she does not identify them as Christ's persecutors, unlike the pilgrims, who state that the Jews "en la crois le leverent" and should be "tüer come chiens" (raised Him to the cross and should be killed like dogs; ll. 6265, 6293). Her use of the passive voice ("Traïs fu et jugiez a tort"; "fu a l'estache liiez") suggests that humanity as a whole ("sacrefion le cors" in version T; "sacrifie l'an le cors" in version A) bears this responsibility, and not a particular individual or faction. She thus reveals to Perceval, in extremis, the function of organized religion, but in a manner that should prevent him from using Christ's Passion as a justification for people's violence against other people.

Without assigning to Chrétien an anachronistic capacity to read the New Testament as a call to end human violence, this nonsacrificial character of the mother's account of Christ's Passion is nonetheless remarkable. In contrast with traditional exegesis, which tends to legitimize the prosecution of Christ's persecutors by invoking Matthew's statement that Christ came on earth not to bring peace, but the sword of division (Matthew 10:34–36),[46] she demystifies any and all forms

of military ideology, especially those that exalt chivalry in support of
the imperatives of revenge. Perceval's entry into the realm of culture
indicates the influential role of maternal nurturing in preventing him,
successfully at first, from imitating the antagonistic behavior that is
the mark of the inhabitants of the land of "ogres." Although his treat-
ment of the Pavilion Damsel, which is a direct result of his ignorance
of courtly etiquette, leads her to interpret his clumsiness as a sign of
aggressive intentions, Perceval remains unaware of the "transgressive"
character of his behavior. His subsequent action is noteworthy. As he
realizes that he has not breakfasted and is dying of hunger,

> Un bouchel trove plain de vin
> Et un hanap d'argent selonc,
> Et voit sor un trossel de jonc
> Une toaille blanche et noeve.
> Il le sozlieve et desoz trove
> Trois bons pastez de chievrol fres,
> Ne li anuie pas cis me.
> Por le fain qui forment l'angoisse,
> Un des pastez devant lui froisse
> Et mengüe par grant talent.
> (Ed. Roach, ll. 738–47)

he finds a cask full of wine and beside it a silver goblet, and then he sees a
fresh white cloth on a bundle of rushes. He picks it up and finds underneath
three fresh-made venison meat pies, which does not displease him. To quell
the hunger that besets him, he breaks open one of the pies and eats with a
vengeance.

In the opening episode of his story, as in this one, Perceval's de-
pendence on his senses is a major and at this point humorous factor
in distinguishing him from traditional chivalric culture. Compared to
the Pavilion Damsel, for whom Perceval's lack of manners indicates
that he is a dangerous individual, the boy neither notices nor inter-
prets her behavior. If his ignorance of social conventions is a source of
tension, this results from the damsel's superior knowledge concerning
"proper" conduct. Yet her expertise at interpretation also leads her to
misjudge Perceval. Both characters here emblematize the difference be-
tween natural law, in reference to a mode of life in which eating and
drinking are spontaneous, life-sustaining activities, and social law, a
mode of communication that, at least in the *Conte*'s traditional chivalric
realm, contributes to a perception of the Other as a potential enemy.

Perceval's behavior as he progresses through the land of "ogres" demonstrates that, until his adventure at the Grail castle, maternal instruction exerts a preponderant influence on his capacity to act as a free and autonomous individual. His action at Biaurepaire confirms the value of his mother's advice in encouraging her son to entertain nonpredatory relationships not only with knights, but also with ladies.

Beyond Reciprocal "Devourment"

As noted in Chapter 1, the reduced role of love in the *Conte* in comparison with Chrétien's earlier works suggests that the primary problem developed in the author's last romance arises not from the presence of conflicting codes of behavior in matters of love and chivalry, but from two contradictory definitions of proper chivalric conduct. In a society such as that depicted in Chrétien's *Conte*, which is essentially governed by aggression and rivalry, love is not a primary concern. More specifically, love is no longer integral to the maturation of the individual, precisely because in this pre- or anti-individualistic society such categories as the "psychological subject" and "character" are not relevant.[47] From the standpoint of the two principal contending factions, for example, Perceval is not assessed as an autonomous entity, but as the potential agent of their respective triumphs in attaining dominance. For Perceval to develop into a mature and responsible knight therefore depends on his capacity to avoid absorption into the realm of contentious chivalry by moving away from the loci (Arthur's court, the Grail castle, the hermitage) associated with the history of strife that inscribes itself in the social landscape of the *Conte*. Biaurepaire, Blancheflor's domain, provides him with such an opportunity insofar as the misfortune besetting Blancheflor and her people calls upon Perceval's personal, rather than factional, involvement in their predicament. Biaurepaire thus constitutes a privileged locus to the extent that, in contrast to the other places charting Perceval's wanderings in the realm of traditional chivalry, it is the sole site where the *niche* is offered the opportunity to use his prowess for defensive and protective purposes. That his action elicits reciprocal love between him and Blancheflor indicates the centrality of the Biaurepaire episode with respect to Perceval's potential role in inaugurating a new kind of chivalric community, away from the "law of the tombs" and in support of peace and prosperity.

The unique character of the *Conte du Graal* thus consists not of reducing or suppressing the love motif that is typical of courtly romance, but, as James Dauphiné observes,[48] of emphasizing the disparity between the ideal articulated in the courtly tradition and the often violent character of the relationships between knights and ladies. In Dauphiné's view, the fact that love is no longer the principal stimulus to chivalric prowess in Chrétien's last romance reflects a new conception of fiction writing that acknowledges the strictly imaginary value of traditional chivalric romance.[49] Yet if love has a different function in the *Conte*, the reason is not, or not merely, that Chrétien recognizes the mendacious character of the courtly ideal as one incompatible with chivalric practices. More specifically, the narration demystifies the ideal of courtly love and of chivalry alike, thereby disclosing the significance of the *quest* (for love *and* for glory) as *conquest*. "Forest" and "court," in that sense, are homologous, not only because the forest is the stage on which courtly heroes parade their value as both knights and "lovers," but primarily because of the predatory nature of what conventional usage, for lack of a better term, designates as "courtly love."

Eros as Hubris

Perceval's first adventure after his departure from the vale of his childhood discloses the incompatibility of love (understood as affective reciprocity) and chivalry in traditional knightly culture. His behavior leads the Pavilion Damsel to assume that the uncouth adolescent has aggressive intentions. If this stranger does not follow the rules of the game, he must come as a "hunter" and view her as his prey.

However, her first words to Perceval reveal that the primary source of her fear is not Perceval himself, but an invisible third party: "Vallet," fait ele, "tien ta voie. / Fui! que mes amis ne te voie" ("Young man," she says, "be on your way. Flee! lest my friend see you"; ed. Roach, ll. 691–92). Whereas Perceval remains oblivious to the existence of the damsel's lover, she assesses the situation from her lover's perspective, thus making him a threatening presence. The scene elaborates a contrast between two types of relationships. The first refers to Perceval's literal perception, which prompts him to see only two individuals face to face (himself and the damsel). The second reflects the damsel's triangular perspective, inducing her to look at Perceval through her lover's eyes. Traditional "courtly love" typically consists of a configuration that comprises two hunters and a prey. Perceval's *nicheté*, however, alters this traditional configuration, which here involves two preys (the damsel and Perceval) and a hunter, that is, her lover. The latter is likely, out of jealousy, to punish her and pursue Perceval, hence her reaction when Perceval endeavors to take her ring:[50]

> Et cele pleure et dist: "Vallet,
> N'en porte pas mon anelet,
> Que j'en seroie malbaillie
> Et tu en perdroies la vie,
> Que qu'il tardast, jel te promet."
> Li vallés a son cuer ne met
> Rien nule de che que il ot,
> Mais de che que jeüné ot
> Moroit de fain a male fin.
>
> (Ed. Roach, ll. 729–37)

And she weeps and says: "Young man, do not take my ring, for I could be ill treated for it, and you could lose your life, sooner or later, I promise you." The boy does not take to heart a word of what he heard, but, because he had not eaten, was feeling consumed with hunger.

That the damsel dreads her lover's reaction indicates that her *amis* is more dominating than loving. Beneath the damsel's lover lurks a possessive tyrant.

The damsel's fear is well founded, as proved by her lover's accusatory behavior when he returns to the pavilion. Seeing the tracks Perceval left, he proceeds to interrogate the damsel:

> Si dist: "Damoisele, je croi,
> A ces ensaignes que chi voi,
> Que chevalier a eü chi."
> "Non a, sire, je vos affi;
> Mais un vallet galois i ot,
> Anïeus et vilain et sot,
> Qui a de vostre vin beü
> Tant com lui plot et bel li fu,
> E menga de vos trois pastez."
>
> (Ed. Roach, ll. 787–95)

And he says: "Maiden, I believe from these signs I see that a knight has been here." "There was none, sir, I promise you; but a Welsh boy was here, a tiresome, uncouth, and foolish one, who drank as much of your wine as he pleased and enjoyed it and ate some of your three meat pies."

The damsel's line of defense, which consists of insisting that no *chevalier* came to her pavilion, only a *vallet*, posits an implicit equivalence between chivalry and aggression. In acknowledging that, by definition, knightly conduct hides predatory intentions, her lover also acknowledges, albeit unwittingly, the proprietary character of his relationship with his "loved" one. This suggests that he prizes the damsel to the extent that she is desired by other knights, leading him to ignore her claim that the visitor was only a *vallet*. The following exchange confirms the lover's rivalrous vision of the Other, effecting the transformation of Perceval, the uncouth boy, into an invisible yet threatening knightly force. Her admission that the visitor went away with her ring provokes great anger in him:

> "Mais je quit qu'il i ot plus fait.
> Se plus i ot, nel celez ja."
> "Sire," dist ele, "il me baisa."
> "Baisa?" "Voire, jel vos di bien,
> Mais ce fu maleoit gre mien."
> "Ainçois vos sist, et si vos plot;
> Onques nul contredit n'i ot,"
> Fait cil cui jalosie angoisse.
> (Ed. Roach, ll. 808–15)

"But I think he did more. If there was more, do not hide it." "Sir," she said, "he kissed me." "Kissed you?" "Yes, I tell you the truth, but it was against my will." "On the contrary, it was as you wished and pleased you well; there was no resistance on your part," he said, tormented by jealousy.

As a punishment for her wicked ways, the lover declares that her horse will not be cared for nor will she be allowed to change the clothes she is wearing, even if this means she will have to follow him naked and on foot, "Tant que la teste en avrai prise;/Ja n'en ferai autre justise" (until I have his head, for I will settle for no less; ll. 831–32). Her accuser ends his threats by sitting down and eating. Unlike Perceval, for whom eating has a strictly nutritional value, the lover's action is, in the context of the reciprocal devourment characterizing interaction in the land of "ogres," also a symbolic gesture. His rage toward the rival "knight" who visited the damsel discloses her function as a prize that may alternately confirm or endanger, as in the present case, his status in the chivalric hierarchy. Suspicion, aggression, and self-interest thus play a similar part in the relationships among *ami chevalier* as between *chevalier* and *amies*.

A subsequent episode in Perceval's story brings the trio back together. The damsel is now in such a sorry state that Perceval fails to recognize the pale, wan, and wretched woman ("descoloree et tainte / Et si chaitive"; ll. 3747–48) he meets on his path and hears lamenting:

> Diex, ensi com tu le sez bien
> Que je n'en ai deservi rien,
> M'envoies tu, se il te siet,
> Qui de ceste paine m'aliet;
> Ou tu de celui me delivre
> Qui a tel honte me fait vivre,
> N'en lui nule merchi ne truis
> Ne vive eschaper ne li puis
> Ne il ne me par velt ocirre.
> Je ne sai por coi il desirre
> Ma compaignie en tel maniere,
> Se por che non qu'il a si chiere
> Ma honte et ma maleürté.
>
> (Ed. Roach, ll. 3757–69)

God, as you know very well, I have done nothing to deserve [this treatment], so send me, should you so please, someone who will free me from this torment; or may you deliver me from the one who makes me live in such shame, in whom I find no mercy, from whom I cannot escape alive, and who refuses to kill me. I do not know why he wants my company in these conditions, unless he relishes my shame and my misfortune.

The damsel's complaint eloquently summarizes the workings of "courtly love" in traditional chivalric culture. Even in her present sorry state, she serves as a decoy to attract other knights, thus providing her lover with the opportunity to challenge his rivals. A "good" knight would undoubtedly feel the urge to avenge her for the obvious mistreatment she endures, thus enabling her lover to prove himself a "better" knight by defending his possession. This is why she presses Perceval to flee while there is still time,

> Que li Orgueilleus de la Lande,
> Qui nule chose ne demande
> Se bataille non et mellee,
> Ne sorviegne a ceste assamblee;
> Que s'il vos trovoit chi alués,
> Certes, il vos ocirroit lués.
> Tant li poise, quant nus m'areste,
> Que nus n'en puet porter la teste,

> Qui en parole me retiegne,
> Poroec que il a tans i viegne.
> N'a gaires qu'il en ocist un.
> (Ed. Roach, ll. 3817–27)

before the Proud Knight of the Heath [Orgueilleux de la Lande], who asks nothing but battle and combat, stumbles across our meeting; for if he should find you here, truly, he would kill you on the spot. He becomes so irate whenever anyone stops me that no one who speaks to me can escape with his head, should he arrive in time. He killed one just a while ago.

The discovery that he is the cause of her present suffering persuades Perceval to stay and confront her irascible and volatile lover. Orgueilleux's thirst for battle and combat is immediately confirmed. Riding out of the wood, he comes "come une foldre / Par le sablon et par la poldre" (like a thunderbolt across the sand and dust; ll. 3833–34) and, although he does not yet know Perceval's identity, challenges him at once. Orgueilleux's defeat testifies to Perceval's role as peacemaker: not only does he remember and obey Gornemant's command never to kill a defeated knight (ll. 3933–36), he also follows his mother's advice to protect ladies and maidens by urging Orgueilleux to repent and make amends for his mistreatment of the damsel. Thanks to Perceval's mediation, the triangle ceases to be a locus of hostility. However, a new triangular configuration emerges, in reference to the absent yet centralizing character of Arthur, to whom Perceval sends Orgueilleux as hostage. Thus, the proprietary relationship between Orgueilleux and his lady is not so much eradicated as it is replaced by another proprietary relationship, one that places Orgueilleux de la Lande under Arthur's control. The outcome of the episode suggests, by anticipation, that the protocols of traditional chivalry will gradually undermine the benefits of maternal instruction.

The role of pursuer is not reserved for the male members of chivalric society, as the relationship between Meliant and Tibaut's elder daughter demonstrates. Her "love" for Meliant is not free, for, as we saw, she values him to the extent that his status as both her father's overlord and the winner of the tournament will enhance and confirm her own at the court of Tintagueil. Courtly love takes the form of an investment that imposes on the loved one the task of proving himself a superior knight. Whether between knights, between ladies, or between ladies and knights, relationships are governed by the desire to dominate, hence the plethora of Orgueilleux and Orgueilleuses in the land of "ogres" and the unstable character of their interaction. In the hierarchical construct that characterizes the chivalric realm outside the vale of Perceval's childhood, one's superiority as "hunter" is only temporary, as is demonstrated when Gauvain overthrows Meliant and effects the younger sister's triumph over her sibling.

If love and chivalry combine, therefore, it is because amorous and chivalric pursuits have a common goal of serving the imperatives of pride and revenge.[51] The motives inducing Orgueilleuse de Logres to humiliate every knight she encounters are symptomatic. In the episode that narrates Gauvain's meeting with Greoreas, she sides with the latter against Gauvain, challenging Arthur's nephew to recapture Greoreas's horse from Orgueilleux de Galvoie. Later on in the text, however, she sides with Orgueilleux de Galvoie, whom Gauvain proceeds to defeat, only to hear Orgueilleuse make a sarcastic comment about armed encounters in which "li febles abat le fort" (the weak defeat the strong; l. 8433). By virtue of her tendency to titillate the vanity of those she encounters, Orgueilleuse plays a major role in provoking aggression among the knightly members of the land of "ogres," including Gauvain. Only in the final section of Chrétien's narrative do we learn the cause of her hostile behavior. As she tells Gauvain, Guiromelant killed her true love,

> Puis me quida tant d'onor faire
> Qu'a s'amor me quida atraire,
> Mais onques rien ne li valut,
> Car al plus tost que il me lut
> De sa compaignie m'emblai
> Et a celui me rasamblai
> A cui tu m'as jehui tolue,
> Dont il ne m'est a une alue.
> Mais de mon premerain ami,
> Quant mors le desevra de mi,
> Ai si longuement esté fole
> Et de si estolte parole
> Et si vilaine et si musarde
> C'onques ne me prenoie garde
> Cui j'alaisse contralïant.
> (Ed. Roach, ll. 8939–53)

then thought to do me great honor by enticing me with his love, but this got him nowhere, for as soon as I could, I escaped from him and joined company with the one [Orgueilleux de Galvoie] from whom you took me today and who means little to me. But ever since death took my first love away from me, I have behaved madly and have said many a rude, wicked, and foolish word, without paying any heed to the one whom I was challenging.

Orgueilleuse's story testifies to the predatory character of "amorous" pairings in the realm of traditional chivalric culture. Their thirst for domination inspires all the *ami chevalier* to act as pursuers, and knightly violence in turn prompts their prey to respond in kind. In the triangular configuration that characterizes social interaction outside the Welsh vale near Valbone, pairing is, in most cases,[52] an alliance that serves to exact revenge against a third party. "Courtly love" is thus part of the contractual type of relationship that marks traditional chivalric culture. Under the rule of Eros the hunter, knights and ladies chase one another not to attain love, but to capture the most prestigious quarry.

Reciprocity as Consensual Exchange: Biaurepaire

The ubiquity of antagonistic relationships in traditional chivalric culture prompts Perceval's mother to wish to protect her son from the realm of reciprocal devourment by providing him with instruction that initiates him into a nonaggressive mode of communication. Once in possession of chivalric armor, Perceval is not only supposed to assist ladies in distress, but also to seek the company of worthy men and pay his respect to God. None of the three elements of the maternal counsel can be separated because they form, as a whole, a model of conduct promoting peaceful alliance and productive union. Unlike Gornemant and unlike the hermit, Perceval's mother does not privilege one type of communication above another, precisely because her vision of social order is neither competitive nor prosecutive. In her view, knights and ladies will become *amis* only when they abandon a mode of interaction focusing on conquest, whether territorial or human.

With ladies, for example, Perceval should not use force, thus avoiding the tyrannical type of relationship exalted in the courtly ideal:

> Se vos trovez ne pres ne loing
> Dame qui d'aïe ait besoi[n]g
> Ne pucele desconseillie,
> La vostre aïde appareillie
> Lor soit, s'ele[s] vos en requierent.
> (Ed. Roach, ll. 533–37)

If you encounter, near or far, a lady in need of help, or a maiden in distress, prepare yourself to aid them, if they call upon you.

An honorable knight does not perceive women in terms of "prize" and "prestigious quarry," but uses his chivalric expertise to protect them, if they so ask. According to Perceval's mother, love between an honorable knight and his lady is grounded in mutual affection and direct communication:

> S'ele a anel en son doi
> Ne a sa corroie almosniere,
> Se par amor ou par proiere
> Le vos done, bon m'ert et bel
> Que vos em portez son anel.
> (Ed. Roach, ll. 550–54)

If she has a ring on her finger or a purse at her belt, and for love or your asking she should give it to you, then in my view it would be good and fair that you should wear her ring.

Perceval's love for this hypothetical lady should blossom outside the triangular configuration that characterizes interaction in traditional chivalry and outside the parasitic interferences imposed by the law of the tombs.[53] At the core of maternal instruction is thus her recommendation that Perceval form with his loved one a consensual, and not a contractual, type of union.

The episode narrating Perceval's adventure at Biaurepaire and his encounter with Blancheflor, which occurs immediately after the protagonist's dubbing by Gornemant, provides Perceval with an opportunity to act on maternal instruction. On his way out from the nobleman's house, Chrétien's protagonist expresses his great desire "Qu'il a sa mere venir puisse" (to return to his mother, l. 1701), signaling that Gornemant's attempt to sever Perceval's ties with his mother left no lasting impression. That the young man heeds his mother's counsel over that of the nobleman appears to be confirmed by his decision to ride through the "forés soutaines, / Car plus i set qu'a terres plaines" (lonely forests, for he is more at ease there than in the open fields; ll. 1703–4). This instinctive preference for the nurturing environment of his childhood enables Perceval to distance himself from the open space of culture, that is, from the stage of ancestral rivalry and lineal prosecution. He soon catches sight of a castle that is "fort et bien seant" (strong and well situated; l. 1707), yet in state of disrepair. The drawbridge is about to collapse; the damsel who greets Perceval is "maigre et pale" (thin and pale; l. 1724); lack of food and sleep marks the retainers who unlock the gate for him. Within the castle, the street are "degastees" (empty; l. 1753) and the houses "decheües" (in ruin; l. 1754), with not a man or woman anywhere. In the two abbeys of the town, the nuns are "esbahies" (distraught; l. 1758) and the monks "esgarez" (bewildered; l. 1759). The walls are "crevez" and "fendus" (crumbling and broken; l. 1762), towers and houses are "descovertes" (roofless; l. 1763), and there is no bread, pastry, wine, or ale. In short, both the land that surrounds the castle, which is described as "terre gaste" (bare and deserted; l. 1709), and the "gaste" (waste; l. 1771) within its walls point to Biaurepaire as a "wasteland."

Biaurepaire therefore shares with the Grail domain a state of desolation and devastation. In view of the narrative juxtaposition of these two episodes in Perceval's story, Biaurepaire seems to constitute a preparatory stage for Perceval's later task as champion of the Grail. Yet a major difference distinguishes his performance at Biaurepaire and at the Grail castle. Whereas Perceval successfully undertakes the restoration of Blancheflor's domain, he fails, according to the Grail messengers, to achieve that of the Grail. Why is he able to act as a worthy knight in one case and not in the other? The answer to this question lies in the messengers' partisan interpretation of Perceval's behavior at the Grail castle, inducing them to accuse the protagonist of unworthy conduct. The Biaurepaire episode discloses the fallacious character of the messengers' exegesis, whose goal, as we saw, is to undercut the value of Perceval's other adventures, including those that appear to support Arthur's rule. Not only does Perceval's action at Biaurepaire testify to his capacity to behave altruistically, thus belying the Grail messengers' accusatory discourse; the episode, which responds to the program of regenerative knightly activities proposed by Perceval's mother, also represents a positive counterpoint to Arthur's order of chivalry. The Biaurepaire adventure is thus of crucial importance for the interpretation of Chrétien's romance, for there we find the key to the enigma of this first Grail text.

The two episodes share a number of elements, such as the isolation marking the domains of Biaurepaire and the Grail, the misfortune that afflicts their inhabitants, and Perceval's silent attitude. These similarities highlight the profoundly antithetical effect that Biaurepaire and the Grail site have on Perceval's discovery of self and Other. Curious about the sorry state of Biaurepaire, just as he will be curious about the procession that crosses the Grail castle, Perceval decides against asking any questions because, in both instances, he remembers well Gornemant's warning against excessive talking. Although Blancheflor's knights pity their guest for being afflicted by dumbness, she realizes

> Que il ne li diroit ja mot,
> S'ele ne l'araisnoit avant.
> Lors dist molt debonairemant:
> "Sire, dont venistes vos hui?"
> (Ed. Roach, ll. 1880–83)

he was not going to say a word to her until she addressed him first. And so she said most courteously: "Sir, where did you come from today?"

Out of consideration for their guest, Perceval's hosts at Biaurepaire opt not to burden him with their worries, inviting him instead to share their meager meal. Perceval's treatment by his Grail hosts presents a striking contrast. If he is the object of a sumptuous reception, this is a measure of the wealth of the domain rather than a mark of generosity. That Perceval's hosts force him to accept a sword confirms that, unlike that of the people of Biaurepaire, their hospitality is not gratuitous.[54] Moreover, Blancheflor's correct interpretation of Perceval's muteness as a sign of inexperience reveals, by anticipation, the groundless nature of the Grail messengers' accusatory interpretation of his silence at the Grail castle. Biaurepaire therefore belies the moral significance of the Grail episode.

A second notable similarity between the two domains is their representation as wastelands. Although Chrétien's text does not directly qualify the Grail site as such, the wound that afflicts its two kings, together with both the cousin's and the Hideous Damsel's accounts of its misfortune, indicate a lack of manpower, if not wealth. Yet, like the hermit's exegesis, these two messengers' respective evocations of the Grail's tragic history also obfuscate the origin of doom. The purpose of the Grail representatives is not to enlighten Perceval, but to present him with a mysterious, hence attractive and worthy, chivalric mission. In contrast to the opaque nature of the Grail castle's doom, the sorry state of Biaurepaire is eminently visible, as the reason for its plight is specific. We learn from Blancheflor that a most evil knight (Enguigeron, who acts on behalf of his lord, Clamadeu of the Isles) has laid siege to this place for an entire winter and summer ("A siege a chi devant esté / Tout un iver et un esté," ll. 2013–14) and that tomorrow, unless God intervenes, this castle will be surrendered to him ("demain, se Diex ne le fait, / Li sera cis chastiax rendus," ll. 2022–23). Her assessment of the siege discloses the predatory character of Clamadeu's attack. His goal is to capture not only the castle, but Blancheflor herself:

> Clamadeus, qui avoir me quide,
> Ja ne m'avra, s'il ne m'a wide
> De vie et d'ame, en nule fin;
> Car je garç en un mien escrin
> Un coutel tot de fin acier,
> Que me volrai el cuer fichier.
>
> (Ed. Roach, ll. 2029–34)

Clamadeu, who hopes to have me, never will in any way, except bereft of life and soul. For I keep in a jewel case of mine a knife of the finest steel, which I plan to plunge into my heart.

Compared to the wound that afflicts the two Grail kings, which invokes the law committing an heir to avenge his ancestors, Blancheflor's determination to kill herself rather than be subjected to Clamadeu's tyranny signifies a negation of both past and future.[55]

That Blancheflor reveals her suicidal intent to Perceval suggests, however, that she still nurtures the hope of a different outcome. Her visit to Perceval on the night before Clamadeu's decisive attack is not entirely innocent because

> Ne vint plorer desor sa face,
> Que que ele entendant li face,
> Fors por che qu'ele li meïst
> En corage qu'il emprëist
> La bataille.
>
> (Ed. Roach, ll. 2041–45)

she had come and wept on his face for no other reason, despite what she gave him to believe, than to induce him to take up the battle.

Is Perceval's gracious hostess herself turning into a pursuer? Contrary to this suggestion, several elements indicate that Blancheflor's ulterior motives in coming to Perceval's chamber contain none of the self-interested components that characterize traditional interaction between knights and ladies. The urgent nature of Blancheflor's predicament demonstrates that her nocturnal visit to Perceval is not a transgression of the rules of hospitality and proper conduct, but a justified reflex of self-survival. Unlike Tibaut's daughter, whose relationship with Meliant is governed by pride, and unlike Orgueilleuse de Logres, who uses her "lovers" as a means to exact revenge, Blancheflor turns to Perceval as a potential protector. Perceval is thus offered the possibility of enacting his mother's definition of an honorable knight by using his prowess to protect a distressed damsel.

Another factor that differentiates the relationship between Perceval and Blancheflor from traditional "courtly" interaction is the significance of their pairing as a consensual rather than contractual type of alliance. Blancheflor neither regards Perceval as her prey nor plans to turn him into a pursuer, as witnessed by the fact that she does not come to Perceval as a "prize." Joining him in his chamber was no easy decision, but one that resulted from her determination to act "Come hardie et corageuse" (with bravery and courage; l. 1955):

> Ha! gentius chevaliers, merchi!
> Por Dieu vos pri et por son fil
> Que vos ne m'en aiez plus vil
> De che que je sui chi venue.
> Por che se je sui pres que nue
> Je n'i pensa[i] onques folie
> Ne mauvestié ne vilonnie.
>
> (Ed. Roach, ll. 1982–88)

Ah, gentle knight, have pity on me! In the name of God and His son, I implore you not to think ill of me for having come here. For although I am nearly naked, I had no thought of folly or sin or wickedness.

Blancheflor's claim of innocence does not invoke a sexual context. At issue, rather, is her sense of isolation ("n'a el monde rien qui vive / Tant dolente ne tant chetive," there is no one living in the world as filled with grief and misery as I; ll. 1989–90), inspiring in her the desire to tell Perceval "De son pensé une partie" (something of her worries; l. 1959). Given Perceval's inability to see beyond the literal, in not telling him "everything," Blancheflor runs the risk of his not responding to her appeal. Remarkably, the slow-witted adolescent's reaction in this instance shows that he is aware of his interlocutor's intention. No less remarkably, his answer to her lament is as elusive as was Blancheflor's request for his help: "Dix, se lui plaist, vos fera mix / Demain que vos ne m'avez dit" (God will send you tomorrow better fortune, if He so pleases, than what you predicted to me; ll. 2052–53). Perceval's restrained response is devoid of calculation, indicating that he does not view her as a prize, but will undertake his defensive role unconditionally.

The nonpredatory character of their interaction as distressed damsel and honorable knight accounts for the transformation of the couple into a loving duo. What was at first a consensual alliance becomes, by the end of the night, a sentimental union. Rejecting Blancheflor's suggestion that he leave Biaurepaire to find better lodging, Perceval promises her that he will not let her enemy harass her any longer:

> Mais se je l'ochi et conquier,
> Vostre drüerie vos quiert
> En guerredon.
> (Ed. Roach, ll. 2103–5).

But if I defeat and kill him, I ask your love as my reward.

Because the couple is now in love, Perceval's request does not represent a condition; it is a confirmation that he plans to liberate her from her aggressor. In his earlier response to her tears, his intention was to protect her, as befit an honorable knight; now he will act out of love. Yet Blancheflor refuses his offer, arguing that Perceval is no match, in age and ardor, for so fearsome, strong, and mighty a knight as Clamadeu ("dur," "fors," and "grant"; ll. 2120–21).

Love thus inspires each partner to act on behalf of the other. Once again, however, Chrétien seems to question Blancheflor's sincerity, noting that she only pretends to plead against Perceval's plan in order better to prod him into action. Yet, once again, the realistic aspect of her predicament[56] justifies Blancheflor's turn to Perceval as a last resort. Furthermore, her reaction once Perceval defeats Enguigeron discloses that she fears more for Perceval's life than for her own. When she realizes that Perceval now intends to challenge Clamadeu, she begs him, in vain, not to do battle. Thus, in striking contrast with the vengeful[57] or egotistical grounds on which traditional associations between *chevalier* and *amies* are founded, the two lovers interact in an altruistic manner. If Perceval and Blancheflor ally against Clamadeu, the reason is not that either one wants to prove his or her preeminence, but that the third party poses a concrete danger. Clamadeu is the embodiment of brute, threatening force rather than a prestigious quarry. Both Perceval's eagerness to do battle against someone who appears to be a superior knight and Blancheflor's eventual attempt to prevent him from challenging her aggressor indicate that they are equally ready to sacrifice themselves for the other's sake. Unlike the sacrificial vision of social order presented in both the Arthurian and the Grail discourses—a vision that imposes on a preordained champion to fight and, if need be, die on behalf of factionalism—Perceval's willingness to sacrifice himself is not part of a scheme to attain preeminence. It is proof of his selfless commitment thus to ensure the survival and well-being of another individual.[58]

Thus, Perceval's behavior at Biaurepaire responds on all counts to the regenerative program delineated by his mother. Of particular interest is the sentimental rather than mimetic basis of the union between Perceval and Blancheflor. If Clamadeu represents an obstacle to the blossoming of the couple's story, his desire for Blancheflor is not the reason that provokes Perceval's love; nor does Perceval's elimination of the obstacle suggest a perception of the Other as rival. With Clamadeu's defeat, the triangular configuration caused by his aggression disappears, and so does Perceval's role as defender of the oppressed. Dueling with Clamadeu is not an end in itself, but a means that effects the survival of the duo. In sharp contrast to the tragic solution invoked, for example, in the legend of Tristan and Yseut, love (*amors*) and death (*mors*) neither rhyme nor combine. Instead of focusing on death as the only means of restoring order and achieving sentimental union, love becomes, for each partner, an incentive to ensure the triumph of life.[59]

My examination of the Biaurepaire episode discloses the significance of the castle as the only site in Perceval's story that offers him the possibility of maturing into a responsible individual. When compared to that at Biaurepaire, Perceval's sojourn at the Grail castle is revealed as an alienating experience, effecting his absorption into the realm of reciprocal devourment. Whereas the desolation of Biaurepaire as a wasteland is grounded in realism, the doom of the Grail site lacks substance, its only visible sign being the illness of Perceval's host. In contrast to Biaurepaire, where free choice is endangered by adversity, adversity becomes, in the Grail experience, an argument to convince Perceval that his destiny is to sacrifice his life in pursuit of invisible enemies.

Yet Perceval's transformation into a "hunter" is a slow process, indicating the influence of his formative years in the vale near Valbone. One protection against predatory chivalry is his ignorance of the code and etiquette that regulate traditional knightly culture. From his perspective, the world outside the Welsh forest does not make sense: chivalric equipment includes not only weapons, but a sumptuous (and, in Perceval's opinion, unmanly) lingerie (ed. Roach, ll. 1161–72, 1611–13); the king "who makes knights" is silent (ll. 924, 926); damsels weep for no reason (l. 729); one is not supposed to mention one's mother (ll.

1675–77); castles mysteriously appear (l. 3051) and their inhabitants mysteriously disappear (l. 3384); total strangers greet one with challenges (l. 1004) and blows (ll. 4254–59); one's feats of arms are at times applauded (ll. 4576–77), at times denounced (ll. 6258–60). Nothing is what it appears to be, so one can easily question the royal identity of a mute and aloof Arthur (ll. 927–30) and take at face value Keu's ironic advice to go and challenge the Red Knight. That Perceval's behavior surprises and dismays the people he encounters serves to measure the distance that separates forest, as natural order, and institutional order.

Maternal instruction is the second, and most important, element that ensures Perceval's uniqueness after his entry into the realm of rival doubles, as is frequently confirmed during his initial adventures outside the Welsh forest. His first reaction when he sees the damsel's courtly pavilion is to remember his mother's advice to go to church and worship the creator (ll. 658–63). After his victory over the Red Knight, he refuses to take off the clothes "Que ma mere me fist l'autr'ier" (that my mother made me the other day; l. 1163). During his encounter with Gornemant, he constantly evokes his mother's teaching; after his departure from his mentor, he expresses his determination to direct his journey in such a way as to return to his mother. Although he appreciates the loving company of Blancheflor, his concern for his mother prompts him to go and search for her and bring her back to Biaurepaire if she is still alive (ll. 2917–67). As he approaches the river running near the Grail castle, he prays to God to help him cross it, for

> Se ceste eve passer pooie,
> Dela ma mere troveroie,
> Mien escïent, se ele est vive.
> (Ed. Roach, ll. 2991–93)

If I cross this water, I am confident that I will find my mother on the other side, if she is still alive.

His desire to return to the vale near Valbone ends when his cousin reveals to him that his mother has died. Perceval responds:

> "Or ait Diex de s'ame merchi,"
> Fait Perchevax, "par sa bonté.
> Felon conte m'avez conté.
> Et des que ele est mise en terre,
> Que iroie jou avant querre?
> Kar por rien nule n'i aloie
> Fors por li que veoir voloie;

Autre voie m'estuet tenir.
Et se vos voliez venir
Avec moi, jel vold[r]oie bien;
Que cis ne vos voldra mais rien
Qui chi gist mors, jel vos plevis.
Les mors as mors, les vis as vis."
(Ed. Roach, ll. 3618–30)

"May God in His goodness have mercy on her soul," Perceval says. "You have told me a sad tale. But because she has been buried, what would be the value of continuing my quest? The sole reason for my journey was my desire to see her; I must take a different course. If you wanted to come with me, I would be very glad, for the one who lies here dead will be of no value to you, I promise you. The dead to the dead, the living to the living."

The *autre voie* he proposes to follow invokes the "sacred trail" of the Grail mentioned in Wolfram's *Parzival* because first Perceval's cousin, then the Hideous Damsel, and finally the hermit eventually succeed in prompting him to undertake the quest. Perceval's journey toward the accomplishment of revenge begins when he learns of his mother's death.[60] His response to his cousin ("The dead to the dead, the living to the living"), an echo of Christ's words ("Let the dead bury the dead"; Luke 10:60), constitutes the last indication that Perceval remembers his mother's advice. Indeed, the end of Perceval's quest for his mother marks the beginning of his absorption into the law of the tombs because he is, from then on, urged to devote his life to the revenge of dead or wounded ancestors. A first step in that direction is the cousin's subtle invitation that he prove his value by avenging the death of her lover. In the end, therefore, the alternative maternal project fails, and the Grail discourse prevails, testimony to the persuasive power of a teaching that valorizes the commemoration of the dead rather than the realm of the living.

The Grail discourse, in that sense, is a palimpsest that erases the life-enhancing value of maternal instruction in order to inscribe a mortuary law of vendetta. In the factional context of Chrétien's romance, this reinscription signals the triumph of rivalry, as reflected in the narrative proximity of two antithetical adventures: the training of Perceval by Gornemant (ll. 1305–698) and his stay at the Grail castle (ll. 2976–3421). Even more revealing is the way these two episodes contain and ultimately submerge the adventure that takes place at Biaurepaire (ll. 1699–2975), for it discloses the totalizing strategy of the two rival discourses in their attempt to superimpose their respective teaching on maternal advice.[61] The Grail experience is thus a key factor in Perceval's acculturation into the law of the tombs, a process that eventually erases in him all memory of his mother's instruction.[62] Biaurepaire as a promise of germination also disappears, signaling the substitution of rivalry for consensual reciprocity. Although the realm of fiction authorizes the possible reunion of Perceval and Blancheflor, Chrétien's *Conte du Graal* suggests a different outcome, one in which Perceval will assume his mission as the prosecutor of his lineage's enemies rather than as the lord of a peaceful and productive chivalric community.[63] As the juxtaposition of the Biaurepaire and Grail episodes forcefully reveals, predatory chivalry is not compatible with love.

The centrality of the Grail episode in Perceval's story points to its determining role in effecting the transformation of Perceval into an avenger of family and clan. Although the immaterial character of the castle, its mysterious atmosphere, and its fleeting appearance contribute to the dreamlike quality of the episode, these elements undermine its traditional investment as the locus from which a regenerated or religious kind of chivalry will emerge. Beneath the mystical resonance of the Grail adventure in Chrétien's last romance, we hear, loud and clear, the sound and fury of a bad dream.

On the basis of the social reading I have developed, the force of the earliest extant Grail narrative appears to lie in the ideological function of discourse at the hands of contending factions as they seek to justify their respective claims to preeminence. While Arthur endeavors to exalt the value of his rule in promoting peace and reconciliation in the land of Logres, the representatives of the Grail lineage resort to a discursive strategy that identifies their primary rival as a "persecutor" and its primary "prey" (the wounded recluse of the Grail castle) as innocent victim. Working on a scheme of virtue, the Grail discourse translates blood feud revenge into ideal chivalry, promotes the protocols of violence to the status of a crusade, and transvalues political agendas into gospels of redemption. Aggression thus invades rhetoric, generating a process of reciprocal accusations the sole constant of which in the end is the perpetuation of antagonism. Deromanticizing, so to speak, the realm of chivalric romance, Chrétien's text provides a trenchant comment on the intoxicating effects of language, reminding its aristocratic audience in a particularly troubled period of its history that, even when they borrow their rhetoric from the lexicon of Christian eschatology, wars of words are never holy.

Conclusion

In the beginning there was violence: such is, in the context of the "social" reading presented in this book, the genesis of the Grail as depicted in Chrétien's *Conte du Graal*. What emerges from my analysis of the intratextual function of the *graal* is not a "holy" dish, but an empty container bereft of intrinsic value. There, in a vacuity that discloses the function of the symbol as a receptacle whose meaning resides entirely with its holders and beholders, lies the enigma of Chrétien's Grail. In this earliest extant Grail narrative, the Grail is both a discourse and a vision, the vehicle of a dream of conquest translated into myth. In the idealizing exegesis of the Grail messengers, it is a content without presence, hence its dreamlike quality and its appeal as the most challenging of all quests. But the Grail is also a presence without content, a mirage concocted by a declining clan, the sum total of its unsatisfied ambitions. In the parallel quest for power replicated in the bipartition of the *Conte du Graal*, will the Grail ideal prove to be more attractive and effective than the Arthurian ideal? Should Perceval ally himself with his lineage or with the king's party? In the historical circumstances surrounding Chrétien's romance, these issues remain undetermined.

Although Chrétien's romance is a forceful account of the dilemma facing young and impoverished knights such as Perceval, subsequent Grail literature deproblematizes, without answering, the *niche*'s choice by transforming his lineal and factional mission into a regenerative or redemptive quest. Thus, none of the sequels responds to the social issues implicit in Perceval's story. To identify the real "continuation" of Chrétien's *Conte du Graal*, we must turn to another work of imaginative literature, one that demystifies, in its turn, any and all forms of idealization and discloses the predatory character of "courtly love": the *Roman de la Rose* by Jean de Meun. Like Chrétien in his last romance, Jean demystifies the "bele conjointure" (beautiful composition; *Erec*, l. 14) of traditional romance by emphasizing the impossibility of harmonious exchange and interaction in a world essentially made up, Jean tells us, of "contreres choses" (contrary things; *Roman de la Rose*, l. 21543). At the heart of both narratives is an acknowledgment that the coexistence of opposites leads to "the strife of contrariety" more often than to "the peace of friendship."[1] Against the affirmation (expressed by Natura) in Alan of Lille's *De planctu Naturae* that under God's law of contraries "plurality made its way back to unity, diversity to identity, discord to concord," such that all things and beings are "harmonized by the chain of an invisible connection,"[2] bipolar opposition serves—in Chrétien's text and, some 80 years later, in Jean's—to emblematize the antagonistic character that tends to define human transactions.

According to Natura in Alan's work, the human propensity to disturb and disrupt the harmony of God's creation is nowhere better evinced than in scriptural practices that countervene the theological principle of mimesis. Because meaning derives from God's word, any human creation is, or should be, both a re-creation and a reproduction, assigning to the artist the status of "copyist."[3] By virtue of its imperfection, however, human language is inescapably subversive. Even when the goal is to name God, as is the case of hagiographic writing like the *Vie de Saint Alexis* (ca. 1040), language never achieves the transparency of the divine Verbum because, as Alexandre Leupin notes, it cannot altogether "redress the rhetorical deviance inherent to terrestrial discourse."[4] Although the *Vie* emblematizes the necessarily "transgressive" status of literature,[5] it also succeeds in redeeming human language simply by acknowledging its limits. By contrast, poets and romance writers of the courtly tradition do not lament so much as they revel in what Alan of Lille qualifies as deviant and sodomic writing.[6] The Tristan legend is the most eloquent illustration of glorifying love outside marriage and lineage and, in Béroul's version, of allowing love to triumph by means of wit and deceptive language.[7]

It is in part the subversive character of both the Tristan legend and the troubadours' lyrical tradition that Chrétien appears to have had in mind in developing the basic story line of each of his first four romances. As their happy endings imply, love can and must combine with chivalry (*Lancelot*) and even with marriage (*Erec*, *Yvain*, *Cligés*); to all appearances, in the latter three narratives the knightly hero ultimately succeeds in being simultaneously a perfect lover, perfect husband, and perfect vassal. At the same time, however, the reliance on hyperbolic comparison[8] to distinguish the hero above and against his knightly companions discloses the competitive character of his quest for chivalric excellence. Not only do the artificial resolutions marking Chrétien's first four romances obfuscate, without solving, the inherent problems of life at court; each narrative, even the genealogically structured *Cligés*, is also remarkably nongenerational. The pleasure of the text therefore lies in the author's capacity to generate the mendacious realm of fiction. The goal here is not to adhere to the theological principle of perfect adequation between words and things. Rather, it is to elaborate a profane and secular kind of genesis, leading to the linguistic fabrication of an ideal and escapist "prelapsarian" world as it is invoked in the happy endings of these narratives. Chrétien's *Yvain* is a typical example of the deproblematizing value of language in traditional romance. Although the narrative posits a conflict between the eponymous hero and Arthur's champion, culminating in the judicial duel that pits Yvain against Gauvain, the outcome of the combat also obfuscates the abusive character of this customary procedure under Arthur's rule. The inconclusiveness of the duel, which terminates in a deadlock (the equivalent of a juridical *non lieu*, that is, "nowhere"), discloses the significance of the happy ending of the episode and ultimately of the romance itself as utopia (that is, "no place").

This utopian element of traditional chivalric romance seems to have inspired Guillaume de Lorris to undertake his own narrative quest for the ultimate *locus amoenus*—the Garden of Love—and for an amorous experience leading to a truly happy ending. The junction of lyric (the love experience) and romance (the quest experience) in Guillaume's text involves two significant recastings of the literary tradition developed in twelfth-century France. On the one hand, Guillaume introduces us to the chivalric realm of *langue d'oil*, but it is a realm that no longer focuses on knightly deeds. The world in which the Lover's adventures take place is one of thought rather than action, as illustrated by the fact that Amant is a dreamer and a mostly passive character. On the other hand, by virtue of his transformation of the Lady into a silent flower, Guillaume also introduces us to the unilateral kind of verbal communication that characterizes the lyrical realm of *langue d'oc*.

Guillaume combines these two literary traditions in a manner that accentuates the dead-end nature of his quest as both lover and writer.[9] Like the troubadour in the lyrical production of southern France, Amant evolves in an oniric realm in which the only response to his prayers is silence. Like the amorous quester of traditional romance or the spiritual quester in many Grail texts after Chrétien, Amant evolves, or wants to evolve, in a prelapsarian realm, away from self-serving chivalric deeds, predatory pursuits, and violence. But this determination to remain a perfect lover also implies that Guillaume will remain an eternal quester. The nonresolution of his text ends with a portrayal of the Lover as victim and of the narrator as a poet confronting the predicament of a postlapsarian world. Violence becomes self-inflicted, and it is against the self-castrating effect of Guillaume's dream that Jean endeavors to resume the narration of Amant's quest for the Rose.

In contrast to Chrétien, who dedicated his *Conte du Graal* to Philippe of Flanders, or to Guillaume de Lorris, who claims to have written his romance in an attempt to entreat an indifferent lady, Jean makes no mention of a patron, suggesting that his text was inspired by strictly personal concerns. In elaborating his *summa* of contemporary society, Jean opens up Guillaume's garden, which becomes the theater of life. Seen against traditional chivalric romance, which depicts the rarefied, insular realm of aristocratic society, Jean's narrative thus takes on a universal character, addressing any and all types of readers. Unlike the "universal" character of many Grail texts after Chrétien, however, the macroscopic world represented in Jean's romance does not seek to deproblematize or altogether reject society; it takes into account the cultural complexities of northern France in the second half of the thirteenth century.

The initial encounter between the Lover and the Rose as narrated in Guillaume's text takes the symbolic form of an arrow that differentiates the Lover as martyr and the Rose as his persecutor. Jean's amplification expands this lethal understanding of interaction and communication through a series of discourses in which the Lover and the Rose are viewed, successively or simultaneously, as either victims or persecutors. The predicament of Jean's protagonist as quester of the Rose is a choice between defeat and victory, between remaining a victim and becoming a persecutor. In contrast with Guillaume's text, the main characteristic of Jean's Amant is to be *niche*,[10] like Perceval, and as such exposed to numerous guides whose respective counsels produce two antithetical views on proper conduct. A striking example is provided by the parallel discourses of Ami (Friend) and the Vieille (the Duenna). According to Ami, women are pursuers whose goal is to "pluck" (*despoillier*, l. 8838; or *escoillier*, emasculate, l. 20020) their male victims, hence his advice to Amant that he protect himself by becoming a pursuer. Conveying a similar, albeit inverted, view, the Vieille maintains that, if women are prey-turned-pursuers, the reason is that men's sole purpose is to "plant" them (*se ficher*, evoked at l. 13236). Should Jean's Lover adopt the rhodophiles' viewpoint (that is, the viewpoint of the figures who defend the Rose against her male persecutors) and venerate the Rose, thus condemning himself to remain an eternal quester? Or should he imitate the rhodophobes (that is, the figures whose rhetoric of manipulation aims at his deflowering of the Rose) and turn into a conqueror? To persuade their pupil, rhodophiles and rhodophobes alike resort to a discourse that glorifies the quest as either a quest for an ideal (in the name of the Rose) or, conversely, as an ideal quest (in the name of the questing Lover). Whether the Rose or the Lover will emerge victorious thus rests on the capacity of both plaintiffs and defendants to convince the Lover of the superior value of their respective causes.

In the second part of the *Roman de la Rose*, therefore, the main protagonist is no longer love, but language itself, insofar as it empowers Jean to bring Guillaume's quest to its successful conclusion.[11] Therein lies the major difference separating Jean as both actor and narrator not only from Guillaume, but also from Chrétien's Perceval: whereas the manipulative use of language at the hands of more learned and astute "educators" is, in Perceval's case, the reason that he appears condemned to remain a *niche*, language is what effects, in Jean's case, the substitution of his individual figure as author for his persona as a *niche*, Amant. Not only does Jean show his awareness that the "contreres choses" of his world do not combine in a complementary manner, as has been maintained,[12] but irreducibly clash and collide. On the basis of his experience of human antagonism, he also questions the mendacious language and realm of traditional romance. Paradoxically, this experience induces him to develop an equally mendacious language, yet one whose idealizing character—unlike that of Guillaume's romance, for example—is governed by an ideology of success. Indeed, Jean's reliance on discourse is integral to a strategy of self-empowerment, as emblematized by the function he assigns to the allegorical figure of Genius in "engineering" the successful conclusion of Amant's quest.

From *gigno*, "to engender," Genius signifies generation in the lineal, sexual, scientific, technical, literary, and artistic sense of the word. Jean's self-praise as a new Genius entails a technique of appropriation that disparages (by encompassing, hence, surpassing) any previous or contemporary generative activities. Jean glorifies the superior value of his text against the self-castrating effect of Guillaume's courtly language, which he repeatedly condemns as a degenerating and degenerate language (*forligniez*; 1. 19752). Rejecting Guillaume's "poetics of obstacle" as the main reason for his failure as both lover and narrator, Jean develops a "dialectic of contradiction" (*engin* as deceitful language) aimed at turning Amant the Dreamer into Amant the Conqueror. The key to the quester's success is thus language. What Jean's *niche* learns from his encounters with the various representatives of the social fabric is that, in a world made up of *contreres choses*, one's status in society is proportional to one's capacity to deceive.

The centrality of *engin* (of the deceitful and manipulative power of language) in Jean's narrative calls attention to its fraudulent use of discourse as a means of proving oneself better, superior, and more deserving of victory than others. As in the case of Chrétien's *Conte*, where comparisons of superiority (*a praestantia*) and inequality (*per contrarium*)[13] are a conspicuous index of the rivalrous motivations that inspire one party to exalt the superior merit of its champion,[14] in Jean's *Roman*, rhodophiles and rhodophobes, and ultimately the author himself, manipulate the art of argumentation for self-serving purposes. Despite Jean's claim to use dialectic in a manner conducive to knowledge and self-control, and despite his[15] and Aristotle's[16] criticism of sophistry, the author shows a propensity to rely on a technique of reasoning the goal of which is to enable the speaker (both Amant and Jean himself) to present a wrong argument as if it were right. In this light, Jean's allusion, through False Seeming, to the thirteen-branch razor of sophistry[17] mentioned in Aristotle's *De sophisticis Elenchis* is eminently ironic. Equally ironic are both Jean's reliance on some of the six linguistic strategies (such as equivocation and ambiguity) criticized by Aristotle and the fact that these strategies play a critical part in the Lover's triumph as conqueror of the Rose. No less remarkable, finally, is the manner in which False Seeming confronts Male Bouche (Evil Tongue, one of the guardians of the Rose's castle), blames him for his hypocrisy, and, after strangling him, cuts out his tongue with a razor (ll. 12117–337). This severing of words and things, of signifier and signified, is proof that, in a world governed by dissimulation, the best way to win is to simulate and use language as a weapon.

Jean's trenchant use of language confirms the saying according to which, in Jean de La Fontaine's words, "la raison du plus fort est toujours la meilleure" (whoever is stronger wins the argument).[18] Here, as in Chrétien's *Conte*, one is "right" in proportion to one's wit and ability to manipulate the other through persuasion. The text of Jean's *Roman* is, in that sense, a texture of deception, elaborating a presentation of mimesis (reproduction) that pretends to be true genesis (production). The dual ending of Jean's narrative discloses the equation between his literary creation and forgery (as opposed to Nature's, or woman's, forge). In the penultimate episode of the *Roman*, the Pygmalion myth allegedly introduces a prelapsarian depiction of lateral exchange as reciprocal lovemaking. To create his perfect mate, however, Pygmalion endeavors to manipulate the natural elements in a manner that undermines the edenic quality of this love story. Far from evoking a return to a past Golden Age, his creation of Galatea places him squarely in the Age of Iron, when men undertook to flay the earth and control the natural environment in order to dominate and control their social environment. In the end, the Pygmalion myth bespeaks not a pre- but a postlapsarian world, as forcefully acknowledged by the second ending of Jean's *Roman*. Ultimately convinced to side with the rhodophobes against the rhodophiles, the Lover, henceforth relinquishing his role as student, also relinquishes the realm of discourse to enter that of action. In the guise of a pilgrim (proof that Amant has finally absorbed the rhodophobes' essential teaching regarding the value of sanctifying ideals as self-serving strategies), he assaults and captures the Rose.

The bipartite pattern that is equally operative in the *Conte* and in the *Roman* prods us to read these narratives as paradigms of the conflictual and competitive character that frequently defines human interaction. Instead of leading to the comforting denouement of traditional chivalric romance or to the sanctifying ending of quest romances such as the *Queste del Saint Graal*, Jean's *Roman* elaborates a resolution grounded in violence, concluding with the "awakening" of Amant as dreamer, that is, with Jean's ultimate self-celebration as the master of a razor-sharp language of deception. Jean's ending indicates, retrospectively, that the dreamlike quality of the Grail is a dream of victory, suggesting that Perceval's "awakening" to the factional realm of the *Conte* will conclude the process of his absorption into the realm of vengeful pursuits. The enigma of Chrétien's unfinished romance therefore appears to find its response in the narrative closure of Jean's *Roman*. In both texts, the significance of the motif of the quest is conquest; in both texts, this quest for power hides itself under the guise of an ideal, the ideal Grail or the ideal Rose; and in both texts, the success of the quest depends on the suppression of the Other as obstacle. This leads to the sacrifice of the Rose in the concluding episode of Jean's narrative and, potentially, to that of Perceval in the *Conte du Graal*, according to a conception of victory that imposes on Chrétien's *niche* the duty to fight and, if need be, die on behalf of lineage.

Jean thus proves to be an astute reader of Chrétien's romance. Yet his text and its sacrificial interpretation of the quest induced his readers a century or so later (around the year 1400) to rekindle the debate between rhodophiles and rhodophobes in what is known as the "Querelle de la Rose." At issue was the pedagogical value of Jean's narrative. In the rhodophiles' view,[19] Jean's text is a warning against predatory pursuits and, consequently, an implicit apology on behalf of virtuous and harmonious interaction. Rhodophobes maintain that the moral of Jean's story is not moral because its extended debate relentlessly exalts hypocrisy as a means of achieving dominance. Among other arguments, rhodophobes, particularly Christine de Pizan, call attention to Jean's narrative resolution as testimony to the significance of his quest as violent conquest. In a reply to Pierre Col, an ardent rhodophile, Christine thus notes:

> I dare to say that if Master Jean de Meun had spoken throughout his book of the inclinations and evil conduct of human nature but had concluded in favor of the moral way of life, then you would have had a greater reason for saying that he did it for a good purpose. For you know that if a writer wishes to use rhetoric properly, he first announces his premises and afterward moves from point to point, touching subjects as he chooses, but then always returns, in his conclusion, to the purpose of his narrative. . . . I consider the book as a single entity, a fact which is sufficient answer in this regard, . . . for the whole work comes to a single purpose in the conclusion.[20]

Beyond the moral arguments invoked by both sides, of particular interest are, on the one hand, the rhodophobes' emphasis on narrative structure as key to the significance of a text and, on the other, the rhodophiles' determination to minimize the meaning of structure. At the heart of the "Querelle," therefore, is the recognition that the bipartite organization of narratives such as Chrétien's *Conte du Graal* and Jean de Meun's *Roman de la Rose* is not gratuitous. For medieval readers, the "truth" of romance lies in its conclusion. Through Jean's recapitulative reading of Chrétien's Grail, the unholy nature of the quest as violent appropriation becomes forcefully clear, in contradistinction to its idealizing reinscription in many medieval and postmedieval sequels.

If in Jean's world the "holy" Grail has disappeared, the reason is that idealism is now recognized as a vacant container. At the core of Jean's *Roman de la Rose* is not an ideal Rose, but an idealization of the Rose as a strategy of conquest. Like the Grail, the Rose is an empty vessel capable of receiving any value according to the motivations of its holders and beholders; like the Grail, the Rose is an intratextual discursive invention, an enigma that holds no other secret than its own vacuity. Although two specifically medieval creations, the mythical Grail and the mythical Rose have lost none of their ideological currency, but remain potent symbols of the magical effects of language when language translates aggression into poetry.

Reference Matter

Notes

Introduction

1. As attested by the massive body of scholarship devoted to Chrétien, the romances of this renowned twelfth-century French poet have generated a wide range of approaches and interpretations, each of which cannot here be given its proper due. Although constituting a richly varied response to Chrétien's production, these commentaries also share a tendency to view the poet's last extant work, the *Conte du Graal*, as a romance notably different in tone and intention from his four previous ones. For a number of critics, the central issue posed by Chrétien's earlier production concerns its cultural value in articulating (and at the same time in idealizing and solving) the problems of the aristocracy that patronized the writing of courtly romances. See Erich Köhler, *Ideal und Wirklichkeit in der höfischen Epik* (trans. E. Kaufholz, *L'Aventure chevaleresque*); Robert W. Hanning, *The Individual in Twelfth-Century Romance*; R. Howard Bloch, *Medieval French Literature and Law*, especially pp. 189–202, and *Etymologies and Genealogies*, especially pp. 186–90; and Eugene Vance, *"Mervelous Signals,"* especially pp. 111–51. What emerges from these analyses is the recognition that the chivalric society depicted in Chrétien's earlier romances "embodies [to cite Donald Maddox's remark on *Erec et Enide*] an acute consciousness of oppositions and tensions, many of which are socioeconomic and political." See Maddox, *Structure and Sacring*, p. 177. As Maddox notes, "At the heart of this courtly identity crisis is the opposition between a conservative feudal monarch . . . and the new alliance of the courtly couple— the 'jeune' and his lady—whose individualistic aspirations do not necessarily coincide with the concerns of the feudal court." The happy resolution that marks the denouement of Chrétien's four earlier romances also indicates their status as what Maddox describes in terms of "problem-solving" romances.

2. According to Köhler, this alienation resulted from the growing hegemony of French monarchy and from its implementation of governmental practices designed to undermine the prerogatives of the aristocracy (*L'Aventure*

chevaleresque, pp. 19–25). In this light, chivalric romances idéalize contemporary reality by inventing a monarch, Arthur, who protects and favors the ambitions of an impoverished nobility (pp. 25–43). By contrast, rather than elaborating a similarly ideal solution to the problems besetting feudal society, in Köhler's view, the *Conte du Graal* acknowledges the fictional character of that solution and thus introduces a notion of quest henceforth understood not in socioeconomic but in spiritual terms: Perceval's mission, like Christ's, is to redeem humanity. Because this mission will be fully achieved only at the end of human history, it explains why Chrétien left his last extant romance unfinished (p. 257). Köhler's view of the redemptive function of Perceval's quest for the Grail in Chrétien's romance is shared by Paule Le Rider. See *Le chevalier dans le "Conte du Graal" de Chrétien de Troyes*.

3. This summary of Perceval's story is based on John Fox, *A Literary History of France*, pp. 163–65. For the sake of consistency, I standardize and, occasionally, modernize or translate the name forms of the places and characters figuring in Chrétien's *Conte*, which vary according to scribes and editors.

4. My project was initially to examine the development of the Grail legend from Chrétien de Troyes's *Conte du Graal* to its various thirteenth-century sequels, including the four verse texts known as the *Continuations* and the five prose narratives known as the Vulgate Cycle (I identify these texts subsequently). Tracing the genesis of the legend eventually led me to concentrate on Chrétien's romance, which thus became the focus of my book. I occasionally refer to those of the *Conte*'s sequels that best illustrate, per contra, the unique status of Chrétien's romance in endowing the Grail with secular significance.

5. Although the dating of Chrétien's last romance has been the subject of controversy (see Douglas Kelly, *Chrétien de Troyes*, p. 120), two events connected with the romancer's noble patrons situate the *Conte*'s composition between 1181 and 1190. The first is the death of Count Henry, husband of Chrétien's previous patron, Marie of Champagne, inducing the poet to join the court of Philippe of Alsace. The second is the latter's departure for the Third Crusade, during which he died in 1191 at the siege of Acre. See Jean Frappier, *Chrétien de Troyes*, pp. 9, 169.

6. Philippe's father, Thierry of Alsace, temporarily installed his son as count when he went to Palestine in 1157. Philippe then succeeded his father at the latter's death in 1167.

7. I am indebted to Professor Gabrielle Spiegel for her advice on this brief evocation of the historical context of Chrétien's romance as well as for making the manuscript of her now published book available to me. See *Romancing the Past*, p. 29. My gratitude goes to Professor Spiegel for the generous and thought-provoking guidance she provided at every stage of my writing.

8. Thus the author of *Flandria Generosa* asserted that the count was "preciuus inter omnes et potentissimus omnium videbatur" (seen as the worthiest

and most powerful of all), eulogizing Philippe after his death as "nobilissimus omnium qui fuerant ante ipsum in Flandria, divitiis et honoribus affluens, prudentia et potentia manus, fervens in iustitia, fortis et probus ad arma" (the most noble of all who lived before him in Flanders, endowed with riches and honors, blessed with prudence and strength, devoted to justice, firm and fair in feats of arms). *Genealogiae Comitum Flandriae*, pp. 327, 329.

9. This quotation refers to William Roach's edition, ll. 11–14. All translations are mine unless otherwise stated.

10. Spiegel, *Romancing the Past*, p. 30.

11. The Plantagenets ruled over a realm that included Anjou, Normandy, Aquitaine, and England, hence the common identification of the Plantagenets as "English" kings.

12. The general contention, to which I subscribe, is that Chrétien wrote the *Conte du Graal* not only for Philippe of Alsace, but also at the latter's court. According to Patricia Stirnemann, however, the fact that none of the *Conte*'s earliest copies has Picard features indicates that Chrétien never left Champagne and began his romance at Troyes. See "Some Champenois Vernacular Manuscripts," pp. 211–12. On Philippe's role in encouraging vernacular literature, see Mary D. Stanger, "Literary Patronage at the Medieval Court of Flanders."

13. See Beate Schmolke-Hasselmann, "Henry II Plantagenêt, roi d'Angleterre, et la genèse d'*Erec et Enide*," and Constance Bullock-Davies, "Chrétien de Troyes and England."

14. Eleanor's marriage to Henry II in 1152 after her repudiation by Louis VII of France, her first husband, had considerably increased the domain of the Plantagenets on the Continent and had by the same token reduced that of the Capetians. Marie's marriage to Henry of Champagne in 1164 reinforced the alliance between the Plantagenets and the house of Champagne.

15. As does Rita Lejeune, "La date du *Conte du Graal* de Chrétien de Troyes."

16. See, for example, Helen Adolf, *"Visio Pacis."* Francis J. Carmody recognizes Philippe of Alsace not behind Arthur but behind Gauvain, the king's nephew, who like Philippe, according to Carmody, finds himself the subject of false accusations and slanders ("Le *Perceval* de Chrétien de Troyes"). Madeleine Blaess suggests a possible connection between Philippe and Perceval—rather than either Arthur or Gauvain—to the extent that both Philippe's and Perceval's familial histories allude to a past of clan rivalry (Philippe's ancestor, Charles of Flanders, was assassinated by Bertulf Eremblad in 1127). Considering that Perceval is himself the heir of a clan (the Grail faction), which "claims encroachment of its rights because of the exile it suffered when Arthur became king," a similar dilemma appears to face Chrétien's young protagonist and his noble patron: at issue, according to Blaess, is whether either figure should undertake to prosecute the enemies of lineage or should forget and forgive

past rivalries and devote himself to ensuring the prosperity of the land. See "Perceval et les 'Illes de Mer.'"

17. See Raymond Desmazières de Séchelles, "L'évolution et la transformation du mythe arthurien."

18. The clan of the Isles also numbers one Clamedeu des Isles, who plays an important part in the Biaurepaire episode (analyzed in Chapter 4).

19. The *Conte du Graal* "survives virtually complete in twelve medieval copies, in extensive fragments in three other medieval manuscripts . . . and in fragments of four others." See ed. Pickens, p. xxv. Terry Nixon provides a detailed description of the manuscripts containing the works of Chrétien de Troyes, including the *Conte du Graal*. See "Catalogue of Manuscripts," pp. 18–85.

20. Alexandre Micha, *La tradition manuscrite des romans de Chrétien de Troyes*, p. 391.

21. Ibid., p. 370.

22. Ed. Pickens, p. xxix.

23. Ibid., p. xxx. For an analysis of the family relations between the *Perceval* manuscripts, see Margot Van Mulken, "*Perceval* and Stemmata."

24. Cluster Delta includes Ms. T (Paris, Bibliothèque Nationale, f. fr. 12576; second half of the 13th c., Picard dialect) and Ms. V (Paris, BN, Nouvelles Acquisitions fr. 6614; last quarter of the 13th c., Picard dialect).

25. Eastern Francian with Champenois admixture.

26. Ranging from Gottfried Baist, *Crestien von Troyes' "Li Contes del Graal"* (*"Percevaus li Galois"*), to Alfons Hilka, *Der Percevalroman ("Li contes del Graal") von Christian von Troyes*, to Félix Lecoy, *Le Conte du Graal (Perceval)*, and, more recently, to Pickens, *Chrétien de Troyes*. (Hilka's edition of the *Conte du Graal* is vol. 5 of Wendelin Foerster's collected works of Chrétien de Troyes, *Christian von Troyes's sämtliche Werke* [Halle: Niemeyer, 1884–1932].)

27. The codex copied by the scribe Guiot is a large collection that "contains all five of Chrétien's romances as part of a thematically arranged sequence of chivalric romances based on ancient and Arthurian history." Nixon, "Catalogue of Manuscripts," p. 29. The letter designation of this codex is Ms. C for *Erec* and *Lancelot*, Ms. A for *Cligés* and *Perceval*, Ms. H for *Yvain* in Foerster's edition, and Ms. A for *Yvain* in Jonin's edition. I designate Guiot's copy as Ms. A.

28. Ed. Pickens, p. xxxi.

29. Ibid.

30. Micha's comparative analysis identifies a number of similarities between Ms. A and Mss. M (Montpellier, Bibliothèque Interuniversitaire, Section Médecine H. 249; end 13th c., Francian), P (Mons, Bibliothèque de l'Université de Mons-Hainaut 331/206 [formerly 4568]; between third and fourth quarter of the 13th c., northeastern dialect), H (London, Heralds Col-

lege, Arundel XIV; mid 14th c., Anglo-Norman), L (London, British Library, Additional 36614; first quarter of the 13th c., Picard), R (Paris, BN, f. fr. 1450; second quarter of the 13th c., Picard), and B (Bern, Burgerbibliothek 354; second quarter of the 13th c., Champenois). See *La tradition manuscrite*. Date attributions of the *Perceval* manuscripts mentioned here reflect those established by Nixon, "Catalogue of Manuscripts," pp. 13–14. Ed. Pickens, pp. xxxii–xxxviii, provides further information on the uniqueness of Ms. A in comparison with other versions of Chrétien's *Conte du Graal*. See also pp. 496–99. The letter designation for Paris, BN, f. fr. 1450 is Ms. H for *Erec*, Ms. B for *Cligés*, Ms. F for *Yvain* and *Lancelot*, and Ms. R for *Perceval*.

31. Tony Hunt, "Chrestien de Troyes," p. 258. Hunt's article is reprinted with minor emendations in Keith Busby et al., *The Manuscripts of Chrétien de Troyes*, vol. 1, pp. 27–40.

32. Charles Potvin's edition is based on Ms. P.

33. Ed. Roach. Hunt's article (1979) predates both the aforementioned edition and English translation of Chrétien's *Conte du Graal* by Pickens and Kibler and the edition and French translation by Charles Méla. For a current list of the *Conte*'s editions, see the bibliography of Busby et al., *The Manuscripts of Chrétien de Troyes*, vol. 2, p. 306.

34. Hunt, "Chrestien de Troyes," p. 269.

35. See ed. Pickens, p. xxxi. Pickens announces here that Keith Busby is preparing a critical edition of Roach's single-manuscript edition. An interesting aspect of Ms. T is that it is the only codex where the *Conte du Graal* is followed by all the verse *Continuations* stimulated by Chrétien's unfinished romance. Ms. T thus comprises the *Conte du Graal* (folio 1–folio 37), the *First Continuation* (possibly composed a decade after Chrétien's romance; folio 37–folio 98), the *Continuation* attributed to Wauchier de Denain (ca. 1220; folio 98–folio 152v), the *Continuation* of Gerbert de Montreuil (ca. 1226–30; folio 152v–folio 220v), the *Continuation* of Manessier (second quarter of the 13th c.; folio 220v–folio 261), the *Mort du Comte de Henau* (added in the mid 14th c.; folio 261v–folio 262), a memorandum of debts (added in the late 13th c.; folio 262), and two romances by the Renclus de Moiliens, *Miserere* (ca. 1230; folio 263–folio 275) and *Carité* (ca. 1224; folio 275v–folio 284v). See Roger Middleton, "Additional Notes," pp. 216–24. A second codex, Ms. V, also contains the four *Continuations*; but numerous folios are missing, the result of which is the loss of much of Chrétien's *Conte* and a single folio for Manessier's text.

36. Three other codices (Mss. R, V, and P) share with Ms. T a northeastern provenance and the Picard dialect. Terry Nixon dates Ms. R from the second quarter of the thirteenth century and Mss. T, V, and P from the fourth quarter of the thirteenth century. See "Catalogue of Manuscripts," p. 13. Keith Busby examines the closeness of Ms. T and Ms. V in "The Scribe of MSS T and V."

37. Nonetheless, as Keith Busby observes, the 9,234 lines of Chrétien's

Conte du Graal "are remarkably stable from a textual viewpoint." See "Text, Miniature, and Rubric," p. 366.

38. I examine the specificity of version T whenever its reading presents a textual alternative germane to my perspective.

39. While picking up the pieces of a sword that was given to him by his host at the Grail castle, which he puts back into the scabbard, Perceval draws the sword that had belonged to the Red Knight and resumes fighting. These twenty lines are edited and translated in ed. Pickens, pp. 506–7. The motif of the broken sword has a central role in the verse *Continuations*. In the *First Continuation*, which focuses on Gauvain as its principal protagonist, Gauvain succeeds in finding the Grail domain but fails to mend the sword. See ed. Roach, ll. 1467–69. In the *Second Continuation* as well as in those of Gerbert and Manessier, Perceval eventually succeeds in returning to the Grail castle and in mending the sword, the result of which is that he becomes lord of the domain.

40. She tells him:

> Gardez ne vos i fiez ja,
> Qu'ele vos traïra sanz faille
> Quant vos venrez en grant bataille,
> K'ele vos volera en pieces.
>
> (Ed. Roach, ll. 3660–63)

Be on your guard, do not trust it, for it will fail you, without a doubt, when you engage in a fierce combat, and will break into pieces in your hand.

41. This is not the case in the verse *Continuations*, three of which focus on Perceval as the eventual hero of the quest. The protagonist of the *First Continuation* is Gauvain, who fails to mend the broken sword because of his imperfect chivalry. The Grail king tells him that the knight who succeeds in this feat and learns the truth about the Grail will have the esteem and praise of the entire realm ("Le pris de tot le monde ara / Et le los"; ll. 1473–74).

42. Two other codices, Ms. A and Ms. R, also juxtapose Chrétien's *Conte du Graal* with semihistorical romances, including Wace's *Roman de Brut* (completed in 1155) and Benoît de Sainte-Maure's *Roman de Troie* (ca. 1165). In Ms. R, all five of Chrétien's romances are inserted in *Brut* at the point when Wace's romance begins to chronicle Arthurian England. Prologues to *Erec* and to the *Conte du Graal* are suppressed, "adding to the illusion that Chrétien's romances are actually part of the *Brut*'s history." See Nixon, "Romance Collections," p. 25.

43. Ms. S also articulates a sociopolitical interpretation of Perceval's story. Produced almost certainly in Paris between 1315 and 1325, the codex contains Chrétien's *Conte*, followed by three of the four *Continuations*. Its iconographic program focuses on King Arthur in a way that induces Sandra Hindman to

read in the manuscript "a nostalgic view of a golden age of Capetian kingship." Rather than implying a collision between two rival principles of sovereignty, the images of the codex exalt "models of political and spiritual kingships in the complementary roles of King Arthur and the Fisher King." See Hindman, *Sealed in Parchment*, p. 164. A confirmation of this interpretation is provided by the last illustration of the codex, which shows Perceval's coronation as narrated by Manessier:

> A un jor de feste Toz Saint
> Fu coronez li bons Galois;
> Le jor i ot quatorze rois
> Coronez par amor de lui.
> (*Third Continuation*, ll. 42478–81)

At the feast of All Saints the good Welshman was crowned. That day fourteen crowned kings [including Arthur] were present in his honor.

The illustration amplifies the text to the extent that it shows Arthur endorsing Perceval's coronation by touching the latter's crown "just as the peers of France touch the king's crown in the French coronation rite." Hindman, *Sealed in Parchment*, p. 167.

44. Micha, *La tradition manuscrite*, p. 260.

45. Alison Stones, "General Introduction," p. 2. For Angelica Rieger, the earliest codex containing Chrétien's *Conte* is not Ms. B, but Ms. T. Cited by Alison Stones, "The Illustrated Chrétien Manuscripts," p. 236.

46. Lori Walters, "The Use of Multi-Compartment Opening Miniatures," p. 341.

47. Stones, "The Illustrated Chrétien Manuscripts," p. 242, n. 69.

48. This miniature is reproduced in Busby et al., *The Manuscripts of Chrétien de Troyes*, vol. 1, p. 344, fig. 6.

49. See Walters, "The Use of Multi-Compartment Opening Miniatures," p. 341.

50. This illustration is reproduced in color in Busby et al., *The Manuscripts of Chrétien de Troyes*, vol. 2, p. 346, plate IVb.

51. Alison Stones argues that the right-hand figure does not hold a lance but a candle. This candle strikingly resembles the one illustrating the Miracle of the Arras Candle contained in BN, fr. 17229, a codex that, like Ms. T, was produced at or near Arras. See "The Illustrated Chrétien Manuscripts," p. 242. On the basis of these visual associations, Stones concludes that the initial Ms. T patrons were members of the bourgeoisie, thus corroborating Roger Middleton's interpretation of names and debts (listed on the leaves between the end of the *Continuations* and the Renclus's texts) in evoking an urban audience. See Roger Middleton, "Additional Notes," pp. 216–24. According to Sandra Hindman, by contrast, this list of obligations "conjures up a vivid

picture of a feudal domain." The iconographic program of the codex focuses on the conflict between earthly chivalry (as evoked in both Chrétien's *Conte* and the *First Continuation*) and spiritual chivalry (in the *Second Continuation*, the *Continuation* of Gerbert, and the Renclus's romances). The story of Perceval is here interpreted as "a story about Perceval's mastery of literate Latin culture," ultimately transforming Chrétien's unlettered and ignorant knight into Perceval, the cleric. See Hindman, *Sealed in Parchment*, pp. 47, 42.

52. Emmanuèle Baumgartner, "Les scènes du Graal," p. 495.

53. The first image is the four-part opening miniature previously mentioned. The second, badly rubbed, depicts Perceval, possibly saddling his horse (folio 1). The third depicts the combat on foot between Perceval and Clamadeu (folio 11v). The fourth shows Perceval, on horseback, and Gauvain, standing (folio 19). In the fifth, Perceval is riding up to his eremitic uncle (folio 25). These five images are reproduced in Busby et al., *The Manuscripts of Chrétien de Troyes*, vol. 2, pp. 430–31.

54. Only two manuscripts, Mss. M and U (Paris, BN, f. fr. 12577; second quarter of the 14th c., Francian), illustrate this episode of Chrétien's romance. The image of Ms. M, which is inserted between the passage of the lance and that of the serving dish, shows a maiden holding the lance. In the compartmented picture of Ms. U, the left-hand sequence shows Perceval as he is given a sword. The right-hand sequence depicts the lance, held by a young man, and the Grail, represented here as a ciborium, which is crowned with a cross and held by a maiden. Two royal characters (a king and a queen) witness this event, but Perceval is absent from the scene. These two images are reproduced in Busby et al., *The Manuscripts of Chrétien de Troyes*, vol. 1, p. 501, figs. 6, 9.

55. Baumgartner, "Les scènes du Graal," p. 498.

56. Of the fifteen manuscripts (excluding fragments) in which the *Conte du Graal* is preserved, only five contain an extensive narrative cycle of miniatures: Mss. M, T, P, U, and S (Paris, BN, f. fr. 1453; second quarter of the 14th c., Francian). Each of those codices includes three or more *Continuations*.

57. Only four (Mss. B, C, F, and H) out of the fifteen *Perceval* manuscripts do not contain any *Continuation*. However, as Keith Busby observes, Ms. F "may have done so, as it breaks off before the end of Chrétien's poem, and [Ms.] H shows knowledge" of the *First Continuation*. See "Text, Miniature, and Rubric," p. 366, n. 5. In addition to Ms. H, described previously, the manuscripts just mentioned are the following: Clermont-Ferrand (Ms. C), Bibliothèque municipale et interuniversitaire 248 (first quarter of the 13th c., no identifiable dialectal features) and Florence (Ms. F), Biblioteca Riccardiana 2943 (second quarter of the 13th c., Eastern dialect).

58. "Explycyt Percevax le viel": Paris, BN, f. fr. 794, folio 394v.

Chapter 1

1. This line appears in the prologue of the *Conte du Graal*, where Chrétien states his intention to tell the "Story of the Grail." In contrast with its figurative significance in the prologue, the *graal* has a concrete meaning throughout Chrétien's text (all line numbers are from the Roach edition):

THE GRAIL EPISODE

Un *graal* entre ses deus mains
Une damoisele tenoit
(Ll. 3220–21)

Quant ele fu laiens entree
Atot le *graal* qu'ele tint
(Ll. 3224–25)

Li *graaus*, qui aloit devant,
De fin or esmeré estoit
(Ll. 3232–33)

El *graal* de maintes manieres,
Des plus riches et des plus chieres
(Ll. 3235–36)

Totes autres pierres passoient
Celes del *graal* sanz dotance.
(Ll. 3238–39)

Et li vallés les vit passer,
Ne n'osa mie demander
Del *graal* cui l'en en servoit
(Ll. 3243–45)

Et li *graals* endementiers
Par devant als retrespassa,
Ne li vallés ne demanda
Del *graal* cui on en servoit.
(Ll. 3290–93)

Par devant lui trespasser voit
Le *graal* trestot descovert
(Ll. 3300–3301)

Et dist qu'aprés als en iroit
Savoir se nus d'als li diroit . . .
Et del *graal* ou l'en le porte.
(Ll. 3397–98, 3401)

THE COUSIN EPISODE

> "Et veïstes vos le *graal*?"
> "Oïl, bien." "Et qui le tenoit?"
>   (Ll. 3556–57)

> "Aloit devant le *graal* nus?"
> "Oïl." "Qui?" "Dui vallet sanz plus."
>   (Ll. 3561–62)

> "Et aprés le *graal*, qui vint?"
> "Une autre pucele." "Et que tint?"
>   (Ll. 3565–66)

> "De che que si t'est mescheü
> Que tu n'as del *graal* seü
> Qu'en en faisoit, n'u on le porte"
>   (Ll. 3603–5)

THE HIDEOUS DAMSEL EPISODE

> Ne del *graal* que tu veïs
> Ne demandas ne n'enqueïs
> Quel preudome l'en en servoit.
>   (Ll. 4659–61)

> Tant que il del *graal* savra
> Cui l'en en sert, et qu'il avra
>   (Ll. 4735–36)

THE HERMITAGE EPISODE

> Et del *graal* que je i vi
> Ne sai pas cui on en servi
>   (Ll. 6379–80)

> T'avient que rien n'en demandas
> De la lance ne del *graal*,
> Si t'en sont avenu maint mal
>   (Ll. 6400–6402)

> Et quant del *graal* ne seüs
> Cui l'en en sert, fol sens eüs.
>   (Ll. 6413–14)

> D'une sole oiste le sert on,
> Que l'en en cel *graal* li porte;
> Sa vie sostient et conforte,
> Tant sainte chose est li *graals*.
> Et il, qui est esperitax
> Qu'a se vie plus ne covient

Fors l'oiste qui el *graal* vient,
Douze ans i a esté issi
Que for[s] de la chambre n'issi
Ou le *graal* veïs entrer.
(Ll. 6422–31)

2. As the use of the article indicates, in Chrétien's romance the grail is a common and not a proper name. I will henceforth capitalize the word when alluding to its symbolic value (the "Grail" as quest), in contradistinction with its concrete significance (the "grail" as serving dish).

3. This tradition is examined and commented upon in the Introduction, which identifies the dates and dialects of thirteen out of the fifteen manuscripts that preserve the "complete" or extensive—as opposed to fragmentary—text of Chrétien's *Conte*. The fourteenth manuscript (Ms. E) is Edinburgh, National Library of Scotland, Advocates' 19. 1. 5 (third quarter of the 13th c., eastern dialect). The fifteenth manuscript is Paris, BN, f. fr. 1429 (last quarter of the 13th c., Champenois dialect). See Terry Nixon, "Catalogue of Manuscripts," pp. 44–45, 61–62.

4. L. 6501 inspired various readings: "se betes non" in Mss. S, T, and V; "se blestes non" in Ms. P; "se herbes non" in Mss. A, C, E, F, M, Q, R, and U; "s'erbetes non" in Ms. B. The emphasis is on the frugal, vegetarian character of the hermit's nourishment.

5. Lacunae in the line numbering of Roach's edition of Ms. T, which reflects that of Hilka's edition of Ms. A, refer to those lines in Ms. A that have no equivalent in Ms. T. An example occurs at l. 6506 of Roach's edition, which is followed by two more lines in Ms. A (as well as in Mss. P, S, and U): "Et estable tel con il dut: / Conreez fu si com estut" (and [his horse] was duly stabled, and given proper attention; see Lecoy's edition of Ms. A, ll. 6281–82). The repetitive character of these added lines convinces Charles Méla that they constitute an unwarranted interpolation (see Méla's edition of Ms. B, note to l. 6428). Yet if we accept the repetition as intentional, these lines can be viewed as indicators of the importance of Perceval's horse (i.e., of chivalric mobility) in enabling him to pursue his mission as reinforcement of the Grail lineage, as I will argue in Chapter 3.

6. Also called the Lancelot Grail Cycle or the Pseudo-Map Cycle, the Vulgate Cycle (ca. 1220–30) is a prose amplification of an earlier prose cycle (ca. 1200–1210), itself based on Robert de Boron's *Roman de l'Estoire dou Graal* (late 12th c.). Robert's *Roman* (preserved in a single manuscript: Paris, BN, f. fr. 20047) may have comprised three verse narratives focusing on Joseph of Arimathea, Merlin, and Perceval, of which only the *Joseph* and fragments of the *Merlin* are preserved. The prose trilogy based on Robert's *Roman* (preserved in two manuscripts, one of which is Paris, BN, f. fr. nouv. acq. 4166, known as the Didot manuscript) comprises the story of Joseph, of Merlin, and of Perceval

(the "Didot Perceval"). In this trilogy, the Grail story inaugurated by Chrétien becomes part of a biblical history, beginning with the recovery of the Grail dish by Joseph of Arimathea, its arrival in insular Britain, Perceval's initiation of the quest, and the eventual demise of Arthur's realm. Probably conceived by a single author, the Vulgate Cycle comprises five prose narratives that recast the Grail story according to the following chronology: *Estoire del Saint Graal*, *Estoire de Merlin*, *Lancelot*, the *Queste del Saint Graal*, and the *Mort le Roi Artu*. The Vulgate Cycle inspired an anonymous author to compose (between 1230 and 1240) his own rendition of the legend, known as the Post-Vulgate Cycle or *Roman du Graal*, that is preserved in scattered French fragments. See Fanni Bogdanow, *The Romance of the Grail*.

7. John Benton, "Consciousness of Self and Perceptions of Individuality."

8. Colin Morris, *The Discovery of the Individual, 1050–1200*, p. 122.

9. Robert W. Hanning, *The Individual in Twelfth-Century Romance*, p. 61.

10. In Chrétien's *Erec et Enide* (ca. 1170), for example, the successful outcome of Erec's quest for both amorous and chivalric perfection induces joy and admiration at Arthur's court: "Granz fu l'asanblee et la presse: / Chascuns d'Erec veoir s'angresse / Et haus, et bas, et povre, et riche" (great were the crowd and the press: everyone, high and low, poor and rich, struggles to see Erec). See Mario Roques's edition of Guiot's copy of Chrétien de Troyes, *Erec et Enide*, ll. 6317–19.

11. That Erec as fighter takes precedence over Erec as lover is corroborated by one of the codices in which Chrétien's romance is preserved: Paris, BN, f. fr. 24403 (fourth quarter of the 13th c., Picard dialect; Ms. V). Ms. V, the only one of the *Erec* manuscripts to be illuminated, presents Chrétien's romance sandwiched between two epic poems (*Garin de Monglane* and *Ogier le Danois*). This particular combination of texts, together with the pictorial cycle illustrating Erec's story, induce Sandra Hindman to see in the codex "a vehicle for the idealization of [Erec]'s excellence at arms." The pictorial cycle, which includes a depiction of the hunt of the white stag, of Erec's combat with three evil knights, and of his battle with two giants, develops an interpretation of Erec's story "as a swift adventure that takes place exclusively in the forest and features knights as warriors." Erec's last adventure pits him against Maboagrain, a formidable knight imprisoned by his beloved lady in the enchanted Brandigan garden, whom Erec defeats. As Hindman observes, "this episode casts Erec as a brave warrior from epic and [Maboagrain] as a fickle hero from courtly romance." See Hindman, *Sealed in Parchment*, pp. 130, 131, 133.

12. On the difference between independent selfhood and interdependent selfhood, see Hazel Rose Markus and Shinobu Kitayama, "Culture and the Self."

13. Ibid., pp. 227, 227–28, 226, 247.

14. What is ingenious in Erec's arrangement, in Hanning's view, is that

it "makes Enide a test of his prowess and insures his full involvement in the quest for honor (through openness to life's adventures) because of, rather than in spite of, his married state." See *The Individual*, p. 133.

15. Chrétien's *Yvain* (between 1171 and 1181) provides an example of craftiness in the character of Lunete, Laudine's lady in waiting, when she traps her lady "in agreeing to help one knight [the mysterious and valorous "knight of the lion"] who turns out to be another," that is, Yvain himself, who thus obtains through trickery Laudine's pardon for his spousal neglect. See ibid., p. 121.

16. As Donald Maddox notes, the central problem articulated in *Erec et Enide* focuses on Arthur's preoccupation with the solidarity of his own court, which is endangered by the self-interested performance of his knights—first of all, Erec—in distant realms and remote lands: if Arthur "initially sanctioned their identity as 'Arthurian knight' by conferring knighthood upon them, his subsequent involvement is largely restricted to their maintenance of *the centripetal ideal of his realm*, that is, the ideal which brought them to him in their youth and which he fervently hopes will keep them with him after their return." See *The Arthurian Romances of Chrétien de Troyes*, p. 25.

17. Hanning, *The Individual*, p. 239.

18. In the course of his adventures as narrated in the *Queste del Saint Graal*, Lancelot comes upon a hermit to whom he acknowledges his sinful love for Guinevere. According to the hermit, Lancelot, whom the Lord graced with supreme wisdom and prowess, misused his talents and is therefore "plus pechierres d'autres pecheors" (the worst of all sinners; *La Queste del Saint Graal*, ed. Pauphilet, p. 68, l. 14).

19. Hanning, *The Individual*, p. 242.

20. In the *Queste del Saint Graal*, Gauvain, Arthur's nephew and the paragon of his chivalry in traditional romance, is the most violent of all the questers. One of the many hermits figuring in the narrative thus admonishes him in these terms: "Ne devez mie cuidier que ces aventures qui ore avienent soient d'omes tuer ne de chevaliers ocirre; ainz sont des choses esperituex, qui sont graindres et mielz vaillanz assez" (you should not think that the adventures that are now taking place concern the slaying of men and killing of knights; to the contrary, these adventures, which are infinitely superior in difficulty and merit, are of a spiritual nature; p. 161, ll. 4–6).

21. See, for example, Pauline Matarasso, *The Redemption of Chivalry*. As Hanning remarks, although the *Queste del Saint Graal* represents an extreme case in "its uncompromisingly religious condemnation of all but holy chivalry," it also shares with other thirteenth-century romances the same view of the "book-as-repository" of historical truth or moral significance. The result of this common concern to remove Arthurian romance from the province of overt fiction is "a complete revaluation (and, in effect, annihilation) of one of the

great achievements of medieval vernacular literature: the imaginary universe of Chrétien de Troyes." See Robert W. Hanning, "Arthurian Evangelists," pp. 359, 355, 361.

22. Hanning, *The Individual*, p. 239.

23. As is sustained by the symbolic analysis of medieval romance inspired by the ground-breaking work of Durant W. Robertson, Jr., *A Preface to Chaucer*.

24. "That is, the Story of the Grail, whose book was given him by the count." Ed. Roach, ll. 66–67.

25. "Chrétien sows and casts the seed of a romance that he begins." Ed. Roach, ll. 7–8. See Michel Zink, *La subjectivité littéraire*, pp. 38–41.

26. "Et li vallés, qui *niches* fu, / Dist: 'Pucele, je vos salu' " (and the boy, who was simple, said: "Hail be to you, maiden"; ed. Roach, ll. 681–82; my emphasis). Perceval, who also receives the attribute of *niche* (or *nice*) in the hands of Arthur (ll. 1012, 1299) and Gornemant (1365), is often qualified as *sos* (fool; e.g., l. 200), *salvage* (ignorant; l. 975), and *fol* (foolish; l. 1173).

27. A hermit thus reminds Lancelot that the virtues required of the adherents of the new order of chivalry include virginity, humility, endurance, integrity, and charity: "Et encor vos comant je que tant come vos seroiz en ceste Queste ne mengiez de char ne ne bevez de vin, et alez toz jorz ou mostier oïr le servise de Nostre Seignor" (and I also order you that as long as you are on this quest you abstain from meat and wine, and go daily to church in order to attend the service of Our Lord; *La Queste del Saint Graal*, p. 129, ll. 13–16).

28. Hanning, *The Individual*, p. 139.

29. In Hanning's use of the term, the subjective *kairos* is "the time within or before which actions must be performed, and awareness sharpened, in circumstances and with effects crucial" to the hero's success as a self-determined individual. Ibid., p. 6.

30. The multicompartment opening miniature in Ms. T introduces the theme of Perceval's *nicheté*, indicating that the planner of the codex considered the protagonist's ignorance to be an important theme of Chrétien's romance. See Lori Walters, "The Use of Multi-Compartment Miniatures," pp. 334–35, and Keith Busby, "The Illustrated Manuscripts of *Perceval*," p. 356. The miniature depicts Perceval's encounter with five armed knights (whom he views as "angels"), his arrival at the court of Arthur (whose cap he knocks off with his horse), and his killing of the Red Knight by piercing him in the eye with a javelin (a nonchivaric weapon). These three images focus on elements in Perceval's story that underscore his ignorance or misperception of knightly culture.

31. In the present state of the narrative, Perceval's last appearance (the hermit episode) occurs in between two of Gauvain's adventures: the Tintagueil episode (during which Gauvain sides with a *niche* damsel against her elder sister) and the Escavalon episode (where Gauvain engages in an amorous

exchange with the daughter of the king of Escavalon—only to find himself attacked by the townsmen, who recognize in him the murderer of their king). At the structural level, the technique of narrative interlacing thus links the two parts of Chrétien's romance. At the level of plot, however, the location of the hermit episode in the midst of Gauvain's adventures appears incongruous, suggesting that the significance of the entire romance lies in the contrast thus elaborated between two vastly different perspectives on chivalry's mission. Although narrative interlacing is a common technique in twelfth-century vernacular literature, including Chrétien's previous romances, according to William W. Ryding, the *Conte du Graal* represents "the first exploitation of it as a structural pattern." See *Structure in Medieval Narrative*, p. 142, n. 35.

32. At the basis of this ambiguous juxtaposition is what Peter Haidu describes in terms of a "process of triangulation," in reference to the "aesthetic distance" that places both poet and public in a position external to the text, whose value is less its status as communicated object than as communication. See "Au début du roman, l'ironie," p. 466.

33. Peter Haidu, *Aesthetic Distance in Chrétien de Troyes*, p. 114.

34. Ibid., pp. 202, 258. Both of Chrétien's protagonists similarly undertake the defense of a helpless damsel, engage in a fight against a "red knight," meet a man in a boat, and confront the hostility of an "Orgueilleux." See ibid., pp. 231–55.

35. See Douglas Kelly, "La spécialité dans l'invention des topiques."

36. The structural organization of Chrétien's romances is also viewed in terms of a tripartite pattern. See Donald Maddox's review of scholarship on this subject, "Trois sur deux."

37. Maddox, *The Arthurian Romances*, p. 16.

38. Not only does the *Conte* comprise the two stories of Perceval and Gauvain. A bipartite pattern equally marks the respective parts of Chrétien's romance, each of which consists of a precrisis phase and a postcrisis phase. For Perceval, the crisis takes place at Arthur's court, with the Hideous Damsel's revelation of his failure at the Grail castle. In the case of Gauvain, according to Maddox, the crisis is initiated at the same locus, but occurs later on, at the remote castle of his maternal kin (La Roche Canguin), when Gauvain fails to assume his seigneurial duties. See ibid.

39.　　　　　Et dist: "Gavains, tu oceïs
　　　　　　Mon seignor, et si le feïs
　　　　　　Issi que tu nel desfïas.
　　　　　　Honte et reproce et blasme i as."
　　　　　　　　(Ed. Roach, ll. 4759–62)

And [Guigambresil] said: "Gauvain, you killed my lord, and you did it without challenging him first. This wins you shame, reproach, and blame."

40.   Par ceste terre dïent tuit,
                      Li blonc et li mor et li ros,
                      Que granz domages est de vos
                      Que vos armes antrelessiez.
                      Vostre pris est molt abessiez.
                             (*Erec*, ll. 2540–44)

Throughout the land they all say, whether with fair hair or with dark or with red, that it is a great pity for you to have put aside your arms. Your worth finds itself greatly reduced because of it.

41.   Yvain, molt fus or oblianz
                      Quant il ne t'an pot sovenir
                      Que tu devoies revenir
                      A ma dame jusqu'a un an.
                    (*Le Chevalier au Lion*, ll. 2748–51)

Yvain, you were carelessly forgetful when you failed to remember that you were supposed to return to my lady within a year.

42.   Et Perchevax redist tout el:
                      Qu'il ne gerra en un hostel
                      Deus nuis en trestot son eage,
                      Ne n'orra d'estrange passage
                      Noveles que passer n'i aille,
                      Ne de chevalier qui miex vaille
                      Qu'autres chevaliers ne que dui
                      Qu'il ne s'aille combatre a lui,
                      Tant que il del graal savra
                      Cui l'en en sert, et qu'il avra
                      La lance qui saine trovee
                      Et que la veritez provee
                      Li ert dite por qu'ele saine.
                         (Ed. Roach, ll. 4727–39)

And Perceval [in contrast to Kahedin] made quite a different oath: he will not spend two nights in the same lodging as long as he lives, nor hear of dangerous passages without crossing them, nor learn of a knight, or even two, more worthy than any other without fighting him, until he knows who is served by the grail, finds the bleeding lance, and is told the true reason it bleeds.

43.   Chiez le Roi Pescheor entras,
                      Si veïs la lance qui saine,
                      Et si te fu si tres grant paine
                      D'ovrir ta bouche et de parler
                      Que tu ne poïs demander

> Por coi cele goute de sanc
> Saut par la pointe del fer blanc;
> Ne del graal que tu veïs
> Ne demandas ne t'enqueïs
> Quel preudome l'en en servoit.
>
> (Ed. Roach, ll. 4652–61)

You entered the castle of the Fisher King and thus saw the Bleeding Lance, but it was too great an effort for you to open your mouth and speak, so that you were not able to ask why that drop of blood flows from the tip of the white blade; neither, regarding the grail that you saw, did you ask or inquire what noble man was thus served.

44. Perceval triumphs successively over Enguigeron, Clamadeu (the king of the Isles), and Orgueilleux de la Lande, each of whom he sends as hostage to Arthur, thereby arousing the king's desire to meet this worthy champion:

> Puis m'a si bien a gre servi
> Que par mon seigneur Saint Davi,
> Que l'en aore et prie en Gales,
> Jamais en chambres ne en sales
> Deus nuis pres a pres ne jerrai,
> Jusques atant que je savrai
> S'il est vis en mer ou en terre,
> Ainz movrai ja por aler querre.
>
> (Ed. Roach, ll. 4133–40)

Since that day [when Perceval killed the Red Knight], he has served me so well that, I swear by Saint David, who is honored and worshiped in Wales, I will never sleep two consecutive nights in a chamber or hall until I know whether he is alive on land or sea; rather, I will immediately set out to find him.

45. The Hideous Damsel incriminates Perceval for having failed, by his silence, to effect the healing of the wounded king, adding:

> Et ses tu qu'il en avendra
> Del roi qui terre ne tendra
> Ne n'iert de ses plaies garis?
> Dames en perdront lor maris,
> Terres en seront escillies
> Et puceles desconseillies,
> Qui orfenines remandront,
> Et maint chevalier en morront;
> Tot cist mal esteront par toi.
>
> (Ed. Roach, ll. 4675–83)

And do you know what will occur on account of this king who will not rule his land nor be cured of his wounds? Ladies will lose their husbands, lands will be ruined, maidens, helpless, will remain orphans, and many a knight will die; all these misfortunes will occur because of you.

46. That the Hideous Damsel sides with the Grail is suggested, first, by the setting (Arthur's court) where she chooses to deliver her indictment of Perceval as a newly acclaimed Arthurian knight and, second, by the effect of her excoriation in inducing Perceval to depart from Arthur's court. But Perceval's departure also fails to produce its intended result. He wanders for five years, we learn eventually, during which he seeks perilous adventures,

> Tant que molt bien s'i esprova.
> Soissante chevaliers de pris
> A la cort le roi Artu pris
> Dedens cinc ans i envoia.
> (Ed. Roach, ll. 6230, 6233–35)

so much so that he tested himself well. Over five years, he sent 60 worthy knights as hostages to Arthur's court.

Roach's line numbering indicates that two lines (ll. 6231–32) are missing in Ms. T (as in Ms. V; see ed. Hilka, note to ll. 1631–32). The number of conquered knights mentioned at l. 6233 (*soissante*) is 50 in Mss. M and V.

47. Contrary to appearances, however, the love motif has a crucial importance in Chrétien's last romance, for, as I argue in Chapter 4, it is his affective interaction with Blancheflor that provides Perceval with the sole means of developing into a mature and responsible individual.

48. In Algirdas Julien Greimas's definition, *actants* are the act- and event-producing forces in a given narrative. See *Sémantique structurale*, pp. 172–91.

49. Fredric Jameson, *The Political Unconscious*, p. 118.

50. This occurs after Yder's defeat by Erec, who summons his anonymous opponent to reveal his identity: "Lors li dist cil, ou voelle ou non: / 'Sire, Ydiers, li filz Nut, ai non'" (And the latter replies, whether he likes it or not: "Sir, my name is Yder, the son of Nut"; *Erec*, ll. 1041–42).

51. Jameson, *The Political Unconscious*, p. 119.

52. This potential outcome implies that Gauvain will continue to act as support and champion of Arthur's cause. In the *Conte*, however (as I show in Chapter 2), the traditional paragon of Arthurian chivalry shows a gradual propensity to neglect his royal mission in favor of self-gratifying pursuits. Considering the weakening of Arthur's power in the temporal setting of the *Conte*, it thus appears that Perceval as the agency of the Grail faction will succeed in effecting his lineage's access to preeminence. Yet this eventual success does not in itself represent a viable solution to the predicament of the *Conte*'s chivalric society because the preeminence of the Grail faction would in turn be chal-

lenged by rival clans or individuals. Chrétien's last romance is, in that sense, a powerful illustration of the cyclical nature of vendetta, indicating the inherent vulnerability and instability of a system of authority that relies on raw force to obtain and retain power.

53. The combat pitting the hero and Gauvain in the penultimate episode of *Yvain* adduces the same potentially lethal outcome because, as Donald Maddox notes, the confrontation brings "the adversaries to the brink of mutual martyrdom." See *The Arthurian Romances*, p. 70.

54. To quote Donald Maddox's assessment of the function of narrative denouement in *Erec et Enide*. See *Structure and Sacring*, p. 177.

55. Jameson, *The Political Unconscious*, pp. 124, 117.

56. Rosemary Morris, "Aspects of Time and Place in the French Arthurian Verse Romances," p. 262.

57. Once Marc's forester discovers the two lovers, according to Béroul, he runs down to the king's castle and tells Marc that "Gel vi *poi* a ensemble o lui" (I *just* saw the lovers asleep side by side); *Les Tristans en vers*, ed. Jean-Charles Payen, p. 61, l. 1866. Chrétien's *Yvain* provides similar evidence of the proximity between court and forest in the episode that narrates how the eponymous hero, after learning from her messenger that he is never to return to Laudine, leaves Arthur's court and immediately enters the woodlands:

> Et il va tant que il fu loing
> Des tantes et des paveillons
>
>   . . .
>
> Les bestes par le bois agueite,
> Si les ocit; et se manjue
> La venison trestote crue.
>
>   (*Le Chevalier au Lion*, ll. 2804–5, 2826–28)

And he goes so far away that he was soon far from the tents and pavilions. . . . He lies in wait for the animals in the woods, kills them, and then eats the game raw.

58. As king of the forest and new proprietor of Laudine's domain, Yvain achieves here a status that might eventually provoke Arthur's desire to come and challenge Yvain. Indeed, the king launches an expedition that takes him and his court to the wondrous fountain of Laudine's domain, where he proceeds to pour water onto its slab, thus setting off a tempest. Yvain comes at once, fully armed, and fights against Keu, whom he defeats. He then reveals his identity to the king. This recognition scene ends Arthur's challenge of the lord of the domain; and, like *Erec*, the narrative concludes with a "happy ending"— the "joie de la cort" episode—that underscores the festive and harmonious quality of the Arthurian community.

59. Jameson, *The Political Unconscious*, p. 117.

60. Maddox, *The Arthurian Romances*, p. 3.

61. Written in 1136 under Plantagenet sponsorship, Geoffrey's Latin chronicle inspired Wace to compose a vernacular adaptation, the *Roman de Brut*, which he reputedly presented to Queen Eleanor around 1155.

62. After Arthur's death, the Saxons came to govern the greater part of the island, "que Loegria uocabatur" (known by the name of Loegria), while Britons took refuge "in occidentalibus regni partibus, Cornubia uidelicet atque Guali[i]s" (in the western parts of the realm, that is, Cornwall and Wales). See Geoffrey of Monmouth, *The "Historia Regum Britannie,"* ed. Neil Wright, p. 134.

63. What characterizes the Other during the inaugural years of Arthur's reign is thus the ethnic difference distinguishing the king's enemies. In the terminal stage of Arthur's reign, the source of evil is no longer external, but comes from within because the cause of the king's eventual demise is his nephew, Mordred. Arthurian chroniclers nonetheless maintain the distinction between Arthur's "right" and the ethical wrong of his adversary by assigning to Mordred the role of absolute villain.

64. Gauvain learns that Guinevere has been abducted by Meleagant, "Uns chevaliers molt forz et granz, / Filz le roi de Gorre" (an extremely tall and mighty knight, the king of Gorre's son). See Mario Roques's edition of Guiot's copy of Chrétien de Troyes, *Le Chevalier de la Charrete*, ll. 638–39.

65. Meleagant keeps in Gorre a number of prisoners who were "del rëaume de Logres né" (born in the kingdom of Logres). See ibid., l. 2055. In "Arthur-izing" the realm of Loegria evoked in Geoffrey's chronicle, traditional romance not only relocates this territory on the west coasts of modern England, but also eliminates the Saxons as foreign invaders and oppressors of the Britons. As a result, Arthur's enemies inhabit the same land and follow the same customs.

66. The weakness of Arthur's kingship in vernacular romance takes into account and amplifies his tragic death or "dormition" in the concluding episode of his history as narrated by Geoffrey and by Wace, respectively.

67. Rupert Pickens rejects the reading of the two lines (6363–64) re-produced in Lecoy's edition of Ms. A. For Charles Méla, these added lines (which are also present in Mss. C, P, S, and U; see ed. Hilka, p. 294 note to l. 6602) appear to constitute an unwarranted interpolation (see Méla's edition of Ms. B, note to l. 6522). In my view, however, these two lines add important information by specifying the aggressive character of the people of Galloway.

68. Ms. A reads: "Li Orguelleus / De la Roche a l'Estroite Voie, / Qui garde les porz de Galvoie" (the Proud [knight] of the Rock of the Narrow Way, who watches over the passes of Galloway; ed. Lecoy, ll. 8384–86). Together these variants combine to underscore both the concrete and human character of the dangers awaiting anyone who attempts to cross the boundary.

69. The reading of Nogres (Norgres) instead of Logres in six of the com-

plete manuscripts preserving the *Conte* suggests on the part of their scribes a reluctance to associate Logres (which designates Arthur's kingdom in traditional romance) with the wicked territory evoked by one of the members of the Escavalon court. That Ms. M reads Nogres and not Logres might also be explained by the fact that the two previously cited lines identifying the kingdom of Logres as formerly the land of ogres are missing in this particular version of the *Conte*. A similar case can be made for Ms. Q because its version of that same passage reads Londres and not Logres. Significantly, in his translation of the version contained in Ms. B, Charles Méla replaces Norgres as Orgueilleuse's birthplace with Logres (trans. of l. 8551).

70. Although Nogres, as Donald Maddox observes, can also be viewed as "a negation of Logres," which would thus refer to an anterior stage of Arthur's kingdom as a "former paragon of justice." See *The Arthurian Romances*, p. 126.

71. Ed. Roach, l. 7179 (noxious maiden). The qualification of Orgueilleuse as *aniouse* in Ms. T reads *ataïneuse* (pernicious) in Ms. B (ed. Méla, l. 7093) and *ranponeuse* (malicious) in Ms. A (ed. Pickens, l. 7137).

72. According to the comment that Matthew Paris, the thirteenth-century St. Albans chronicler, wrote on his maps of Britain, Galloway is peopled with "gens montana" who are "ferocious and wild." See Morris, "Aspects of Time and Place," p. 273.

73. An episode in Perceval's story narrates his confrontation with one Orgueilleux de la Lande (the Proud [knight] of the Heath; ed. Roach, l. 3817). Gauvain confronts the hostility of both Orgueilleux de Galvoie and his friend, Orgueilleuse de Logres. The common term ("Orgueilleux") designating the "proud" knights who inhabit the *Conte* "rearranges the letters of the word 'Logres' into the negative field of *orgueil*." See Donald Maddox, *The Arthurian Romances*, p. 126.

74. Lancelot's actions address the law of love rather than that of Arthur. See Maddox, *The Arthurian Romances*, p. 52.

75. See Morton W. Bloomfield, *The Seven Deadly Sins*, and Lester K. Little, "Pride Goes Before Avarice."

76. As G. D. West remarks, the Orkney Isles mentioned in vernacular romances were "not necessarily thought of as such but as a kingdom in Bretaigne." See *An Index of Proper Names in French Arthurian Prose Romances*, p. 238. However, I suggest that Orquenie in Chrétien's *Conte* invokes a northern, albeit imprecise, part of Logres.

77. Ibid., p. 261.

78. "Es illes de mer n'ot lignage / Meillor del mien en mon eage" (in the isles of the sea there was no finer lineage than mine in my day; ed. Roach, ll. 425–26).

79. Madeleine Blaess, "Perceval et les 'Illes de Mer,'" p. 72. References to the "Isles" also appear in Chrétien's previous romances: *Erec* contains an

allusion to one "Bruianz des Illes," a knight who gave two thrones as a gift to Arthur and the queen (l. 6668); in *Yvain*, the hero learns that "li rois de l'Isle as puceles"—a born fool—is the reason 300 maidens are kept imprisoned at the castle of Pesme-Aventure (*Le Chevalier au Lion*, ll. 5251, 5254). Bruiant's generosity toward Arthur, together with the disparaging characterization of the king of the Isle of the Maidens, indicate that here the people of the Isles present no threat to Arthur's rule.

80. Geoffrey's *Historia* situates this campaign in the inaugural years of Arthur's reign. The first event is the death of Utherpendragon, which induces the Saxons to renew their aggression against the Britons. Arthur, as the latter's newly crowned king, launches an attack against the invaders, whom he defeats at the battle of Kaerluideoit (Lincoln), forcing them to flee to Caledonian Wood (Scotland), where he besieges them until they surrender and agree to return to Germany. Arthur then leads his army to Moray in order to fight the Picts and the Scots. Although Geoffrey's topography lacks precision, his charting of Arthur's northern campaign is consistent with Matthew Paris's four maps of Britain. In the perspective of both Geoffrey and Matthew Paris, "Wales and the Scottish borders are juxtaposed, and Carlisle is in Wales." See Morris, "Aspects of Time and Place," p. 264. The centrality of Carlisle (Kaerleil in the *Historia*) in this geographical configuration suggests that Geoffrey's Arthur might have used the city as a base against the Picts and Scots. See ibid., p. 266.

81. Geoffrey of Monmouth, *The "Historia Regum Britannie,"* p. 105.

82. See the edition by I. D. O. Arnold and M. M. Pelan of Wace, *Roman de Brut*, ll. 938–48.

83. Blaess, "Perceval et les 'Illes de Mer,' " p. 72.

84. Ed. Pickens, p. 453.

85. The nature of the wound afflicting Perceval's father varies in the manuscript tradition. He is struck between the "gambes" (legs) in Mss. P and A; between the "hanches" (hips) in Mss. M, Q, R, and U; in the "jambe" (in the singular) in Ms. T; and in the "[h]anche" (singular) in Mss. B, C, and H. See ed. Hilka, note to l. 436. The variant of Ms. S ("hauberc"; hauberk), although representing an obvious misreading of "hanches," is nonetheless noteworthy in that it underscores the military circumstances during which Perceval's father was mutilated. As I show in Chapter 3, a similar wound debilitates the Grail king, although the sexual character of his mutilation tends to be even more explicit: first, because variants share an allusion to the afflicted part of his body in the plural ("jambes"; hanches); second, because one variant (Ms. T) specifies that he was struck between the thighs ("quisses").

86. One would expect that Perceval's mother, herself a victim of Arthur's unfair aggression, would incriminate the king as the cause of her present misfortune. That she does not accuse but praises Arthur is remarkable indeed. Although her reference to "good King Arthur" does not cohere with the latter's

behavior during the campaign in Scotland as narrated by Wace, it is nonetheless consistent, as I suggest in Chapter 4, with her desire to protect Perceval from such customs as those that require a noble heir to assume the prosecution of his lineage's enemies.

87. Arthur makes this claim during his campaign in Gaul, after his victory over the monster of Mont-Saint-Michel: "dicebat autem se non inuenisse alium tante uirtutis postquam Rithonem gigantem in Arauio monte interfecit" (he said that he had not found anyone so strong since the time he killed the giant Rithon on Mount Aravius). Geoffrey of Monmouth, *The "Historia Regum Britannie,"* p. 119.

88. See William A. Nitze and Harry F. Williams, *Arthurian Names in the Perceval of Chrétien de Troyes*, pp. 289–90. Snowdon is the only mountain that figures in Matthew Paris's maps. See Morris, "Aspects of Time and Place," p. 263.

89. "Uocatis denique magis suis consuluit illos iussitque dicere quid faceret. Qui dixerunt ut edificaret sibi turrim fortissimam que sibi tutamen foret cum ceteras munitiones amisisset. Peragratis ergo quibusdam locis ut eam in congruo loco statueret uenit tandem ad montem Erir." Geoffrey of Monmouth, *The "Historia Regum Britannie,"* p. 71. The Mount Aravius associated with the giant Rithon and the Mount Erith of Vortigern are one and the same. See Geoffrey of Monmouth, *The History of the Kings of Britain*, trans. Lewis Thorpe, p. 298. Mount Aravius/Erith may refer to the Welsh "Dinas Emrys," whose meaning is the Fort of Ambrosius, in reference to the second name of Geoffrey's Merlin, Ambrosius. See Geoffrey Ashe, *The Landscape of King Arthur*, p. 89; see also Geoffrey of Monmouth, *The History of the Kings of Britain*, p. 187, n. 1.

90. The manuscript tradition proposes a profusion of variants for l. 298 of Roach's edition: "de Vaucoigne" (Ms. B); "de Valonne" (Ms. F); "d'Escandone" (Ms. H); "de Vaugonne" (Ms. Q); "de Valdonne" (Mss. S and U); "notre home" (our dwelling place; Ms. C). See ed. Hilka, note to l. 298. On the basis of Ms. H, some scholars associate the site Perceval mentions with the mountain passes of Snowdon ("d'Escandone," i.e., "de Scaudone"). For others, the reading of Ms. H represents a *lectio difficilior*, considering that the variants give priority to "Val-" (or "Vau," instead of "Scau-") as an initial syllable echoing the last one of Perceval's name (Perce-"val"). For still others, Val-"done" refers to the gorge of the "Done" on the boundary of Galloway. See Nitze and Williams, *Arthurian Names*, pp. 291–92.

91. Lenora D. Wolfgang, "Prologues to the *Perceval* and Perceval's Father," p. 87. Wolfgang also notes that *Bliocadran* (early 13th c.) reinforces Chrétien's distinction between Perceval's birthplace and the dwelling in the waste forest and that *Perlesvaus* (early 13th c.) gives Perceval's mother two separate residences.

92. Calogrenant's narration of his own adventure in the opening episode

of Chrétien's *Yvain* is emblematic. Calogrenant the storyteller begins by evoking his persona as adventure seeker: "Il m'avint plus a de set anz / Que je, seus come païsanz, / Aloie querant aventures" (More than seven years ago, it happened that I, alone like a peasant, was wandering in search of adventures; *Le Chevalier au Lion*, ll. 173–75). His path leads Calogrenant to encounter a villain, of whom he asks the way to find "Avanture, por esprover / Ma proesce et mon hardemant" (adventure, in order to test my prowess and courage; ll. 362–63), to which the villain replies: "D'aventure ne sai je rien, / N'onques mes n'en oï parler. / Mais si tu voloies aler / Ci pres jusqu'a une fontainne" (I know nothing about adventure, nor have I ever heard about it. But if you wanted to go to a nearby fountain; ll. 368–71). What follows is a detailed description of Laudine's fountain, the central adventure of Yvain as the hero of the romance.

93. Hearing Calogrenant's tale, Arthur decides that in a fortnight he and his knights will go to test themselves against the wondrous fountain. Yvain's reaction to the king's decision is significant: "Mes qui qu'an soit liez et joianz, / Mes sire Yvains an fu dolanz, / Qu'il i cuidoit aler toz seus" (But while everyone at court was happy and joyful, my lord Yvain was greatly saddened, for he had thought to go there on his own [in order to receive alone the honor of the test]; *Le Chevalier au Lion*, ll. 677–79).

94. "Au roi qui fait les chevaliers" (ed. Roach, l. 494).

95. Morris, "Aspects of Time and Place," p. 272.

96. Following the fisher's instruction, Perceval seeks, in vain at first, the lodging that is supposed to sit beyond "cele roche," "en un val" (this rock, in a vale; ed. Roach, ll. 3030, 3032). Then he suddenly sees the tip of its tower (l. 3051). When he wakes up the following morning, the castle is empty (l. 3359–85); and as he crosses the bridge on his way out, the bridge draws up under the front hooves of his horse ("Mes ains qu'il par fust jus del pont, / Les piez de son cheval amont / Senti qu'il leverent en haut"; ed. Roach, ll. 3403–5).

97. Morris, "Aspects of Time and Place," p. 270. The brief topographical survey presented in this paragraph is based on Rosemary Morris's detailed identifications of the *Conte*'s place names.

98. Ibid., p. 272. Two indices point forward to the median location of the Grail castle in the coastal landscape of the *Conte*. The first is the possible connection, as Rosemary Morris suggests, between the fictive Biaurepaire and the fortified port of Chester. The second is the proximity of Biaurepaire and the Grail castle, considering that Perceval comes upon the Grail castle after less than one day's ride from Biaurepaire. The castle thus stands midway between the geographical poles of the landscape charted in the romance.

99. Gauvain's route ends at La Roche Canguin, a castle located a short distance from the city of Orquenie (extreme northwest), where we last see Arthur holding court (ed. Roach, l. 9101).

100. Far from confirming Gauvain's traditional role as Arthur's most faithful deputy, in the *Conte*, as I argue in Chapter 2, the circular character of his journey signals his gradual transformation into a knight-errant exclusively interested in the pursuit of self-serving deeds.

101. Morris, "Aspects of Time and Place," pp. 271–72.

102. Ibid., p. 272.

103. Jameson, *The Political Unconscious*, p. 110.

104. Ibid., pp. 112, 111, 113.

105. See ed. Pickens, p. 454.

Chapter 2

1. Donald Maddox, *The Arthurian Romances of Chrétien de Troyes*, p. 133. In the section concluding his analysis, Maddox examines the interest of Chrétien's usage of customs within the sociohistorical sphere. See "Literary Customs and the Socio-historical Question," pp. 133–40.

2. Harold J. Berman, *Law and Revolution*, pp. 465, 535. With the ensuing decline of the aristocracy, feudal law as an autonomous legal system governing both the law of fiefs and the law of lord-vassal relations was destined to fade and "to remain as a fossil." Ibid., p. 533. On the development of the judicial system of bailiffs from Philip Augustus, see Emile Chénon, *Histoire générale du droit français public et privé des origines à 1815*, vol. 1, pp. 606–19.

3. Berman, *Law and Revolution*, p. 315.

4. Ibid., p. 471. On the growing preeminence of royal justice, see also Chénon, *Histoire générale du droit français public et privé*, pp. 519–23.

5. Berman, *Law and Revolution*, p. 417. On the gradual containment of feudal law by royal law, see also Adhemar Esmein, *Cours élémentaire d'histoire du droit français*, pp. 351–54.

6. John of Salisbury's *Policratius* (dating from 1159) distinguishes between a good prince, who rules according to law, equity, and the principle of the common welfare, and a bad prince, or tyrant, who rules by force. See Berman, *Law and Revolution*, p. 281.

7. See Maddox, *The Arthurian Romances*, pp. 32 and 130. On Arthur's depiction as an ineffective royal figure in vernacular literature, see also Edward Peters, *The Shadow King*, pp. 170–209, and Barbara Nelson Sargent-Baur, *"Dux bellorum / res militum / roi fainéant."* An illustration of the weakening of Arthur's rule in the temporal setting of Chrétien's *Conte* is his defeat at the hands of Rion, whereas Wace's *Roman de Brut* narrates how the king succeeds in defeating and killing Rion, who appears here as a giant, Rithon. See G. D. West, *An Index of Proper Names in French Arthurian Verse Romances, 1150–1300*, p. 138.

8. Maddox, *The Arthurian Romances*, p. 136.

9. Ibid.

10. Ibid., p. 139.

11. For an analysis of the opening episode of Chrétien's first extant romance, see Donald Maddox, *Structure and Sacring*, pp. 101–19.

12. For a review of critical analyses of the contrastive roles of love and prowess in Chrétien's *Erec et Enide*, see Sara Sturm-Maddox, "*Hortus non conclusus.*"

13. *Desresnier* suggests the notion of a disputation that can be verbal ("sanz bataille") or can, as is the case here, involve recourse to combat. See Maddox, *The Arthurian Romances*, pp. 71–72.

14. In an early episode of *Yvain*, Arthur decides to avenge the humiliation incurred by the hero's cousin, Calogrenant, at the hands of the lord of the domain of the fountain. As soon as the king and his companions agree to undertake this punitive enterprise, the animosity that marked the king's court in the narrative's opening section disappears and, with it, the danger of internecine violence.

15.   Tuit s'escrïent a une voiz:
            "Par Deu, sire, ne par sa croiz,
            Vos poëz bien jugier *par droit*
            Que ceste la plus bele soit."
            (*Erec*, ll. 1777–80; my emphasis)

They all cry out in unison: "In the name of God and His cross, sire, you are entitled to claim *by right* that she is the fairest of all."

16. An absolutist tenor marks the entire oration, which represents Arthur's longest discourse in Chrétien's romances. See Maddox's perceptive analysis of this oration in *The Arthurian Romances*, pp. 25–31.

17. According to Bernard Guenée, in the Middle Ages, customs inherited from "time immemorial" were measured in relation to man's capacity to remember, a "time of memory" covering approximately a century. See "Temps de l'histoire et temps de la mémoire." The best custom was one so ancient that its origins were no longer known. See Jean Barbey, "Genèse et consécration des lois fondamentales," p. 77; John Gilissen, *La Coutume*, pp. 29–30; and Paul Ourliac, "Coutume et mémoire," p. 117.

18. As Donald Maddox convincingly argues, manipulation is a constitutive property of late-twelfth-century romance. See "Roman et manipulation au 12e siècle." Not only is the audience presented with the creation of a make-believe world; vernacular romancers also endow their characters with the same talent to persuade and deceive because *engin*, as I show in Chapter 1, is the hero's best asset in empowering him to control the outer and inner circumstances of his story. In the *Conte du Graal*, whose twin protagonists are agents rather than *actants*, the art of creating an illusory or false "reality" belongs to figures such as Arthur, through Gauvain, his principal spokesman, who resort to a semiotics of deceit in order to justify their respective claims to hegemony.

19. As Daniel Poirion observes, the denouements of Chrétien's romances are not entirely convincing, indicating that the poet's talent lies in his ability to underscore, rather than solve, the problems besetting traditional chivalry. See "Du sang sur la neige," p. 163.

20. The emphatic use of the personal pronoun in Arthur's kingly oration reaffirms his preeminence at court: "*Je* sui rois" (It is *I* who am king; *Erec*, l. 1749; my emphasis).

21. Described in the penultimate episode of the romance, this custom perpetuates aggression among the knights of the realm. In abolishing the bad Brandigan custom, Erec restores peace and order in this part of the land, whence the joyful celebration at Arthur's court (in the final joie de la cort episode).

22. Maddox, *The Arthurian Romances*, pp. 6, 120, 89.

23. Taken together, *loial* (loyal) according to l. 7129 of Roach's edition and *leal* (legal) in the reading of Mss. A and B combine the idea of faithfulness and lawfulness. Gauvain's assessment of Arthurian justice thus points to the disinterested character of the king's adjudicative function in maintaining order without contravening the custom of the land.

24. In the context of the episode, Perceval's ignorance of the "lois" (laws; l. 236) mentioned by the knight appears to evoke both his linguistic and behavioral deficiency with respect to the protocols of chivalry.

25. As Pierre Legendre points out, *institution* is a legal term used by Roman jurists to define the principles (*institutiones*) imposed on the political subject. See *L'amour du censeur*, p. 24.

26. Words such as *sanc* (blood), *combatre* (fight), and *ocire* (kill) appear with a much greater frequency in his story than in Gauvain's. See Jacqueline Cerquiglini et al., "D'une quête l'autre," pp. 275, 287.

27. In the last decades of the twelfth century, the tournament differed little from warfare: a pitched battle between two armies, it was often deadly even though, because the aim was booty, each participant attempted "to capture rather than harm his opponent." See Larry D. Benson, "The Tournaments in the Romances of Chrétien de Troyes and *L'Histoire de Guillaume le Maréchal*," pp. 7–8. Benson cites the case of a tournament in 1170 between Baldwin of Hainaut and Godfrey of Louvain that degenerated into a bloody rout as an example proving that the game could "get out of hand and turn into a small civil war" (p. 11). See also Richard W. Barber, *The Knight and Chivalry*, pp. 167–77. Beginning with Chrétien, according to Larry Benson, courtly romance changed the tournament "from a mere rough sport into admirable chivalric activity," endowing the game "with all the authority of Arthurian history" (pp. 14, 17).

28. As Georges Duby notes, a battle is "a procedure of peace" in that it puts an end to war and spectacularly demonstrates on which side right stands.

See *Le dimanche de Bouvines*, pp. 145–46. See also John Beeler, *Warfare in Feudal Europe, 730–1200*, pp. 44–45.

29. The two men identified by Tibaut's counselor as Arthur's "knights" are in reality Gauvain and his squire. According to Jacqueline Cerquiglini et al., "D'une quête l'autre," the fact that Gauvain's identity becomes known only after his victory over Meliant calls into question the former's value as an autonomous knight (p. 284). In my view, however, this belated revelation of the champion's Arthurian identity serves to emphasize Gauvain's function as royal deputy.

30. In Larry Benson's view, Tibaut finally agrees to tourney with Meliant's men because his counselor reminds him "that he has many good archers and men-at-arms." See "The Tournaments," p. 13. I would suggest, however, that the counselor's advice, hence, Tibaut's eventual decision, results from the fortuitous arrival on the scene of "two" representatives of Arthurian chivalry whose renowned prowess carries with it the promise of victory.

31. Gauvain's intervention evokes an act of *disseisin*, that is, "the forcible dispossession of a man from his enjoyment of rights in land or other valuable perquisites." See W. L. Warren, *The Governance of Norman and Angevin England, 1086–1272*, p. 112. Henry II's invention of the *novel disseisin* (an inquisitorial procedure whose aim was to determine justified or unjustified dispossession) was one important way of settling land disputes outside the hazardous custom of trial by combat. The *novel disseisin* also played a significant role in demonstrating the peacemaking merits of Henry II's royal arbitration (ibid., pp. 112–16).

Arthur never actively participates in tournaments, for his function is one of judge and impartial spectator. It does not befit a king to engage in such profane and lucrative activities, and this is why Louis VII allowed his younger sons to joust, but not Philip Augustus, his heir presumptive. At the battle of Bouvines in 1214 opposing the French and their princely and imperial rivals, Philip Augustus was thus the sole actor who had never once tourneyed. See Duby, *Le dimanche de Bouvines*, p. 118.

32. In *Cligés*, for example, Fenice's wet nurse, Thessala, possesses the ability to concoct wondrous potions (see *Cligés*, ll. 3156–74 and 5394–5402). In *Yvain*, the lady of Norison owes to Morgan le Fay her possession of an unguent capable of curing mental diseases (*Le Chevalier au Lion*, ll. 2948–51).

33. This substratum can be traced in legends, like that of Mélusine, whose protagonist is a woman endowed with a fairylike power over nature. According to Laurence Harf-Lancner, the many ladies-of-the-lake figuring in Arthurian literature are, like Mélusine, distant heirs to the goddesses of Celtic mythology and share with her the same chthonian origin. See "Une Mélusine galloise." See also Robert Sherman Loomis, *Celtic Myth and Arthurian Romance*, Part D, "Brides of the Sun," and Jean Markale, *Le roi Arthur et la société celtique*.

34. See Jessie L. Weston, *From Ritual to Romance*, pp. 106–10, who evokes Gauvain's possession of medical knowledge in such romances as the Dutch poems *Moriaen* (late 13th c.) and *Lanceloet* (ca. 1300).

35. See *Triads of Britain*, p. 50. As Malcolm Smith notes in the introduction, the triads—mnemotenics that may date from the Roman occupation—were used in the barbic schools to recall the British heroic age; the oldest surviving collections of triads are preserved in thirteenth-century manuscripts (p. 9).

36. In *Erec et Enide*, Chrétien mentions that Arthur received from Morgan, his sister, an unguent capable of curing any wounds (ll. 4193–4200). The prose rendition of Robert de Boron's *Merlin* specifies that Morgan, the daughter of Ygerne and the Duke of Tintagueil, learned so well that she "sot merveille d'un art que l'en apele astronomie et molt en ouvra toz jorz et sot molt de fisique, et par celle mastrie de clergie qu'ele avoit fu apelee Morgain la faee" (mastered the art that is called astronomy, which she practiced daily, and also mastered the art of physics, and because of her control in the science of clerks, was known as Morgan le Fay). See Robert de Boron, *Merlin*, ed. Alexandre Micha, p. 245, ll. 10–13.

In contrast to the description of fairy characters in twelfth-century romances, which converge on the *fées'* supernatural power, thirteenth-century romances echo the Church's view of women as "fickle, insatiable, [and] dangerous" and present the *fées'* power in terms of unnatural, hence, evil, knowledge. See Kathryn S. Westoby, "A New Look at the Role of the *Fée* in Medieval French Arthurian Romance."

37. According to *Culhwch and Olwen*, a Welsh tale preserved in a fourteenth-century manuscript. See *The Mabinogi and Other Medieval Welsh Tales*, tr. Patrick K. Ford, p. 132.

38. Wounded by a falcon's attack, a goose has bled three drops of blood on the snow, a sight that brings to Perceval's mind the "vermel" color of Blancheflor's cheeks in her white face: "Si pense tant que il s'oblie" (he thus becomes so lost in his contemplation that he forgets himself; l. 4202). As Henri Rey-Flaud notes, Perceval's novel capacity to forget himself, which goes in tandem with his novel awareness of the Other, here signals the emergence of his autonomous self. See "Le sang sur la neige," p. 22. I examine both the blood on the snow scene and the multiple commentaries it has inspired further in relation to the significance of Blancheflor in Perceval's story in Chapter 4.

39. That Perceval is sleeping indicates that a knight immobile on his horse is an unusual sight from the perspective of Arthur's men, just as it is unusual—and, indeed, problematic in the context of Arthur's sovereign status—that the king is sleeping in his tent. In this light, distinction in traditional chivalric society is proportional to one's capacity to demonstrate one's prowess. However, although Arthur is sleeping, such is not the case of Perceval, whose

apparent catalepsy is really a contemplative stance. The misinterpretation of Arthur's men here discloses the significance of prowess as demonstrated martial expertise in chivalric culture. Their judgment of Perceval confirms the incompatibility of love and prowess in traditional knightly society because it misreads amorous contemplation in terms of a passivity resulting in loss of chivalric status. The way the courtiers confuse appearances and realities stands in striking contrast to Perceval's developing ability to see beyond the literal. As Grace Armstrong remarks, the protagonist is no longer the buffoon who first arrived at Arthur's court; at this point in his story, Perceval has in reality "surpassed [the courtiers'] *courtoisie* by becoming fully aware of the complexities involved in courtly service." See "The Scene of the Blood Drops on the Snow," p. 144. And because Perceval's love for Blancheflor distances itself from the rival ground of amorous pursuits in the hands of Arthur's *ami chevalier*, as I show in Chapter 4, love here represents a powerful antidote to the violent impulses governing the inhabitants of the Land of Ogres.

40. The Welch Gwalchmai is described as a golden-tongued knight, one "so mellifluous and eloquent" in all his addresses that "no one could refuse to grant [him] what [he] desired." See *Triads of Britain*, p. 70.

41. See Alice Planche, "La Dame au sycomore," pp. 495–516.

42. Vernacular texts provide various interpretations of the second element (*-mor*) contained in the word, which is sometimes understood as death, sometimes as madness (in reference to the Greek *moros*), and sometimes placed in rhyming parallel with love (*amor*). See ibid., pp. 502, 511.

43. As Erec eventually learns from Maboagrain, his beloved's intention was to keep him forever her prisoner, for "Ne cuidoit pas que a nul jor / Deüst an cest vergier antrer / Vasaus qui me deüst outrer" (She thought that the day would never come when a knight able to overcome me would enter this orchard; *Erec*, ll. 6042–44).

44. The common designation of necromancy as black magic results from a confusion between the Greek root *nekros* and the Latin *niger*.

45. Since Pepin the Short in 751, Carolingian leaders were crowned through a progressively elaborate ritual involving public anointment by bishops. See Marc Bloch, *Les rois thaumaturges*, p. 69. On the sacred character of medieval kingship, see also Robert Folz, *Les saints rois du moyen âge en Occident (VIe–XIIIe siècles)*, and Andrew W. Lewis, *Royal Succession in Capetian France*.

46. The Capetians were apparently the first to profess the miraculous effect of their royal touch. See Duby, *Le dimanche de Bouvines*, p. 47. Henry II of England was praised for having cured cases of scrofula and even for having freed his people from the plague. See Bloch, *Les rois thaumaturges*, pp. 41–42, 246.

47. Although Arthur claims, as he does in the oration quoted from *Erec et*

Enide, that his law is right and true, as Donald Maddox observes, the king never asserts that his custom is also good: "rather than prescribe ethical attributes," the king's customary regulation of chivalric behavior provides "a juridical model founded more on ritualized action than on a set of invariable values." See *The Arthurian Romances*, pp. 138–39. Remarkably, the Grail spokesmen make no mention of Gauvain's power, a silence that contrasts eloquently with the sanctifying exaltation of Grail kingship in their discourse, particularly in the discourse of Perceval's eremitic uncle (analyzed in Chapter 3).

48. Greoreas's wounds caused him to become blind. Through Gauvain's intervention, he recovers not only his health, but also his sight. He is thus enabled to identify his healer as Arthur's nephew.

49. The last four lines of the quotation appear in Mss. A, C, F, P, S, and U only. In Rupert Pickens's view, these lines are not an unwarranted repetition, but underscore Greoreas's "ability to regard himself from another's, that is, his lady's, point of view, and in a rather touching way at that." See ed. Pickens, p. 466.

50. In contrast to his role as accuser in this episode of Chrétien's *Conte*, Gauvain is forced into the role of the accused in the *First Continuation*. The episode begins with Gauvain's discovery of a beautiful maiden, lying inside a pavilion. He asks for her love and she gives herself to him. When her father learns that she is no longer a maiden, he challenges Gauvain, who kills him. Soon thereafter, Bran de Lis, the girl's brother, pursues Gauvain and accuses him of being a rapist and a murderer. See the *First Continuation*, ll. 2592–987.

51. See Georges Duby, "Les 'jeunes' dans la société aristocratique dans la France du Nord-Ouest au XIIe siècle."

52. Within the nobility, any lord who planned to marry had to consult his vassals; conversely, these could not choose their spouse without their lord's consent. See Georges Matoré, *Le vocabulaire et la société médiévale*, p. 194. In Arthur's case, royal control of matrimonial unions was a unilateral law.

53. As Warren has demonstrated, the result of Henry II's juridical innovations was that his principle of the rule of law "taught his subjects the remedy against the abuse of power." See *The Governance of Norman and Angevin England*, p. 396. Both Henry II and Philip Augustus were instrumental in developing the notion of the rule of law. Bracton in England (early 13th c.) could thus state that the king is under God and the law, and Philip of Beaumanoir in France (late 13th c.) insisted that a judge must disobey his lord rather than carry out an order contradicting God's law. See Berman, *Law and Revolution*, pp. 293, 479, and Philippe de Beaumanoir, *Coutumes de Beauvaisis*, vol. 1, p. 18.

54. A chance encounter with Erec arouses in Keu the desire to force the hero to come to Arthur. Erec resists and criticizes the king's seneschal for attempting to take him "par force" and "sanz desfiance" (by force and without

challenging him first; *Erec*, ll. 4006–7). Here, as in the blood on the snow episode of the *Conte*, Keu's action brings forward Arthur's intention to rally the best knights of the realm to reinforce his authority.

55. The purpose of the attacker's challenge (*défi*), an essential part of the ritual regulating armed encounters in chivalric society, was to provide the opposing party with adequate time to prepare his defense, thus ensuring fairness in combat. See Matoré, *Le vocabulaire et la société médiévale*, p. 297.

56. The dispute between Gauvain and Guigambresil indicates the highly litigious character of both the *Conte*'s chivalric society and contemporary feudal aristocracy. Indeed, as Friedrich Heer notes, "litigation was second only to feuding and warfare as a form of conflict favoured by the baronage." See *The Medieval World*, p. 21.

57. According to the legist Glanvill (late 12th c.), a murder is "done secretly, out of sight and knowledge of all but the killer and his accomplices." Quoted by Warren, *The Governance of Norman and Angevin England*, p. 60. Philippe de Beaumanoir states that such a crime deserves capital punishment. See *Coutumes de Beauvaisis*, vol. 1, p. 824.

58. The improbable character of Gauvain's first hypothesis reveals that he does not value cases of reconciliation achieved through pacific means. Resembling a combat between two violent contestants, the verbal dispute opposing him and Guigambresil indicates that they both seek to settle the issue by means of a martial confrontation. That their verbal debate is a stage of combat is another illustration of the litigiousness characterizing contemporary nobility, for whom, as Friedrich Heer remarks, "trial by battle and trial by law were both forms of single combat. 'God and my right': let God determine the issue, in the duel and in the ordeal." See *The Medieval World*, p. 21.

59. As Georges Matoré notes, Philippe de Beaumanoir refers to the judicial duel as "gages de bataille" (gages of combat). See *Le vocabulaire et la société médiévale*, p. 193, n. 15.

60. To borrow R. Howard Bloch's expression. See *Medieval French Literature and Law*, p. 119.

61. The recourse to champions constitutes the grounds on which the duel as legal procedure was ultimately abandoned and replaced by inquests and jury trials. On the practice of inquest by the royal French court, see John W. Baldwin, *The Government of Philip Augustus*, pp. 141–44. On the use of jury trial under Henry II, see Warren, *The Governance of Norman and Angevin England*, p. 212–14. On the corruption of the procedure as represented in vernacular literature, see Huguette Legros, "Quand les jugements de Dieu deviennent artifices littéraires, ou la profanité impunie d'une poétique," and Pierre Jonin, *Les personnages féminins dans les romans français de Tristan*.

62. The solution arises in the form of a verbal ruse as Arthur succeeds

in manipulating the wrongdoer into admitting her guilt. As Donald Maddox notes, here, as in the concluding episode of *Yvain*, the resolution involves "the deceptive solicitation of speech acts." See *The Arthurian Romances*, p. 76.

63. All manuscripts concur with the identification of the deceased as being Guigambresil's lord, except for Ms. A, wherein he is the plaintiff's own father ("mon pere"). Both Hilka (note to l. 4760) and Lecoy (note to l. 4734) reject this reading. The identity of the dead lord as the king of Escavalon is revealed during the episode narrating Gauvain's arrival at Escavalon.

64. See Gustave Cohen, "Le duel judiciaire chez Chrétien de Troyes," p. 524.

65. According to René Louis, the pseudoprefix *es-* in words such as Arthur's Escalibor, his father, Espandragon, and the kingdom of Escavalon merely emphasizes the martial or heroic value of the proper name. See "Le préfixe inorganique es- dans les noms propres en ancien français."

66. See, for example, the prose rendition of the Perceval story known as the Didot Perceval (ca. 1200–1210; thus named in reference to the former owner of one of the two manuscripts in which the text is preserved), which states: "Et si fu li rois Arthus navrés a mort, car il fu ferus d'une lance parmi le pis, et lors mena on grant duel entor Artu. Et Artus lor dist: 'Laissiés ester le duel, car je ne morrai pas. Je me ferai porter en Avalon por mes plaies meciner a Morghain, me seror'" (and thus the king was mortally wounded, for he was struck by a lance in the middle of his chest, on account of which the grief was great around him. And Arthur told his men: "Put aside your grief, for I shall not die. I will have myself carried to Avalon to have my wounds cured by Morgan, my sister"). See *The Didot Perceval According to the Manuscripts Modena and Paris*, ll. 2642–46.

67. For a summary of the Irish and Welsh origins of the island of Arthur's dormition, see William A. Nitze and Harry F. Williams, *Arthurian Names in the Perceval of Chrétien de Troyes*, p. 272, and the entry "Avalon" in Norris J. Lacy, ed., *The Arthurian Encyclopedia*, pp. 32–35. That Ablach (i.e., rich in apple trees) is replete with apples, a traditionally magic fruit, also accounts for the otherworldly character of the island.

68. The beheading game consists of the following challenge: he who volunteers to cut off the giant's head will earn the right to govern but will himself be beheaded a year later. The last aspect of the challenge serves only as a test of the champion's bravery, hence its significance as transferal of power.

69. Other champions of the beheading game include Cûchulainn and Karadawc, mythical heroes of the Celtic tradition, and Chrétien's Lancelot, who overcomes Meleagant, the heir presumptive of the otherworldly land of Gorre. As Jean Markale notes, in most of these texts, transferal of power is clearly Arthur-oriented. See *Le roi Arthur et la société celtique*, p. 343. The

beheading game appears in the *First Continuation* when an unknown knight presents himself at Arthur's court and challenges the king and his companions. No one responds to his challenge, hence his scorn:

> Or poëz veoir, rois Artus,
> Que vostre cors n'est pas si riche
> Come chascuns dist et affiche;
> N'i a nul chevalier hardi.
>
> (Ll. 3374–77)

It is by now clear, King Arthur, that your court is not as strong as everyone says and maintains; you do not have a single courageous knight.

These contemptuous words induce Carados to respond to the knight's challenge by striking off his head.

70. See Roger Sherman Loomis, *Arthurian Tradition and Chrétien de Troyes*, p. 480, and Jean Marx, *Nouvelles recherches sur la littérature arthurienne*, p. 149. According to Jacques Ribard, for whom the topography of the Arthurian textual tradition does not have a referential significance, the Escavalon of Chrétien's *Conte du Graal* (whose prefix signifies, in his view, the "marches" of Avalon) represents a symbolic "ladder" allowing Gauvain access to the Other World. See "Ecriture symbolique et visée allégorique dans le *Conte du Graal*," p. 104.

71. According to Jean Markale, the term *Glas* really refers to a Saxon ethnic group settled at Glastonbury. See *Le roi Arthur et la société celtique*, p. 128.

72. As already noted (see the Introduction), Philippe Ménard interprets Gauvain's trial at Escavalon differently. In his view it betokens a dispute opposing the Escavalon faction not with Arthur, but with the Grail lineage, the result of which is that the Grail lineage and Gauvain (hence Arthur) are allies. See "Problèmes et mystères du *Conte du Graal*," p. 65.

73. This lineal tie between Ban and Galahad is identified by Ulrich von Zatzikhoven in his *Lanzelet* (ca. 1200). See Nitze and Williams, *Arthurian Names in the Perceval of Chrétien de Troyes*, p. 267. That Galahad's completion of the quest for the Grail marks the beginning of the end of Arthur's reign is frequently noted in Grail literature after Chrétien. An example is the opening episode of the *Queste del Saint Graal*, which narrates how Galahad's arrival at Arthur's court induces in every knight there the desire to answer the call of the Grail quest. Hence the king's lament over the departure of "la plus bele compaignie et la plus loial que je onques trovasse, et ce est la compaignie de la Table Reonde. Car quant il departiront de moi, de quelle ore que ce soit, je sai bien qu'il ne revendront ja mes tuit arriere, ains demorront li plusor en ceste Queste" (the finest and most loyal companionship that I could ever find, that is, the companionship of the Round Table. For when they decide to depart from me, regardless of the time, I know well that they will not all return here,

and that many of them will keep on this Quest). See *La Queste del Saint Graal*, ed. Albert Pauphilet, p. 17, ll. 2–6.

74. Rosemary Morris, "Aspects of Time and Place in the French Arthurian Verse Romances," p. 272.

75. As Rupert Pickens notes, Gauvain's incongruous courting of the daughter of a man whom he is accused of having murdered discloses the less than heroic significance of Chrétien's second protagonist. See ed. Pickens, p. 463. Gauvain's philandering is the cause of a potentially nefarious chain of events that cumulatively underscores the profound deficiency of Arthur's nephew in Chrétien's *Conte*. His exposure as the murderer of the king of Escavalon compels Gauvain the lover to resume his persona as knight; however, because he has left part of his weapons outside the maiden's chamber, Gauvain finds himself forced to make a shield from a chessboard and to rely on the help of his lady friend, who flings the chess pieces at their assailants. Significantly, the passage in question is excised in Ms. A (ll. 5852–991 in ed. Pickens reproduce the reading of Ms. T), which thus obfuscates Gauvain's display here of chivalric inadequacy. Neither does Gauvain show himself an adequate lover because, as Peter Haidu remarks, his dalliance with the young king's sister, like all of his flirtations throughout the romance, qualifies as a case of "unconsummated conquest." See *Aesthetic Distance in Chrétien de Troyes*, p. 215.

76. I disagree on this point with Paule Le Rider, for whom Gauvain's quest for the Bleeding Lance is a quest for repentance. See *Le chevalier dans le "Conte du Graal" de Chrétien de Troyes*, pp. 305–21. In the *First Continuation*, Gauvain eventually returns to the Grail castle, where he learns about the significance of the Bleeding Lance. Longinus used it to strike the son of God in the side. Since that fatal blow, the lance "Toz jors a puis sainié adés, / Et saineras durablement / Entrusqu'al jor del finement" (has bled and will continue to bleed until Judgment Day; ed. Roach, ll. 13474–76). The Grail king assigns the origin of the realm's misfortune not to the lance, but to the now broken sword of the Grail: "Li roialmes de Logres fu / Destruis, et toute la contree, / Par le cop que fist ceste espee" (the kingdom of Logres and the entire realm were ruined by the blow this sword dealt; ll. 13506–8). The king's chronicle differs from Chrétien's narration in that it situates this event in the past and thus eliminates the factional connotation that Logres receives in the Escavalon episode.

77. As Keith Busby shows in his insightful analysis, the representation of Gauvain undergoes several stages from Geoffrey of Monmouth to 1230. Epitomizing perfect knighthood under Arthur's imperial leadership, in the Vulgate Cycle, for example, Gauvain emblematizes the problems inherent in the chivalric ideal. Thus "the history of the figure of Gauvain illustrates many of the aspects of the history of Arthurian romance, and the rise and fall of Gauvain is the rise and fall of the Arthurian world." See *Gauvain in Old French Literature*,

p. 402. Chrétien's romances reflect this transformation: in contrast with *Erec*, where Gauvain acts as the king's faithful and sagacious guide (for example, questioning Arthur's wisdom in reviving the Custom of the White Stag), the futile or even lethal character of his performance in the *Conte*, although undermining Gauvain's effectiveness as royal advisor, also discloses the defects and inadequacies of the Arthurian principle of chivalric behavior. In the context of the French Arthurian tradition of the twelfth century, what makes Chrétien's *Conte* unique is that it appears to be the sole text in which Gauvain is confronted with outright enemies. See E. H. Ruck, *An Index of Themes and Motifs in Twelfth-Century French Arthurian Poetry*, sec. L-a. 18, p. 92.

78. This mention of the *pais* evokes the peace movements (God's Truce and God's Peace) by means of which ecclesiastical and secular rulers in the eleventh and twelfth centuries attempted to control military aggression. See Marc Bloch, *La société féodale*, pp. 569–79, and Thomas Head and Richard Land, eds., *Essays on the Peace of God*. In the context of the Tintagueil episode, however, the comment has a derogatory implication.

79. From the perspective of the merchants, whose function was *negotium* (i.e., an occupation that is *not idle*), nobles were often viewed as social parasites. See Jacques Le Goff, *Pour un autre Moyen Age*, p. 96. By contrast, the nobility idealized its function in terms of a commitment to defend and protect the realm. In the context of the Tintagueil episode, the sarcastic comments inspired by Gauvain's idleness, which prompts the ladies to identify him as a tradesman, constitute an implicit inversion of the merchants' perspective: if Gauvain sits idly while the tournament takes place, this indicates that he belongs not to chivalric but to economic society.

80. This danger accounts for the role of courtly romance in attempting to obfuscate the martial character of chivalry. As Eugene Vance perceptively demonstrates in his analysis of Chrétien's *Yvain*, the thrust of metaphor in the narrative discourse of chivalric romance "is to 'translate' warlike impulses into the impulse to love: that is, to subvert the *proprietas* of chivalric war by making it 'figurative.'" See "*Mervelous Signals*," p. 121. The significance of the *Conte*'s mercantile similes is examined by Marc Shell, who sees the grail as the image of a "boundless gift" that was appropriated both by "financial wizards beginning to dabble in credit economics" and by the tenants of "the dying [feudal] aristocracy." See "The Blank Check," p. 24. This is why Shell refers to Chrétien's romance as the "Account of the Grail." Sandra Hindman interprets the iconographic program of Ms. P (a codex "copied and illustrated in the area of the counties of Flanders and Hainaut probably between 1275 and 1285") as indicating a reading of Perceval's story in genealogical terms. The idealization of dynastic lineage here suggests "an antiroyal, anti-Capetian stance," articulating the desire of the Flemish aristocracy to exalt, if not preserve, its

prestige and autonomy. One of the factors weakening its status was the gradual blurring of the social lines between nobility, knighthood, and bourgeoisie, considering the way "knighthood came to be purchasable, like a commodity." See Hindman, *Sealed in Parchment*, pp. 89, 123, 120. The image of Perceval as the heir of a family of the upper aristocracy accounts for the favorable reception of Chrétien's *Conte* and its *Continuations* at the court of Flanders. Manessier thus dedicates his narrative to Johanna (Philippe of Alsace's grandniece, Countess of Flanders from 1206 to 1244), whom he extols as a noble lady graced with "sens," "valeur," "biauté," "cortoisie," "loiauté," "franchise," "largesce," and "pris" (wisdom, valor, beauty, courtesy, loyalty, nobility, generosity, and worth; *Third Continuation*, ll. 42647–49). "Ai en son non finé mon livre. / El non son aiol conmença" (I have done my book in her name. It was begun in the name of her ancestor [Philippe of Alsace]; ll. 42652–53).

81. The *First Continuation* undercuts Gifflet's boast in Chrétien's *Conte* that he will demonstrate his knightly superiority at the Chastel Orgueilleus. Arthur accuses his knights of treason for having failed to rescue Gifflet from the Chastel Orgueilleus, where he has been imprisoned for three years: "S'en ai al cuer molt grant dolor, / C'ainc ne vi chevalier meillor" (I greatly suffer in my heart, because I never had a better knight than he; ll. 8997–98).

82. There is no point in duplicating Haidu's penetrating assessment of Gauvain's story, which my own comments therefore summarize. See *Aesthetic Distance in Chrétien de Troyes*, pp. 203–50.

83. Wace, *Roman de Brut*, for example, identifies Orquenie as the kingdom of Loth. For other references, see West, *An Index of Proper Names*, p. 126.

84. Consistent with the reproach he addresses to the eponymous hero of *Yvain*, Gauvain does not want to "anpirier" (degenerate) by remaining idle in one place. His attitude at La Roche Canguin thus puts into action the advice he gives his companion in Chrétien's previous romance: "Or ne devez vos pas songier, / Mes les tornoiemanz ongier" (instead of wasting your time in [amorous] dreams, you must preoccupy yourself with the pursuit of tournaments; *Le Chevalier au Lion*, ll. 2505–6).

Chapter 3

1. Donald Maddox, *The Arthurian Romances of Chrétien de Troyes*, p. 131. Maddox links this ideal anterior order not to the inaugural years of Arthur's rule, but to the reign of his father, Utherpendragon. Considering the abusive character of Uther's rule in such accounts as that of Robert de Boron, however, this anterior order qualifies as "ideal" only within the context of a proroyal discourse. The relative insignificance of Uther within Chrétien's chronicle indicates that Arthur laments the erosion of his power and the disappearance of his hegemony, rather than his father's.

2. Ibid., p. 132 (my emphasis).

3. So ensconced is he in worries that cause him to be *pensis* and *mus* (preoccupied and silent; l. 911), Arthur does not notice Perceval's arrival at court.

4. In the reading of Mss. C, R, and U. See ed. Hilka, note to l. 1243. In my view, as in that of Rupert Pickens (who rejects *valet* in favor of *chevalier* in his edition of Ms. A), this latter variant represents a better reading insofar as it underscores the centrality of martial talent in ensuring one's identification as an Arthurian knight.

5. See Wace, *Roman de Brut*. Hereafter cited as *Brut*.

6. David A. Fein, "*Le Latin Sivrai*," p. 582.

7. Maddox, *The Arthurian Romances*, p. 134.

8. Gabrielle M. Spiegel, *Romancing the Past*, p. 266.

9. Jean Flori, *L'idéologie du glaive*, pp. 100–102, 168–73.

10. Jean Flori, *L'essor de la chevalerie, XIe–XIIe siècles*, pp. 268–89.

11. Ibid., pp. 302–3.

12. Ibid., pp. 270–71.

13. Tony Hunt, "The Emergence of the Knight in France and England, 1000–1200," pp. 7, 19.

14. See Georges Duby, *Le dimanche de Bouvines*, pp. 122–24.

15. In his seminal analysis, "Chrétien's *Yvain* and the Ideologies of Change and Exchange," Eugene Vance posits that one of the purposes of romance as "fiction" was "to accelerate the transformation of twelfth-century chivalric conduct into a class exercise whose archaic warlike function was becoming more an emblem or a sport than a form of direct political coercion." In translating the warlike impulses into the impulse of love, in subverting "the *proprietas* of chivalric war by making it 'figurative,'" the goal of romances such as Chrétien's *Yvain* was to inaugurate "a new casuistry based upon the rigorous perception of equivalences of value among people, services, or objects to be metamorphosed or exchanged in the economy of love." See "*Mervelous Signals*," pp. 121, 129.

16. This is sustained in the episode describing how the king proceeds to dub 400 knights and more,

> Toz filz de contes et de rois:
> Chevax dona a chascun trois,
> Et robes a chascun trois peire,
> Por ce que sa corz mialz apeire.
> Molt fu li rois puissanz et larges.
>
> . . .
>
> Alixandres, qui tant conquist
> Que desoz lui tot le mont mist,
> Et tant fu larges et tant riches,
> Fu anvers lui povres et chiches.
>
> (*Erec*, ll. 6601–5, 6611–14)

all sons of counts and kings: to each of them he gave three horses and three pairs of robes in his desire to enhance the appearance of his court. The king was as powerful as he was generous. . . . Alexander, who conquered so many lands that he subjugated the whole world, and who was so liberal and wealthy, was poor and mean compared to [Arthur].

The reaffirmation of Arthur's power in the concluding episode of *Erec* ends in obfuscating in extremis the reality of the king's weakening status in the face of rival knights, such as Erec himself, as evoked in the narrative's "premier vers." This suggests that behind the glorification of the wealth and generosity of Philippe of Alsace ("Qui valt mix ne fist Alixandres"; l. 14) in the *Conte*'s prologue lies similarly the reality of the count's growing disempowerment in the face of his rival, Philip Augustus. That the fictional attributes of King Arthur now glorify Chrétien's noble patron posits an equally ironic use of hyperbole for purposes of aggrandizing beyond measure both the legendary and the historical rulers.

17. In contrast with l. 1016 in Roach's edition of Ms. T, Ms. A proposes a slightly different version of the passage: "Ancor puet preuz *et saiges* estre" (he can still become brave *and wise*; ed. Pickens, l. 996; my emphasis). I think Ms. T provides a better reading to the extent that Arthur's allusion to the future transformation of the *niche* into a *vassax* is consistent with the king's desire to channel military prowess in support of his rule.

18. "Cinc jors antiers," according to Ms. A in ed. Pickens (l. 288); eight days, according to Mss. H and S. See ed. Hilka, note to l. 288. "Cinc ans entiers" in Ms. T in ed. Roach (l. 288) as well as in Mss. F, L, Q, and R.

19. Extratextual evidence also tends to question the validity of this alternative, considering that the Welsh tale *Peredur* identifies one of the knights Perceval encounters as Gauvain: "One day three knights came down the bridle path alongside the forest: Gwalchmei son of Gwyar, Gweir son of Gwestyl and Owein son of Uryen." See *The Mabinogion*, trans. Jeffrey Gantz, p. 219. It seems dubious that the traditional paragon of Arthurian chivalry could ever be portrayed in terms of a newly dubbed knight. Considering Gauvain's gradual indifference toward the plight of his royal uncle in the *Conte*, his putative appearance in the vale near Valbone could serve as a preliminary illustration of the non-Arthurian direction of his journey in the section of Chrétien's narrative devoted to his adventures.

20. These bonds are crucial in the context of the *Conte*'s criticism of traditional chivalry, for it is from his mother alone, as I explore in Chapter 4, that Perceval is presented with a type of instruction encouraging him to use his prowess in a disinterested manner and for truly defensive and protective purposes. With this perspective in mind, I disclose in this chapter the violent character of the chivalric ideal in the discourse of the Grail spokesmen as in that of Arthur. My goal in developing throughout the hypothesis that Chré-

tien's narration is grounded on a prediegetic history of rivalry is not to replace, so much as to supplement, parallel readings of Chrétien's last romance in the hope of contributing to the understanding of this richly enigmatic and complex work.

21. The scene of Perceval's dubbing is innovative on several counts. First, it includes some details, such as the conferral of the right spur, which Gornemant attaches to Perceval (l. 1625), the mentor's mention of the "ordre de chevalerie" (l. 1637), and his blessing of the new knight (l. 1694), that here make their first appearance in vernacular literature. Second, the ceremony takes place in the context of a narration that amplifies the function of the ritual in glorifying the class distinction of aristocratic society, as well as its significance in ensuring the newly dubbed knight's promotion within that society. Finally, the ritual concludes with advice (duty of protection and adherence to courteous behavior; ll. 1639–70) that gathers together for the first time all the elements that constitute the ideal of chivalry as it becomes henceforth the very emblem of the aristocratic order. As Jean Flori observes, "This is the rite of admission into Chivalry, a chivalry that takes pride in itself and ascribes to itself an ideology that justifies its own privileged existence, even at a time when military and economic conditions no longer justified the social preeminence that chivalry now more than ever claimed for itself." See "Pour une histoire de la chevalerie," p. 44. The illustration of Perceval's dubbing in Ms. P emphasizes the secular component of the ceremony "by paying special attention to the delivery of the sword and belt." See Sandra Hindman, *Sealed in Parchment*, p. 93.

22. An example is Perceval's triumph over Clamadeu: in rescuing Blancheflor against Clamadeu's abusive exercise of force, not only does Perceval defend the rights of the weak; he also compels Clamadeu to submit to Arthur's rule.

23. For Louis VII and Philip Augustus, the resort to military force was a royal prerogative whose aim was "the defense and vengeance of the poor." See Duby, *Le dimanche de Bouvines*, p. 96.

24. Gornemant provides his pupil with the following code of conduct in combat:

> Se vos en venez al desus,
> Que vers vos ne se poïst plus
> Desfendre ne contretenir,
> Ainz l'estuece a merchi venir,
> Gardez que merchi en aiez
> N'encontre che ne l'ociiez.
>
> (Ed. Roach, ll. 1643–48)

If you get the advantage and [your opponent] can no longer defend himself or resist, but finds himself forced to beg for mercy, be careful to grant him mercy instead of killing him outright.

25. My interpretation of the strategic use of clemency under Arthur's rule differs from that of Donald Maddox in his assessment of the peacemaking value of prowess in the hands of either Perceval or Gauvain. Examining, for example, how Perceval effects, without coercion, the reintegration of Orgueilleux de la Lande into Arthurian society, Maddox sees Perceval's action as an index of the protagonist's role in rescuing society from its tradition of aggression: "punishing the offender by inflicting the same offense that constituted the crime [in reference to Orgueilleux as transgressor of the law of courteous behavior] would only prolong the cycle" of violence. See *The Arthurian Romances*, p. 108. I do not believe that Perceval, any more than Gauvain (see ibid., pp. 117–18), emblematizes the emergence of a new order insofar as both protagonists fail to update and, on the contrary, adhere to a code of conduct that, in the case of Gauvain, has a self-serving direction and that, in the case of Perceval and until his encounter with the hermit, tends to favor the resurgence of Arthur's power. As for Arthur, the "mercy" he displays toward the transgressors of his customary protocols once they submit to his rule is "born of indifference to their crimes, not of charity." See Rupert T. Pickens, *The Welsh Knight*, p. 67.

26. L. 1658 in Roach's edition of Ms. T ("Ou soit *orfenins* ou soit dame") presents an interesting contrast to the reading provided by all the other manuscripts ("Ou soit *dameisele* ou soit dame"; ed. Hilka, note to l. 1658). Despite its singularity in the context of the *Conte*'s manuscript tradition, the reading of Ms. T appears preferable insofar as it confirms the ideological significance of the chivalric ideal as appropriated by contemporary aristocracy, which thus revendicated as its own a task (the protection of widows and orphans) that was traditionally (from the second half of the tenth century) entrusted to the kings. See Jean Flori, *L'idéologie du glaive*, p. 93.

27. A possible illustration of the alienating effect of Perceval's induction into Arthurian chivalry is the transformation of his former identity as "Perchevax li Galois" (as the protagonist names himself; ed. Roach, l. 3575) into "Perchevax li chaitis" (as Perceval's name is corrected by his cousin, l. 3582). According to Henri Rey-Flaud, the substitution of *chaitis* (in the sense of captive) for *gallois*, which contains the notion of joy (Old French *gai*), marks "the immediate alienation of the subject, who nonetheless has acquired the capacity to name himself." See "Le sang sur la neige," p. 22. From the standpoint of Arthurian society, in Rupert Pickens's analysis, "to be Welsh is to be uncivilized," considering that *gallois* and *chaitis* "are virtually synonyms" in Arthurian usage. See *The Welsh Knight*, p. 116. Conversely, from the standpoint of Perceval's cousin as one of the Grail representatives, it is in view of his failure at the Grail castle that "Perceval is no longer worthy of being called Gallois" (ibid.). For Pickens, Perceval's dual naming "highlights the hero's paradoxical character and the paradoxical nature of his existence and destiny" (ibid., p. 117): only by becoming an Arthurian knight, and then by transcending this imperfect

form of socialization, can Perceval hope to regain the essence of the *gallois*, that is, "a kind of childlike [rather than childish] innocence" (ibid., p. 132). Although I concur with this interpretation of Perceval's possible evolution, I also see the protagonist's dual naming in terms of an antithetical, rather than paradoxical, tension between two similarly totalizing investments of chivalry by both Arthur and the Grail faction: a prerequisite to Perceval's eventual maturation into a responsible knight—in answer to his mother's hope—is that he avoid the alienating effect of his induction into traditional chivalry, that glorified either by Arthurian or by Grail representatives.

28. Maddox, *The Arthurian Romances*, p. 111.

29. The custom of mercy in combat, which prescribes that defeated knights must be sent as hostages to Arthur's court, illustrates the self-serving character of chivalric service under the king's rule. In Donald Maddox's view, it is therefore not coincidental that Perceval's discovery of the Grail ideal occurs "on the very day that commemorates the *liberation* of time-bound prisoners in Christ's Harrowing of Hell." See ibid.

30. It is also significant that Gornemant's general warning against excessive loquacity is soon given specific relevance: in Gornemant's parting words to his pupil (ll. 1675–84), the mentor orders Perceval not to mention any longer that his mother told him this or that. As we saw, Gornemant's order seeks to sever Perceval's lineal links to the Grail in order to secure his bonds of allegiance to Arthur.

31. To suggest that Perceval "is unresponsive to strange impressions is to misread the text," for, as Grace Armstrong observes, the sight of the Bleeding Lance, for example, impresses him so deeply that he twice promises himself to inquire in due time about its meaning. See "The Scene of the Blood Drops on the Snow," p. 138.

32. Both Perceval's cousin and the Hideous Damsel allude not to two royal characters, but to a single Grail king. I analyze the significance of their perspective as opposed to that of Perceval's eremitic uncle, who reveals to his nephew the ties that link both Perceval and himself to the Grail lineage, later in this chapter.

33. Perceval shows on several occasions that he is sensitive to visual impressions. In the blood drops scene, for example, the color red conjures up in him the image of Blancheflor's face ("La fresche color li resamble / Qui ert en la face s'amie," the bright color resembles the complexion of his friend's face; ll. 4200–201). As Daniel Poirion notes, Perceval's capacity to compare demonstrates that "he knows the difference between poetic language and the reality of things." See "Du sang sur la neige," p. 150. Similarly, when Perceval observes that his mother was lying *as though* she had fallen dead, the comparison expresses his opinion that she has fainted, not that she has died.

34. The Hideous Damsel's goal in renaming Perceval *li maleüreus* (l. 4665)

is identical to that of the protagonist's cousin when she changes Perceval *li Galois* into Perceval *li chaitis* (l. 3582) before assigning to him the attribute of *maleüros* (l. 3583). Contrary to the Arthurian perspective, in which *Galois* and *chaitis* have a derogatory meaning, both Perceval's cousin and the Hideous Damsel invest his "Welsh" origins with positive value. In this connection, Perceval no longer deserves his former identification as a member of the "Welsh" clan because of his new pledge of allegiance to Arthur. From the standpoint of these two Grail representatives, Perceval's induction into Arthurian chivalry has an alienating effect (invoked in the term *chaitis*) insofar as it prevents him from serving the cause of lineage, whose misfortune (invoked in the term *maleüreus*) must thus endure. Perceval's dual naming here articulates a definition of one's identity grounded on social and factional, rather than on personal, considerations.

35. The Hideous Damsel's allegiance to the Grail faction is demonstrated, first, by her implicit denunciation of Arthurian chivalry and, second, by her attempt to deprive Arthur of his companions by challenging them with what she presents as highly dangerous and worthy chivalric tasks (ll. 4688–714), a challenge that, as I showed in Chapter 1, appeals to the vanity of the king's Round Table.

36. Pickens, *The Welsh Knight*, p. 46.

37. Maddox, *The Arthurian Romances*, pp. 111–12.

38. Pickens, *The Welsh Knight*, p. 129.

39. Ibid., p. 47.

40. Ibid., p. 46.

41. Several incidents in Perceval's story (such as the protagonist's departure from Arthur's court in quest of his own adventure, his lapse into madness upon discovery of his failure, and the hermits' role in helping him recover his sanity) evoke that of the eponymous hero of *Yvain*. See ibid., pp. 47–48. In this connection Perceval may be bound to cross paths with Gauvain, implying that the protagonist will engage, as does Yvain, in a judicial duel against Arthur's nephew (leading, in the *Conte*'s potential ending, not to the deadlock alluded to in *Yvain*, but to a deadly outcome).

42. This is a prayer "Que nomer ne doit bouche d'ome, / Se par paor de mort nes nome" (that man's mouth should never utter, except in peril of death; ll. 6487–88). According to Donald Maddox, Chrétien here acknowledges that the meaning of his romance is not theological: his narrative "places transcendence at a remove by passing over in silence the holy words that are supposed to signify it." See "Roman et manipulation au 12e siècle," p. 190.

43. See Etienne Delaruelle, "La culture religieuse des laïcs en France aux XIe et XIIe siècles," and Michel Zink, *La prédication en langue romane avant 1300*, pp. 446–49.

44. In a thirteenth-century hagiographic poem on Saint Juliana, the devil

acknowledges that one of his most successful temptations is disturbing believers during mass by making them think they would do better to go home, work, get rich, and give alms. See *Li ver del Juïse*, ll. 725–44. The Avignon Council in 1209 denounced members of the laity who talk and play during mass. See *Sacrorum conciliorum et decretum*, vol. 2, col. 809.

45. Gornemant's mention of the service to *orfenins* or *dame* appears only in version T, l. 1658. But the hermit's reference to *veve dame* or *orfenine* (l. 6467) is present throughout the manuscript tradition, with the exception of version A. His allusion to two types of social weakness (widowhood and orphanhood), which are emblematized by both Perceval and his mother, indicates the hermit's desire to convince Perceval that his primary duty is to assist his family.

46. Although Perceval's adherence to "shadow-knighthood idealized in the Arthurian kingdom causes him to fail at the Grail castle, it also, in consequence of that failure, brings him to cognizance of his identity and of his essential nature in guessing his name. . . : if knowledge and consciousness are possible only through Arthurian experience, full understanding is possible only in the world of the Grail." See Pickens, *The Welsh Knight*, p. 133.

47. Jean-Charles Payen, "Encore la pratique religieuse dans le *Conte du Graal*," pp. 121–32. Perceval's cousin links his failure at the Grail castle to the sin he committed against his mother: "Por le *pechié, se saches tu,* / De ta mere t'est avenu, / Qu'ele [est] morte del doel de toi" (By the *sin, know it well*, you committed against your mother, who died of sorrow on your account; ed. Roach, ll. 3593–95). This calls into question the validity of the hermit's remark that Perceval committed a sin *of which he knows nothing*. But the hermit focuses perhaps not on Perceval's unawareness or filial indifference so much as on his ignorance in matters of ethics. The *Continuation* of Gerbert de Montreuil gives an interesting assessment of Perceval's sin. Before rescuing Gornemant from the attacks of demon knights, Perceval relates to his mentor his discovery of the Grail castle. There he saw the *graal* and the Bleeding Lance, but "Trop malvaisement me gardai . . . / Quant nule rien n'en demandai" (I was dreadfully cautious when I asked nothing about them; ll. 5097, 5100). The Grail king refused to reveal to him the secrets of the broken sword, which worries him, "Que *ne sai* par quel mesestanche / Ne *par quel pechié* ce me vient" (because *I do not know* what wickedness or *sin of mine* is to blame; ll. 5126–27; my emphasis). Perceval can think of only one sin he has not confessed and done penance for: "une covenance / Que je ai a une pucele / Qui molt est avenans et bele" (a promise of marriage I gave to a most beautiful and lovely girl; ll. 5132–34). In Gerbert's text, Perceval's sin is linked not to his mother, but to Blancheflor. He makes amends by returning to his lover and marrying her. But a voice enjoins him to resume his quest for the Grail. He thus leaves Blancheflor, finds the Grail castle, mends the broken sword, and becomes lord of the domain.

48. The nature of the fisher's wound varies: struck between the thighs

("quisses ambesdeus") in Ms. T; between the hips in Ms. A ("hanches") and Ms. B ("anches"); or, in Mss. H, L, and R, between the legs ("jambes"), thus "making the consequent sexual mutilation somewhat more explicit." See ed. Pickens, p. 453.

49. See ed. Hilka, note to l. 4661. The *Continuations* also underscore the wealth of the Grail domain. See the *First Continuation*, ll. 1249–1323; the *Second Continuation*, ll. 32278–99; the *Continuation* of Gerbert de Montreuil, ll. 16840–17086.

50. The hermit makes no mention of a wound, an omission the significance of which I explore further in this chapter. The wound motif, which applies to both father and son (hence their reliance on a boat as the only adequate mode of transportation), is integral to Perceval's assigned mission as reinforcement of the Grail kingdom.

51. See, for example, Donald Maddox, *The Arthurian Romances*, pp. 111–12, 132.

52. To use Brian Stock's felicitous expression. See *Listening for the Text*, p. 4.

53. Before narrating an adventure he had experienced several years before, Calogrenant, one of Arthur's knights, reminds the court that "Les oroilles sont voie et doiz / Par ou s'an vient au cuer la voiz" (the ears are the route and channel by which the voice reaches the heart; *Le Chevalier au Lion*, ll. 165–66). As Eugene Vance notes, Calogrenant's remark is directly reminiscent of Augustine's theory that God speaks to man through the inner "ears of the heart." See *From Topic to Tale*, p. 14. Calogrenant (Chrétien) invites his audience to go beyond the surface of his narration, that is, its literal meaning, indicating that the truth of romance lies in its figurative meaning, which the audience is invited to discover.

54. Joan Tasker Grimbert, "Misrepresentation and Misconception in Chrétien de Troyes," p. 50.

55. Ibid.

56. To cite Amelia A. Rutledge, from an article in which she reviews the scholarly debate on the significance of the hermitage episode. See "Perceval's Sin," p. 53.

57. Sister M. Amelia Klenke, *Liturgy and Allegory in Chrétien's "Perceval,"* and "The Spiritual Ascent of Perceval," pp. 1–21.

58. David G. Hoggan, "Le péché de Perceval"; Jean Frappier, *Chrétien de Troyes et le mythe du Graal*.

59. As is maintained by, among others, Paul Imbs, "L'élément religieux dans le *Conte du Graal* de Chrétien de Troyes," Edmond Faral, "Note sur la nature du Gral," David C. Fowler, *Prowess and Charity in the "Perceval" of Chrétien de Troyes*, and John Bednar, *La spiritualité et le symbolisme dans l'oeuvre de Chrétien de Troyes*.

60. Alexandre Micha, "Le *Perceval* de Chrétien de Troyes (roman éducatif)."

61. Sister M. Amelia Klenke, "Cups, Dishes, and the Holy Grail." The wounded king is also identified as Melchisedec (see Urban T. Holmes and Sister M. Amelia Klenke, *Chrétien, Troyes, and the Grail*) or as Adam, before or after the sin (see Myrrha Lot-Borodine, "Le *Conte du Graal* de Chrétien de Troyes et sa présentation symbolique," p. 257).

62. Helen Adolf, "Le Vieux Roi, clef de voûte du *Conte del Graal*," p. 951. Adolf also resorts to extratextual arguments, noting how, from the eighth to the tenth centuries, the biblical figure of Hezekiah was, along with David and Solomon, frequently invoked as an exemplary model for Merovingian and Carolingian kings (p. 952).

63. The duration of the king's ascetic existence varies in the manuscript tradition: eleven years in Mss. M and Q; twelve years in B, F, H, R, T, and V; fifteen years in A, E, and L; and twenty years in C, P, S, and U. Despite its imprecision, this manuscript tradition clearly seeks to situate the origin of the weakening of the Grail kingdom in a remote past. Rupert Pickens rejects the reading of Ms. A (fifteen years), presumably because of the greater frequency of the allusion to the king's twelve-year reclusion in his chamber. See ed. Pickens, note to l. 6395, p. 489.

64. Jean Marx, *La légende arthurienne et le Graal* and *Nouvelles recherches sur la littérature arthurienne*.

65. Michelle Freeman, "Jean Frappier et le Mythe du Graal," pp. 132–33.

66. Amelia A. Rutledge concludes her review of the scholarly interpretations of Perceval's sin by opting in favor of the protagonist's psychological guilt. See "Perceval's Sin," pp. 58–59.

67. Perceval's description of the castle's splendor leads his cousin to guess the identity of Perceval's host at the Grail castle: that Perceval found lodging in what he describes as the best "hostel" (l. 3492) indicates to her that he was welcomed "Chiez le riche Roi Pescheor" (at the house of the rich Fisher King; l. 3495). Perceval's cousin proceeds to narrate how Perceval's host was wounded in battle and henceforth forced to inaction.

68. A *graal* (from *gradale*, by stage) designates the platter "brought to the table at various stages during a meal." See Norris J. Lacy, ed., *The Arthurian Encyclopedia*, under the entry "grail," p. 257.

69. In the *Third Continuation* of Manessier, for example, the appearance of the "Saint Graal" (l. 42490) during the festivities of Perceval's coronation as the new Grail king has a food-producing effect:

> Lors furent de mes delitables
> Trestotes les tables garnies
> Et si gentement replenies

Que honme nonmer ne seüst
Nul mes que trouver ne peüst.
(Ll. 42502–506)

Then the tables were covered with delectable dishes and so splendidly provided that there was no dish one could name without seeing it appear.

The procession of the Grail has the same effect in the *Queste del Saint Graal*: "Come il trespassoit par devant les tables, estoient eles maintenant raemplies endroit chascun siege de tel viande come chascuns desirroit" (As it moved along the tables, these were at once filled such that each place was furnished with whatever kind of food its occupant would desire; *La Queste del Saint Graal*, ed. Albert Pauphilet, p. 15, ll. 25–27). See also Stith Thompson, *Motif-Index of Folk Literature*, sec. D: 1472.1. 19–33.

70. By Urban T. Holmes and Sister M. Amelia Klenke, *Chrétien, Troyes, and the Grail*.

71. In this retrospective interpretation of the gospel, the New Testament was not so much "new" as it was better, hence a tendency to oppose Christ's law to all other laws and the eventual use of the gospel for sectarian purposes. See Beryl Smalley, *The Study of the Bible in the Middle Ages*, p. 25.

72. See Roger Dragonetti, *La vie de la lettre au Moyen Age*, p. 131.

73. Examining the polysemic significance of Yvain's lion, Peter Haidu thus concludes: "The semiological field of religion is treated here as a source among others, all equally generative of meaning, a source in competition with other equally accessible and worthy fields. And, as with other symbolic values, the meaning produced by exegetical allegory [the lion as Christ] can be denied." See *Lion-Queue-Coupée*, p. 72.

74. "For Chrétien's art is essentially paradoxical. His symbolism is anti-symbolic and leads the reader to the phenomenal level of life as well as to the literal level of literature." Ibid., p. 82.

75. See Maurice Keen, *Chivalry*, pp. 43–63.

76. See Maddox, *The Arthurian Romances*, pp. 112–13.

77. Ibid., pp. 132, 112.

78. Jean Gouttebroze, "Cousin, cousine," p. 79. Curiously, however, Gouttebroze makes no reference to the sword and asserts that the doom of the Grail kingdom has a sexual origin, invoking the threat of endogamy: Perceval's silence at the castle represents a healthy refusal to marry his cousin.

79. According to Dragonetti, *La vie de la lettre*, pp. 142, 169–71, 184–85. The first sword Perceval obtains is the one he takes from the Red Knight; Gornemant bestows the second on him during the dubbing ceremony; and he is "given" the third at the Grail castle.

80. In a manner similar to Perceval's dubbing by Gornemant, the hermit's induction of Perceval into "spiritual" chivalry takes the form of a ritual

rather than a training, invoking an initiation that does not instruct the young protagonist so much as it redirects his martial energy.

81. According to Charles Méla, *"Perceval,"* p. 271.

82. This nongratuitous, forced "gift" is an example of what is known as "don contraignant." See Jean Frappier, "Le motif du don contraignant dans la littérature du Moyen Age." See also Marcel Mauss's seminal "Essai sur le don."

83. Not only does Perceval use the Grail sword against the interests of his Grail host; the fact that he also breaks it, according to the reading of version T (as narrated in the twenty lines inserted between ll. 3926 and 3927 of Roach's edition), discloses even more forcefully—from the viewpoint of the Grail faction—the transgressive character of his action.

84. See Gary Macy, *The Theologies of the Eucharist in the Early Scholastic Period,* pp. 55–60.

85. Canon 21 of the fourth Lateran Council in 1215, which reminds the laity of its obligation to commune at least once a year, also insists that one must first confess privately to one's parish priest. See *Conciliorum Oecumenicorum Decreta,* p. 245.

86. See Keen, *Chivalry,* p. 61. Only two manuscripts, M and U, contain an illustration of the Grail episode (reproduced in color in *The Manuscripts of Chrétien de Troyes,* vol. 2, plate IVc, p. 347; plate Va, p. 348). In Ms. M, which provides no representation of the *graal,* the Bleeding Lance does not bleed and is carried not by a young man, but by a maiden. Ms. U, which is thus the sole codex to represent the *graal,* juxtaposes the three principal elements of the Grail episode. A tower divides the image into two sequences. On the left-hand register, a royal character gives a sword to Perceval. On the right-hand register, a royal couple witnesses the procession of the lance and the *graal,* but Perceval is absent. Qualified by the rubric as "holy," the dish is here a ciborium crowned with a cross, indicating a Christian reinscription of the scene. See Emmanuèle Baumgartner, "Les scènes du Graal," p. 492. The iconographic silence of most *Perceval* manuscripts with respect to the Grail episode attests to a general reticence in visualizing sacred or religious motifs such as the *graal.* See Angelica Rieger, "Le programme iconographic du *Perceval* montpelliérain," pp. 398, 403. By contrast, the *Continuations* inspired abundant illustrations of otherworldly adventures such as the last apparition of the *graal* at the end of Manessier's text, which is illustrated in Ms. T (reproduced in color in *The Manuscripts of Chrétien de Troyes,* vol. 2, plate IVb, p. 347). See Laurence Harf-Lancner, "L'image et le fantastique," pp. 460–72. The iconographic contrast between Chrétien's romance and its sequels indicates a determination on the part of the manuscripts' producers to distinguish between the secular significance of the *Conte* and its Christian reinscription in the hands of many of Chrétien's followers.

87. Bonnie Buettner, "The Good Friday Scene in Chrétien de Troyes' *Perceval*."

88. Unusual in Chrétien's work, the expression also appears in *Cligés*, where "molt sainte chose" (l. 6012) describes Fenice's supposed corpse. The intention here is clearly ironic, which, in Peter Haidu's view, is obviously not the case in the *Perceval* phrase, although it shares with the *Cligés* usage the characteristic of incongruity. See *Aesthetic Distance in Chrétien de Troyes*, pp. 220–30. According to Haidu, the hermit's simplistic sanctification of the Grail recluse takes into account the simplicity of his penitent *niche*: he offers "simple spiritual food to one who is still a simpleton" (p. 223). Although helping Perceval gain access to "the full life of man in society" (p. 226), the narrative value of the hermitage episode is limited, articulating only "a particular view of Perceval and his actions which, if not exclusively correct, provides one more aspect of the hero" (p. 228).

89. To use Rupert Pickens's expression. See *The Welsh Knight*, p. 48.

90. According to Roger Sherman Loomis, the transformation of the Grail from a cornucopian vessel (as the motif frequently appears in Welsh folklore) into a sacred dish results partly from a misinterpretation of the Old French word for horn (*cors*, of cornucopian significance). See *Arthurian Literature in the Middle Ages*, pp. 293–94. The fact that *cors* in the nominative case could have such meanings as "coin," "court," "course," and "body," together with the fact that the legendary context favored this last meaning, explains its eucharistic significance in many Grail texts after Chrétien, as contained in the designation of the Grail domain as Corbenic ("holy body") in Manessier's *Third Continuation* (l. 42455) and, in the *Queste del Saint Graal*, of Pellés's Grail castle as Corbenyc (p. 79, l. 17).

91. Jacques Stiennon, "Bruges, Philippe d'Alsace, Chrétien de Troyes et le Graal," p. 12. In Manessier's *Third Continuation*, the Grail king recounts to Perceval how Longinus struck Christ with a lance when He was on the cross:

> Li *sans precïeus* qui se lance
> Dou fer qui est desus la lance,
> Qui si est tres bel et tres blanc,
> Ce est li *sains precïeus senc*
> Qui dou costé Dieu descendi
> Quant Longis dou fer lou feri.
>
> (Ll. 32663–68)

The *precious blood* that flows from the head of the [Bleeding Lance], which is most beautiful and white, is the *holy, precious blood* that ran down from God's side when Longinus struck him with it (my emphasis).

That Manessier dedicates his narrative to Johanna of Flanders suggests that the description of the blood as *precious* is here intentional, the result of which is to connect the Grail legend with both the cult of the precious blood and Flemish sovereignty.

92. See Jean Marx, *La légende arthurienne et le Graal*. At issue was the Capetian kings' claim "to rule by the grace of God," as emblematized by their traditional anointment with the holy oil that, according to the legend, "had been miraculously delivered from heaven to Saint Remi, the bishop who baptized Clovis." See John W. Baldwin, *The Government of Philip Augustus*, pp. 374–80. An example is Philip Augustus's anointment by the archbishop of Reims on November 1, 1179.

93. Jacques Le Goff, *La civilisation de l'Occident médiéval*, p. 335. However, the recognition of the sacerdotal character of French kingship was so customary that, although a number of princes (e.g., the dukes of Normandy and Aquitaine) sought to appropriate some aspects of the ceremony, they never dared imitate the practice of anointment. See Marc Bloch, *Les rois thaumaturges*, pp. 194–245.

94. The Grail mystique derives not from Chrétien's text, but from Robert's trilogy, which inspired "magnificent literary works" by adding to Chrétien's romance, according to Jean Marx, a "more spiritual dimension." See *Nouvelles recherches sur la littérature arthurienne*, p. 152.

95. The hermit's sanctifying account focuses on the *graal*, a "Tant saint chose" (eminently holy thing; ed. Roach, 1. 6425), because it contains the Host. The expression "saint Graal" (Holy Grail) appears not in Chrétien's romance, but in its sequels. See, for example, the *First Continuation* (1. 1363) and the *Second Continuation* (1. 32400).

96. The significance of Perceval's name is enigmatic, leading to various interpretations according to the reception of the Grail legend by both medieval and modern readers. An example is provided by Ms. T, whose textual and pictorial composition induces Sandra Hindman to read the codex as a story focusing on Perceval's gradual transformation from a knightly figure to a clerical one. In her perspective, a fascinating aspect of Ms. T is how performative (knightly and illiterate) culture and nonperformative (clerical and literate) culture "appear to coexist in the text, the miniatures, and even the layout of the manuscript." The performative culture is represented in historiated initials in which a knight on horseback dominates, thus "giving visual form to Perceval's name, *par cheval*" (on horseback). The nonperformative culture appears in the miniature (depicting Perceval dressed in clerical garb) that concludes Manessier's *Continuation* as the last text of the entire Perceval cycle contained in the codex. This miniature underscores the literate and clerical reinscription of Perceval's story by Manessier, as summarized in his epilogue, when he invites his reader to verify the authenticity of his story by going to Salisbury and seeing his "escrit" (written word; *Third Continuation*, 1. 42664): "Encore le puet on veoir la / Tot seellé en parchemin, / Cil qui errent par le chemin" (All

those who travel the road can still see [the story] there, sealed in parchment; ll. 42666–68). The mounted knight (*par cheval*) of performative culture "becomes a metaphor for the reader whose travel (*par le chemin*) is equated with the act of reading on the surface of the page (*parchemin*)." See Hindman, *Sealed in Parchment*, pp. 42, 44, 45.

97. See Rupert Pickens, *The Welsh Knight*, p. 127.

98. During the attack of Chastel Orgueilleus by Arthur and his knights as narrated in the *First Continuation*, Bran de Lis reminds the king that there can be no fighting from noon on Saturday until Monday morning. See the *First Continuation*, ll. 11720–42. The Truce of God formulated by the Church in 1027 prohibited any warfare and attacks between the last hour of Saturday and the first hour of Monday, a restriction soon to include the three days commemorating Christ's Passion. Secular leaders (first the counts of Flanders and the dukes of Normandy in the eleventh century, then the Capetian kings in the twelfth century) in their turn claimed the right to regulate the bearing of arms as a testimony to their God-given pacifistic mission. See Georges Duby, *Le dimanche de Bouvines*, pp. 82–99. French kings claimed their right to regulate armed encounters by presenting themselves as the representatives of the King of Judgment Day. Ibid., p. 92.

99. The penitent knights Perceval encounters have their heads covered by hoods, are walking barefoot, and are wearing hair shirts "por salvement de lor ames" and "Por les pechiez que fais avoient" (for the salvation of their souls and for the sins they had committed; ed. Roach, ll. 6250, 6252). Four manuscripts (P, M, S, and U) contain an illustration of this episode. The image in Ms. U represents the penitent knights as fully armed (reproduced in *The Manuscripts of Chrétien de Troyes*, vol. 2, fig. 325, p. 510). Although it misinterprets Chrétien's text at the literal level, this illustration may constitute an accurate, albeit unintentional, gloss of the scene. In this perspective, the "sins" committed by the penitents would be of the same nature as Perceval's "sin" for having sided with Arthur rather than his lineage. Their encounter with Perceval's eremitic uncle would have persuaded them to "repent" by forsaking their Arthurian allegiance and joining the ranks of the Grail faction.

100. After he learns that Laudine has rejected him, Yvain escapes into the forest. Naked, alone, and "having lost his senses," he owes his survival to a hermit, who cooks for him the stags and does of his hunt (*Le Chevalier au Lion*, ll. 2804–80). For Robert Harrison, knights of medieval romance such as Yvain "are at bottom wild men who have become heroes of the social order, yet who must periodically return to the forests in order to rediscover within themselves the alienated source of their prowess. . . . The natural prowess of the wild man is the same *realigned* power that preserves a precarious social order against the dangers that threaten it both from within and without." See *Forests*, pp. 66, 68. I suggest a reverse interpretation of the forest of medieval romance: knights

of medieval romance are at bottom wild men inasmuch as they become heroes of Arthurian society and champions of an order governed by royal ambitions. An example of the bewildering effect of Arthurian society is Yvain's course of action when he learns that Laudine has rejected him: he decides to flee Arthur's companions because he knows that he will "lose his sense and reason" if he stays among them. In contrast to the dictates of a social order that values violence as a source of empowerment, the forest is a "rational" locus to the extent that it provides choice: between the snake and the lion, between self-serving aggression and altruistic service. Another example of the bewildering effect of Arthur's law is, later in the narration, the way the king resorts to "force and intimidation," rather than persuasion, to conclude a dispute between two sisters. Law at court *is* the law of the "forest" in that it responds to aggression with aggression, thus indulging, rather than containing and controlling, the violent impulses of human nature.

101. Mentioned and analyzed by Archer Taylor, "The Three Sins of the Hermit." See also Angus J. Kennedy, "The Hermit's Role in French Arthurian Romance" and "The Portrayal of the Hermit-Saint in French Arthurian Romance"; and Jean-Charles Huchet, "Les déserts du roman médiéval."

102. See Jean Becquet, "L'érémitisme clérical et laïc dans l'Ouest de la France," and Jean Leclercq, "L'érémistisme et les cisterciens," pp. 182–202, 573–75.

103. Considering the sociopolitical significance of the tension between court and forest in the *Conte*, it is tempting to evoke here the regulations over the woodland (forest law) developed by contemporary rulers. On the appropriation of woodlands by Henry II, see W. L. Warren, *Henry II*, pp. 389–96, and Charles R. Young, *The Royal Forests in Medieval England*, pp. 33–73. On the appropriation of Norman woodlands by Philip Augustus in 1219, see Roland Bechmann, *Des arbres et des hommes*, p. 282. Under forest law, only the king and his court had the right of access to certain areas of the forest and to chasing such game as the red deer, the fallow deer, the roe, and the wild boar. After Henry II's edict in 1184, it was forbidden to enter his forest with bows, arrows, or dogs. See Jacques Le Goff and Pierre Vidal-Nacquet, "Lévi-Strauss en Brocéliande," p. 541. In addition, the cutting of timber, agricultural clearings, pannage, and pasturage were severely taxed and infractors severely punished. At the core of the forest dispute stood the fact that "the law was not true law at all but the expression of arbitrary will." By the admission of the king's own treasurer, "what is done in accordance with that law is not called 'just' without qualification but 'just according to forest law.'" See Warren, *Henry II*, pp. 394–95. Local inhabitants, particularly the monks, resented these royal exactions, which deprived them of important sources of revenue.

104. According to the Cistercian Helinand of Froimond (late 12th c.), Grail tales exist only in French and are in the hands of noble lords. A Flemish

cleric, Jacob van Maerlant (late 13th c.), denounces Grail narratives as lies and inventions. Jean Frappier, who cites these two texts, concludes that the Grail myth was addressed to, and read by, the nobility. See "Le Graal et la chevalerie," pp. 208–10. This appears to be the case of most of the manuscripts in which Chrétien's *Conte du Graal* is preserved. Of the twelve manuscripts containing the "complete" or extensive text of Chrétien's romance that were copied in the thirteenth century, only two provide information of contemporary ownership. Ms. L belonged to Robert of Cassel (ca. 1275–1331), the second son of Robert de Béthune, Count of Flanders. See Roger Middleton, "Index of Former Owners," pp. 127–28. According to Middleton, the first owner of Ms. T may have been not a noble, but a merchant living at Amiens between about 1270 and about 1290. See "Additional Notes on the History of Selected Manuscripts," p. 223. For a diverging attribution of ownership, see Sandra Hindman, *Sealed in Parchment*, p. 47.

105. As Jean Flori points out, noble knights were threatened, on the one hand, by the growing use of mercenary soldiers as military reinforcement in the conduct of war and, on the other, by the increasing influx of wealthy and learned bourgeois at royal courts. See *L'essor de la chevalerie*, pp. 270, 341.

106. The distinction between chevalerie and *preudomie* was rooted in the need to defend the aristocracy from both the threat of an emerging monetary society and the internecine forces endangering the feudal order. Thus Erich Köhler remarks that "the *preudomie* that allows chivalry to constitute itself as a moral elite at the heart of the feudal system results so to speak from the necessity it is met with of defending itself against the forces at work within the feudal system itself. These forces discredit chivalry by upsetting the order it has established for itself. . . . Only the *preudome* is the true knight. If *preudomie* formerly seemed to be a natural outgrowth of chivalry, this same *preudomie*, which from now on possesses its own laws, will determine in its turn the true nature of chivalry. . . . At a time when bourgeois spirit is undertaking to appropriate *preudomie* for itself, the nobility precisely adheres to the religious sense of the chivalric ideal." See Köhler, *L'aventure chevaleresque*, pp. 153–54, 156.

107. Also noteworthy is Chrétien's dedication of his romance to Count Philippe of Flanders, whom he praises as "le plus preudome / Qui soit en l'empire de Rome" (the most noble man in all the empire of Rome; ll. 11–12), a praise expressing, in part, the poet's hope that "avra bien salve sa paine" (his efforts will be rewarded; l .61) and that his patron will exercise his "charity" on his account.

108. Hence the Church's tendency to associate chivalric pride with envy and cupidity. According to the moralist Jacques de Vitry (early 13th c.), for example, the nobility is guilty of oppressing the weak and the just, of misusing might, and of implementing "bad customs" detrimental to the welfare of society. Significantly, in his sermon "Ad potentes et milites," Vitry uses chiv-

alry as a metaphor for the seven deadly sins. See the excerpt of Vitry's sermon in Jacques Le Goff, *L'imaginaire médiéval*, pp. 258–61.

109. Both *preus* (prowess) and *preudomie* derive from the Latin *prodis*, designating alternately a material and an abstract form of worth.

110. Keen, *Chivalry*, p. 62.

111. In Wolfram von Eschenbach's *Parzival* (ca. 1200–1210), for example, the hero's eremitic uncle, Trevrizent, is not a priest, but an aged knight.

112. Whether *Peredur* is a sequel to Chrétien's romance or whether Chrétien based his narrative on a similar Celtic tale is still a matter of scholarly debate. For the passage under consideration, see *The Mabinogion*, tr. Jeffrey Gantz, pp. 226–57.

113. Jean-Claude Lozachmeur, "Recherches sur les origines indo-européennes et ésotériques de la légende du Graal," p. 47.

114. Madeleine Blaess, "Perceval et les 'Illes de Mer.'"

115. Manessier's *Third Continuation* amplifies the theme of vengeance that Jean-Claude Lozachmeur sees as integral to the primitive stage of the Grail legend (Archetype A in terms of Lozachmeur's categories). Thus Perceval learns from the Grail king the evil origin of the broken sword: his brother was murdered by Partinal "li devez" (the wild; *Third Continuation*, l. 32954), who struck a grievous blow that caused his sword to break in two. Perceval vows to take revenge upon Partinal (ll. 32941–48), but his journey takes him through a series of adventures during which he kills many knights "Por pris et por honor conquerre" (to increase his worth and ensure his renown; l. 37784). The hermit to whom Perceval relates his quest for honor and glory admonishes him to change his ways, enjoining Perceval

> Que de ce s'alast bien gardant
> Que, se n'est sus lui desfandant,
> Que jamés home n'oceïst
> Ne si grant pechié ne feïst.
>
> (Ll. 37855–58)

henceforth to avoid committing any such crime as killing a man, except in self-defense.

A chance encounter with Partinal presents Perceval with the opportunity to fulfill his vow. He severs Partinal's head clean from the trunk (ll. 41832–33) and carries off his opponent's head to the Grail king (ll. 41846–47), who feels great relief and comfort to see his brother's death thus avenged:

> La sus desus ma maistre tor
> Metrai ceste teste trainchie,
> La amont en un pel fichie,
> En ennor et en remenbrance
> Que de celui est pris venjance

> Qui a tort ot, et sanz raison,
> Mon frere ocis en traïson.
>
> (Ll. 41908–14)

I will affix this severed head up there on top of my main tower, in honor and memory of the revenge taken against the knight who killed my brother wrongfully and treacherously.

Then the king orders that a meal be prepared, during which the "Saint Graal" and the "sainte lance" appear (ll. 41952–53), held by two maidens who pass before the tables. It is noteworthy that Manessier's text, which is the most Christianized of the four *Continuations*, reinscribes Chrétien's romance in a way that amplifies the vengeful direction of Perceval's quest for the Grail. The Grail king's joy when he sees the severed head of his brother's killer, together with the ensuing appearance of the Holy Grail, articulate a partisan perspective of Grail chivalry. Perceval's role as the avenger of Grail kingship indicates that the hermit does not condemn violent chivalry as much as any use of military expertise that does not further the Grail interests. Although Perceval eventually becomes a priest, the central element in his transformation from knight to cleric is his exploit in killing Partinal.

116. The enigma of the *graal* in Chrétien's romance centers on the question Perceval failed to ask during his stay at the Grail castle: "n'osa mie demander / Del graal *cui* l'en en servoit" (he did not dare ask *who* was served by the Grail; ed. Roach, ll. 3244–45; my emphasis). As Emmanuèle Baumgartner observes, the emphasis here is on the recipient of the Grail service (*cui*), in contradistinction to the *Continuations*, where the question focuses on the nature of the Grail service: "*que* an an sert" (*what* does it serve). The result of this modification is a presentation of Perceval's quest stressing its cognitive value. See Baumgartner, " 'Del Graal cui l'an an servoit': variations sur un pronom," pp. 140–43.

117. Version A (along with F and P; see ed. Hilka, note to l. 6422) stresses the sanctifying character of the Grail recluse. Thus the hermit tells Perceval that "li *sainz hon*" (the *holy man*) is sustained "D'une seule oiste" (by a single Host) that is brought to him in the *graal* (ed. Pickens, ll. 6388–89; my emphasis). Compare this reading with that preserved in Ms. T: "D'une sole oiste *le sert on* / Que l'en en cel graal li porte" (*he is served* a single Host, which is brought to him in that grail; ed. Roach, ll. 6422–23; my emphasis). L. 6422 of version T reads *le sert l'on* in versions S and U and *ceo savoms* in version P. In version R, the old king is designated as *li prodom*.

118. Israel was the chosen people not because it was the greatest of the nations, but because it was unjustly enslaved by the pharaoh. See Robert McAfee Brown, *Religion and Violence*, p. 95.

119. Perceval's silence also results from Gornemant's warning against excessive loquacity.

120. Peter Brooks, *Reading for the Plot*, p. 93.

121. R. I. Moore, *The Formation of a Persecuting Society*, p. 138.

122. An example in the persecuting discourses Moore analyzes is the way heretics, Jews, lepers, and prostitutes were said to present the same threat: "Through them the Devil was at work to subvert the Christian order and bring the world to chaos." Ibid., p. 130.

123. Ibid., p. 109.

124. Henry II was the first king to enact secular legislation against heretics and prostitutes. Philip Augustus at times exploited the Jews as a source of profit, at times persecuted them in support of his territorial ambitions. See ibid., pp. 38, 43.

125. Ibid., p. 65.

126. Anti-Semitic propaganda played an important part in the development of rational thinking, as illustrated in attempts made, for example, by Fulbert of Chartres, Anselm, and Abelard to convince the Jews of the superiority of the Christian faith. See Charles M. Radding, *A World Made by Men*, pp. 154–72. What may have begun as a dialectical effort to persuade unbelievers contributed to what R. I. Moore perceives as the permanent transformation of Western Europe into a persecuting society.

127. The strategy contained in the Grail messengers' discourse of accusation evokes what Léon Poliakov aptly describes as a process of "diabolical causality." See *La causalité diabolique*.

128. Chivalric equipment effects Perceval's transformation from a rustic Welshman into a mirror image of the knights who inhabit the land of Logres. Interestingly, the word *Welsh* derives from the Saxon *wealh* (foreigner), designating all those who were not Saxon and, by extension, the earlier inhabitants of occupied Wales. See Joseph T. Shipley, *Dictionary of Word Origins*, p. 129.

Chapter 4

1. See the edition and translation of version A in ed. Pickens, l. 8136.

2. See Nigel Bryant, trans., *Perceval: The Story of the Grail*, p. 86.

3. See the glossary of Lecoy's edition, p. 153: "religion (or nation), that is, any group united by the same religion or language."

4. Pierre Gallais, "Métonymie et métaphore dans le *Conte du Graal*," p. 226, n. 57.

5. For example, the troubadour Bernart de Ventadorn (Bernard de Ventadour; second half of 12th c.) begins one of his songs with this traditional opposition between man and nature:

> Lo gens tems de pascor
> Ab la frescha verdor
> Nos adui folh' e flor
> De diversa color,

Per que tuih amador
Son gai e chantador
Mas eu, que planh e plor,
C'us jois no m'a sabor.
(*Bernard de Ventadour, troubadour
du XIIe siècle*, canso 17, p. 124)

The gentle season of Easter brings us, along with its fresh greenery, leaves and flowers of various colors; therefore all lovers and singers are happy, except me, who laments and weeps, for no joy has any delight for me.

6. In the *Conte*, for example, it is Pentecost when Arthur holds his court at Dinasdaron (l. 2785) and, later on, at Orquenie (ll. 8888, 9103).

7. See Laurent Ajam, "La forêt dans l'oeuvre de Chrétien de Troyes," p. 125.

8. Although Perceval's desire focuses on chivalric weaponry as equipment and not status symbol, it nonetheless marks his entry into mimetic chivalry. As he tells Arthur, he wants not only to obtain the Red Knight's armor, but also to become a "chevaliers vermeus" (red knight; l. 997). The illustrations of the *Perceval* manuscripts faithfully reflect the symbolism of Perceval's dress in Chrétien's romance. Thus the codices consistently depict Perceval as a Welsh boy until his encounter with the Red Knight and as a knight with red armor thereafter. In Ms. S, Perceval is represented as a knight with red armor throughout the *Perceval* cycle and Gauvain as a knight with red armor in both the second part of Chrétien's romance and the *First Continuation*. According to Laurence Harf-Lancner, the color red symbolizes the characters' association with the Other World. See Harf-Lancner, "L'image et le fantastique," p. 472. For Michel Pastoureau, the color of the Red Knight's armor ("de gueules plain," in heraldic terminology) underscores the character's violent nature. The symbolism of the armor takes on a new significance when Perceval acquires it: no longer signifying blood-letting violence, the color red henceforth evokes the blood of Christ's Passion. See Pastoureau, "Les armoiries arthuriennes," p. 245.

9. Omer Jodogne, "Le sens chrétien du jeune Perceval dans le *Conte du Graal*," p. 120.

10. Charles Méla, "*Perceval*," p. 260.

11. Sara Sturm-Maddox, "Lévi-Strauss in the Waste Forest," p. 94.

12. In his inaugural lecture to the Chair of Social Anthropology at the Collège de France, January 5, 1960. See Claude Lévi-Strauss, *Anthropologie Structurale Deux*, pp. 33–35.

13. See Jacques Le Goff and Pierre Vidal-Naquet, "Lévi-Strauss en Brocéliande." Yet, whereas in the case of Erec, Yvain, Cligés, and Lancelot, political rivalry occurs in the generation that precedes their own, in the *Conte du Graal*,

clan rivalries are not yet resolved, creating the possibility that Perceval's life will be absorbed into the cycle of revenge.

14. In an attempt to prevent Perceval's identification as a member of the opposition, she has him dress in a manner that hides his Welsh origin: "Ses gavelos en velt porter, / Mais deus en fist sa mere oster / Por che que trop semblast Galois" (He wants to take his three javelins, but his mother had two of them be taken from him because he looked too much like a Welsh; ed. Roach, ll. 607–9).

15. Her examination of Ms. P leads Sandra Hindman to read the codex as an exaltation of genealogy and lineage. For example, the miniatures indicate that the producer's interest was in Perceval's knightly progress rather than his adventures in connection with the Grail castle, none of which is represented. See Hindman, *Sealed in Parchment*, p. 93. This emphasis on Perceval as future lord of the Grail domain is reinforced by the producer's insertion of *Bliocadran*, an anonymous 800-verse prologue to the story of Perceval, in place of Chrétien's opening dedication of his romance to Philippe of Flanders. (Ms. L also contains the *Bliocadran* prologue, but the producer of this codex maintained Chrétien's own prologue, which precedes *Bliocadran*.) The anonymous prologue recounts the story of Perceval's father, Bliocadran, one of eleven brothers descended from one of the richest and most powerful families in Wales. But Bliocadran is killed in the course of a tournament. Three days later, his wife gives birth to a son, Perceval. Determined to protect her son from the dangers of chivalry, she retires to the waste forest. Fourteen years pass. Then one day she decides to warn her son against certain kinds of men he might meet in the forest:

> Se vos une gent veïés
> Qui sunt isi aparelliés
> Con s'il fuissent de fer covert,
> C'est diables tout en apert,
> Qui sont felon et enpené;
> Tost vos aroient devoré.
> (*Bliocadran*, ll. 755–60)

If you were to see men dressed as if they were covered with iron, know that these are winged devils, most baneful creatures, who would soon devour you.

Her fear of chivalric aggression echoes that of Perceval's mother in Chrétien's romance. But an incident before her departure indicates that, against her wishes, Perceval is to return to the family's domain. Her steward persuades her to assemble her people and request of them that they swear allegiance to her son as their lord-to-be (ll. 551–64).

16. Lenora D. Wolfgang, "Prologues to the *Perceval* and Perceval's Father," p. 85.

17. Roach's numbering of this ten-line quotation reflects those lines in Hilka's edition of Ms. A (ll. 131–32) that are missing in Ms. T.

18. For the sake of clarity, this analysis standardizes the heroes' names, which vary in the different versions of the legend.

19. The following observations on venatic imagery in Gottfried's *Tristan* are based on Marcelle Thiébaux's seminal analysis: *The Stag of Love*, pp. 128–43.

20. In primitive cultures, reassembling the carcass represented an attempt to obfuscate the violence of the hunt, transforming death into life. See Walter Burkert, *Homo Necans*, p. 16.

21. Compared to other renditions of the legend, such as Thomas's poem (ca. 1160–70), Béroul's narrative proposes a less courtly or noncourtly ("common," "vulgar") version of the legend to the extent that the poet sides with the two lovers against Marc and his court and glorifies love as a source of joy rather than suffering. See Jean Frappier, "Structure et sens du *Tristan*."

22. Béroul, ll. 1405–697, in *Les Tristans en vers*, ed. Jean-Charles Payen.

23. As R. Howard Bloch notes, "the fate of the feudal world hangs in the balance of Marc's raised sword." Once he discovers the fugitives, the king is under the obligation to punish them as transgressors of order: "In refusing to slay the couple and in disregarding the wishes of his barons, both of which would have further bound him to the feudal past, [Marc] lays the foundation of a modern notion of state," that is, the gradual substitution of private right for collective right. See *Medieval French Literature and Law*, p. 241.

24. Ulle E. Lewes, *The Life in the Forest*, pp. 66–67.

25. Friend is one of the many allegorical figures who endeavor to assist the Lover in his quest for love, represented by the Rose. See Félix Lecoy's edition of Jean de Meun and Guillaume de Lorris, *Le Roman de la Rose*, vol. 2, ll. 8325, 8424, 9463–95.

26. In Jean's version of the Golden Age myth, as Paul B. Milan remarks, "vice and corruption brought about a departure from this primitive state and [led] to the establishment of a coercive government and private property to maintain law and order." According to Milan, Jean uses the conventional topos of the Golden Age myth for rhetorical purposes: this is "not a program of radical social reform," and it cannot "with any degree of certainty be equated with [the author's] personal views." See Paul B. Milan, "The Golden Age and the Political Theory of Jean de Meun," pp. 144, 148.

27. Burkert, *Homo Necans*, p. 43.

28. See Eugene Vance, "Sylvia's Pet Stag."

29. Unlike both the *jus primae noctis* custom introduced in the sixteenth-century revival of seigneurialism and Arthur's symbolic deflowering of Enide, which have a proprietary significance, the deflowering of virgins by substitutes had a truly ritual function in primitive societies: in Walter Burkert's words,

"defloration turn[ed] into sacrifice mainly because of the exclusively human phenomenon of shedding blood in first intercourse." See *Homo Necans*, p. 62.

30. As Marcelle Thiébaux observes, "a hawk is customarily a pursuer, while a stag is pursued." See *The Stag of Love*, p. 112.

31. As Peter Haidu remarks, Gauvain prepares himself in a manner "thoroughly inappropriate to the job of hunting down a fleeing deer." Like Perceval, he reduces chivalric armor (e.g., the lance) to the utilitarianism of the hunter; unlike Perceval, however, his riding a war-horse and using a heavy lance are here attempts "to raise the level of the hunt to that of knightly exploit." The parallel between the two protagonists is intentionally ironic: whereas Perceval the hunter achieves a knightly exploit by killing the Red Knight with a javelin, Gauvain fails in the hunt, as he "will fail in the love adventure." See *Aesthetic Distance in Chrétien de Troyes*, p. 213.

32. Norris J. Lacy, "Gauvain and the Crisis of Chivalry in the *Conte del Graal*," p. 158.

33. See Jean Markale, *Le Graal*, pp. 231–34. According to Markale, the name of Arthur (whose Indo-European root signifies "to plough") comes from *Artus*, "the bear," which sleeps during the winter and wakes up with the seasonal germination of nature ("Pentecost").

34. Bloch, *Medieval French Literature and Law*, p. 201.

35. Thiébaux, *The Stag of Love*, p. 176.

36. An example occurs in the episode narrating Parzival's arrival at the hermitage of his uncle, Trevrizent: "Der rît nu ûf die niwen slâ, / Die gein im kom der rîter grâ" (sec. 455, ll. 23–24,), ("He is now riding along the fresh tracks left by the grey knight that met with him"; tr. Hatto, p. 233).

37. "Gotes vart" (sec. 446, l. 29).

38. "Spor" (sec. 448, l. 21).

39. As Marcelle Thiébaux observes, Wolfram underscores the sacredness of Parzival's quest by contrasting it with the mundane character of Gâwâân's hunting activities, for example, when a track, all bloodied as if a stag had been shot on it, leads Arthur's nephew to his lover, Orgeluse (*Parzival*, sec. 507, l. 25). See *The Stag of Love*, p. 175.

40. Combining "hell" and "akin," the world *Hellequin* means "that which relates to hell." See Henri Dontenville, *La France mythologique*, p. 159.

41. According to Elizabeth J. Bik and Ria Lemaire, "Roi-elfe et reine mère," p. 117.

42. False Seeming, another allegorical figure introduced in Jean's text, is the emblem of hypocrisy.

43. Such is the case of Mario Roques, "Le Graal de Chrétien et la demoiselle au Graal." Omer Jodogne's criticism, by far the most virulent, states that the mother deliberately opted not to take Perceval to a church. See "Le sens chrétien," p. 120. Jean-Charles Payen maintains that, if Perceval does not

know what a church is, this is merely because there is no consecrated chapel in the Welsh vale near Valbone. See "Encore la pratique religieuse dans le *Conte du Graal*," p. 122.

44. Per Nykrog, "Two Creators of Narrative Form in Twelfth-Century France," pp. 266–67.

45. The penitent Perceval encounters before his meeting with the hermit remind him of the necessity to commemorate Christ's Passion. However, because the penitents owe their expertise to the hermit, their sectarian interpretation of Christ's Passion appears to reflect the hermit's view. See Chapter 3, "The 'Holy' Grail: Exegesis as Manipulation."

46. According to Marie Balmary, in Matthew's expression, "division" (*diamerismos* in the Greek text, that is, "distribution") does not mean dissension, as is customarily interpreted, but distinction, in reference to a process of identification recognizing the unique value of each individual. See *Le sacrifice interdit*, pp. 93–100.

47. To quote Fredric Jameson. See *The Political Unconscious*, p. 124.

48. James Dauphiné, "Le thème de l'amour dans le *Conte du Graal*." In Chrétien's first four romances, according to Dauphiné, manifestations of "feudal" love (that is, chivalric practices) take place in the forest, the symbolic locus of violent seduction, and "courtly" love blossoms at Arthur's court, the stage of harmonious communication (p. 116).

49. "The *Conte du Graal* offers the image of a fictional realm that attests to the power of language at the same time that it casts doubt on it and mistrusts it." Ibid., p. 119. In contrast to Dauphiné's view, Jean-Charles Payen asserts that Chrétien's implicit contrast between ideal and practice has a strictly narrative value: only with the development of Arthurian romances in the thirteenth century did this contrast take on a pedagogic and ideological significance. See "La destruction des mythes courtois dans le roman arthurien," pp. 214, 216.

50. Ms. M is the only codex to illustrate this episode, which is represented by two images. The first image shows two lovers tenderly embracing each other. In the second, the maiden offers to her lover a ring garnished with an emerald. As Angelica Rieger observes, these miniatures misinterpret Chrétien's text to the extent that they eliminate the noncourtly character of Perceval's behavior. Taken together, the illustrations contained in the codex indicate a reading of the *Perceval* cycle that idealizes courtly culture. See Rieger, "Le programme iconographique du *Perceval* montpelliérain," pp. 391–92, 406.

51. Analyzing military imagery in Chrétien's romances, Eugene Vance posits that chivalric activities focus on the attainment of love. See "Le combat érotique chez Chrétien de Troyes." In the *Conte*, however, the confluence of military and sexual imagery tends to put forward the equally aggressive character of chivalric and amorous pursuits. An example, in the opening lines of the blood drops episode, is the description of a falcon's hunt of a goose. After

striking the goose so hard that it falls on the ground, the falcon flies off, "Qu'il ne s'i volt liier ne joindre" (because he does not want to unite or join; l. 4183) with the goose. In Daniel Poirion's view, "the falcon's attack on a goose, the way the former hits and crushes it to the ground, and the falcon's flight away from what could have been an embrace ("lïer ne joindre") articulate a language that stands midway between the military and the sexual," indicating that the *Conte*'s critique of courtly love calls into question the adverse effects its law exerts on what Poirion characterizes as "the natural joy of love." See "Du sang sur la neige," pp. 160, 164. This confluence of military and sexual imagery suggests that "love" in the courtly tradition is not an end in itself, but a means to demonstrate one's superior prowess.

52. Guiromelant's love (as "amour de loin") for Clarissant, Gauvain's sister, seems to represent an exceptional case. However, the fact that Gauvain's and Clarissant's father killed Guiromelant's jeopardizes the possibility of their sentimental union. Guiromelant's dead father has thus a parasitic function, effecting the substitution of the duel between Guiromelant and Gauvain for the potential duo of Guiromelant and Clarissant.

53. In Daniel Poirion's view, maternal instruction thus reflects the emergence of a new concept of social exchange, one that rejects the essentially despotic, virile, and territorial desire that marks feudalism. See "L'ombre mythique de Perceval dans le *Conte du Graal*."

54. The "constraining" gift of the sword places Perceval in his donator's debt, assigning to him the restoration of the Grail faction.

55. Blancheflor's evocation of the bloody outcome that will free her from Clamadeu's threat is an index of the lethal repercussions of pursuits in traditional chivalric culture. In addition to the Bleeding Lance of the Grail castle, other, more direct evocations of the deadly character of knightly performance include Perceval's killing of the Red Knight as narrated by Yvonet and the presentation of Perceval's cousin holding the bleeding body of her dead lover in her arms. In the blood drops scene, by contrast, the color red is associated with the forces of life and regeneration. As Grace Armstrong observes, the emphasis here is neither on slaughter (as suggested by the fact that "the wild goose is able to fly off after the attack") nor on bloodshed (because Perceval's trance focuses on *three* blood drops), but on the protagonist's "developing sensitivity" as awakened through the love experience. See "The Scene of the Blood Drops on the Snow," pp. 131, 138.

56. Although maintaining that Blancheflor functions as Perceval's initiator into adulthood, Pierre Gallais obfuscates the realistic elements contained in the episode by invoking the "oriental" origin and significance of the love between Chrétien's two protagonists. See *Perceval et l'initiation*.

57. Like the townsmen of Escavalon, Blancheflor's people have a violent sense of justice: after Perceval's victory over Enguigeron, they wonder why he

did not cut off their enemy's head (ll. 2334–37). Both Enguigeron and Clama-
deu, who killed not only many knights of Biaurepaire but Blancheflor's father,
are aware of their enemies' murderous disposition toward them and thus refuse
Perceval's offer that they submit to imprisonment in Biaurepaire.

58. The Biaurepaire episode contains an allusion to Christ's Passion that
reflects a realistic rather than sectarian assessment of the persecuting effect of
Clamadeu's aggression. As Perceval leaves Biaurepaire to combat Enguigeron,
the people pray for him, telling him:

> Biax sire, icele vraie crois,
> Ou Diex soffri pener son fil,
> Vos gart hui de mortel peril
> Et d'encombrier et de prison,
> Et vos ramaint a garison
> En liu ou vos soiez a ese,
> Qui vos delit et qui vos plaise.
> (Ed Roach, ll. 2154–60)

Fair sir, may that true cross, on which God allowed His son to suffer, protect
you today from mortal danger and misfortune and capture and lead you back
safely to where you may rest at ease, in happiness and pleasure.

59. In Lori Walters's perspective, "It is highly likely that Chrétien envi-
sioned Perceval and Blanchefleur eventually marrying and reigning jointly over
a kingdom—either Biaurepaire, the Grail domain, or a combination of the
two—after Perceval's completion of another visit, this time successful, to the
Grail Castle." Walters deduces this eventuality from the iconographic program
of Ms. M, which consistently depicts Blancheflor as a romance heroine: "Not
only does Blanchefleur appear there more often than in any other manuscript
containing the Grail cycle, but a good number of miniatures in which she is
not represented directly develop romance themes associated with her." An ex-
ample is the depiction of the procession of the Bleeding Lance, which is carried
not by a young man, but by a maiden whose headdress and clothing "recall
those worn by Blanchefleur" in the miniature depicting her nocturnal visit to
Perceval. See Walters, "The Image of Blanchefleur," pp. 440, 439, 447. But
the interpretation of Perceval's story by the producer of the codex does not
necessarily reflect Chrétien's intention. Although I concur with Walters's em-
phasis on Blancheflor's profound significance for Perceval, I do not believe that
Chrétien meant to develop an "analogy between romantic love and those tran-
scendent truths figured by the objects in the Grail procession." Ibid., p. 447.
In my view, Biaurepaire and the Grail domain are two antagonistic rather than
complementary sites. The first provides Perceval with the opportunity of as-
suming his dynastic responsibilities; the second imposes on him the task of
avenging his ancestors.

60. As Rupert T. Pickens observes, "with knowledge that his mother is dead, Perceval is a knight without a quest object—a knight, therefore, who is unmotivated, who has no longer a reason for movement." See *The Welsh Knight*, pp. 29–30. Hence, the effect of the Grail messengers' discourse is to persuade Perceval to assume the quest for the *graal*.

61. The reading proposed here of Chrétien's *Conte* as a pessimistic account of the protocols of traditional chivalry agrees on many counts with that developed by Donald Maddox in *The Arthurian Romances of Chrétien de Troyes*. However, I differ from Maddox by arguing that nothing differentiates the Arthurian order and social order according to the Grail because both rival factions contribute to their own weakening by adhering to the same obsolescent and inadequate system of customs. I thus situate the transtextual coherence of Chrétien's oeuvre in a representation of protocols and codes of behavior that dramatizes their inadequacies "as an institution for the maintenance of order" (ibid., p. 139). Like Arthurian custom, "a practice of long standing" (p. 54), which the king attempts to enforce throughout the realm (p. 134), custom as observed at the remote locus of the Grail castle is not a practice of more recent inception (p. 66), but one equally marked by "longevity" (p. 94). The key element here is the centrality of prediegetic history (from the time of Utherpendragon's death) in dictating a preordained type of conduct, signaling the ineluctability of Perceval's transformation into the avenger of his Grail lineage. To cite Maddox's seminal remark, "what is known of twelfth-century techniques of composition enhances the likelihood that the wealth of thematic relationships which customs maintain both within and among Chrétien's romances results from consistent application of conscious poetic processes" (p. 123), revealing "a close relationship between poetic technique and a developmental ethical coherence within the textual ensemble" (p. 162, n. 11). The prevailing custom operative throughout Chrétien's fictional world is one that perpetuates violence and rivalry among all the knightly inhabitants of the land of "ogres," including the Grail faction.

62. In contrast with the whiteness of the snow in the blood drops scene, which functions as a screen where "Perceval the subject" appears for the first—and perhaps last—time (see Henri Rey-Flaud, "Le sang sur la neige," p. 21), the "blankness" of Perceval's mind once the Grail messengers succeed in imposing on him the law of lineal revenge signals the disappearance of his emerging autonomy as loving son, devoted lover, and responsible knight. Although he is henceforth asked to redress past familial grievances, this past is also never fully revealed to him. Perceval's "educators" thus intentionally fail to provide him with the kind of information that would have helped him understand the meaning of his mission, and this is why his journey is inscribed in space rather than time. If the scene of the falcon chasing the goose emblematizes the possibility of Perceval's fruitful union with Blancheflor, then the fact that the falcon does not "join" with the goose emblematizes the effect of traditional chi-

valric culture in separating two characters whose love had held the promise of a reconciliation between Arthur's faction (considering Blancheflor's lineal ties with Gornemant) and the Grail. Significantly, the manuscript tradition tends to explain the falcon's departure from the goose in terms of a missed opportunity: "Mais trop fu *main*, si s'en parti, / Qu'il ne s'i volt liier ne joindre" (But it was too *early* in the day, and the falcon flew off because he does not want to unite or join with the goose; version T, ed. Roach, ll. 4182–83; my emphasis). Compared to l. 4182 of version T, version B reads "mes par fu *nois*" (it was too dark), and version A in Lecoy's edition, "mes trop fu *tart*" (it was too late). See ed. Hilka, note to l. 4182. Rey-Flaud sees the cause of this missed opportunity in Perceval, who, like the falcon, refuses to acknowledge his sexual desire ("Le sang sur la neige," p. 20). However, if it is always too early or too late for Perceval to act properly, as Daniel Poirion notes ("Du sang sur la neige," p. 161), the reason is not Perceval himself, but external influences, as in the case of Gornemant, whose instruction induces the *niche* to defer his inquiry about the objects of the Grail procession until the following morning. In the blood drops scene, the belatedness of Perceval's yearning for Blancheflor's company points to the effect of the Grail messengers in redirecting Perceval's journey, suggesting that, in Chrétien's narration, he will never return to Biaurepaire.

63. Reinscribing Perceval's story as introduced in the *Conte du Graal*, two of the four *Continuations* narrate how Chrétien's protagonist returns to Biaurepaire and marries Blancheflor. In the *Second Continuation*, Perceval announces to his lover that he will leave her after the marriage ceremony and resume his quest for the Grail, promising to return to her at the completion of his mission (ll. 22895–99). But the text ends after the episode of Perceval's successful return to the Grail castle, as does the *Continuation* of Gerbert de Montreuil. Only with Manessier's *Continuation* does Perceval's story receive closure. The narrative recounts how he avenges the death of the Grail king's brother, but refuses the king's offer to become lord of the domain. He then returns to Arthur's court, where he learns that the Grail king has died and bequeathed his kingdom to him. Arthur accompanies him to Corbenic and attends his coronation. After seven years, Perceval retires to a hermitage, and the holy Grail, the holy lance, and the holy silver trencher go there with him (*Third Continuation*, ll. 42561–63). He becomes a priest after five years and dies five years later·

> Fu el ciel ravi sanz doutance
> Et le Saint Graal et la lance
> Et le bel tailleor d'argent,
> Tout en apert, voiant la gent,
> Onc puis ne fu, tant seüst querre,
> Nus hom qui le vëist en terre
> Puis que Perceval fu finnez.

(Ll. 42617–23)

He was carried off to heaven, most certainly, and with him, the Holy Grail, the lance, and the beautiful silver trencher, in full view of everyone. Since the day of his death, no man ever saw the Grail on earth again, search as he might.

Blancheflor plays a minimal part in the story of Perceval as reinscribed by Manessier. Her name is first mentioned during the episode of Perceval's temptation by the devil, who assumes the guise of Blancheflor (ll. 38150, 38318–24). Perceval meets her again when he returns to Biaurepaire, where he conducts himself as Blancheflor's protector rather than as her lover. Despite her grief (ll. 39316–17, 39348), he departs from Biaurepaire, and there is no further mention of Blancheflor in the remainder of Manessier's narrative. Manessier thus develops a negative portrayal of Blancheflor to the extent that she is potentially an obstacle on Perceval's road to sanctity. Like the *Conte du Graal*, the *Continuation* distinguishes between Biaurepaire and Corbenic as two opposite and irreconcilable sites with respect to Perceval's chivalric acculturation. Unlike Manessier's text, however, Chrétien's romance endows Biaurepaire with positive value, in contrast to the effect of the Grail domain in forcing Perceval to devote his life to the avenging of his ancestors.

Conclusion

1. To cite Alan of Lille's allegorical figure of Natura in *De planctu Naturae* (ca. 1160–70), who claims that God "in amicicie pacem litem repugnantie conmutauit." See Nikolaus Haring's edition of Alan of Lille, *De planctu Naturae*, p. 840; and *The Plaint of Nature*, trans. James J. Sheridan, p. 145.

2. According to Natura, "subtilibus igitur inuisibilis iuncture cathenis concordantibus ad unitatem pluralitas, ad idemptitatem diuersitas, ad consonantiam dissonantia, ad concordiam discordia, unione pacifica remeauit." *De planctu Naturae*, p. 840; *The Plaint of Nature*, p. 145.

3. See Alexandre Leupin, *Barbarolexis: Medieval Writing and Sexuality*, p. 41.

4. Ibid., p. 48.

5. Also noteworthy is the "transgressive" stance of the saint as hero, which calls upon Alexis's capacity to transcend and surpass normative standards of conduct—by rejecting, for example, his duty as a noble heir charged with the task of perpetuating lineage, property, and renown. See Brigitte Cazelles, "Outrepasser les normes: L'invention de soi en France médiévale."

6. That the troubadours' poetry is intentionally subversive is best summarized by Arnaut Daniel, when he states, "Ieu sui Arnautz q'amas l'aura, / E chatz la lebre al lo bou / E nadi contra suberna" (*Canzoni*, canso 10, ll. 43–45; I am Arnaut, who amasses the wind, who chases the hare with an ox, and who swims against the tide). See also Brigitte Cazelles, "Mots à vendre, corps à prendre et les troubadours d'Aquitaine."

7. On the role of verbal ruse in enabling Yseut to claim her innocence

against the charge of adultery, see Pierre Jonin, *Les personnages féminins dans les romans français de Tristan.* According to Jonin, the vulnerability of customary procedure as it found itself open to abuse and manipulation constituted the grounds for the development of inquests and jury trials during the thirteenth century. See also Jean-Charles Payen, "Lancelot contre Tristan: La conjuration d'un mythe subversif."

8. Hyperbolic comparison plays a central part in Chrétien's narrative technique of the "surenchère" (outbidding) as a means of identifying his romances' heroic figures. See Don A. Monson, "La 'surenchère' chez Chrétien de Troyes."

9. In Guillaume's *Roman de la Rose,* Amant's quest ends in an impasse to the extent that the Rose remains unresponsive, hence his failure as quester, his laments in the face of a tyrannical Rose (in the narrator's perspective, the sufferings he endured as Lover are bound to cause his death; see l. 4014), and the inconclusiveness of Guillaume's text.

10. Although Amant is never characterized as *niche* (nice) in Guillaume's text, in Jean's text, this becomes his principal attribute. For example, see Reason's assessment of her pupil, l. 5341.

11. Although, in Jean's text, the source of power is first and foremost verbal persuasion, the narration of Amant's quest for the Rose is not violence-free. That debate is a form of combat is vividly illustrated in the episode narrating the assault that the God of Love and his host launch against the castle of the Rose. See ll. 15273–96.

12. For instance by Nancy Freeman Regalado, who interprets Jean's representation of the cosmos as a harmonious conflation of "contreres choses." See "*Des contraires choses*: La fonction poétique de la citation et des *exempla* dans le *Roman de la Rose* de Jean de Meun."

13. For a description of these two rhetorical figures, see Eugene Vance, "Le combat érotique chez Chrétien de Troyes: De la figure à la forme," p. 545.

14. An example is the debate between the two sisters regarding Meliant's relative value.

15. The criticism of the sophists' technique of reasoning appears in the discourse of Faux Semblant (False Seeming, who joins the God of Love's army):

> Il font un argument au monde
> Qu conclusion a honteuse
>
> · · ·
>
> Cist argumenz est touz f ïeus,
> Il ne vaut pas un coustel troine:
> La robe ne fet pas le moine.
> Ne porquant nus n'i set respondre,
> Tant face haut sa teste tondre,
> Voire rere au rasoer d'Elanches,
> Qui barat tremche en .xiii. branches;

Nus ne set si bien distinter
Qu'il en ose un seul mot tinter.
(*Roman de la Rose*, ll. 11022–23, 11026–34)

They present an argument to the world that leads to a shameful conclusion. . . .
This argument is entirely specious, not worth a knife of privet; the habit does
not make the monk. Nonetheless, no one knows how to reply to it, no mat-
ter how high he tonsures his head, even if he shaves it with the razor of the
Elenchis, which cuts up fraud into thirteen branches. No one has sufficient
knowledge on how to set up distinctions to dare utter a single word against it.

16. Aristotle's *De sophisticis Elenchis* is mentioned by False Seeming at
l. 11032. The word *elenchus* ("Elanches" in Faux Semblant's speech, l. 11031)
refers to a pearl in the shape of a pear, an image of the abusive argumentation
characterizing sophistic reasoning.

17. In his treatise, Aristotle distinguishes between two major modes of
false argumentation: one, which involves external factors such as the inter-
locutor's ignorance, comprises seven ways; the other, which is connected to
language, comprises six "methods of producing false illusion" (*De sophisticis
Elenchis*, trans. E. S. Forster, p. 17), hence the thirteen-branch razor invoked
by False Seeming.

18. To cite the opening line of the fable entitled "Le loup et l'agneau." See
Jean de La Fontaine, *Fables*, p. 67.

19. In the context of the "Querelle," "rhodophiles" designate those who
undertook to defend Jean's text, including Jean de Montreuil, secretary to the
king of France (Charles VI), Gontier Col, first notary to the king, and Pierre
Col, canon of Paris. The principal accusers of Jean's romance (the "rhodo-
phobes") were Jean Gerson, chancellor of the University of Paris, and Christine
de Pizan.

20. "Se maistre Jehan de Meung, se je l'ose dire, eust parlé parmy son livre
de plusseurs choses a quoy nature humainne est encline et qui adviennent, et
puis rameinné au propos et fait sa conclusion en meurs de bien vivre, tu eusses
plus grant cause de dire que il le fist affin de bien; et car tu sé se ung dicteur
veult user d'ordre de rethorique, il fait ses premisses de ce que il veult traictier,
et puis entre de propos en propos et parle de plusseurs choses s'il luy plaist,
puis revient a sa conclusion de ce pour quoy il a faite sa narracion. . . . Je tiens
tout ung mesme edifice. Et souffit pour responce a cest chapitre . . . car tout
vient a une fin." Quoted in Eric Hicks, ed., *Le débat sur le Roman de la Rose*, pp.
134–35. Trans. in Joseph L. Baird and John R. Kane, *La Querelle de la Rose:
Letters and Documents*, p. 132.

Works Cited

Chrétien de Troyes's *Perceval ou le Conte du Graal*

Baist, Gottfried, ed. *Crestien von Troyes' "Li Contes del Graal" ("Percevaus li Galois")*. Freiburg im Breisgau: In Kommission G. Ragoczy (K. Nick), 1911.

Bryant, Nigel, trans. *Perceval: The Story of the Grail*. Totowa, N.J.: Rowman and Littlefield, 1982.

Hilka, Alfons, ed. *Der Percevalroman ("Li contes del Graal") von Christian von Troyes*. Halle: Niemeyer, 1932.

Lecoy, Félix, ed. *Le Conte du Graal (Perceval)*. Paris: Champion, vol. 1, 1973; vol. 2, 1975.

Méla, Charles, ed. *Le Conte du Graal ou le Roman de Perceval: Edition du manuscrit 354 de Berne {Ms. B}*. Paris: Librairie Générale Française, 1990.

Pickens, Rupert T., ed. *Chrétien de Troyes: The Story of the Grail {Li Contes del Graal} or Perceval*. Trans. William Kibler. New York: Garland Publishing, 1990.

Potvin, Charles, ed. *Perceval le Gallois ou le Conte du Graal*. 6 vols. Mons: Desquesne-Masquillier, 1865–71.

Roach, William, ed. *Le Roman de Perceval ou le Conte du Graal publié d'après le Ms. fr. 12576 {Ms. T} de la Bibliothèque Nationale*. Geneva: Droz, and Paris: Minard, 1959 [1956].

Perceval Continuations

La Continuation de Perceval [The *Continuation* of Gerbert de Montreuil]. Eds. Mary Williams (vols. 1 and 2) and Marguerite Oswald (vol. 3). Paris: Champion, vol. 1, 1922; vol. 2, 1925; vol. 3, 1975.

The Didot Perceval According to the Manuscripts Modena and Paris. Ed. William Roach. Philadelphia: University of Pennsylvania Press, 1941.

The First Continuation: Redaction of Mss. T, V, D. Ed. William Roach. Philadelphia: University of Pennsylvania Press, 1949.

The Second Continuation. Ed. William Roach. Philadelphia: American Philosophical Society, 1952.

The Third Continuation by Manessier. Ed. William Roach. Philadelphia: American Philosophical Society, 1983.

Other Medieval Works

Alan of Lille. *De planctu naturae.* Ed. Nikolaus M. Häring. In *Studi Medievali,* 3rd series, 19.2 (1978): 797–879.

———. *The Plaint of Nature.* Trans. James J. Sheridan. Toronto: Pontifical Institute of Mediaeval Studies, 1980.

Arnaut Daniel. *Arnaut Daniel: Canzoni.* Ed. Gianluigi Toja. Florence: G. C. Sansoni, 1960.

Bernard de Ventadour. *Bernard de Ventadour, troubadour du XIIe siècle: Chansons d'amour.* Ed. Moshé Lazar. Paris: Klincksieck, 1966.

Bliocadran. Ed. Lenora D. Wolfgang. Tübingen: Niemeyer, 1976.

Chrétien de Troyes. *Le Chevalier au Lion (Yvain).* Ed. Mario Roques. Paris: Champion, 1982 [1960].

———. *Le Chevalier de la Charrete.* Ed. Mario Roques. Paris: Champion, 1983 [1958].

———. *Cligés.* Ed. Alexandre Micha. Paris: Champion, 1978.

———. *Eric et Enide.* Ed. Mario Roques. Paris: Champion, 1973 [1952].

Conciliorum Oecumenicorum Decreta, pp. 227–71. Ed. Giuseppe Alberigo et al. Bologna: Instituto per le Scienze Religiose, 1973.

Genealogiae Comitum Flandriae. Continuatio Claromariscensis: Flandriae Generosa. In *Monumenta Germaniae historica, Scriptores,* vol. 9: 326–34.

Geoffrey of Monmouth. *The "Historia Regum Britannie" of Geoffrey of Monmouth. I. Bern. Bürgerbibliothek, Ms. 568.* Ed. Neil Wright. Cambridge, Eng.: D. S. Brewer, 1985.

———. *The History of the Kings of Britain.* Trans. Lewis Thorpe. New York: Penguin Books, 1979 [1966].

Jean de Meun and Guillaume de Lorris. *Guillaume de Lorris et Jean de Meun: Le Roman de la Rose.* Ed. Félix Lecoy. Paris: Champion, vol. 1, 1974; vol. 2, 1973; vol. 3, 1982 [1970].

"Li ver del Juïse" en fornfransk Predikan. Ed. Hugo von Feilitzen. Upsala: Akademiska Boktryckeriet, 1883.

The Mabinogi and Other Medieval Welsh Tales. Trans. Patrick K. Ford. Berkeley: University of California Press, 1977.

The Mabinogion. Trans. Jeffrey Gantz. New York: Dorset Press, 1985 [1976].

Philippe de Beaumanoir. *Coutumes de Beauvaisis.* Ed. A. Salmon. Paris: Picard, 1899–1900.

La Queste del Saint Graal: Roman du XIIIe siècle. Ed. Albert Pauphilet. Paris: Champion, 1984 [1923].

Robert de Boron (pseud.). *Robert de Boron: Merlin, roman du XIIIe siècle.* Ed. Alexandre Micha. Geneva: Droz, 1979.

Sacrorum conciliorum et decretum. Supplementum. Ed. Giovanni Domenico Mansi et al. 6 vols. Lucae: Ex typographia J. Salani, 1748–53.

Sir Gawain and the Green Knight. Ed. John Ronald Revel Tolkien and Eric Valentine Gordon. Oxford: Clarendon Press, 1925.

Triads of Britain. Ed. Iolo Morganwg. Trans. W. Probert. London: Wildwood House, 1977.

Les Tristans en vers: Tristan de Béroul, Tristan de Thomas, Folie Tristan de Berne, Folie Tristan d'Oxford, Chèvrefeuille de Marie de France. Ed. Jean-Charles Payen. Paris: Garnier, 1974.

Vie de Saint Alexis. Ed. Gaston Paris. Paris: Champion, 1974 [1903].

Wace. *La partie arthurienne du Roman de Brut.* Ed. I. D. O. Arnold and M. M. Pelan. Paris: Klincksieck, 1962.

Wolfram von Eschenbach. *Parzival.* Ed. Gottfried Weber. Darmstadt: Wissenschaftliche Buchgesellschaft, 1963.

———. *Parzival.* Trans. A. T. Hatto. New York: Penguin Books, 1980.

Scholarly Works

Adolf, Helen. "Le Vieux Roi, clef de voûte du *Conte del Graal.*" In *Mélanges offerts à Rita Lejeune*, pp. 945–55. Dembloux: Duculot, 1969.

———. *"Visio Pacis": Holy City and Grail, an Attempt at an Inner History of the Grail Legend.* University Park: Pennsylvania University Press, 1960.

Ajam, Laurent. "La forêt dans l'oeuvre de Chrétien de Troyes." *Europe* 642 (1982): 120–25.

Aristotle. *De sophisticis Elenchis.* In *On Sophistical Refutations, on Coming-To-Be and Passing-Away, on the Cosmos*, trans. E. S. Forster. Cambridge, Mass.: Harvard University Press, 1955.

Armstrong, Grace. "The Scene of the Blood Drops on the Snow: A Crucial Narrative Moment in the *Conte du Graal.*" *Kentucky Romance Quarterly* 19 (1972): 127–47.

Ashe, Geoffrey. *The Landscape of King Arthur.* New York: Henry Holt, 1988.

Baird, Joseph L., and John R. Kane, trans. *La Querelle de la Rose: Letters and Documents.* Chapel Hill: University of North Carolina Press, 1978.

Baldwin, John W. *The Government of Philip Augustus: Foundations of French Royal Power in the Middle Ages.* Berkeley: University of California Press, 1986.

Balmary, Marie. *Le sacrifice interdit: Freud et la Bible.* Paris: Grasset, 1986.

Barber, Richard W. *The Knight and Chivalry.* London: Scribner, 1970.

Barbey, Jean. "Genèse et consécration des lois fondamentales." *Droits: Revue Française de Théorie Juridique* 3 (1986): 75–86.

Baumgartner, Emmanuèle. " 'Del graal cui l'an an servoit': Variations sur un pronom." In Philip E. Bennett and Graham A. Runnalls, eds., *The Editor and the Text*, pp. 137–44. Edinburgh: Edinburgh University Press, 1990.

————. "Les scènes du Graal et leur illustration dans les manuscrits du *Conte du Graal* et des *Continuations*." In Keith Busby et al., eds., *The Manuscripts of Chrétien de Troyes*, vol. 1, pp. 489–503. Amsterdam: Rudopi, 1993.

Bechmann, Roland. *Des arbres et des hommes: La forêt au moyen âge*. Paris: Flammarion, 1984.

Becquet, Jean. "L'érémitisme clérical et laïc dans l'Ouest de la France." In *L'eremistismo in Occidente nei secoli XI e XII*, pp. 182–202. Milan: Centro di studi medieoevali, 1965.

Bednar, John. *La spiritualité et le symbolisme dans l'oeuvre de Chrétien de Troyes*. Paris: Nizet, 1974.

Beeler, John. *Warfare in Feudal Europe, 730–1200*. Ithaca, N.Y.: Cornell University Press, 1971.

Benson, Larry D. "The Tournaments in the Romances of Chrétien de Troyes and *L'Histoire de Guillaume le Maréchal*." In Larry D. Benson and John Leyerle, eds., *Chivalric Literature: Essays on Relations Between Literature and Life in the Later Middle Ages*, pp. 1–24. Kalamazoo, Mich.: Medieval Institute Publications, 1980.

Benton, John. "Consciousness of Self and Perceptions of Individuality." In Robert L. Benson and Giles Constable, with Carol D. Lanham, eds., *Renaissance and Renewal of the Twelfth Century*, pp. 263–95. Cambridge, Mass.: Harvard University Press, 1982.

Berman, Harold J. *Law and Revolution: The Formation of the Western Legal Tradition*. Cambridge, Mass.: Harvard University Press, 1983.

Bik, Elizabeth J., and Ria Lemaire. "Roi-elfe et reine mère." *Poétique* 81 (1990): 115–25.

Blaess, Madeleine. "Perceval et les 'Illes de Mer.'" In *Mélanges de Littérature du Moyen Age au XXe Siècle Offerts à Jeanne Lods*, vol. 1, pp. 69–77. Paris: Collection de l'Ecole Normale Supérieure de Jeunes Filles, 1978.

Bloch, Marc. *Les rois thaumaturges*. Paris: Gallimard, 1983 [1924].

————. *La société féodale*. Paris: Albin Michel, 1978 [1939].

Bloch, R. Howard. *Etymologies and Genealogies: A Literary Anthropology of the French Middle Ages*. Chicago: University of Chicago Press, 1983.

————. *Medieval French Literature and Law*. Berkeley: University of California Press, 1977.

Bloomfield, Morton W. *The Seven Deadly Sins*. East Lansing: Michigan University Press, 1952.

Bogdanow, Fanni. *The Romance of the Grail: A Study of the Structure and Genesis of a Thirteenth-Century Arthurian Prose Romance*. Oxford: Manchester University Press, 1966.

Brooks, Peter. *Reading for the Plot: Design and Invention in Narrative*. New York: Knopf, 1984.

Brown, Robert McAfee. *Religion and Violence*. 2nd ed. Philadelphia: Westminster Press, 1987.

Buettner, Bonnie. "The Good Friday Scene in Chrétien de Troyes' *Perceval*." *Traditio* 36 (1980): 415–26.

Bullock-Davies, Constance. "Chrétien de Troyes and England." *Arthurian Literature* 1 (1981): 1–61.

Burkert, Walter. *Homo Necans: The Anthropology of Ancient Greek Sacrificial Ritual and Myth*. Trans. Peter Bing. Berkeley: University of California Press, 1983 [1972].

Busby, Keith. *Gauvain in Old French Literature*. Amsterdam: Rodopi, 1980.

———. "The Illustrated Manuscripts of Chrétien's *Perceval*." In Keith Busby et al., eds., *The Manuscripts of Chrétien de Troyes*, vol. 1, pp. 351–63.

———. "The Scribe of MSS T and V of Chrétien's *Perceval* and Its *Continuations*." In Keith Busby et al., eds., *The Manuscripts of Chrétien de Troyes*, vol. 1, pp. 49–65.

———. "Text, Miniature, and Rubric in the *Continuations* of Chrétien's *Perceval*." In Keith Busby et al., eds., *The Manuscripts of Chrétien de Troyes*, vol. 1, pp. 365–76.

Busby, Keith, et al., eds. *The Manuscripts of Chrétien de Troyes*, 2 vols. Amsterdam: Rodopi, 1993.

Carmody, Francis J. "Le *Perceval* de Chrétien de Troyes: Lexique et sources." *Actas del XI Congreso Internacional de Lingüística y Filología Románicas*, vol. 2, pp. 729–35. Madrid: Revista de Filología Española, 1968.

Cazelles, Brigitte. "Mots à vendre, corps à prendre et les troubadours d'Aquitaine." *Stanford French Review* (Spring 1983): 27–36.

———. "Outrepasser les normes: L'invention de soi en France médiévale." *Stanford French Review* (Spring-Fall 1990): 69–92.

Cerquiglini, Jacqueline, Bernard Cerquiglini, Christiane Marchello-Nizia, and Michèle Perret. "D'une quête l'autre: De Perceval à Gauvain ou la forme d'une différence." In *Mélanges de Littérature du Moyen Age au XXe Siècle Offerts à Jeanne Lods*, vol. 1, pp. 269–96. Paris: Collection de l'Ecole Normale Supérieure de Jeunes Filles, 1978.

Chénon, Emile. *Histoire générale du droit français public et privé des origines à 1815*. Paris: Sirey, vol. 1, 1926, vol. 2, 1929.

Cohen, Gustave. "Le duel judiciaire chez Chrétien de Troyes." *Annales de l'Université de Paris* 8 (1933): 510–27.

Dauphiné, James. "Le thème de l'amour dans le *Conte du Graal*." *Europe* 642 (1982): 114–20.

Delaruelle, Etienne. "La culture religieuse des laïcs en France aux XIe et XIIe siècles." In *I Laici nella "Societas Christiana" dei secoli XI e XII*, pp. 548–81. Milan: Società Editrice Vita e Pensiero, 1968.

Desmazières de Séchelles, Raymond. "L'évolution et la transformation du mythe arthurien." *Romania* 78 (1957): 182–98.

Dontenville, Henri. *La France mythologique*. Paris: Veyrier-Tchou, 1966.

Dragonetti, Roger. *La vie de la lettre au Moyen Age: Le "Conte du Graal."* Paris: Seuil, 1980.

Duby, Georges. *Le dimanche de Bouvines*. Paris: Gallimard, 1973.

———. "Les 'jeunes' dans la société aristocratique dans la France du Nord-Ouest au XIIe siècle." *Annales, Economies, Sociétés, Civilisations* 19 (1964): 835–46.

Esmein, Adhemar. *Cours élémentaire d'histoire du droit français*. Paris: Larose, 1895.

Faral, Edmond. "Note sur la nature du Graal." In *Les Romans du Graal aux XIIe et XIIIe siècles*, pp. 59–62. Paris: Centre National de la Recherche Scientifique, 1956.

Fein, David A. "*Le Latin Sivrai*: Problematic Aspects of Narrative Authority in Twelfth-Century French Literature." *French Review* 66 (1993): 572–83.

Flori, Jean. *L'essor de la chevalerie, XIe–XIIe siècles*. Geneva: Droz, 1986.

———. *L'idéologie du glaive: Préhistoire de la chevalerie*. Geneva: Droz, 1983.

———. "Pour une histoire de la chevalerie: L'adoubement dans les romans de Chrétien de Troyes." *Romania* 100 (1979): 21–53.

Folz, Robert. *Les saints rois du moyen âge en Occident (VIe–XIIIe siècles)*. Brussels: Société des Bollandistes, 1984.

Fowler, David C. *Prowess and Charity in the "Perceval" of Chrétien de Troyes*. Seattle: University of Washington Press, 1959.

Fox, John. *A Literary History of France: The Middle Ages*. New York: Barnes and Nobles, 1974.

Frappier, Jean. *Chrétien de Troyes*. Paris: Hatier, 1968.

———. *Chrétien de Troyes et le mythe du Graal: Etude sur "Perceval ou le Conte du Graal."* Paris: SEDES, 1972.

———. "Le Graal et la chevalerie." *Romania* 75 (1954): 165–210.

———. "Le motif du don contraignant dans la littérature du Moyen Age." *Travaux de Linguistique et de Littérature* 7 (1969): 7–46.

———. "Structure et sens du *Tristan*: Version commune, version courtoise." *Cahiers de Civilisation Médiévale* 6 (1963): 255–80.

Freeman, Michelle. "Jean Frappier et le Mythe du Graal." *Oeuvres et Critiques* 5 (1980–81): 129–34.

Gallais, Pierre. "Métonymie et métaphore dans le *Conte du Graal*." In *Mélanges . . . offerts à Jeanne Lods*, vol. 1, pp. 213–48. Paris: Collection de l'Ecole Normale Supérieure de Jeunes Filles, 1978.

———. *Perceval et l'initiation: Essais sur le dernier roman de Chrétien de Troyes, ses correspondances "orientales" et sa signification anthropologique*. Paris: Sirac, 1972.

Gilissen, John. *La Coutume*. Turnhout: Brepols, 1982.

Gouttebroze, Jean. "Cousin, cousine: Dévolution du pouvoir et sexualité dans le *Conte du Graal*." In *Chrétien de Troyes et le Graal*, pp. 77–87. Paris: Nizet, 1984.

Greimas, Algirdas Julien. *Sémantique structurale*. Paris: Larousse, 1966.

Guenée, Bernard. "Temps de l'histoire et temps de la mémoire." *Bulletin de la Société de l'Histoire de France* 87 (1976–77): 25–35.

Haidu, Peter. *Aesthetic Distance in Chrétien de Troyes: Irony and Comedy in Cligés and Perceval*. Geneva: Droz, 1968.

————. "Au début du roman, l'ironie." *Poétique* 36 (1978): 443–66.

————. *Lion-Queue-Coupée: L'écart symbolique chez Chrétien de Troyes*. Geneva: Droz, 1972.

Hanning, Robert W. "Arthurian Evangelists: The Language of Truth in Thirteenth-Century French Prose Romances." *Philological Quarterly* 64 (1985): 347–65.

————. *The Individual in Twelfth-Century Romance*. New Haven, Conn.: Yale University Press, 1977.

Harf-Lancner, Laurence. "L'image et le fantastique dans les manuscrits des romans de Chrétien de Troyes." In Keith Busby et al., eds., *The Manuscripts of Chrétien de Troyes*, vol. 1, pp. 457–88. Amsterdam: Rodopi, 1993.

————. "Une Mélusine galloise: La Dame du Lac de Brecknock." In *Mélanges de Littérature du Moyen Age au XXe Siècle Offerts à Jeanne Lods*, vol. 1, pp. 322–38. Paris: Collection de l'Ecole Normale Supérieure de Jeunes Filles, 1978.

Harrison, Robert Pogue. *Forests: The Shadow of Civilization*. Chicago: University of Chicago Press, 1992.

Head, Thomas, and Richard Land, eds. *Essays on the Peace of God: The Church and the People in Eleventh-Century France*. Waterloo, Ontario: University of Waterloo Press, 1987.

Heer, Friedrich. *The Medieval World: Europe, 1100–1350*. Trans. Janet Sondheimer. New York: World Publishing, 1962 [1961].

Hicks, Eric, ed. *Le débat sur le Roman de la Rose*. Paris: Champion, 1977.

Hindman, Sandra. *Sealed in Parchment: Rereadings of Knighthood in the Illuminated Manuscripts of Chrétien de Troyes*. Chicago: University of Chicago Press, 1994.

Hoggan, David G. "Le péché de Perceval: Pour l'authenticité de l'épisode de l'ermite dans le *Conte du Graal* de Chrétien de Troyes." *Romania* 93 (1972): 50–76, 244–75.

Holmes, Urban T., and Sister M. Amelia Klenke. *Chrétien, Troyes, and the Grail*. Chapel Hill: University of North Carolina Press, 1959.

Huchet, Jean-Charles. "Les déserts du roman médiéval. Le personnage de l'ermite dans les romans des XIIe et XIIIe siècles." *Littérature* 60 (1985): 89–108.

Hunt, Tony. "Chrestien de Troyes: The Textual Problem." *French Studies* 33 (1979): 257–71. Repr. in Keith Busby et al., eds., *The Manuscripts of Chrétien de Troyes*, vol. 1, pp. 27–40. Amsterdam: Rodopi, 1993.

————. "The Emergence of the Knight in France and England, 1000–1200." In William Henry Jackson, ed., *Knighthood in Medieval Literature*, pp. 1–22. Woodbridge, Suffolk: Brewer, 1981.

Hurley, Margaret. "Saints' Legends and Romance Again: Secularization of Structure and Motif." *Genre* 8 (1975): 60–73.

Imbs, Paul. "L'élément religieux dans le *Conte du Graal* de Chrétien de Troyes." In *Les Romans du Graal aux XIIe et XIIIe siècles*, pp. 31–53. Paris: Centre National de la Recherche Scientifique, 1956.

Jameson, Fredric. *The Political Unconscious: Narrative as a Socially Symbolic Act.* Ithaca, N.Y.: Cornell University Press, 1981.

Jodogne, Omer. "Le sens chrétien du jeune Perceval dans le *Conte du Graal.*" *Lettres Romanes* 14 (1960): 111–21.

Jonin, Pierre. *Les personnages féminins dans les romans français de Tristan.* Gap: Orphys, 1958.

Keen, Maurice. *Chivalry.* New Haven, Conn.: Yale University Press, 1984.

Kelly, Douglas. *Chrétien de Troyes: An Analytical Bibliography.* London: Grant and Cutler, 1976.

————. "La spécialité dans l'invention des topiques." In Lucie Brind'amour and Eugene Vance, eds., *Archéologie du signe*, pp. 101–26. Toronto: Pontifical Institute of Medieval Studies, 1983.

Kennedy, Angus J. "The Hermit's Role in French Arthurian Romance (c. 1170–1530)." *Romania* 95 (1974): 54–83.

————. "The Portrayal of the Hermit-Saint in French Arthurian Romance: The Remoulding of a Stock-Character." In Kenneth Varty, ed., *An Arthurian Tapestry: Essays in Memory of Lewis Thorpe*, pp. 69–82. Glasgow: French Department of the University, 1981.

Klenke, Sister M. Amelia. "Cups, Dishes, and the Holy Grail." *The Catholic Educational Review* 51 (1953): 404–10.

————. *Liturgy and Allegory in Chrétien's "Perceval."* Chapel Hill: University of North Carolina Press, 1951.

————. "The Spiritual Ascent of Perceval." *Studies in Philology* 53 (1956): 1–21.

Köhler, Erich. *Ideal und Wirklichkeit in der höfischen Epik: Studien zur Form der frühen Artus- und Graldichtung.* Tübingen: Niemeyer, 1956. Trans. E. Kaufholz, *L'Aventure chevaleresque: Idéal et réalité dans le roman courtois.* Paris: Gallimard, 1974.

Lacy, Norris J. "Gauvain and the Crisis of Chivalry in the *Conte del Graal.*" In Rupert T. Pickens, ed., *The Sower and His Seed: Essays on Chrétien de Troyes*, pp. 155–64. Lexington, Ky.: French Forum, 1983.

————, ed. *The Arthurian Encyclopedia.* New York: Garland Publishing, 1986.

La Fontaine, Jean de. *Fables.* Paris: Livre de Poche, 1964.

Le Goff, Jacques. *La civilisation de l'Occident médiéval.* Paris: Arthaud, 1967.

————. *L'imaginaire médiéval*. Paris: Gallimard, 1985.

————. *Pour un autre Moyen Age: Temps, travail et culture en Occident*. Paris: Gallimard, 1977.

Le Goff, Jacques, and Pierre Vidal-Naquet. "Lévi-Strauss en Brocéliande." *Critique* 325 (1974): 541–71.

Le Rider, Paule. *Le chevalier dans le "Conte du Graal" de Chrétien de Troyes*. Paris: SEDES, 1978.

Leclercq, Jean. "L'érémistisme et les cisterciens." In *L'eremistismo in Occidente nei secoli XI e XII*, pp. 27–44. Milan: Centro di studi medieoevali, 1965.

Legendre, Pierre. *L'amour du censeur: Essai sur l'ordre dogmatique*. Paris: Seuil, 1974.

Legros, Huguette. "Quand les jugements de Dieu deviennent artifices littéraires, ou la profanité impunie d'une poétique." *La Justice au Moyen Age (Sanction ou Impunité?)*, *Senefiance* 16 (1986): 197–212.

Lejeune, Rita. "La date du *Conte du Graal* de Chrétien de Troyes." *Moyen Age* 60 (1954): 51–79.

Leupin, Alexandre. *Barbarolexis: Medieval Writing and Sexuality*. Trans. Kate M. Cooper. Cambridge, Mass.: Harvard University Press, 1989.

Lévi-Strauss, Claude. *Anthropologie Structurale Deux*. Paris: Plon, 1973.

Lewes, Ulle E. *The Life in the Forest: The Influence of the Saint Giles Legend on the Courtly Tristan Story*. Chattanooga: University of Tennessee, 1978.

Lewis, Andrew W. *Royal Succession in Capetian France: Studies on Familial Order and the State*. Cambridge, Mass.: Harvard University Press, 1981.

Little, Lester K. "Pride Goes Before Avarice: Social Changes and the Vices in Latin Christendom." *American Historical Review* 76 (1971): 16–49.

Loomis, Robert Sherman. *Arthurian Literature in the Middle Ages: A Collaborative History*. Ed. R. S. Loomis. Oxford: Clarendon Press, 1959.

————. *Arthurian Tradition and Chrétien de Troyes*. New York: Columbia University Press, 1949.

————. *Celtic Myth and Arthurian Romance*. New York: Columbia University Press, 1927.

Lot-Borodine, Myrrha. "Le *Conte du Graal* de Chrétien de Troyes et sa présentation symbolique." *Romania* 77 (1956): 225–88, and 78 (1957): 142–43.

Louis, René. "Le préfixe inorganique es- dans les noms propres en ancien français." In *Festgabe Ernst Gamillscheg zu seinem fünfundsechzigsten Geburtstag am 28. Oktober 1952*, pp. 66–76. Tübingen: Niemeyer, 1952.

Lozachmeur, Jean-Claude. "Recherches sur les origines indo-européennes et ésotériques de la légende du Graal." *Cahiers de Civilisation Médiévale* 30 (1987): 45–63.

Macy, Gary. *The Theologies of the Eucharist in the Early Scholastic Period: A Study of the Salvific Function of the Sacrament According to the Theologians, c. 1080–c. 1220*. Oxford: Clarendon Press, 1984.

Maddox, Donald. *The Arthurian Romances of Chrétien de Troyes: Once and Future Fictions*. Cambridge, Eng.: Cambridge University Press, 1991.

———. "Roman et manipulation au 12e siècle." *Poétique* 66 (1986): 179–90.

———. *Structure and Sacring: The Systematic Kingdom in Chrétien's "Erec et Enide."* Lexington, Ky.: French Forum Publishers, 1978.

———. "Trois sur deux: Théories de bipartition et de tripartition des oeuvres de Chrétien de Troyes." *Oeuvres et Critiques* 5 (1981): 91–102.

Marcus, Hazel Rose, and Shinobu Kitayama. "Culture and the Self: Implications for Cognition, Emotion, and Motivation." *Psychological Review* 98 (1991): 224–53.

Markale, Jean. *Le Graal*. Paris: Retz, 1982.

———. *Le roi Arthur et la société celtique*. Paris: Payot, 1976.

Marx, Jean. *La légende arthurienne et le Graal*. Paris: Presses Universitaires de France, 1952.

———. *Nouvelles recherches sur la littérature arthurienne*. Paris: Klincksieck, 1965.

Matarasso, Pauline. *The Redemption of Chivalry: A Study of the "Queste del Saint Graal."* Geneva: Droz, 1979.

Matoré, Georges. *Le vocabulaire et la société médiévale*. Paris: Presses Universitaires de France, 1985.

Mauss, Marcel. "Essai sur le don: Forme et raison de l'échange dans les sociétés archaïques." In *Sociologie et anthropologie*, pp. 145–279. Paris: Presses Universitaires de France, 1980 [1923–24].

Méla, Charles. "*Perceval*." *Yale French Studies* 55–56 (1977): 253–79.

Ménard, Philippe. "Problèmes et mystères du *Conte du Graal*: Un essai d'interprétation." In *Chrétien de Troyes et le Graal*, pp. 61–76. Paris: Nizet, 1984.

Micha, Alexandre. "Le *Perceval* de Chrétien de Troyes (roman éducatif)." In René Nelli, ed., *Lumières du Graal: Etudes et textes*, pp. 122–31. Paris: Cahiers du Sud, 1951.

———. *La tradition manuscrite des romans de Chrétien de Troyes*. Geneva: Droz, 1966 [1939].

Middleton, Roger. "Additional Notes on the History of Selected Manuscripts." In Keith Busby et al., eds., *The Manuscripts of Chrétien de Troyes*, vol. 2, pp. 177–243.

———. "Index of Former Owners." In Keith Busby et al., eds., *The Manuscripts of Chrétien de Troyes*, vol. 2, pp. 87–176.

Milan, Paul B. "The Golden Age and the Political Theory of Jean de Meun: A Myth in *Rose* Scholarship." *Symposium* 23 (1969): 137–49.

Monson, Don A. "La 'surenchère' chez Chrétien de Troyes." *Poétique* 70 (1987): 231–46.

Moore, R. I. *The Formation of a Persecuting Society: Power and Deviance in Western Europe, 950–1250*. Oxford: Blackwell, 1987.

Morris, Colin. *The Discovery of the Individual, 1050–1200.* Toronto: Toronto University Press, 1987 [1972].

Morris, Rosemary. "Aspects of Time and Place in the French Arthurian Verse Romances." *French Studies* 42 (1988): 257–77.

Nelson Sargent-Baur, Barbara. "*Dux bellorum / res militum / roi fainéant*: La transformation d'Arthur au XIIe siècle." *Medium Aevum* 90 (1984): 357–73.

Nitze, William A., and Harry F. Williams. *Arthurian Names in the Perceval of Chrétien de Troyes.* University of California Publications in Modern Philology, vol. 38. Berkeley: University of California Press, 1955.

Nixon, Terry. "Catalogue of Manuscripts." In Keith Busby et al., eds., *The Manuscripts of Chrétien de Troyes*, vol. 2, pp. 1–85.

———. "Romance Collections and the Manuscripts of Chrétien de Troyes." In Keith Busby et al., eds., *The Manuscripts of Chrétien de Troyes*, vol. 1, pp. 17–25.

Nykrog, Per. "Two Creators of Narrative Form in Twelfth-Century France: Gautier d'Arras—Chrétien de Troyes." *Speculum* 68 (1973): 258–76.

Ourliac, Paul. "Coutume et mémoire: Les coutumes françaises au XIIIe siècle." In B. Roy and P. Zumthor, eds., *Jeux de mémoire: Aspect de la mnémotechnie médiévale*, pp. 111–22. Montréal: Les Presses de l'Université de Montréal, and Paris: Vrin, 1985.

Pastoureau, Michel. "Les armoiries arthuriennes." In Keith Busby et al., eds., *The Manuscripts of Chrétien de Troyes*, vol. 2, pp. 245–47.

Pauphilet, Albert. *Le legs du moyen âge: Etudes de littérature médiévale.* Melun: D'Argences, 1950.

Payen, Jean-Charles. "La destruction des mythes courtois dans le roman arthurien: La femme dans le roman en vers après Chrétien de Troyes." *Revue des Langues Romanes* 78 (1969): 213–28.

———. "Encore la pratique religieuse dans le *Conte du Graal*." In *Chrétien de Troyes et le Graal*, pp. 121–32. Paris: Nizet, 1984.

———. "Lancelot contre Tristan: La conjuration d'un mythe subversif (réflexions sur l'idéologie romanesque au moyen âge)." In J. Dufournet and D. Poirion, eds., *Mélanges de langue et de littérature offerts à Pierre Le Gentil*, pp. 617–32. Paris: SEDES, 1973.

Pellegrini, Carlo. "Per l'interpretazione del *Perceval* di Chrétien de Troyes." In *Studi di Varia Umanita in Onore di Francesco Flora*, pp. 109–18. Milan: Mondadori, 1963.

Peters, Edward. *The Shadow King: Rex Inutilis in Medieval Law and Literature.* New Haven, Conn.: Yale University Press, 1970.

Pickens, Rupert T. *The Welsh Knight: Paradoxicality in Chrétien's "Conte du Graal."* Lexington, Ky.: French Forum, 1977.

Planche, Alice. "La Dame au sycomore." In *Mélanges de Littérature du Moyen Age au XXe Siècle Offerts à Jeanne Lods*, vol. 1, pp. 495–516. Paris: Collection de l'Ecole Normale Supérieure de Jeunes Filles, 1978.

Poirion, Daniel. "Du sang sur la neige: Nature et fonction de l'image dans le *Conte du Graal*." In Raymond J. Cormier, ed., *Voices of Conscience: Essays on Medieval and Modern French Literature in Memory of James D. Powell and Rosemary Hodgins*, pp. 143–65. Philadelphia: Temple University Press, 1977.

————. "L'ombre mythique de Perceval dans le *Conte du Graal*." *Cahiers de Civilisation Médiévale* 13 (1973): 197–98.

Poliakov, Léon. *La causalité diabolique: Essai sur l'origine des persécutions*. Paris: Calmann-Lévy, 1980.

Pollmann, Leo. *Chrétien de Troyes und der "Conte del Graal."* Tübingen: Niemeyer, 1965.

Radding, Charles M. *A World Made by Men: Cognition and Society, 400–1200*. Chapel Hill: University of North Carolina Press, 1985.

Regalado, Nancy Freeman. "*Des contraires choses*: La fonction poétique de la citation et des *exempla* dans le *Roman de la Rose* de Jean de Meun." *Littérature* 41 (1981): 62–81.

Rey-Flaud, Henri. "Le sang sur la neige: Analyse d'une image-écran de Chrétien de Troyes." *Littérature* 37 (1980): 15–24.

Ribard, Jacques. "Ecriture symbolique et visée allégorique dans le *Conte du Graal*." *Oeuvres et Critiques* 5 (1980–81): 103–9.

Rieger, Angelica. "Le programme iconographique du *Perceval* montpelliérain, BI, Sect. Méd. H 249 (M)." In Keith Busby et al., eds., *The Manuscripts of Chrétien de Troyes*, vol. 1, pp. 377–435.

Robertson, Durant W., Jr. *A Preface to Chaucer: Studies in Medieval Perspectives*. Princeton, N.J.: Princeton University Press, 1962.

Roques, Mario. "Le Graal de Chrétien et la demoiselle au Graal." *Romania* 76 (1955): 1–27.

Ruck, E. H. *An Index of Themes and Motifs in Twelfth-Century French Arthurian Poetry*. Cambridge, Eng.: D. S. Brewer, 1991.

Rutledge, Amelia A. "Perceval's Sin: Critical Perspectives." *Oeuvres et Critiques* 5 (1980–81): 53–60.

Ryding, William W. *Structure in Medieval Narrative*. The Hague: Mouton, 1971.

Schmolke-Hasselmann, Beate. "Henry II Plantagenêt, roi d'Angleterre, et la genèse d'*Erec et Enide*." *Cahiers de Civilisation Médiévale* 24 (1981): 241–46.

Shahar, Shulamith. *The Fourth Estate: A History of Women in the Middle Ages*. Trans. Chaya Galai. New York: Methuen, 1983.

Shell, Marc. "The Blank Check: Accounting for the Grail." *Stanford French Review* (Spring 1983): 5–25.

Shipley, Joseph T. *Dictionary of Word Origins*. Totowa, N.J.: Littlefield, Adams, 1979.

Smalley, Beryl. *The Study of the Bible in the Middle Ages*. Notre Dame, Ind.: University of Notre Dame Press, 1978 [1964].

Spiegel, Gabrielle M. *Romancing the Past: The Rise of Vernacular Prose Historiography in Thirteenth-Century France.* Berkeley: University of California Press, 1993.

Stanger, Mary D. "Literary Patronage at the Medieval Court of Flanders." *French Studies* 11 (1957): 214–29.

Stiennon, Jacques. "Bruges, Philippe d'Alsace, Chrétien de Troyes et le Graal." In *Chrétien de Troyes et le Graal*, pp. 5–15. Paris: Nizet, 1984.

Stirnemann, Patricia. "Some Champenois Vernacular Manuscripts and the Manerius Style of Illumination." In Keith Busby et al., eds., *The Manuscripts of Chrétien de Troyes*, vol. 1, pp. 195–226.

Stock, Brian. *Listening for the Text: On the Uses of the Past.* Baltimore: Johns Hopkins University Press, 1990.

Stones, Alison. "General Introduction." In Keith Busby et al., eds., *The Manuscripts of Chrétien de Troyes*, vol. 1, pp. 1–8.

———. "The Illustrated Chrétien Manuscripts and Their Artistic Context." In Keith Busby et al., eds., *The Manuscripts of Chrétien de Troyes*, vol. 1, pp. 227–322.

Sturm-Maddox, Sara. "*Hortus non conclusus*: Critics and the *Joie de la Cort*." *Oeuvres et Critiques* 5 (1980–81): 61–71.

———. "Lévi-Strauss in the Waste Forest." *L'Esprit Créateur* 18 (1978): 82–94.

Tasker Grimbert, Joan. "Misrepresentation and Misconception in Chrétien de Troyes: Nonverbal and Verbal Semiotics in *Erec and Enide* and *Perceval*." In Julian N. Wasserman and Lois Roucy, eds., *Signs, Sentence, Discourse: Language in Medieval Thought and Literature*, pp. 50–79. Syracuse, N.Y.: Syracuse University Press, 1989.

Taylor, Archer. "The Three Sins of the Hermit." *Modern Philology* 20 (1922): 61–94.

Thiébaux, Marcelle. *The Stag of Love: The Chase in Medieval Literature.* Ithaca, N.Y.: Cornell University Press, 1974.

Thompson, Stith. *Motif-Index of Folk Literature: A Classification of Narrative Elements in Folk-Tales, Ballads, Myths, Fables, Medieval Romances, Exempla, Fabliaux, Jest-Books and Local Legends*, vol. 2. Bloomington: Indiana University Press, 1956.

Vance, Eugene. "Le combat érotique chez Chrétien de Troyes: De la figure à la forme." *Poétique* 12 (1972): 544–71.

———. *From Topic to Tale: Logic and Narrativity in the Middle Ages.* Minneapolis: University of Minnesota Press, 1987.

———. "*Mervelous Signals*": *Poetics and Sign Theory in the Middle Ages.* Lincoln: University of Nebraska Press, 1986.

———. "Sylvia's Pet Stag: Wilderness and Domesticity in Virgil's *Aeneid*." *Arethusa* 14 (1981): 127–38.

Van Mulken, Margot. "*Perceval* and Stemmata." In Keith Busby et al., eds., *The Manuscripts of Chrétien de Troyes*, vol. 1, pp. 41–48.

Walters, Lori. "The Image of Blanchefleur in MS Montpellier, BI, Sect. Méd. H 249." In Keith Busby et al., eds., *The Manuscripts of Chrétien de Troyes*, vol. 1, pp. 437–55.

———. "The Use of Multi-Compartment Opening Miniatures in the Illustrated Manuscripts of Chrétien de Troyes." In Keith Busby et al., eds., *The Manuscripts of Chrétien de Troyes*, vol. 1, pp. 331–50.

Warren, W. L. *The Governance of Norman and Angevin England, 1086–1272*. Stanford, Calif.: Stanford University Press, 1987.

———. *Henry II*. Berkeley: University of California Press, 1973.

West, G. D. *An Index of Proper Names in French Arthurian Prose Romances*. Toronto: University of Toronto Press, 1978.

———. *An Index of Proper Names in French Arthurian Verse Romances, 1150–1300*. Toronto: University of Toronto Press, 1969.

Westoby, Kathryn S. "A New Look at the Role of the *Fée* in Medieval French Arthurian Romance." In Glyn S. Burgess and Robert A. Taylor, eds., *The Spirit of the Court*, pp. 373–85. Cambridge, Eng.: D.S. Brewer, 1985.

Weston, Jessie L. *From Ritual to Romance*. Garden City, N.Y.: Doubleday Anchor Books, 1957 [1919].

Wolfgang, Lenora D. "Prologues to the *Perceval* and Perceval's Father: The First Literary Critics of Chrétien Were the Grail Authors Themselves." *Oeuvres et Critiques* 5 (1980–81): 81–90.

Young, Charles R. *The Royal Forests in Medieval England*. Philadelphia: University of Pennsylvania Press, 1979.

Zink, Michel. *La prédication en langue romane avant 1300*. Paris: Champion, 1976.

———. *La subjectivité littéraire: Autour du siècle de saint Louis*. Paris: Presses Universitaires de France, 1985.

Index

In this index an "f" after a number indicates a separate reference on the next page, and an "ff" indicates separate references on the next two pages. A continuous discussion over two or more pages is indicated by a span of page numbers, e.g., "57–59." *Passim* is used for a cluster of references in close but not consecutive sequence.

Library of Congress Cataloging-in-Publication Data

Cazelles, Brigitte.
    The unholy Grail : a social reading of Chrétien de Troyes's Conte
du Graal / Brigitte Cazelles.
        p. cm. — (Figurae)
Includes bibliographical references and index.
ISBN 0-8047-2481-4
    1. Chrétien, de Troyes, 12th cent. Perceval le Gallois.
    2. Perceval (Legendary character)—Romances—History and criticism.
    3. Arthurian romances—History and criticism.   4. Grail—Romances—
History and criticism.   5. Literature and society.   6. Chivalry in
literature.   I. Title.   II. Series: Figurae (Stanford, Calif.)
PQ1445.P2C39   1996
841'.1—dc20   95-1781
                                                                        CIP

⊗ This book is printed on acid-free, recycled paper.

DATE DUE

DEMCO 38-297